Compositional Theory
in the
Eighteenth Century

# Compositional Theory
# in the
# Eighteenth Century

JOEL LESTER

HARVARD UNIVERSITY PRESS

Cambridge, Massachusetts

London, England

1992

Publication of this volume has been assisted by a grant from the
Publications Program of the National Endowment for the Humanities,
an independent federal agency.

This book is printed on acid-free paper, and its binding materials
have been chosen for strength and durability.

*Library of Congress Cataloging-in-Publication Data*

Lester, Joel.
Compositional theory in the eighteenth century / Joel Lester.
p.     cm.
Includes bibliographical references and index.
ISBN 0-674-15522-X (alk. paper)
1. Music—Theory—History—18th century. 2. Composition (Music)—
History—18th century. I. Title.
ML430.L46     1992
781.3′09′033—dc20

92-5083
CIP   MN

# Acknowledgments

A COMPREHENSIVE SURVEY such as this work is possible only because of innumerable earlier studies, for which I am unremittingly grateful. I have been researching this material in various forms for two decades. As a result, it is more than likely that ideas I have incorporated into my own thinking may have come from an article or dissertation I read years ago. In addition, I have frequently drafted a passage only to find its tenets in a subsequent publication. I have tried wherever possible to cite sources, especially where a reader may profit from a more detailed discussion of an individual topic than space allows here. I apologize in advance for any unintended omissions. The Bibliography, extensive as it is, is intended not as a comprehensive survey of the primary or secondary literature but as a list of those items referred to in the text.

I also owe heartfelt thanks to a number of individuals: to Margaretta Fulton, Humanities Editor at Harvard University Press, who proposed that I write this book and who has been supportive and knowledgeable at every step; to Donna Bouvier, who steered this book through production; to David Lewin, who made uncommonly keen suggestions on an earlier draft; to Thomas Christensen, who has been an inexhaustible source of information on eighteenth-century theory; to Frank Samarotto, for his handsome musical orthography; to Don Franklin, for providing facsimiles of a Bach manuscript; to David Kornacker, for assistance with the translations from French; to Rebecca Pechefsky, for assistance in editing; to students in my history-of-theory seminars at The Graduate School of The City University of New York, whose questions stimulated my thinking; and, most of all, to my family, who patiently allowed me to work and who listened to and commented on numerous passages. An award from the Research Foundation of CUNY provided for the purchase of research materials. And an Eisner Research Award from the Humanities Division at The City College released me from some duties, allowing me to begin work. Last, without the collection of the Music Research Division at the New York Public Library at Lincoln Center and the assistance of the librarians there I would hardly have dared to undertake this work.

# Contents

*We have the good fortune to live in a century in which most sciences and arts have risen to such a high degree of perfection.*
Preface by Johann Ernst Bach to
*Anleitung zu der musikalischen Gelahrtheit*
(1758) by Jacob Adlung

*There are two opposing dangers to be avoided when proposing a system of harmony: one is to censure those things that are constantly and successfully used in any number of ways; the other to extend rules to cases that cannot be used, or that can be used only with special precautions.*
Alexandre-Théophile Vandermonde,
*Second Mémoire sur un nouveau système d'harmonie applicable à l'état de la musique*
(1778), p. 2

# Introduction

*The picture any age forms of a section of the past is never totally independent of the controversies of its own time, in which it seeks to ascertain the nature of its own historical essence. There is a danger that (since every historian is also a child of his own time) historical judgements will be based indiscriminately and uncritically on the norms we all (necessarily) use to orientate ourselves in our own time. The best way to avoid or at least reduce the danger is to recognize it and thus seek to neutralize it, instead of allowing it to seep into the investigation of a past epoch in the form of implicit assumptions.*
*Dahlhaus 1985, p. 2*

MANY INTRODUCTIONS begin by explaining the need for yet another book on the topic at hand. Such comments are not pertinent here. No other comprehensive history details what eighteenth-century writers on compositional theory said, when and how they said it, and what they meant in the context of their own times.

Such a study was less urgent prior to recent years. But the increasingly prevalent belief that analysis of and scholarship on the music of past ages should at least acknowledge the thinking of those ages has made a comprehensive and critical survey of that theory a pressing concern. Unless theory of a former age is understood in its own context, its issues are eviscerated and its theorists turned into shades merely foreshadowing modern theoretical positions or cardboard figures standing in for modern theoretical disputes.

By being aware of its context, we can become aware of the resplendence of eighteenth-century theory. This was the era in which many features of modern theory first emerged and in which theorists first began grappling in modern terms with issues that remain challenging today—the nature of the interaction between lines and harmonies, the nature of the interaction between melodic motives and phrasing and harmonies, the factors that make music mobile and the best ways to understand them, the relation between point-to-point connections and larger structures, and the presence of structural foundations lying below the compositional surface.

It is central to this study that the first priority of a historian of ideas is to understand how the original authors thought. Writers of past eras, when formulating their thoughts in ways that seem problematic to modern readers, were not trying to state our modern ideas in clumsy fashion; they were stating their own ideas in their own terms. Only by being sensitive to their terminology, to their perspectives, and to their theoretical agendas can we avoid unwittingly misinterpreting the import of their ideas. A full exploration of terminology, perspectives, and agendas is the subject matter of this study as a whole. But one instance of each can foreshadow the issues involved.

*Modulation* is a term that has lost a once-common meaning. Nowadays it denotes a change of key or the process of key change. In the eighteenth century (and well into the nineteenth), it also commonly denoted what seems to us the contradictory meaning of reinforcing a sense of the current key. An eighteenth-century musician understood an underlying unity encompassing *modulating within a key* and *modulating from one key to another*—a family of ideas including the notions of a melody or progression that has a sense of direction (establishing one key or moving to another), a melody in general, a chord progression or voice leading in general, the substance from which a melody or a chord is made, and so forth. Thus Johann Gottfried Walther, when he talks about why a proper scale has a mixture of whole steps and half steps, says if there were no half steps, the resulting whole-tone scale would be a "modulation without modulation . . . a pure mishmash" in the sense of a melodic structure without structure (Walther 1732, article *modus musicus;* Lester 1989, p. 212): neither "modulation" here denotes change of key.

No single modern term encompasses what we regard as these separate meanings. Yet if we are to understand eighteenth-century musicians, we must try to grasp the family resemblance recognized by them among what we regard as separate tenets. Construing a term solely in its modern sense or transferring only a part of its meaning to a single modern term inevitably distorts the meaning of the original. In this study, discussions of individual theorists adhere wherever possible to the terminology of the original source. When *modulation* or a similar term occurs in a citation, it is generally rendered by a modern equivalent along with the original term. The original meaning emerges by trying to think in terms of the original vocabulary, not merely by trying to find a modern term that perhaps is relatively close to that original term but invariably carries some unwarranted connotations and excludes others.

Likewise, complexes of ideas often carried different connotations in the eighteenth century than they do nowadays. For instance, after the middle of the eighteenth century, the intervals in species counterpoint were understood as parts of chords and chord progressions by many musicians, Mozart and Beethoven among them, not as purely intervallic voice leading. But this does not necessarily mean that they were thinking along the lines of a late-nineteenth-century harmony text, placing chord numbers willy-nilly beneath the exercise and thinking of each verticality outside its linear context. Counterpoint represented to them the interaction of lines, even though they thought of the intervals between those lines as complete or incomplete statements of chords.

Finally, a theorist may have introduced an explanation to resolve a problem hardly remembered by modern musicians. Consider the issue of suspensions. Nowadays, we easily parse the surface of a piece into triads and seventh chords and sort out nonharmonic suspensions. It is hard for us to imagine the music world before triads, seventh chords, and their inversions were recognized as the standard harmonies and other tones conceived of as additions to them. But that was the situation confronting early-eighteenth-century musicians. Innumerable rules and exceptions dealt with the treatment of dozens of verticalities containing suspended notes—some indicated by different thoroughbass figurings and some sharing the same thoroughbass figurings in any of a large number of idiosyncratic systems of thoroughbass numbering; some resolving down and some resolving up; some forming what we consider seventh chords and therefore not resolving until several other voices also moved, and others resolving without other voices moving; and some even being consonances over the bass though they nevertheless had to resolve as suspensions (such as the fifth in a 6/5 chord).

To simplify this situation Rameau developed his theory of chords by subposition (ninth and eleventh chords), explaining how the resolution of virtually all suspended dissonances could be understood by a single rule. From an early-eighteenth-century perspective, he was trying to rationalize suspended dissonances and give a linear context to verticalities that thoroughbass theory simply considered entities capable of being juxtaposed with numerous other entities. It is easy for a modern musician to see only the resulting ninth and eleventh chords reminiscent of the absurdly stacked thirds of later harmonic theory and wonder what a theory with ninth and eleventh chords has to do with early-eighteenth-century music. Only by understanding the situation that motivated Rameau's theoretical formulation can we understand his constructs.

To be sure, terms, ideas, and slogans do change. And an important part of their meaning today is what those changes inspired. Perhaps an eighteenth-century political slogan can demonstrate this point more dramatically than a musical term. "All men are created equal" has resounded through the last two centuries. But it has clearly meant different things to different people at different times. Many Americans in the eighteenth and nineteenth centuries, possibly including the author of the phrase, saw little conflict between espousing the slogan and owning slaves, excluding women and those who did not own property from full citizenship rights, and so forth.

Jefferson's words, taken in their own eighteenth-century context, reflect an attitude that we today may regard as internally inconsistent. But those words also helped people become aware of inequalities (a role the slogan still plays) and thereby inspired and continue to inspire them to change their practices and attitudes so as to conform more closely to the slogan. The same is true of musical theoretical terms, ideas, and slogans.

Ideas may well have lives quite independent of their original context, but it is ultimately misleading to take an idea as it has developed in a later era and apply that formulation to the original context. It often distorts the original idea to such an extent that it seems no reasonable person could have thought that way.

Any study will necessarily view the past through the agenda of its present. Historians address only issues that they conceive of as issues. Thus Hugo Riemann acknowledges in the preface to his impressive *Geschichte der Musiktheorie im IX.–XIX. Jahrhundert* (1898), the closest approximation to a comprehensive history of theory, that he intended not a comprehensive, objective history, but a chronicle tracing theoretical tenets from their genesis to their place in his own theory of harmony. Likewise, Matthew Shirlaw's perceptive *Theory of Harmony* (1917) concentrates on speculative harmonic theory, primarily by those who treat "The Natural Principles of Harmony" (subtitle), excluding important writers, ignoring crucial theoretical traditions (counterpoint and the study of melody), and largely bypassing practical aspects of theory and the practical applications of speculative tenets.

Many studies of eighteenth-century theory address issues from the perspective of functional harmony and overlook many discussions of voice leading and hierarchical structure to which a Schenkerian perspective awakens us. To take a glaring example, Riemann's and Shirlaw's studies, different as they are, dismiss or ignore species counterpoint as a force in eighteenth-century musical thinking. The linear concerns of the eighteenth century were simply not as important in Riemann's and Shirlaw's time as they have become since. Some modern European scholars of eighteenth-century theory—Peter Benary, Arnold Feil, and Carl Dahlhaus among them—have also been less concerned with the implications of many linear and hierarchical ideas in eighteenth-century theory than some American scholars are. It is inevitable that the present study, which does address these issues, will fail to address other concerns of interest in the present or in the future.

In short, objectivity is an elusive goal in history. Indeed, it has become fashionable in some disciplines to deny altogether that objectivity is a proper goal of historical research. But as stated in the epigraph at the head of this Introduction, awareness of one's biases can help one avoid potential pitfalls.

Surveying the writings of approximately a century of musicians and comparing all these works has inevitably brought new items to light. For instance, it is now clear that numerals placed next to the chords in an example to analyze the root movements first appeared in print earlier than has hitherto been believed: in 1766 in a book published by John Trydell in Dublin and then widely propagated via its inclusion in the 1771 *Encyclopaedia Britannica*. Of greater significance than such facts is the extent to which it is now evident that many tenets or discoveries long associated with a single theorist actually appeared widely in print much earlier. For instance, many ideas central to Rameau's theory—not only triadic inversions and the notion of a chordal root, but also directed motion as evaded cadences, the association of specific chord types with specific scale degrees, and so forth—appeared in many earlier works.

These and other findings have led to the discovery of a larger degree of agreement than has previously been thought to exist among different eighteenth-century schools of thought. Despite numerous and acrimonious theoretical disputes, representatives of various theoretical traditions such as species counterpoint, thoroughbass, and harmony shared many more underlying tenets than has been recognized, especially in terms of practical applications.

This study deals intensively with the period from the 1720s through about 1790, that is, from three treatises considered classics in their theoretical traditions—Rameau's 1722 treatise on harmony, composition, and accompaniment; Fux's 1725 manual on counterpoint, fugue, and composition; and Heinichen's 1728 manual on thoroughbass and composition—through the *Versuch einer Anleitung zur Composition* by Koch (1782–1793). To cover the background of the earlier works, the historical survey begins with Zarlino, the great theorist of the second half of the sixteenth century, whose works remained influential into the eighteenth century.

The emphasis is on compositional theory to the extent that it can be separated from speculative theory, aesthetics, or performance theory. Issues of speculative theory (the origins of notes, intervals, chords; representations of the divine in music; and so forth) and aesthetics are discussed only where necessary to understand the practical application of a writer's ideas or the climate in which a theorist worked. Sources whose primary focus is performance, especially thoroughbass manuals, are invoked as they illuminate composition. Even publications intended for amateurs can shed light on the spread of ideas within the music world. This information is central to the vision of history of theory in the present study. It is one thing to present what Rameau, for instance, articulated in his works. It is quite another to see how those ideas affected the music primers of the time. Although some of Rameau's ideas were avidly debated over the decades but never left the hothouse of speculative treatises and their rebuttals, other ideas quickly joined everyday musical discourse.

Composition is construed here rather broadly to include everything from musical rudiments, intervals and chords, the study of harmony and voice leading, considerations of melody, musical phrasing and form, and the actual process of working out a composition. The relationship between music and text (including most aspects of text setting) is considered an aspect of musical aesthetics and is therefore bypassed. To have included it would have expanded an already large study.

Finally, this work should be regarded as a preliminary sketch of a history of eighteenth-century theory. The field is vast and, despite many strides taken in the past few decades, still contains numerous large patches that mapmakers of old labeled *terra incognita*. My aim is to present a comprehensive view of the century, fill in many gaps, correct misconceptions, and make it easier for future scholars to orient themselves within the field.

Compositional Theory in the Eighteenth Century

CHAPTER ONE

# Zarlino and His Legacy

*Zarlino: A celebrated writer on music whom M. de Brossard calls "the prince of modern musicians."*
*Rameau 1722, Table of Terms*

THE OPENING DECADES of the eighteenth century present a plethora of seemingly disparate theoretical approaches to the materials of musical composition. There were methods of traditional counterpoint (intervals and their interactions), a method of species counterpoint, methods of thoroughbass, and studies of harmony. These works, as well as dictionaries and journals, described several approaches to melodic construction, phrasing, and those aspects of music that nowadays fall under the heading of form: rhetoric underlay discussions of cadences, of dissonant configurations, of the parsing of pieces, and of melodic construction in general; variations applied to thoroughbass voice leadings created all sorts of compositions; and there were discussions of imitation, canon, and fugue, descriptions of the events within various types of movements, and ad hoc discussions of melodic contour and rhythmic continuity. Several different systems of modes and various formulations of the major-minor keys co-existed. While some writers continued to invoke numerical ratios to explain the basics of music, others appealed to the new science of acoustics, and still others specified no particular model to account for the musical elements. If this were not sufficient diversity, every new work seemed to present its own idiosyncratic mixture of these elements.

Despite this wide range of content, approach, purview, and conceptual model, most of these traditions can be traced to common roots in mid-sixteenth-century theory and in the profound changes in musical style that took place at the end of that century. Both species counterpoint as offered by Johann Joseph Fux (1660–1741) and the harmonic theories of Jean-

Philippe Rameau (1683–1764) are deeply indebted to the great sixteenth-century theorist Gioseffo Zarlino (1517–1590). The controversies over musical style that split the world of composition into *prima pratica* and *seconda pratica* (controversies in which Zarlino was an early participant) were crucial to the rise of thoroughbass, the evolution of major and minor keys, the continued existence of contrapuntal theory alongside growing harmonic perspectives, and also the use of rhetoric to explain the ordering and content of musical compositions. As a result, although Zarlino is far removed from the eighteenth century chronologically and conceptually, it is appropriate to begin a study of eighteenth-century theory with his ideas as they appeared in the mid-sixteenth century. This discussion concentrates solely on those aspects of Zarlino's ideas that are important to an understanding of eighteenth-century theory.

## Zarlino as Theorist

Among the many excellent sixteenth-century writers on music, Zarlino alone was preeminently influential on later theorists in numerous countries. His formulations, transmitted via his own magnum opus, the *Istitutioni harmoniche* of 1558, via manuscript translations, and via the writing of his pupils and others influenced by him, were authoritative for musicians in Italy, France, Germany, and England by the early seventeenth century. More than 160 years after its publication, ideas from the *Istitutioni* permeate early-eighteenth-century writings in several different theoretical traditions. And as late as the end of the nineteenth century, Hugo Riemann cited Zarlino as a source of parts of his harmonic theories (even though Riemann misconstrued the role of these tenets in Zarlino's work).

Zarlino's authority and influence derive from his erudition as well as his practical knowledge. He was a composer as well as a scholar—a student of Adrian Willaert (c. 1490–1562) and *maestro di cappella* at Saint Mark's in Venice from 1565 until his death in 1590, succeeding in that post Willaert, who held it from 1527 to 1562, and fellow Willaert pupil Cipriano de Rore (1516–1565). Later musicians found Zarlino's writings stimulating because he was primarily concerned with human music *(musica humana)*; hearing and the practices of composers were both central issues and also important criteria in deciding theoretical matters. But Zarlino's humanism, which also encompasses the first detailed discussion of text setting, did not endorse all compositional practices. Music did not exist for him solely to titillate the listener. Along with Plato, Zarlino believed that music should be enjoyed prudently because it has the capacity to arouse evil as well as good (Zarlino 1558, Part 1, Chapter 3; Plato's *Republic* in Strunk 1950, pp. 7–8). He repeatedly insisted that music should contain pleasing sounds combined with skill, and he rejected what he

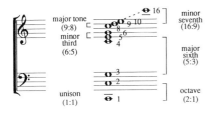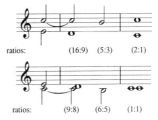

*Example 1-1.*

deemed excessive and improper dissonances, improper melodic intervals, and undue chromaticism. It is therefore not surprising that the most prominent musician to challenge these apparent extravagances in monodies early in the next century was Zarlino's pupil Giovanni Maria Artusi (c. 1540–1613).

Platonic-Pythagorean numerology provided a systematic basis for Zarlino's conception of proper and improper usages. The ancient Greeks had realized that in music there was a direct correlation between low-numbered string ratios and the simplest musical intervals (1:1 for the unison, 2:1 for the octave, 3:2 for the fifth, and so forth). This placed music in striking contrast to other quantifiable domains, where everyday relationships were often represented by quite complex numbers. In geometry, for instance, the radius and diameter of a circle relate to the circumference and area via the irrational pi, and the hypotenuse of a right triangle is the square root of the sum of the other sides, generally an irrational number. From antiquity through the beginning of the modern era, the ratios of musical intervals, where there was a one-to-one relationship between simple structures and simple proportions, were invoked in cosmology and other sciences, as well as in theories to explain musical structure. Intervals represented by simple ratios were the most consonant. And the progression from relatively complex ratios through simpler ratios to ratios close to unity explained the functional progression from a suspended dissonance to a third or sixth to the perfection of a cadential unison or octave (see Example 1-1). The directionality of such cadential voice leadings in both musical terms and also mathematical terms (as the ratios progress toward unity) provided the basis for a rudimentary functional theory of intervallic-harmonic progression.

Humanistic concerns and Platonic-Pythagorean reasoning coexist but do not always agree as the conceptual underpinnings of Zarlino's theoretical perspective. Like all theorists who have sought to explain music via a systematic theory, Zarlino had to strike a balance between music in a particular style created by and heard by humans and music as a construction based on abstract and eternal principles. For instance, since Zarlino

*Example 1-2.*

believed that smaller-number ratios were more consonant than larger-number ratios, the inexorable logic of numbers led him to argue that what we call a major 6/4 chord (represented by the proportion 5:4:3) is more consonant than what we call a minor 6/3 chord (8:6:5) (Zarlino 1558, Part 3, Chapter 60); see Example 1-2. Zarlino's argument is not entirely irrelevant to sixteenth-century practices, since there are occasional "major 6/4 chords" in his own compositions and those of his contemporaries in which the dissonant fourth is treated more leniently than it is in other combinations.[1] Yet Zarlino readily acknowledges that the 6/4 chord is "little esteemed by musicians," and elsewhere he does not insist on its use.

Zarlino's special genius, then, lay in his ability to organize the comprehensive practical knowledge of his age according to speculative principles, and at the same time to look beyond the boundaries of those principles to acknowledge practical realities, occasionally including novel insights that challenge the very bases of his theoretical conceptions.

## Aspects of Zarlino's Compositional Theory, Sixteenth-Century Music, and Later Adaptations

Zarlino's *Istitutioni* lays out the compositional practices of the sacred music of his own time. The style he surveys is not, therefore, that of his slightly younger contemporary Palestrina (c. 1525–1594), most of whose compositions postdate the first edition of *Istitutioni,* but that of his teacher Willaert (even though on many matters, Zarlino's explanations do in fact agree with usages of the Palestrina-Lassus generation). Zarlino frequently applies a perspective on voice-leading concerns somewhat different from the one that modern musicians might apply and even different from that of the seventeenth- and eighteenth-century musicians who cited him as an authority. Thus, when later theorists borrow or adapt tenets from the *Istitutioni,* it is important to recognize the differences between the formulation and placement of the tenet within Zarlino's own works, the

1. In Zarlino's madrigal *Amor mentre dormia* (Zarlino 1562, p. 25, m. 21) and in Part 2 of Palestrina's *Beatus Laurentius* (*Werke,* 5, p. 55), suspended fourths that are part of "major 6/4" chords last twice as long as other suspensions.

Major thirds        Minor thirds        Major sixths        Minor sixths

*Example 1-3.* Zarlino 1558, Part 3, Chapter 29

often different formulation of the tenet within the later work, and the sometimes different formulation of that tenet in modern theory.

Zarlino's discussion of consecutive consonances is representative. In addition to the familiar prohibition on parallel octaves and perfect fifths, he bans two major thirds or two minor sixths in succession and only barely tolerates consecutive minor thirds or major sixths (Part 3, Chapter 29)—proscriptions that Zarlino may have received from his teacher Willaert (Berger 1987, pp. 111–112).

Zarlino gives three reasons for these proscriptions. First and foremost, consecutive consonances violate the principle of variety. Promoting variety, which "brings pleasure and delight" (Part 3, Chapter 55), is a goal of many of Zarlino's compositional recommendations. In addition to proscribing consecutive consonances of the same size, Zarlino also bans repeated melodic motives (Chapter 55), urges avoiding unisons since they contain no variety (Chapter 41), and praises the harmonic perfection of what we call the root-position triad (without using that term)[2] because it contains a variety of consonances: the major and minor thirds within a fifth (Chapter 31).

Because of variety, Zarlino tolerates two minor thirds or two major sixths in succession only when the parts move by step, because in this case the interval in each of the two parts differs in the system of just intonation he proposes: one part moves by a major tone (9:8), while the other moves by a minor tone (10:9). He prohibits minor thirds or major sixths in succession when skips are involved.

Zarlino's second reason for banning parallel consonances is that there should be a semitone (literally or contained within a skip) somewhere in any interval-to-interval connection. The lack of a semitone arises when both parts in an interval succession move by whole tones; see Example 1-3. When thirds or sixths of different qualities follow one another by

2. The term *triad (trias harmonica)* was coined by Johannes Lippius (1585–1612) in the seventeenth century. References in modern scholarship to Zarlino's use of the term are erroneous.

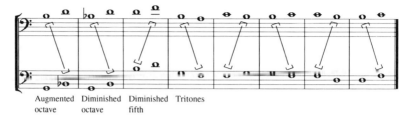

Augmented    Diminished    Diminished    Tritones
octave       octave        fifth

*Example 1-4.* Zarlino 1558, Part 3, Chapter 30

step or skip, a semitone arises or is passed through somewhere in the voice leading.

More troubling for Zarlino is his third reason: what he calls the lack of a harmonic relationship can arise when two thirds or sixths of like quality follow one another by step or skip, or in other interval successions; see Example 1-4. The proscriptions of the cross relations and the diminished fifth are understandable in terms of later theory. But the lack of a harmonic relationship in some of the other instances highlights voice interactions on which later theorists do not focus much attention, although these interactions were clearly of interest to Zarlino as a sixteenth-century composer and theorist. Zarlino is interested not only in the intervals formed as simultaneities, but also in the "diagonal" relations among the four notes involved in any interval succession.

Surprisingly, although Zarlino uses diagonal tritones and diminished fifths to proscribe various voice leadings among consonances, he uses the same procedure to insist that a diminished fifth may appear as a vertical interval, even in two-part note-against-note writing, because when that interval moves to a major third no false interval occurs diagonally: "the parts can be exchanged without any discomfort" (see Example 1-5).

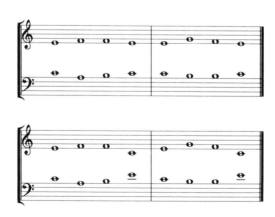

*Example 1-5.* Zarlino 1558, Part 3, Chapter 30

Compositional Theory in the Eighteenth Century

*Example 1-6.*

Whatever his reasons, and whatever the relationship of his recommendations to compositional practice in the sixteenth century, Zarlino's proscription of parallel major thirds and parallel minor sixths was frequently cited by seventeenth- and eighteenth-century theorists, who then proceeded to explain that this rule need not be followed. Christoph Schröter (1699–1782) still mentions this proscription in his 1772 thoroughbass treatise, and Johann Georg Albrechtsberger (1736–1809) suggests that two major thirds should not appear in conjunct succession in the strict style (Albrechtsberger 1790, Chapter 7).

A further voice-leading recommendation suggested by Zarlino that was routinely cited and just as routinely dismissed by later theorists concerns major and minor intervals. Zarlino suggests that the upper note of major intervals should ascend and the upper note of minor intervals should descend (Part 2, Chapter 5). Although Zarlino himself pretty much ignores this advice elsewhere and does not follow it in his own compositions, the tenet lived on in theory as a troublesome idea for quite a while. Many seventeenth-century writers respected Zarlino's authority enough to repeat the remark, almost always disclaiming its applicability to modern practice. Rameau was sufficiently intrigued by the notion to apply Zarlino's advice to what he regarded as the two dissonances in a dominant seventh chord: the leading tone, which he called the *major dissonance* (because it is a *major* third over the root), always ascended to resolve, and the chord seventh, which he called the *minor dissonance* (a *minor* seventh over the root), always descended. The stature of Zarlino 130 years after his death is nowhere more apparent than in Rameau's pride in explaining this well-known remark of Zarlino's that others had found inexplicable.

Another voice-leading recommendation of Zarlino's is a legacy of earlier theory. Amid a wide-ranging discussion of various consonant successions that are recommended or proscribed, Zarlino urges that when imperfect consonances move to perfect ones, they should proceed from the one closer in size: for instance, a third or sixth expanding to an octave should be major (Part 3, Chapter 38). Only when a diagonal tritone would arise between parts, as in the motion of a major third to a perfect fifth over a stepwise descending tenor, does Zarlino make an exception (see Example 1-6).

On another voice-leading matter not much remarked on by future theorists, Zarlino does not allow the resolution of a dissonant suspension to

*Example 1-7.* Zarlino 1558, Part 3, Chapter 42

*Example 1-8.* Jeppesen 1970, p. 78

be sustained and become a perfect interval (see Example 1-7). Zarlino explains that here the "dissonance resolves coldly" since the ear is not adequately compensated for "the offense of the dissonance" (Part 3, Chapter 42).

In addition to restricting voice leadings that did not trouble later theorists, Zarlino also approves of acceptable sixteenth-century voice leadings that bothered later theorists. For instance, he selectively approves of various hidden fifths and octaves, even in two-voice writing (Chapter 36), agreeing with Palestrina's practice (Jeppesen 1970, pp. 295–301). Zarlino's examples also consistently apply various sixteenth-century melodic and rhythmic norms, such as the near total absence of ascending skips from quarter notes on a strong beat (ibid., pp. 61–73),[3] and the total absence of the quarter-note figure shown in Example 1-8) (ibid., pp. 78–80).

The concerns outlined here, when compared to seventeenth- and eighteenth-century texts that purport to teach counterpoint in the *stile antico,* indicate how different sixteenth-century theory and practice were from such eighteenth-century theory. In his *Gradus ad parnassum* (1725), for instance, which the eighteenth and nineteenth centuries viewed as a manual in sixteenth-century style, Fux does not mention Zarlino's ban on parallel major thirds and minor sixths, he does not mention the need for a semitone within interval successions, he is not troubled by most of Zarlino's non-harmonic relations (except for chromatic cross relations), he prohibits diminished fifths in note-against-note counterpoint except at cadences in more than two voices, he does not mention Zarlino's recommendation to

3. Only two such skips occur in the *Istitutioni:* in Marco and Palisca 1968, Ex. 87, first example, m. 12, and Ex. 118d, upper voice in m. 13. In the latter instance, the skip occurs in a part that has been intervallically inverted to demonstrate a particular type of invertible counterpoint.

proceed to a perfect interval from the imperfect interval closest in size, he does not proscribe holding the resolution of a suspension to become a perfect consonance, he does not allow similar motion into perfect consonances in two voices, and he incorporates many melodic patterns unknown to the sixteenth century. Similarly, the discussion of strict style in the *Tractatus compositionis augmentatus* (c. 1655) by Christoph Bernhard (1627–1692), even though it was written much closer to the end of the sixteenth century than Fux's *Gradus,* also differs in innumerable matters from sixteenth-century practice.

## Successive Composition, Tenor vs. Bass Primacy, and Chords

Zarlino's sixteenth-century perspective is once again evident when he recommends that the voices in a texture be composed successively (Part 3, Chapter 58): "most of the time musicians are accustomed to begin all their compositions with the tenor and then add to it the soprano, joining to these the bass and finally the alto."[4] Common sense and other sixteenth-century theorists inform us that the fully imitative textures characteristic of mid-sixteenth-century music cannot be composed in such a manner. But Zarlino hews to this traditional approach to composition. One voice, usually the tenor, which "governs and regulates the composition and maintains the mode," is composed first as a subject (*soggetto:* "that part against which the composer derives the invention of the other parts," Part 3, Chapter 26). Even if the composer works out all the parts together, the part composed first is the *soggetto* of that passage. Zarlino does not describe any other method of composing.

For instance, when in Chapter 58 he explains dozens of ways of combining four voices to make a consonant sonority, he begins in each case with the soprano-tenor dyad and adds all the other possible voice combinations (see Table 1).[5] The approach to chords in this table differs from later chordal theory in several ways. The chords are a composite of several intervals built from the tenor. And there is no differentiation of what later theory would know as separate inversions or even major and minor chords. This method of explaining multivoiced chords continued to appear in treatises even as late as the *Historia musica* (1695) by Andrea Bontempi

4. Although Zarlino recommends this practice, he does not follow earlier theorists such as Johannes Tinctoris (1436–1511), who had insisted that the rules of proper voice leading were more important when against the tenor than between other voices, even allowing consecutive fifths between outer voices not involving the tenor (Seay 1978, p. 133)!

5. Lester 1989, pp. 18–19, contains the entire table and a translation into musical notation.

*Table 1.* Chords that are found between the parts of compositions

| From the unison: | |
|---|---|
| If the soprano makes and the bass makes the alto can be | a unison with the tenor, a third below the tenor; a fifth or sixth above the bass. |
| But if the bass makes the alto makes | a fifth below the tenor, a third or tenth above the bass. |
| Likewise if the bass be the alto can be | a sixth below the tenor, a third or tenth above the bass. [Etc.] |

*Source:* Zarlino 1558, Part 3, Chapter 58.

(c. 1624–1705) (pp. 227–228),[6] long after a theory of triads and their inversions had been published. And the notion of composing against a *soggetto* (Fux's *cantus firmus*) remained alive through the eighteenth century in both strict and free styles. For instance, the very first rule that Rameau gives for composing is that "we normally write a single part, called the subject" (Rameau 1722, Book 3, Chapter 43). Later in the eighteenth century, both Joseph Riepel (1709–1782) and Heinrich Christoph Koch (1749–1816) imply that a composer in the *galant* style begins by writing a main part against which the remainder of the texture is composed.

Zarlino knows well that the lowest voice, not the tenor, plays a crucial role in determining the sonority of a harmony: it is the bass *(basso)* or lowest voice as well as the basis *(basa)* or foundation (Part 3, Chapter 58). But his theoretical perspective does not allow him to treat the bass as a primary determinant of harmony. As just discussed, harmony for him arises from a variety of intervals against the tenor that join to make a concordance, not from a harmony built on the lowest pitch.

Nevertheless, Zarlino realized that his tenor-oriented perspective was inadequate to illuminate important aspects of musical structure. In Chapters 30 and 31, amid a long digression concerning cross relations and consecutive consonances, he stresses that such nonharmonic relationships be avoided in two voices. But he realizes that it is virtually impossible to do so in many-voiced textures because there are so many diagonal voice interactions in any succession of simultaneities. When more than two voices are present,

6. Bontempi's explanation occurs in the section on *practica moderna*. He credits a 1588 treatise by Zarlino's pupil Orazio Tigrini (c. 1535–1591) for his table.

Compositional Theory in the Eighteenth Century

the variety of harmony . . . does not consist solely in the variety of the consonances which are found between two voices, but also in the variety of the harmonies—which [variety] is determined by the position of the note which makes a third or tenth above the lowest voice of the composition. Either these [intervals] are minor, and the harmony which arises is determined by or corresponds to the arithmetical proportion or division; or they are major, and such a harmony is determined by or corresponds to the harmonic mean. On this variety depends all the diversity and perfection of harmonies. (Part 3, Chapter 31)

In this famous passage, Zarlino not only acknowledges the primary role played by minor and major "triads" in "root position," to use modern terminology, but he also uses the bass as the voice from which he builds the chords.[7]

Zarlino does not and cannot place these structures in positions of prominence in his treatises; they do not appear in chapter headings, and they are not the basis of compositional instruction. Nor does he relate "inversions of triads" to their "root-position form." Such recognitions are predicated on the bass as the primary determinant of harmonic structure and that multipitch sonorities are a unity greater than the sum of the intervals that constitute them. These are stances incompatible with interval structures based on the tenor as the basis of composition.

To be sure, Zarlino is aware of the invertibility of all intervals within an octave (seconds becoming sevenths, thirds becoming sixths, and fifths becoming fourths). But this notion appears only once in all his voluminous treatises: amid a long explanation on the consonance of a fourth in the *Dimostrationi harmoniche* (1571) (p. 77). He argues by analogy that since consonant thirds invert to become consonant sixths, and since dissonant seconds invert to become dissonant sevenths, therefore the perfect fourth, which is an inversion of the consonant perfect fifth, should be consonant. Franchino Gafori (1451–1522) had also noted the octave invertibility of intervals within an octave, mentioning how major thirds become minor sixths and minor thirds become major sixths (Gafori 1496, Chapter 7). But for Gafori as well as for Zarlino, a harmonic, bass-oriented perspective stands outside the overall theoretical framework.

Yet Zarlino's hesitancy in this matter surfaces once again in Chapter

---

7. Dahlhaus 1957 interprets this passage somewhat differently, arguing that the term *harmony* in this passage refers to the harmoniousness of the proportions; hence Zarlino still understands the concordance as the result of pairs of intervals and not as a chord in the modern sense. But even if Zarlino intended by *harmony* only the harmoniousness of the proportionality of these concordances, he explicitly refers to the harmoniousness of the entire sonority as built from the bass, not merely of the constituent intervals. Rivera 1979 and Lester 1989 (pp. 14–15) discuss tentative antecedents of Zarlino's recognition of these harmonies.

59, when he repeats that a multivoice sonority is best when there is a fifth and third over the lowest voice but that a sixth can replace the fifth over the lowest voice. Here again, although he bypasses an inversional explanation of what we call first-inversion triads, he explains the concordance (a chord of the sixth) by the intervals over the bass, not against the tenor.

Zarlino's tenor-oriented theoretical framework affects even the way the intervals are derived. Zarlino, like other theorists of his and earlier generations, generates intervals by dividing them, adding them, or subtracting them, but not by inverting them: the division of the octave (2:1) yields the perfect fifth (3:2) and perfect fourth (4:3); the division of the perfect fifth yields the major and minor thirds (5:4 and 6:5); the division of the major third yields the major and minor tones (9:8 and 10:9); and the division of the minor third yields a major tone and a diatonic semitone (16:15). Sixths, by contrast, are not explained in this manner. Rather, they arise by adding a perfect fourth and a third (Part 1, Chapter 13).

This method of interval generation does not relate thirds to sixths as complementary intervals. In fact, it contradicts the inversional relationship among thirds and sixths by using the *major* third to generate the *major* sixth (perfect fourth + major third = major sixth) and using the *minor* third to generate the *minor* sixth (perfect fourth + minor third = minor sixth). For this reason, Zarlino would consider E-G-C, what we call a "first-inversion major triad," as a *minor* harmony because of the minor third and minor sixth over the lowest voice; likewise, C-E-A, a "first-inversion minor triad," would be for him a *major* harmony. Thus, even if he had conceived of triadic inversions, Zarlino might well have rejected the idea since a "triad" would change its affect when inverted. Not until the early seventeenth century do theorists begin to generate all intervals along with their complements, thereby relating thirds and sixths as inversions by their manner of generation.

## Cadences

In general, Zarlino's explanations of contrapuntal structure proceed on a note-by-note basis. He never suggests explicitly (as do some later theorists) that in the process of composing one should look ahead, plan on crucial goals, and then fill in the resulting gaps. In general, as long as a point-to-point voice leading does not break any rules, it is acceptable. In two areas, however, he provides explanations that go beyond this. Both areas concern cadences and strongly influenced later theorists.

Zarlino joins a long-standing tradition of theorists who explain that not just any interval succession will end a phrase or a piece in a proper manner. A section must end not only with a proper perfect consonance (a unison or octave in two voices, for instance), but with a particular type of approach leading to that final resting point. The unison is to be preceded by a minor third, with chromatic alteration, if necessary; the octave by a major sixth (Part 3, Chapter 53).[8] In this one area, theory traditionally provided a functional harmonic preference rather than just the option of any interval succession. That cadences are formulas in which the penultimate sonority must move to the concluding sonority implies an underlying harmonic functionality; within a phrase any verticality succession is possible if its presence does not violate voice-leading rules, but at cadences only specific progressions are allowed.

The second area in which Zarlino adds a functional perspective builds on this understanding of cadences. He notes that cadences "were devised to mark off full sections of a larger harmonic composition and to punctuate the complete sentences of the text . . . But to make intermediate divisions in the harmony and text . . . we may write those cadences which terminate on the third, fifth, sixth, or similar consonances. Such an ending does not result in a perfect cadence; rather this is now called evading the cadence (*fuggir la cadenza*)" (Part 3, Chapter 53). That is, the figuration of the parts will often imply an impending cadence. But before the cadence is reached, one or another voice will move in such a manner that a perfect cadence is evaded. As Zarlino writes, "It is fortunate that we have such evaded cadences. They are useful when a composer in the midst of a beautiful passage feels the need for a cadence but cannot write one" (ibid.). This suggestive idea was not new with Zarlino. Nicola Vicentino (1511– c. 1576) antedates Zarlino with a similar passage (Vicentino 1555, Book 3, Chapter 24, pp. 51–52; commented on in Berger 1987, p. 136).

The idea that a composer "feels the need for a cadence"—that is, a voice leading appears that functionally implies a specific goal—but evades the cadence to continue the motion until heading toward a later goal, appears in many seventeenth-century treatises. But prior to Rameau, no theorist specified that this implies a functionality potentially present in mid-phrase progressions as well as at cadences. Rameau adopted this notion of evaded cadences and made it his principal explanation for the continuity of harmonic progressions within phrases.

## Zarlino and the *Seconda Pratica*

Zarlino and his pupils Artusi and Tigrini extoled the sacred style of Josquin and Willaert and its evolution in the music of Palestrina—a style in which variety is carefully measured, in which dissonances are relatively fleeting and serve to enhance the consonances to which they lead, and in which

---

8. Earlier in Part 3, one example ends with a final octave preceded by a perfect fifth (Marco and Palisca 1968, Ex. 39).

control over texture, line, and harmony has remained ever since a model of classic purity. During Zarlino's lifetime, however, other composers and theorists began to challenge this tradition, especially in secular music. The chief issues of contention concerned dissonance treatment, texture, and the relationship of text to music. A complete account of the resulting controversies would constitute a history of music and theory during much of the sixteenth and seventeenth centuries. Only a brief survey of the issues most pertinent to eighteenth-century theory appears here.[9]

DISSONANCE TREATMENT

Zarlino and his predecessors generally understood dissonances as momentary disruptions in a consonant musical surface. Dissonances provided variety and emphasized the perfection of the consonances by a temporary acerbity: "a dissonance causes the consonance which follows it to sound more agreeable. The ear then grasps and appreciates the consonance with greater pleasure, just as light is more delightful to the sight after darkness" (Zarlino 1558, Part 3, Chapter 57). Contemporaneous theorists of the newer styles challenged that view, arguing that dissonances were the most important part of counterpoint and should be considered for their own sake, not merely as incidental to consonances (Galilei 1581, 1588; discussed in Palisca 1956).

At the very beginning of the next century, Zarlino's pupil Artusi clearly articulated the underlying issues in an essay "on the imperfections of modern music" (1600) by analyzing various excerpts from the as-yet unpublished fifth book of madrigals by Claudio Monteverdi (1567–1643). Artusi was no mere pedant attacking the new. He recognized the important role played by dissonance in music, having published the first treatises devoted primarily to dissonance treatment (Artusi 1589, 1598), in which he relaxed some traditional restrictions on dissonance.

Artusi's discussion of Monteverdi's madrigals shows that even at the inception of the dispute, defenders as well as critics of the new practices understood them as elliptical instances of traditional voice leadings. The argument between the defenders and the critics was over the propriety of these ellipses. Artusi cites the passage from Monteverdi's *Cruda amarilli* shown in Example 1-9. The problematic dissonances are the A and F in the highest voice: a ninth against the bass without a preparation or a resolution, and then an unprepared seventh on a strong beat, occupying half a measure. Artusi examines the explanations proposed by supporters of Monteverdi, illustrates separately a simpler soprano part that is presumably the basis of the A and F, and finds the explanation of each

9. Palisca 1956, Palisca 1972a, Palisca 1983, and Federhofer 1964 offer more complete accounts of various aspects of the disputes summarized here.

*Example 1-9.* Strunk 1950 pp. 395, 397

dissonance inadequate. The A, he is told, is supposed to arise as a neighbor to the tenor G, and the F as a passing dissonance merely lengthened. Both explanations argue from missing notes either in the same or a different register. And it is on this issue that Artusi takes exception: "The sense of hearing does not perceive what it does not hear . . . How absurd it is to say that the tenor sustains a note in one register while the soprano, immediately afterward in a higher register, produces the effect the tenor should have produced . . . especially after the rest" (Strunk 1950, p. 397).

When Monteverdi published *Cruda amarilli* in his *Fifth Book of Madrigals* (1605), he responded to Artusi in the Preface. His brother Giulio Cesare Monteverdi then published a "declaration" at the end of Claudio's *Scherzi musicali* (1607). Claudio promised to write a formal work explaining the new practices, a promise he repeated as late as 1633.

But despite continuing polemic published from Rome to Warsaw over the next few decades, a comprehensive rationale for the new dissonance usages did not appear until the mid-1650s. The author was German composer and theorist Christoph Bernhard (1627–1692), a pupil of Heinrich Schütz (1585–1672) and Paul Siefert (1586–1666). Bernhard's manuscript, *Tractatus compositionis augmentatus* (c. 1655), circulated widely in German-speaking areas.[10] A composer in both the newer and older styles, Bernhard imitates rhetorical treatises by expressing each type of dissonance as a musical *figure* ("a way of employing dissonances," p. 77),

10. Hilse 1973, p. 4, discusses dating the *Tractatus*. Federhofer 1958 discusses its seventeenth-century circulation. Lester 1990 discusses the appearance of Bernhard's figures in Stierlein 1691, itself the source for articles in Walther 1732.

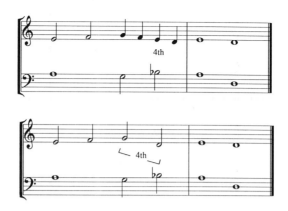

*Example 1-10.* Hilse 1973, pp. 81–82

conferring on each a Latin or Greek name.[11] He illustrates each dissonance and shows its origin in strict voice leading, beginning with the relatively simple usages of the strict style *(stylus gravis),* such as *transitus* (unaccented passing tone or neighbor), *quasi-transitus* (passing tone on a weak beat), and *syncopatio* (suspension). His explanation of the origin of the *quasi-transitus* is representative (see Example 1-10).

The voice-leading reductions to simpler structures become ever more complex for figures in the more elaborate style *(stylus luxurians),* which contain skips in and out of dissonances, consecutive dissonances, and the like. Some of these are shown in Example 1-11.

More extreme possibilities arise in the theatrical style *(stylus theatralis),* including the *ellipsis* ("the suppression of a normally required consonance," p. 112), the *abruptio* (a rest between a dissonance and its resolution), and, especially, the *heterolepsis:* "the seizure of a second voice" (p. 118) (see Example 1-12).

In these and other examples, Bernhard demonstrates a sophisticated understanding of voice leading, especially with his clear distinction between a part and the various voices that are implied by that part. The *Tractatus* is in this sense the work that explains the newer dissonance usages as elaborations of strict voice leading, thereby demonstrating the underlying unity of all musical dialects of the mid-seventeenth century. By

11. Dahlhaus notes that Bernhard's *Figurenlehre* reflects a German tradition in which cantors were also often Latin teachers, knew their Quintilian, and used the difference between grammar and rhetorical license to explain the foreign Italian style. Dahlhaus concludes that Bernhard's approach is thus separate from the Italian tradition that gave rise to the *seconda pratica* (Dahlhaus 1989, pp. 140–141). But Bernhard's method, although more comprehensive than Monteverdi's and Artusi's and using the apparatus of *Figuren,* is essentially the same as that of these Italians. The differences Dahlhaus cites are in the clothing of the ideas, not in their essence.

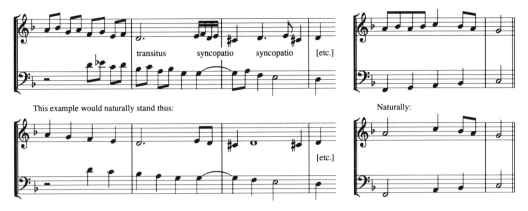

*Example 1-11.* Hilse 1973, pp. 92, 100

the end of the century, theorists could finally list what had been antago-nistic positions about dissonances in a dispassionate manner. Thus, Charles Masson, in his influential composition treatise of 1699, calmly notes three reasons to use dissonances, borrowing one reason from proponents of the newer styles and the other two from defenders of the older style: to project harshness and a sad text, to add ornaments, and to fill in melodic intervals (pp. 58–59).

### TEXT SETTING AND TEXTURE

Although much of the heated controversy between the new and old styles concerned dissonances, the underlying issues concerned text setting and musical texture. Ironically, both sides traced their positions to the same phrase in Plato's *Republic:* the exhortation that "the harmony and the

*Example 1-12.* Hilse 1973, pp. 118–119

rhythm must follow the words" (Strunk 1950, p. 4).[12] Zarlino read Plato's declaration in conjunction with the Greek philosopher's warning that music must not contain excesses and believed that an ideal setting of a text would combine all the elements of music in a polyphony that projected the text while maintaining a proper balance of variety, consonance and dissonance, rhythm, and so forth. But Galilei was convinced that monody and not polyphony was the ideal vehicle for expression of the text. The Monteverdis defended the new dissonances by appealing to the expression of the text. Artusi, in turn, did not regard textual expression as a justification and omitted the text from the excerpts he cited.

### PRIMA PRATICA AND SECONDA PRATICA

As a result of these disputes, it was obvious to all by the very early years of the seventeenth century that two separate musical languages coexisted. The terms *prima pratica* and *seconda pratica* (first and second practices) were apparently so widespread by the turn of the century that Artusi used *seconda pratica* in print for the first time in 1603 without defining it (Artusi 1603, p. 16).

Even though some of the conflicts between the styles were reconciled when Bernhard showed that dissonances in both shared a common ground, the stylistic split remained a feature of the musical world in some form or other into the eighteenth century. In addition to *prima* vs. *seconda pratica* or *stile antico* vs. *stile moderno,* the contrast between relatively stricter and freer styles was variously termed *contrapunto osservato* vs. *contrapunto commune* by Girolamo Diruta (c. 1554–after 1610) and Adriano Banchieri (1568–1634), *musica antica* vs. *musica moderna* by Marco Scacchi (c. 1602–c. 1685), and *contrapunctus gravis* vs. *contrapunctus luxurians* by Bernhard.

The *stile antico,* used primarily for sacred music, remained an active style well into the eighteenth century by Catholic and Protestant composers alike[13] and long remained a basis for teaching composition, whether via species counterpoint or merely by recognizing a style with greater restrictions on dissonances and voice leading. Well into the eighteenth century, theorists continued to categorize acceptable types of dissonances and melodic lines according to the style of a composition.

The increased emphasis on the bass as a supporting voice in monodies promoted the early development of thoroughbass, although the earliest publication using the term *basso continuo* was actually a sacred collection close to *prima pratica* in its dissonance treatment. Although thoroughbass

12. Marco and Palisca 1968, pp. xxii–xxiii, and Palisca 1983, especially pp. 153–155, discuss this in more detail.

13. Wolff 1968 discusses J. S. Bach's use of the *stile antico.*

as a performance technique was applied to music in the *stile antico* as well as in the newer styles, musicians regarded thoroughbass as more closely allied with the newer dissonance usages and voice leadings.

The new emphasis on the bass as a structural foundation, the resulting need of thoroughbass performers, and the separate need of organists to be able to accompany Lutheran chorales in a homophonic texture fostered a growing awareness of chordal combinations. Theorists at the very beginning of the seventeenth century developed the first fully harmonic theories, classifying chords, recognizing triadic inversions, redefining modes in terms of major and minor according to the triad built on the tonic, and recommending composition by connecting the notes from one triad to the next (discussed in Chapter 4).

Finally, the emphasis on text that first appeared as a humanistic concern and that later resonated throughout the battles over the *seconda pratica* called attention to relationships between language and music. Various aspects of rhetoric were used to explain melodic construction, melodic figures, and larger aspects of musical phrasing and continuity (aspects that we nowadays treat under the subject of musical form).

Thus, the results of the stylistic split between *prima* and *seconda pratica*, which itself grew out of the humanistic view of music promoted by Zarlino and his predecessors, remained alive in the eighteenth-century theoretical traditions enumerated at the opening of this chapter. The following chapters explore each of these traditions in turn as they appeared in the early eighteenth century.

# CHAPTER TWO

# Species Counterpoint and Fux's *Gradus*

*The way I teach counterpoint to our students is this: first I teach it to them note against note, so that they learn to land on the consonances; then with half notes and some syncopated whole notes against the cantus firmus, mixing dissonances with consonances if one can, avoiding and sometimes alighting on perfect cadences (which are on the octave, the fifteenth, or the unison). Finally, I teach them diminished [counterpoint], syncopated to such an extent that no entire beat ever occurs as a whole note or a dotted half note. But when the counterpoint passes through three or even four parts, I do not hold them to such strictness.*

Lanfranco 1533, p. 119

TEACHING COUNTERPOINT by isolating different types or *species* of voice interactions goes back at least to the early sixteenth century. Although Giovanni Maria Lanfranco (c. 1490–1545) includes no musical examples with this earliest-known description, his text clearly describes note against note, two notes against one with occasional ties or suspensions, and florid species, corresponding to first, second/fourth, and fifth species in Fux's classic *Gradus ad parnassum* (1725), published nearly two centuries later.

To modern musicians, Fux's pedagogical method appears so compelling that the terms *counterpoint* and *species counterpoint* seem to be indissolubly linked. But Fuxian species were by no means universal in counterpoint pedagogy either before or after 1725. Some theorists simply listed all the possible successions from one consonance to another: all the ways a unison could move to a minor third, to a major third, to a perfect fifth, and so forth. Dissonance configurations were then listed separately. It is hard to imagine how such a catalog of recommended, tolerable, and prohibited interval successions could have been learned other than by sheer rote memorization. In addition, this atomistic approach seems to preclude any systematic discussion of structures larger than note-to-note successions or involving more than two voices. Yet this tradition remained alive and well from Johannes Tinctoris in the late fifteenth century to Christoph Bernhard in the seventeenth century to Johann Mattheson (1681–1764) in the mid-eighteenth century. A separate tradition of counterpoint instruction, Zarlino's differentiation into *simple* counterpoint (note against note), *diminished* counterpoint (one florid part against long notes), and *free* counterpoint (two florid parts), was the basis of innumerable seventeenth- and eighteenth-century methods. Finally, many discussions of counterpoint before and after Fux were based on elaborations of a multivoiced harmonic texture, whether a thoroughbass realization, as in Friderich Erhard Niedt (c. 1674–1708), or a harmonic progression, as in Johannes Lippius (1585–1612) or Heinrich Christoph Koch (1749–1816).

Each of these counterpoint methods has its own strengths and weaknesses and its own implications. This chapter concentrates on species counterpoint, its evolution, various features of its presentation in *Gradus,* and its influence.

## Seventeenth-Century Formulations of Species

Among seventeenth-century writings concerned primarily with teaching the fundamentals of music, several presented species counterpoint in some form. An early example is the concise second part of *Il transilvano* (1609) by the Venetian musician Girolamo Diruta (c. 1554–after 1610), one of the models for Fux's *Gradus.* Like *Gradus, Il transilvano* is in dialogue format (the student being a Transylvanian—hence the title). Attempting to avoid the countless rules and exceptions that characterize other treatises, Diruta encapsulates the principles of consonant voice leading via four types of movement *(movimento):*

From a perfect consonance to another perfect consonance, move in contrary [including oblique] motion.
From an imperfect consonance to another imperfect consonance, move freely.
From a perfect consonance to an imperfect consonance, move freely.
From an imperfect consonance to a perfect consonance, move by contrary motion and by a semitone [in one voice].
(Diruta 1609, p. 2; facsimile in Palisca 1958, col. 1538)

Innumerable later writers testify to the advantages of such brief universal rules by adopting some formulation of them.

Diruta differentiates seven species of counterpoint against a *cantus fir-*

*mus* in whole notes: whole notes, two half notes, consonant tied half notes, dissonant tied half notes (suspensions), quarter notes, varied rhythms with dissonances treated strictly *(osservato),* and varied rhythms with dissonances treated more freely *(commune).* This species approach allows Diruta to introduce both rhythmic complexities and new types of dissonances one at a time. This is in contrast to Zarlino's method, where a student learned whole-note-against-whole-note writing with consonances in simple counterpoint, and then had to absorb rhythmic complexities and all sorts of dissonances all at once in florid counterpoint. As Diruta introduces each new species, he offers an example, labels all the intervals (just as Fux later did), and explains the voice leading note by note. Zarlino's influence is often felt (as in the suggestion to avoid consecutive consonances of any size on p. 5), but the clarity and concision is entirely Diruta's.

Lodovico Zacconi (1555–1627), a Venetian colleague of Diruta's, incorporated many of Diruta's examples in Book 2 of his *Prattica di musica seconda parte* (1622, pp. 57–128) and consolidated Diruta's seven species into what became Fux's five: whole notes, half notes, quarter notes, tied notes, and mixed note values. Book 3 (pp. 129–248) treats counterpoint without a *cantus firmus,* including imitation, canon, and invertible counterpoint. *Gradus* copies not only Zacconi's five species but also his organization, with separate sections for preliminary matters, species counterpoint, and imitative counterpoint.

Neither Diruta nor Zacconi deals with the dissonances of the *seconda pratica.* In fact, Italian theorists publishing composition methods in the seventeenth century dealt primarily with sacred music. As a result, there are no discussions of *seconda pratica* dissonances akin to Bernhard's within the species counterpoint writers of this period. But newer practices did gradually enter into treatises, such as those by Giovanni Maria Bononcini (1642–1678) and Angel Berardi (c. 1636–1694). For instance, Bononcini's popular *Musico prattico* (Bologna, 1673 and 1688; Venice, 1678; partial German translation, 1701) includes both the standard resolutions of suspensions and the ones shown in Example 2-1. Among the more modern features are consecutive dissonances (first and fourth excerpts), the ascending resolution of a suspended note with both voices moving (second excerpt), skips from a suspension (third excerpt), and also the presence of thoroughbass figures (fourth excerpt). This last feature makes it clear that for Bononcini, the two voices shown do not necessarily represent a two-part texture, but rather an outer-voice frame.

Berardi published two major treatises, one adopting Zarlino's differentiation of simple and diminished counterpoint (*Documenti armonici,* 1687), the other using a species approach to an extent unknown elsewhere, with dozens of species (*Miscellanea musicale,* 1689, Book 1): some counterpoints contain only steps or only skips, some use ostinatos (pitch ostin-

*Example 2-1.* Bononcini 1673, pp. 65–67. X represents a sharp.

atos, rhythm ostinatos, or both combined), some exclude any repetitions, some omit various scale steps or intervals or use only a few scale steps or intervals, some include imitations, some use a very wide range of intervals, and so forth. The earlier work introduces twenty-four rules of counterpoint, the first four modifying Diruta's four rules, some of the remaining ones derived from Zarlino (proscribing consecutive thirds or sixths of the same quality), and others being original. Fux found many of these rules overly restrictive, although he often cited them without crediting Berardi (as in the case of *ottava battuta;* Mann 1965a, pp. 37–38).

In addition to his exhaustive study of traditional counterpoint, Berardi also introduces usages suggesting contemporary instrumental styles. Example 2-2 is "in a more modern manner" reminiscent of Arcangelo Corelli (1653–1713), who had lived in Bologna and who published his works for the first time just a few years before this treatise.

*Example 2-2.* Berardi 1687, p. 143

The treatises by Diruta, Zacconi, Bononcini, and Berardi are the major published works on species counterpoint preceding Fux's *Gradus*. Many aspects of *Gradus* are already present in one or more of them: the five species, the four rules for consonances introduced at the beginning, use of the various species to introduce rhythmic complexities and dissonances, the dialogue format, the emphasis on *stile antico*, various specific usages, the gradual ascent from simple species exercises in two voices toward imitation and fugue, and the introduction of more modern usages based on variants of strict counterpoint. But none of these seventeenth-century authors was able to match Fux's achievement—the consolidation of the species approach into a comprehensive and convincing whole.

## IMPROVISED SPECIES COUNTERPOINT

In addition to these works presenting species counterpoint in terms of written composition, there are others that use contrapuntal species to teach vocal improvisation—singing "above the book" *(super librum)* as Tinctoris called it. For many centuries such extempore vocal improvisation was probably an important training ground for composers. Vicente Lusitano (?–?) presented the first methodical instructions for vocal improvisation in 1553, applying note against note, then two, three, and four notes against one to vocal improvisation against a *cantus firmus* in two, three, and more voices (1561 edition, fols. 12$^r$–12$^v$, fols. 15$^r$–16$^v$). Lanfranco, quoted at the beginning of this chapter, also probably referred to improvised and not written counterpoint in 1533, in that he teaches his students "to land on the consonances" *(cadere su le Consonanze)*. Such improvised species counterpoint lasted into the eighteenth century in at least some locations. Brossard 1703 discusses *"chanter sur le Livre,"* and Padre Martini heard four-voiced vocal improvisations *(contrappunto alla mente)* in 1747 in Rome (Martini 1774–1775, Vol. 1, pp. 57–59). Madin 1742 gives instructions even while the author, a priest in Paris, acknowledges that it was no longer practiced in many countries (p. 1). Yet Madin also reports on the "veritable confusion from the mixture of intervals [that results] from 30 or so musicians intoning it all at the same time, some correctly and others utterly randomly" (pp. 6–7).

Another aspect of vocal improvisation, adding ornaments to composed pieces, was recognized as an important influence on composition in counterpoint manuals of all types. For instance, Stierlein 1691 introduces many of Bernhard's dissonant figures as vocal ornaments (Lester 1990), and Fux cites vocal improvisation as the origin of various dissonance usages. But by the latter part of the seventeenth century, thoroughbass practiced at the keyboard had replaced singing above the book and vocal ornamentation as the primary medium for compositional training via improvisation. Although the very largest outlines of this development seem clear, the detailed study that will chronicle this momentous transformation in compositional process and its affects on musical styles has yet to be written. In any event, Fux's *Gradus* offers no hint that the species method is to be used for anything other than learning written composition.

## *Gradus ad parnassum* and the Pedagogy of Counterpoint

Of all the major theoretical treatises in the Western tradition, *Gradus ad parnassum* (Vienna, 1725) by Johann Joseph Fux (1660–1741) in its original text or literal translation has remained in practical use the longest. It was quickly hailed as a pedagogic classic by Fux's contemporaries, even by those who disagreed with Fux on one or another matter;[1] was rendered during the eighteenth century from its Latin original into German, Italian, French, and English, either in literal translation or paraphrase; and was used by numerous prominent eighteenth-century musicians, among them Haydn, Mozart, and Beethoven (Mann 1965a, pp. xi–xiv; Mann 1967, 1973, 1978–1979, 1987). It has been a model or at least a point of departure for many works on counterpoint since its publication and, via mid-twentieth-century translations into German and English, has remained in use as a textbook down to the present time.

The lasting success of *Gradus* is based not only on the species method but also on the work's pedagogic organization and endearing literary style. Fux published it in his sixty-fifth year, drawing on a lifetime's experience teaching not only composition but also the fundamentals of music to choirboys at Saint Stephens in Vienna, where he was Kapellmeister from 1704. Fux extended the species approach to three and four voices. He avoided the intricacies of Berardi's twenty-four rules or Zarlino's multiple rules spread over dozens of chapters and interrupted by extended digressions by offering a reformulation of Diruta's four rules of consonant voice leading, reordered and no longer requiring a semitone in one voice when moving from an imperfect to a perfect consonance. Fux's formulation of these four rules recurs in innumerable works throughout the century, regardless of their orientation. Even the 1756 treatise by Johann Friedrich Daube (c. 1730–1797), which teaches thoroughbass via Rameau-inspired

---

1. Mattheson, who engaged Fux in an acerbic correspondence concerning modes, major-minor keys, and solmization systems (Mattheson 1725, pp. 185–205), penned an ode in honor of a never-completed German translation of *Gradus* by Georg Philipp Telemann (1681–1767) (Mattheson 1731, p. 181). Lorenz Mizler (1711–1778) translated *Gradus* into German in 1742, although his annotations show that he disagreed with Fux on many matters. J. S. Bach apparently owned a copy of the *Gradus* (Benary [1961], p. 78). C. P. E. Bach reports that his father "started his pupils right in with what was practical, and omitted all the *dry species* of counterpoint that are given in Fux and others" (David and Mendel 1966, p. 279).

harmony, praises Fux's rules (preface). Some later musicians noted that the four rules could be reduced further. Beethoven suggested two rules (one for motion into perfect consonances and one for imperfect consonances); Padre Martini noted that the only prohibition is direct motion into a perfect consonance (Mann 1965a, p. 22). Finally, Fux attempted to reduce the influence of changing musical styles on the rules of counterpoint by insisting that vocal style, not the instrumental influences seen in Bononcini and Berardi, was its proper foundation.

For Fux, all that is needed to begin counterpoint is a list of consonances and the four rules of voice leading. From this simple basis, Fux proceeds through species counterpoint in two, three, and four voices; turns to imitation, fugue, and invertible counterpoint; and concludes the treatise with a survey of musical figures and affects and the requirements of various contemporary styles. He relegates to a forty-two-page introduction those matters (such a interval generation) still deemed necessary in a formal treatise. As a result, the student learns local interactions of intervals via the species; the *cantus firmus* and repetitious rhythms of the individual parts remove from consideration such issues as texture and rhythmic relations among the parts. The section on imitation and fugue focuses on precisely these issues and also the use of motives. When the student has mastered all this, Fux imparts his advice on modes and on a range of stylistic issues.

The body of the work (Fux 1725, pp. 43–279) is cast as a dialogue between Josephus (Fux as an eager student) and Aloysius, representing Palestrina, the master "to whom I owe everything that I know of this art" (Mann 1965a, p. 18).[2] Throughout the dialogue, Josephus puts into practice the precepts handed down by Aloysius, continually raising the sorts of questions a student would have and occasionally making mistakes and correcting them or having them corrected by Aloysius. Numerous earlier works had illustrated good and bad voice leadings. But no other work so realistically portrays a pupil progressing to a substantial composer under constant tutelage. Readers, conscientiously working out all the examples, could easily imagine themselves, as the young Haydn probably did, studying along with a colleague under the guidance of a master: "[Haydn] worked his way through the whole method, did the exercises, put them by for several weeks, and looked them over again and polished them until he thought he had got them right" (Griesinger 1810, p. 10; Gotwals 1963, p. 10).

Fux introduces all rules and voice-leading recommendations via the exercises and their emendations, imparting only what a student needs to

2. At one point, Fux forgets this pose and Aloysius refers to Palestrina in the third person (Lester 1989, p. 195).

know at any given point in order to do the exercises and gain compositional experience. Absent are extended preliminary discussions of rules as in Diruta 1609 and Bononcini 1673 (such as the rhythmic circumstances in which consecutive perfect consonances might or might not be acceptable, and how best to use consecutive thirds or sixths).

This relaxed manner in which Fux introduces and modifies his rules is both one of the signal merits of *Gradus* and one of its most maddening features. For instance, Fux explains that a counterpoint should begin with a perfect interval; but when Josephus begins his second counterpoint exercise in the D-mode with a G in the lower voice, Aloysius must briefly explain that this particular fifth is unacceptable because it violates his sense of modal propriety (Mann 1965a, p. 31). A full explanation of modes, which would certainly have interrupted the beginning exercises if placed here, does not occur until quite a bit later, after the study of fugue and imitation (Fux 1725, pp. 221–231; Lester 1989, pp. 189–196). Similarly, not until Josephus needs the information for three-part writing does Aloysius explain why the rule prohibiting similar motion into a perfect interval needs to be relaxed in writing for more than two voices (Mann, 1965a, pp. 76–77).

This very approach, however, yields numerous passages where the lack of systematization and formal rules leads to confusion over the criteria involved. For instance, at the very end of first species in two voices, there is a discussion of the propriety of raising the leading tone three measures before the end of an exercise so that F♯-G-F♯-G will occur instead of the "harsh relation" F-G-F♯-G (p. 39). A careful student will have noted that the identical "harsh relation" had arisen previously and arises later without correction or comment.

Likewise, a careful reader might wonder about skips outlining a tritone. In the fourth exercise, Aloysius emends the ascending skip F-B to F-C (p. 35). Two exercises later, Josephus uses the ascending succession F-A-B♭. When should B♭ be used? When C? And why does Aloysius let stand the ascending succession F-G-B-D not long afterwards (p. 47)? Fux probably avoided an explicit discussion because it would have involved balancing complex modal and contrapuntal issues: B♭ is not appropriate in the first instance because the exercise is in the E-mode, just before a stepwise line leading to the final; the second instance is in the F-mode, where B♭ is generally preferable to B; in the third instance B♭ is not possible because of a sustained E in the *cantus firmus,* and the melodic pattern F-G-C-D would have been more problematic.

Similar issues arise throughout the treatise. Eighteenth-century musicians were aware of these problems. Nicolas Framery (1745–1810), a French musician active in founding the *Conservatoire* (Gessele 1989, Chapters 2 and 5), probably spoke for many eighteenth-century musicians when he criticized "the obscurity of the principles and their developments. All that one can admire is the marvelous sagacity of the student who comprehends at the first word things that masters themselves would understand only with difficulty" (Azopardi 1786, p. 11).

In Fux's defense, this very lack of systematization is the essence of his method—to develop ever-greater sophistication as students approach compositional problems of ever greater complexity, leading them to realize that as composers they will constantly have to weigh alternatives. Consider the discussion where Josephus avoids a potential tied note in fourth species because it would lead to a "bad repetition" (Mann 1965a, pp. 60–61). Repetitions occur in earlier and later exercises. Fux's point is not to prohibit them but to introduce yet another criterion to the developing composer's sense of discrimination. Marginalia by Haydn and Beethoven, commenting on various voice leadings in Fux's examples, confirm that they used *Gradus* in just this way.[3] To the extent that *Gradus* succeeds either as a pedagogical text or a source for structural counterpoint, this is one of its signal strengths.

Another superior feature of Fux's pedagogy is the length and variety of his *cantus firmi*. In contrast to a single inordinately long *cantus firmus* or merely an ascending and descending scale, as found in some other treatises, Fux maintains a different *cantus firmus* for each mode. The melodies are about a dozen notes in length—long enough to allow for a variety of motions between the circumscribed opening of the phrase and the obligatory cadence, but not so long that flabby lines will be inevitable (although surely many of the quarter-note exercises do wander aimlessly).

A final aspect of *Gradus* that has enhanced its status as a pedagogic classic is its relative abstraction from any particular compositional style. Zarlino had written about compositional practices of the generation preceding his. Later writers on counterpoint had attempted to keep up to date in their recommendations. Fux's approach is different. Although the inclusion of sections discussing contemporary styles toward the end of *Gradus* clearly illustrates his intent to write for a contemporary audience, he also strongly believed that the underlying basis of musical composition should be unaffected by stylistic mannerisms. He concludes the treatise with a parable relating musical styles to fashions in dress and architecture:

> If one were to dress today in the style of fifty or sixty years ago, certainly he would expose himself to ridicule. Music, too, should be suited to the times. But never have I found a tailor familiar with the new fashions, nor have I heard tell of one, who attached shirt sleeves to the thigh or to the knee; nor of any architect who was so foolish as to put the foundation of a building

3. Many of Haydn's comments appear in the critical report to the 1967 facsimile edition of *Gradus;* some of Beethoven's comments appear in Mann 1965a, especially pp. 125–126.

on top of the roof. Yet we see and hear such things everywhere in music, not without bringing disappointment to those of taste, and shame to art when the fundamental precepts of nature and art are inverted from their proper place, and the foundation is put above while the other parts are put below without regard for the proper foundation. Indeed, Joseph, no matter how much you strive for novelty and invention by exerting all the powers of your times, nothing can overturn, much less destroy, the rules of art which imitate nature and which achieve the ends of nature. (Lester 1989, p. 209)

Fux aimed to present what he considered this undying foundation of musical structure, believing it was exemplified in the music of Palestrina. In this sense Fux stands as the last important theorist of the *prima pratica* tradition, following the line running from Zarlino and Artusi through many of the seventeenth-century Italian writers. As a composer, Fux wrote in both practices—operas and trio sonatas in the latest style and *a cappella* liturgical music.

It is clear from modern scholarship, especially that of Jeppesen, that the usages in *Gradus* do not agree in numerous ways with either the details or the spirit of Palestrina's music. In addition, it is significant that when Fux refers to music of the sixteenth century, he cites only Palestrina. Earlier theorists, closer to that era chronologically, refer to a much wider range of composers; Bernhard, for instance, cites Palestrina as well as Josquin (c. 1440–1521), Willaert (c. 1490–1562), Morales (c. 1500–1553), Gombert (c. 1500–c. 1556), and Francesco Soriano (1549–1621). By Fux's lifetime, the music of Palestrina's time had become more of a venerated symbol of idealized polyphony than a known repertoire.

One seemingly archaic aspect of *Gradus,* however, was not included solely in homage to the past. Fux based the entire work on the six authentic church modes because that was what he considered to be the sole basis of contemporary music. As discussed in Lester 1989, Fux's use of modes was only one part of a complex of traditions that kept the church modes alive as an aspect of contemporary music well into the eighteenth century, especially in German-speaking areas. Eight years after defending the modes against Mattheson's call for the adoption of major and minor keys, Fux does not even mention the keys anywhere in *Gradus,* not even when Josephus asks about those who hold differing opinions on nature of the modes (Lester 1989, p. 189). Fux was thereby in agreement with Italian contrapuntal theory in the seventeenth century, which by and large did not deal with the major-minor keys either.

## *Gradus* and the Discipline of Species Counterpoint

In recent decades, partly because of the central role it plays in Schenkerian perspectives on tonal music, species counterpoint has acquired significance apart from the historical importance of Fux's treatise and of species as a pedagogical method within the eighteenth century. Schenker's works, in addition to using concepts drawn from species counterpoint, include provocative commentaries on *Gradus* (especially in Schenker 1987). Schenker treats tenets of species counterpoint apart from their context within Fux's work and within the eighteenth century. Schenker seems to have believed that the species method originated with Fux (Schenker 1954, p. 180), and he also was apparently unaware of other types of contrapuntal writings circulating during Fux's lifetime, even Bernhard's *Tractatus* (published in 1926), which seemingly would have been of great interest to him with its suggestive notions of simple structures underlying complex dissonance patterns (Federhofer 1982). Furthermore, Schenker seems not to have paid much attention to the later portions of *Gradus* where Fux considers more contemporary styles, leading Schenker to consider *Gradus* primarily as a work on strict counterpoint rather than as a composition method.

Interest in the role of *Gradus* in the eighteenth century has also focused on the intense interest of the major composers of the Classical era in counterpoint. Earlier generations of historians, noting the relative absence of polyphonic surface textures in Classical music (at least in comparison to the music of J. S. Bach), often stressed the harmonic roots of the classical style. But it is now clear that Haydn, Mozart, and Beethoven shared an abiding interest in contrapuntal aspects of voice leading as it affected their own music (Mann 1973). Furthermore, contrapuntal passages in their music often mimic species exercises (such as the opening of the finale of Mozart's *String Quartet*, K. 387).

As a result, many of the concepts in *Gradus* have gathered meanings that are not quite those that they have in the context of Fux's work in the early eighteenth century. Considering all these meanings as they appear in modern theory and history would take the present study far from its course. Chapter 7 discusses the application of Fuxian counterpoint later in the eighteenth century. The current discussion is directed instead primarily to defining two central issues as they appear within *Gradus:* first, the extent to which Fux considers motion among consonances to be a structural frame within which both consonant and dissonant diminutions arise; and second, the extent to which simultaneity-to-simultaneity successions arise from the voice leading of individual lines rather than the progression of chords.

THE STRUCTURAL FRAME AND DIMINUTION

In a Schenkerian perspective, counterpoint controls voice leading between structural points at each level of a composition. Many musicians today believe that this process of diminution is implicit in the species approach itself: after learning note-against-note interactions using only consonant

*Example 2-3.* Mann 1965a, p. 41

whole notes, the student learns how to put additional events between these downbeats in the quicker-moving counterpoints of later species. But although this mode of thinking plays an important role in other theoretical traditions of the time, it is not central in *Gradus*. And the relatively limited areas where it does appear in *Gradus* are those in which the concept had been used for many generations.

Composition via diminution is the core of Part 2 of Niedt's thoroughbass manual (1706). As discussed more fully in Chapter 3 of this study, Niedt generates several complete dance movements by applying ever more complex variations to a brief chordal thoroughbass realization. In addition, harmonic theorists, from Lippius in the early seventeenth century through Rameau's followers in the eighteenth century, demonstrate how elaborations of a given chordal structure can produce complex textures.

Fux considered such elaborative methods inimical to what he was trying to teach via species counterpoint. He disparaged thoroughbass approaches that claimed they could teach a student to compose after a few months of study. For him composition was not to be learned by applying elaborations to an underlying structure. Rather, it required long study of voice leading and texture—slow ascent of the *Steps to Parnassus,* as stated in the title. Thus Fux never applies diminution to the actual composition of counterpoint (either with or without a *cantus firmus*). When the task is to compose a new counterpoint on a given *cantus firmus,* the object is to create a new counterpoint, not to rework a previous exercise.

Fux does use diminution to explain the origin of various types of dissonances. For instance, an unaccented passing tone in second species, the very first dissonance-type introduced, is a diminution "filling out the space between two notes that are a third distant from each other" (Mann 1965a, p. 41) (see Example 2-3). Similar examples reduce quarter-note passing tones and neighbors to "their original forms" (p. 51) and tied notes to their basis "if the retardation were removed" (p. 56).

After the study of the species and of imitation and fugue, Fux uses diminution to explain two additional dissonance patterns—*variation* and *anticipation:*

[Variation] differs from regular diminution in that regular diminution arises only when notes progress by skips of a third: [see Example 2-4]. Variation arises when notes proceed by step [see Example 2-5]. This example demon-

*Example 2-4. Lester 1989, p. 185*

strates clearly that variation departs from the common rules of counterpoint in that it proceeds by skips from a consonance into a dissonance [at E to C], and then from a dissonance into another dissonance [at C to A]—this is certainly not allowed in counterpoint, but is commonly allowed in composition. (Lester 1989, pp. 185–186)

After showing several other similar types of variations, Fux treats anticipations as shown in Example 2-6.

That is the extent of Fux's understanding of dissonances by diminution. He is not even sure of the propriety of variations and anticipations. These "departures from the rules of counterpoint" arose because singers "were so little content with regular diminutions and so fond of showing off the flexibility of their voice" (Lester 1989, p. 188). Using as his evidence these rather tepid dissonant figures, Fux launches a vociferous condemnation of singers for their "destruction of the harmony."

He returns to dissonances one last time in the discussion of recitatives (Lester 1989, pp. 204–209), offering an example, (2-7), to which Josephus reacts with horror: "It seems that the instrumental chords, which consist mostly of dissonances, depart from all the rules of counterpoint."

Instead of attempting to explain the dissonances as elaborations of a simpler structure, as Artusi and Bernhard had done with such sophistication generations earlier, Fux argues that in effect there is no explanation. These dissonances are simply "considered good according to the nature

*Example 2-5. Lester 1989, p. 186*

*Example 2-6. Lester 1989, p. 187*

Compositional Theory in the Eighteenth Century

*Example 2-7.* Lester 1989, p. 205

of recitative . . . In this style one should pay attention less to the harmonies than to the expression of the meaning of the words." Examples ensue illustrating common recitative patterns that express various sentiments and various types of grammatical constructions (complete sentences, question marks, commas, etc.).

Fux thus joins the *prima pratica* tradition running back through Zarlino in which dissonances are relatively brief disruptions of consonant voice leading, even when they create a progressive functionality leading to a cadence. From that perspective, Fux could only consider his mild variations and anticipations as violations of the strict style. For the rest, it was as if the *seconda pratica* and its theory had never existed. He endured the dissonances common in early eighteenth-century recitatives as given rhetorical figures to be learned by rote—set a question this way, an answer that way; set a king's speech this way, a knave's that way. In brief, his

*Example 2-8.* Diruta 1609, p. 3

understanding of dissonant diminution techniques does not extend beyond the simplest patterns.

Early-eighteenth-century theoretical traditions other than species counterpoint imparted to dissonance additional important roles in musical structure. Thoroughbass theorists, for instance, knew that an overwhelming majority of possible bass figurings included dissonances. Because of their required preparation and resolution, these dissonances played a major role in determining the harmonic context in which a chord could appear. Rameau built on this tradition, treating dissonances as crucial and necessary to determine harmonic function and direction. Thus, an eighteenth-century musician seeking a contemporary understanding of dissonances more complex than simple passing tones, neighbors, and suspensions would turn to thoroughbass or harmonic writers but not to Fux.

Diminution techniques also arise in *Gradus* to explain various nondissonant voice leadings. Thus, Fux includes the traditional explanation for proscribing hidden fifths and octaves: diminution reveals the concealed voice-leading problem. Fux's examples (Mann 1965a, p. 33) are similar to those in Diruta 1609 (see Example 2-8).

Apart from diminution techniques, one might seek evidence of working from a structural frame in Fux's repeated admonitions that students should look ahead as they work out exercises: "consider the ending before you start to write" (Mann 1965a, p. 42); "I should like to urge you . . . not only to pay attention to the measure upon which you are working but also to those following" (p. 48). In the hands of the some thoroughbass writers, this long-range perspective occasionally leads to insights into a large-scale voice-leading frame for simultaneity-to-simultaneity progressions. By contrast, Fux offers his advice to avoid problems on the compositional surface of the music: "I want to remind you again to pay the utmost attention to measures following; otherwise, you may sometimes find yourself unable to go on" (p. 53); "it is most important to consider whether a correct progression will be possible from the chord of the first measure built up this way, to the second, third, or even fourth measures" (p. 111).

Countless additional passages confirm that Fux's primary focus is di-

*Example 2-9.* Mann 1965a, p. 51

rected toward the musical surface, not toward any abstractions drawn from that surface, no matter how they are conceived. For instance, he includes the cambiata figure shown in Example 2-9 not because it is symbolic of any structural meaning, but because it is a part of the surface of sixteenth-century music. In fact, the rhythm in which Fux cites the cambiata figure is comparatively rare in Palestrina's music (Jeppesen 1970, p. 212).

In sum, modern musicians have found suggestions of diminution in Fux's explanations of simple dissonance patterns sanctioned by centuries of use, and then extended these principles to include a host of diminution techniques. But these extensions, which may indeed be quite useful in many ways, lay outside of Fux's conceptual universe. With more comprehensive approaches to dissonances readily available elsewhere, it is hardly likely that eighteenth-century musicians turned to *Gradus* or to species counterpoint for information on how complex motions of any sort (consonant or dissonant) could arise within a given voice-leading frame. They found in *Gradus* a clear method for learning to manipulate intervals and for dealing with lines, rhythms, motives, and textures, and a provocative gateway to the romance of counterpoint of the Golden Age. But their approach to freer dissonances (even the most commonly used dissonances) and to large-scale diminutions could not have come from species counterpoint or Fux's *Gradus*. Those features were simply not present there in the eighteenth century.

### INTERVALLIC VOICE LEADING AND HARMONY

The basis of Fux's species counterpoint seems to lie in composing two voices that relate to each other intervallically and then learning to control additional voices in the same manner. But several aspects demonstrate both that Fux's approach is less consistently intervallic than it may seem and that because of his limited vocabulary for dealing with harmonies, Fux seems at times unable to express himself clearly on various harmonic matters that he chose to raise.

The most revealing passage appears at the beginning of the discussion of three-part counterpoint. Fux is faced with the age-old problem of explaining how more than two voices relate to one another. He must give guidance before allowing Josephus to begin writing three-part counterpoint because some interactions that are consonant against the bass, such as a simultaneous fifth and sixth, will produce unwanted dissonances. Fux could have explained that all voice interactions should be checked for dissonances. But that would have required a further discussion of why the fourth, which is dissonant against the bass, is acceptable between upper voices. Fux's solution is temporarily to abandon working from a *cantus firmus* while he explains the *triad (trias)*.

Fux at first defines the term *triad* quite literally as a third and a fifth over the bass. Although "the harmonic triad should be employed in every measure if there is no special reason against it" (Mann 1965a, p. 71), this is not always possible. "Occasionally, for a better melodic line, one uses a consonance not properly belonging to the triad, namely, a sixth or [NB!] an octave" (p. 72). Fux uses the concept of the triad here not to explain how pitches or intervals belong to harmonies but primarily to control texture by urging the presence of three pitch classes in as many simultaneities as possible (to use modern terms)—hence the octave is "a consonance not properly belonging to the triad." In this passage Fux's notion of the triad is quite close to Zarlino's *perfect harmony* except that Zarlino, of course, had never used the term *triad*.

Immediately thereafter, Fux considerably expands his triadic perspective to include the first inversion. He illustrates a C-major triad with C in the bass, and then with E in the bass and C on top, explaining that in a harmony with a third and sixth over the bass, the note making a sixth over the bass "should be considered as if it were moved from its proper place [in the bass] to an unusual one [in an upper voice] . . . in its proper place [it] establishes the harmonic triad" (Mann 1965a, p. 74). Fux thus shows his awareness of a theory of triadic inversions dating back at least as far as Otto Siegfried Harnish (c. 1568–1623) in 1608 and Johannes Lippius (1585–1612) in 1610, both of whom explicitly recognized inversions of the triad in terms of the removal of the bass note to another position (Lester 1989, pp. 31–33, 39–41).

To illustrate all this, Fux introduces a unique example. In contrast to every other such exercise in the entire dialogue on species counterpoint, no voice is specified as a *cantus firmus*. And instead of beginning a discussion with the D-mode (as he invariably does elsewhere), Fux writes the example, shown in 2-10, in the C-mode, with a fundamental harmonic progression more like a progression in C-major than voice leading in the C-mode.

There are triads, in Fux's definition of the term, only in measures 1 and 5, and an inverted triad in measure 4. Josephus wonders why full triads are not possible in additional measures, proposing the emendation of

*Example 2-10.* Mann 1965a, p. 72

measures 2 and 3 shown in Example 2-11. Aloysius replies, "Your alteration is not bad and your example is not to be considered wrong." But
he clearly prefers the version in Example 2-10. Some of the reasons he
offers for this preference do not stand up to scrutiny. He notes that the
tenor in Example 2-10 moves by step at first, which is better than the skip
that begins Example 2-11. Furthermore, the tenor in Example 2-10 has
only one A, whereas Josephus' alteration has two, violating the principle
of variety. Unfortunately for Aloysius' argument, the overwhelming majority of exercises in *Gradus* would have to be rewritten if these were the
standards for good lines.

Aloysius is also concerned with the harmony in measure 3 of Example
2-11, explaining that over solmization syllable *mi* (in this case, the bass E
in measure 3) a sixth is preferable to a fifth when the bass progresses from
*mi* to *fa* (that is, ascends a semitone). Fux apparently hears the E+G of
measure 3 as implying an E-minor triad, not the desired C-major triad
with E in the bass. The recommendation to use a sixth over *mi* is commonplace in thoroughbass manuals of the period, where it explains how
the third and seventh degrees in major keys best support first-inversion
triads. But it is anomalous in *Gradus*. It is a harmonic, not an intervallic
explanation. And it concerns scale steps in a major key, which Fux does

*Example 2-11.* Mann 1965a, p. 73

*Example 2-12.* Mann 1965a, p. 76

not acknowledge. He applies this recommendation most consistently in the C-mode, the F-mode, and the G-mode—the modes closest to major scales. In the E-mode he commonly harmonizes an E in the bass with a fifth, not a sixth, even in the succession E-F (Mann 1965a, pp. 114–115).

Josephus tries his hand at two more emendations of the progression in Example 2-10 amid growing confusion about Fux's reasons for introducing this discussion. See Example 2-12. Aloysius remarks on the diminished fifth between middle and upper voices in measure 2 of the first exercise but not on the comparable augmented fourth of the second example. But he does not mark any of these examples as being wrong. (Fux uses a "first-inversion diminished triad" as the standard cadential approach-chord when the *cantus firmus* is in the bass [pp. 80, 83, and 84, passim]. But he never addresses the consonance-dissonance of this cadential sonority, in which the sixth over the bass, a dissonant tone against the third over the bass, resolves a suspension.)

It seems that Examples 2-10, 2-11, and 2-12 are more in C major than in the C-mode and that Fux is searching for reasons to promote "I-vii$^{o6}$-I$^6$" instead of "I-ii-iii" or "I-ii-I$^6$" in the first three measures. This was a major issue at the time. Not long before 1725, the *règle de l'octave* in thoroughbass treatises began to enshrine "I-vii$^{o6}$-I$^6$" as the standard progression over a rising or descending bass involving scale-steps 1, 2, and 3, rejecting the older notion that the normal chord over any bass note was a "root-position" triad. Half a century later, Padre Martini confirmed this historical development, using similar progressions ("I-ii-I" vs. "vii$^{o6}$-I") to illustrate the difference between the old-fashioned and modern ways of writing chords over a stepwise bass (Martini 1774–1775, Vol. 1, pp. 224–225).

But Fux—without a clear sense of key, which other theorists of his and an earlier period had, and without a more systematic way of dealing with harmonic structures and progressions—has no working vocabulary to offer this advice. A puzzling question is why he introduced these examples at

*Example 2-13.* J. S. Bach, *Well-Tempered Clavier I: Prelude in C major*, mm. 1–4, voice leading

all, since they seem to be out of place in his discussion of species counterpoint. But whatever his reason for placing this discussion at the very beginning of the discussion of three-voice writing, its presence is revealing. First, it shows the limitations of his perspective to give advice on choosing among harmonic possibilities. And second, it shows his awareness of harmonic progressions and their importance despite his difficulties in explaining these matters.

Another matter concerning harmony is Fux's implicit understanding that the bass is the voice supporting the structure. Unlike Zarlino and other theorists of counterpoint through Bontempi (1695), who had calculated the notes in multivoiced chords in relation to the tenor, Fux always seems to assume that if the *cantus firmus* is not in the bass, then the bass is the first voice to be worked out against the *cantus firmus*. How could one know whether an upper-voice fourth, augmented fourth, or diminished fifth were possible unless one knew the bass note? Significantly, Fux never raises the issue. It was an underlying assumption of the eighteenth century that did not have to be mentioned because it was so universally held.

Finally, Fux's limited chordal perspective makes it impossible for him to deal with consonant diminutions, which are explained by other eighteenth-century approaches as arpeggiations. Albrechtsberger, when he taught species counterpoint later in the century, considered all interactions—even first species in two parts—to represent complete chords. And Mozart, when he taught species counterpoint, thought the same way (as discussed in Chapter 7). Arpeggiation as an explanation for skips was a possibility for Albrechtsberger and Mozart and was an important part of thoroughbass and harmony treatises, but was outside of Fux's domain.

EIGHTEENTH-CENTURY HARMONIES ABSENT FROM *GRADUS*
The voice-leading patterns imposed by the species approach combined with Fux's own limited harmonic vocabulary leave many commonplace early-eighteenth-century harmonic usages outside the boundaries of *Gradus*. These include all sorts of "nonharmonic tones" and second-inversion triads (which will not arise with only one voice moving in a note-against-note texture except over a bass pedal; Mann 1965a, pp. 98–99). And although some types of suspension patterns do arise, other common manifestations that make "seventh chords" do not (see Example 2-13). In fact,

no systematic treatment of seventh chords, even of the 6/5 chord (which arises occasionally even in Palestrina's music), is possible, although occasional passing "chord sevenths" occur (Mann 1965a, p. 122). These and a host of other voice-leading patterns faced theorists of the early eighteenth century. Thoroughbass theory attempted with differing degrees of success to organize them into rational categories. And the problems that remained unsolved by contrapuntal and thoroughbass theorists were one of the factors motivating Rameau's harmonic perspective.

## Gradus and Its Heritage

The very traits that made it possible for Fux to have written *Gradus* were also the source of many of the aspects of the work discussed above. Fux was a conservative man, respectful of tradition—the son of a peasant, who by hard work rose to hold the most exalted musical positions in imperial Austria. His reverence for tradition is nowhere more clearly set forth than in his correspondence with Mattheson. Not only will he have nothing to do with what he thought of as the newfangled idea of major and minor keys (regarding them as an impoverishment of musical resources because they are merely transpositions of two modes), but he insists that the early medieval system of six-syllable solmization, complete with hexachordal mutation, remains the best method for teaching children how to sing, citing the medieval Guido d'Arezzo as his source of authority and his lifetime of practical experience teaching this method as proof. Indeed, it is likely that Haydn learned to read music via six-syllable solmization in this very way when he was a choirboy at Saint Stephens in Vienna.

Fux's reverence for the past led him to spend a lifetime honing the traditions of the *prima pratica,* handed down from Zarlino through the Italian theorists of the seventeenth century, into the work that we know as *Gradus.* Even in a matter as relatively minor as naming the modes, Fux is the sole theorist after the middle of the seventeenth century to adopt Zarlino's idiosyncratic reading of the Greek theorists, calling the D-mode Ionian, the E-mode Dorian, the F-mode Phrygian, and so forth, bypassing the universally accepted names for the modes (Lester 1989, p. 11). Fux was practical enough to avoid confusion in *Gradus* by generally referring to the modes by the pitch name of their final. That he was aware of these names is another sign of his reverence for what he regarded as an ancient authoritative truth, even if contemporary practice did not recognize it. But Fux, while maintaining Zarlino's modal names, abandoned Zarlino's revised ordering of the modes and returned to an even earlier tradition that put the D-mode in first place. The same reverence for past authorities, once again going back past Zarlino, is probably the root of Fux's choice to publish *Gradus* in Latin—the last major practical music theory treatise to appear in that language. In homage to the Latin language and to the creative process, Fux borrowed his title from a 1688 poetical thesaurus of Latin synonyms, epithets, and poetical phrases by Paul Aler that appeared under this title in numerous prints from 1688 through the twentieth century.

One of the fundamental changes taking place in eighteenth-century thought concerned the status of innovations. For the new spirits of the Enlightenment, innovativeness was a positive trait, an opportunity to sweep out ideas that reasoned examination no longer found useful. Fux would have nothing to do with this notion. He held onto the older attitude toward innovation: it was something to be wary of and to be measured against the standard of ancient authority.

Theorists and teachers in the eighteenth century, despite their admiration for *Gradus,* did not hesitate to emend Fux's approach in substantial ways. Mizler, in his 1742 German translation, was faithful to Fux's text but added numerous annotations to make the work more relevant to modern styles. He explained that it was more important to know major-minor keys than the modes, remarked on the inadequacy of Fux's discussion of triads, and commented on numerous issues of voice leading. Later writers and teachers concerned with species counterpoint and the *stile antico*—including such figures as Martini, Mozart, Albrechtsberger, and Beethoven—made much more fundamental changes, insisting on chordal rather than intervallic explanations for voice interactions, viewing even two-part counterpoints as the representations of complete chords, and treating the resulting chords in terms of the harmonic progressions they created. As a result, even though much lip service was paid to *Gradus* and the species methodology was maintained, musicians during the second half of the century did not view many crucial issues as Fux himself did and certainly did not perceive Fuxian species counterpoint as presenting some sort of true musical essence untainted by chord-to-chord harmonic theories.

There is a telling difference in emphasis between Fux's preface and Mizler's preface to the German translation—a difference that highlights the divergence between Fux's intentions and the use to which later generations of eighteenth-century musicians used his work. Fux makes it clear he has written of the eternal bases of music in large part because of "the unrestrained insanity" of contemporary music (Mann 1965a, p. 17). Mizler, by contrast, stresses that Fux erects his pedagogy on the basis of the *stile antico* so that one studying his book will have "such a firm foundation that he can build upon it whatever he wishes" (p. 3)—presumably even "unrestrained [but firmly based!] insanity."

The role played by *Gradus* in its own era, later in the eighteenth century, and in later periods has been a subject of much debate. One thing is clear—that in any assessment of Fux's intentions, judgment should be based on the entire treatise. Although many readers may have used it primarily as a treatise on species counterpoint or on fugue, Fux clearly thought of *Gradus* as a comprehensive work designed to educate students through carefully graded exercises and higher-level discussions until they were capable of composing music, not merely writing counterpoint exercises (Federhofer 1962, p. 113; Wollenberg 1970).

Riemann's characterization of *Gradus* as out of date before it was published (Riemann 1898, p. 415) and similar sentiments expressed by others (Benary 1961, p. 80; Feil 1957) likewise ignore the richness of seventeenth-century theory and the coexistence of a variety of musical styles in the early eighteenth century. Certainly the value that eighteenth-century musicians (as well as later generations) found in the work is evidence enough that it was far more timely than many more supposedly up-to-date treatises that have been long forgotten. It is a document of its own era, as well as a testament to eternal verities. It is neither a work that explains many aspects of contemporaneous music, nor one that deals with structural counterpoint. Rather, it is a thoughtful and pedagogically sound early-eighteenth-century text in the *prima pratica,* displaying much of the musical knowledge accumulated by that tradition over nearly two centuries.

If Fux had not been so taken with tradition, it is probable that he never would have undertaken a work such as *Gradus* and that we might know another treatise (perhaps Bononcini 1673?) as the classic that taught the eighteenth century about the *stile antico*. However enjoyable it may be to imagine the ways music in the eighteenth century might have differed without a work like *Gradus* as an influence, such an exercise is ultimately idle speculation. The work is no anomaly, but the summation of a centuries-long musical and pedagogical tradition.

# CHAPTER THREE

# Thoroughbass Methods

*Thoroughbass is the beginning of composing; indeed, it may be called an extemporaneous composition.*

J. S. Bach (Spitta 1889, Vol. 2, p. 917)

AMID THE HEATED POLEMIC over *prima pratica* and *seconda pratica*, musicians around 1600 could hardly have realized that one apparently minor innovation of the time—an abbreviated musical notation—would be the age's most long-lived technical legacy. Features loudly touted to support the *seconda pratica* were soon softened: persistent monody gave way to more diverse musical textures, and extreme dissonances came to be seen as variants of *prima pratica* voice leading. But *basso continuo* transcended the stylistic split, since it acknowledged the bass as determinant of harmony and voice leading in all new music. In fact, the term was first applied in print not to music of the *seconda pratica* but to ecclesiastical music close to the *prima pratica* in its treatment of dissonance and chromaticism (Viadana 1602). In Viadana's collection, the *basso seguente* (an organ part duplicating the lowest sounding part) became an independent bass part in which occasional accidentals (but no numerals) help indicate the chords to be played. Basses with numerals first appeared around the same time in *seconda pratica* monodies.

Thoroughbass,[1] more than a mere notational innovation, confirms the

---

1. Of the various English terms, the most useful to this study is *thoroughbass,* a translation of *basso continuo* and akin to the German *Generalbass* (with or without a hyphen) as used in Praetorius 1619 and Albert 1643. Locke 1673, the earliest English publication on the subject, used *Continued-Bass,* a locution that did not survive. *Through Bass* occurs in a manuscript treatise by John Blow (1649–1708) that may actually antedate Locke (Arnold 1931, p. 163). *Figured bass,* as a generic term for the practice and its theory (as in Shirlaw 1917), omits by definition the study of basses without figures, one of the most theoretically interesting portions of this literature.

change from the tenor-oriented intervallic polyphony of an earlier era to the bass-oriented chordal voice leading of later periods. As with all such momentous changes in perspective, it was not a change wrought overnight. By the mid-sixteenth century, growing awareness of the importance of the bass led Zarlino to write about major-minor and multivoiced harmonic entities. By the first decade of the seventeenth century, several theorists adopted a chordal perspective on musical structure. And by the last decade of the seventeenth century, the change to bass-oriented thinking was so engrained that it erased memory of any earlier practices. Thus, in 1694, when Henry Purcell (1659–1695) explained that "Modern Authors Compose to the *Treble* when they make *Counterpoint* or *Basses* to Tunes or Songs," he contrasted this with the only older practice he knew: "Formerly they used to Compose from the *Bass*" (Purcell 1694, p. 151).

The existence of compositions for which a performer had to furnish harmonies and voice leadings above a bass necessitated a new species of text—the thoroughbass manual. Scores of such publications and reprints appeared in a remarkable variety of formats and approaches from the earliest years of the seventeenth century into the early nineteenth century, complemented by an even greater number of manuscript methods. They range in length from a single broadsheet (Bianciardi 1607) to 960 pages (Heinichen 1728); they appeared in collections of published music (Viadana 1602, Albert 1643, Telemann 1730), as part of composition treatises (Ebner 1653, Penna 1684), as the second part of keyboard treatises (St. Lambert 1707, Bach 1762, Türk 1791), and as independent publications. They were written by major composers like François Couperin (1668–1733), Georg Philipp Telemann (1681–1767), and C. P. E. Bach (1714–1788), as well as by authors whose names survive only through their treatises (St. Lambert).

Their contents vary enormously. Some works are merely concerned with the mechanics of figures and how to realize them (Couperin undated, Mattheson 1735) or concentrate on transposition (Treiber 1704), while others apply thoroughbass to composition (Niedt 1706, Heinichen 1728). Some works are primarily for beginners or amateurs, while others are so encyclopedic they probably daunted many an experienced practitioner (Heinichen 1728, Bach 1762). Some treatises are not based on any single system of harmony, while other works, especially those from after the middle of the eighteenth century, are organized according to Rameauian harmonic theories (Daube 1756, Türk 1791).

Thoroughbass practices varied from generation to generation and from place to place. Differences include the harmonies intended by a given notation, the rigor of voice-leading strictures, the freedoms accorded the performer, the recommended figurings, the types of dissonances to be used, and so forth. Some differences between treatises reflect the age and circumstances of the theorists. In 1698, Andreas Werckmeister (1645–1706), a church organist and composer, was primarily interested in German sacred music of the late seventeenth century, while just thirteen years later the much younger Johann David Heinichen (1683–1729) drew on his experience with operas in Hamburg and Dresden in the early years of the eighteenth century; C. P. E. Bach based his 1762 treatise on the *Galant* style of the midcentury. Other differences reflect personal tastes.

Modern scholarship on thoroughbass has concentrated on realizations performed on keyboard instruments. But throughout Europe, plucked string instruments (lute, theorbo, and even harp) and strummed string instruments (guitar) were commonly used in thoroughbass realizations. More portable than keyboard instruments, plucked and strummed instruments were widely used to accompany soloists and small ensembles. Many treatises on thoroughbass were written by players of plucked and strummed instruments or deal with such instruments, including Delair 1690, with extensive directions for unfigured basses; two manuscript treatises from Salzburg around 1700 with "tiorba" realizations (discussed in Kohlschütter 1978); Campion 1716, containing the complete *règle de l'octave* for the first time; Baron 1727, by a musician prominent in the Berlin circle at midcentury; Kellner 1732, which was reprinted through 1796 and was translated from its original German into Swedish, Dutch, and Russian, and Daube 1756, applying Rameauian harmonic theories to thoroughbass.

Thoroughbass realization on plucked and strummed instruments brings to the fore various issues that are less prominent on keyboard instruments. Most important, voicing of chords on a fingerboard is often much more restricted by the nature of the instrument than on a keyboard. Standard fingerboard positions for some harmonies gave rise to what we would call an inversion, known then as a *renversement*. Treatises from the early seventeenth century acknowledged these standard positions via *Alfabeto* notation instead of thoroughbass figures: any of a variety of lists of chords for strummed instruments (especially guitar) in which letters were assigned arbitrarily to chords and a performer simply applied the standard chord position whenever a given letter appeared (surveyed in Christensen 1992a). *Alfabeto* notation strengthened the notion inherent in any thoroughbass method that each harmony is a discrete vertical unit.

A major factor differentiating treatises written before the middle of the eighteenth century from later works concerns how closely a thoroughbass realization should reflect the features of a polished composition. Seventeenth-century and early-eighteenth-century manuals, reflecting everyday experience, were generally more understanding of lapses in voice leading such as consecutive fifths and octaves, skips by augmented intervals, poorly resolved dissonances (Arnold 1931, pp. 248–249, 252–253, 281–283, passim), or the degree to which a performer could play a chord other than the one indicated "so long as the thoroughbass player does not play conflicting chords that cannot stand together with the chords of the work in question" (Heinichen 1728, pp. 731–732). Concerning parallel octaves, Rameau, who recognizes the importance of their avoidance in a written composition where "a composer can vary at leisure all the parts of a harmony to his liking," frankly states that in keyboard accompaniment they "are perceptible only to musicians who have been warned about this point, and even then the musicians' ear is usually struck by them only after their eyes have told them about them" (Rameau 1732, pp. 60–61; Hayes 1974a, pp. 87–88). By contrast, later treatises, notably Bach 1762, apply to improvised accompaniments the voice-leading standards that hold for finished compositions, probably reflecting the gradual disappearance of extempore thoroughbass realizations.

In sum, there is no single School of Thoroughbass. Thoroughbass was not tied to any instrumentation, style of music, style of performance, or specific approach to theory. Nevertheless, despite their diversity and the fact that they were designed primarily to inform performers how to read the various symbols used to figure basses and how to deal with basses where the figuring was incomplete, erroneous, or lacking altogether, thoroughbass methods reveal much about attitudes toward composition from the way they give instructions, from the way they explain various voice leadings and harmonic structures, from what they include, and from what they omit. In all thoroughbass methods, the bass is the foundation of harmony and chords are discrete vertical units that follow one another. All thoroughbass methods promoted an attitude in which improvisation was central, in which less attention was paid than in contrapuntal methods to the rhythmic independence of voices and the contour and integrity of the highest voice in the texture, and in which pitches not included in thoroughbass figures (especially melodic passing tones, neighbors, and arpeggiations) were not deemed essential to the harmony. Such topics, not performance directions, are the focus here.

Among the many treatises, four are central to this chapter. Heinichen's 960-page *Der General-Bass in der Composition* (Dresden, 1728) is the most encyclopedic and informative thoroughbass manual of the age. The second part of the *Musicalische Handleitung* (Hamburg, 1706) by Friderich Erhard Niedt (c. 1674–1708) details more fully than any other work how thoroughbass leads to composition. The brief *Traité d'accompagnement et de composition* (Paris, 1716) by François Campion (c. 1686–1748) treats the relationship between harmony and the expression of a key. And the second part of the *Versuch über die wahre Art das Clavier zu spielen* (Berlin, 1762) by C. P. E. Bach is an authoritative work by a major composer of the middle and late century.

# Chords

Thoroughbass writers dealt with harmonies as units built above the bass. By abandoning the earlier tenor orientation and by viewing harmonies as units instead of as combinations of intervals, they came closer to the modern perspective of a chord with rearrangeable, octave-equivalent members. But many differences, both obvious and subtle, remained. In classifying the various chords arising from thoroughbass signatures, many writers dealt first with what we call root-position triads, then other consonant chords, and lastly with dissonant chords, which is the order followed here.

## THE TRIAD

Thoroughbass writers, following Zarlino and others in the late sixteenth century, recognized a fifth and third over the bass as the normal harmony. It was the only chord whose presence was routinely indicated by the absence of figures, although it could require an indication if it included a note not found in the key signature or if there were several harmonies over one bass note (Delair 1690, p. 23, offers six ways to indicate a triad). Most thoroughbass writers endow it with a special name: the harmonic triad (*trias harmonica* in Niedt 1700), the perfect chord (*l'accord parfait* in Couperin), the common chord (*comon corde* in Blow c. 1670?, *concentus ordinarius* in Muffat 1699, *Ordinar-Satz* or *Ordinar-Griff* in Werckmeister 1702, *ordinair Accord* in Heinichen 1728), and, with Mattheson's characteristic bombast, the "perfect, fully consonant, harmonic triad or chord" (1735).

Since good voice leading could mandate different right-hand positions, thoroughbass writers urged performers to practice the triad in the right hand with any of its notes on top. Mattheson 1735 refers to these voicings of what we call the root position triad as the "three positions of the chord" (*drey Ordnungen der Accorde*) while Heinichen 1728 calls them the "three principal chords" (*drey Haupt-Accorde*). Werckmeister 1702 bestows three different names on what we call root-position triads: *Ordinar-Sätze* for triads with the right hand in close position, *zerstreuten* (dispersed) *Ordinar-Sätze* for triads with the right hand in open position, and *Extraordinar-Sätze* for open-position chords doubling the third or fifth (pp. 3–5). Such terminology indicates both a change from a sixteenth-century perspective and lingering aspects of that perspective: any chord was now an entity that could appear in any arrangement over the bass, but different names for different voicings still implied that these different voicings were separate entities, not different forms of one entity.

Theorists differed over the relationship between triads and other harmonies. Earlier writers simply stated that all chords not 8/5/3 required figures because they were "special chords" or "exceptions" (*sonderbahren*

*Sätze* or *exceptiones,* Werckmeister 1702, pp. 8–9). J. S. Bach, in the *Clavierbüchlein für Anna Magdalena Bach,* likewise differentiates "true" *(eigenthümlich)* chords or 8/5/3 from all other chords, which are "borrowed" *(entlehnet).* The assumption that 8, 5, and 3 are the standard intervals above a given bass note even led the author of a popular manual on singing, playing "all sorts of instruments," realizing a thoroughbass, and composing instrumental and vocal music to list sixths among the dissonances (Speer 1697, p. 180).

Many eighteenth-century writers, showing a greater awareness of the placement of different types of harmonies on different scale degrees, rejected this dichotomy, arguing that the proper chord above most notes of the scale was something other than a simple triad. For instance, Lorenz Mizler (1711–1778) criticized the 1715 edition of Werckmeister 1698, arguing that in C major, D should carry a 6/4/3 chord, E a 6/3/8 or 6/3/6 chord, and so forth—these should not be thought of as exceptions but as the regular chords for those degrees (Mizler 1736–1754, Vol. 2, pp. 50–51). This is the same issue that Fux had grappled with in his discussion of triads in *Gradus.* This way of thinking about harmony and key structure was promoted by the *règle de l'octave* and other ways of dealing with unfigured basses (discussed later in this chapter), thereby preparing the way for many of Rameau's ideas about the proper placement of harmonies within a key.

OTHER CONSONANT CHORDS

After discussing triads, thoroughbass writers generally turned to the other consonant chord, 6/3. Some theorists, echoing Zarlino's perspective, explained that in a 6/3 chord "instead of the fifth there is a sixth" (Muffat 1699, p. 41). Other writers simply listed the notes of a 6/3 chord, giving no explanation of its origin or relation to other chord types (Gasparini 1708, Chapter 2).

Many writers, though, related the 6/3 chord to the 5/3 triad. Sometimes such explanations do not imply understanding of triadic inversions, as in Keller 1717: "A Common Cord to any note makes third Sixth & Eighth to ye third above it or sixth below it, A Common Cord makes a fourth sixth & Eighth to ye fifth above it or fourth below it" (p. 7). As suggestive as this remark is, it is clear from what follows immediately that Keller does not intend an inversional or functional relationship between the chords; he is simply offering a mnemonic device to relate different figurings that yield the same notes in the right hand: "A Common Cord makes a third fifth & seventh to the sixth above it or third below it, A Common Cord makes fourth sixth & second to the seventh above it or second below it" (see Example 3-1). Surely, a C-major triad is not the origin of an A-minor seventh chord. Many writers utilized such mnemonic methods,

*Example 3-1*. Keller 1717, p. 7

whether by listing different figurings that yield the same right-hand patterns (Delair 1690, St. Lambert 1707, Hesse 1776) or by stating that 6/3 chords have the same notes as 5/3 triads a third lower (Bach 1762, Chapter 3; Mitchell 1949, p. 209).

Other writers, both before and after Rameau's *Traité* of 1722, explicitly recognize the 6/3 chord as a triadic inversion. Werckmeister 1702, for instance, explains a C♯/E/A chord by noting that "A must truly be the root [*Wurtzel*] of this chord." Hence doubling the C♯ would be bad "because these two C♯s would stabilize the bass [*das Fundament stabiliren*], which is not the proper root of this chord . . . Thus whenever a sixth stands above a note, the lower third is assumed below it [*profunda mento gesetzet*]" (p. 76). *Wurtzel* is probably a translation of the Latin *radix* for the root of an interval or triad in Lippius 1610 (fol. B3ᵛ).

Heinichen 1728 similarly discusses how inversion *(Verkehrung)* explains both the origin and the common doubling of a 6/3 chord (pp. 140–141). Here it is likely, though not provable, that the explanation derives from Rameau's *Traité* (1722), not from the Lippius tradition reflected in Werckmeister. First, there is no comparable discussion in Heinichen's earlier thoroughbass treatise of 1711. Second, Heinichen's discussion is close to Rameau's terminology, referring like Rameau to inversion but not to chord roots. Third, Heinichen discusses inversions of seventh chords (which no theorist before Rameau did) in a passage where he seems to be explaining the notion of inversion as something new to himself as well as to his reader, feeling his way among the terms "rearrange" *(verwechseln)*, "invert" *(verkehren)*, and "exchange" *(vertauschen)* and not entirely sure whether the result is "an entirely new chord" or "a rearrangement of the previous harmony":

Before we ask how one can rearrange the harmony before the resolution of a dissonance, we must first know what a rearrangement of the harmony really is . . . [I]n the general sense, it is nothing other than an inversion or rearrangement of the notes so that some are placed below and others above . . . Since musical harmony is changed only a bit if only the upper voices are exchanged while the bass remains, so more specifically or in its true meaning a real rearrangement of the harmony only occurs where the bass-note or the basis itself is rearranged and exchanged with the other notes so that an entirely new chord and harmony arises, which one can therefore properly call a rearrangement of the previous harmony, because just those preceding notes are repeated in a changed ordering. (pp. 622–623)

Finally, the placement of these tenets within Heinichen 1728 suggests that they were late additions to the text. The earlier portions of the treatise, which do not mention Rameau or Rameauian ideas in the body of the text, were set in type for as long as six years prior to publication (Heinichen 1728, p. 938). Explicit references to Rameau occur late in the treatise (pp. 763–766 and in the addenda on pp. 948 and 960). The discussion of inverted seventh chords occurs in the body of the text rather late in the treatise. But the inversional explanation of the triad occurs in a footnote running under pp. 140–143, attached to the traditional rule on what to double in a 6/3 chord. Footnotes were commonly used to insert information to a text already set in type, implying that the footnote might have been added after Heinichen had read Rameau's *Traité*. In the *Vorrede* to his 1728 work, Heinichen notes that among the changes he made to his 1711 treatise was the incorporation of hitherto unknown materials from German, Italian, and French authors (fol. f'); decades later, Marpurg cited this very statement as proof that Heinichen learned chord inversions from Rameau (Marpurg 1776, pp. 271–272).

In sum, it is difficult to gauge knowledge of triadic inversions. Writers of fingerboard thoroughbass manuals talked of *renversements* and the conservative church musician Werckmeister freely talked about chord roots, while Heinichen, active in the latest operatic styles, seemingly learned inversions from Rameau.

### OTHER CHORDS OF THE SIXTH

Thoroughbass was supposed to allow a performer to see a figure and play a chord. As pointed out by William Mitchell, a theory of harmony hampers this process by requiring a performer to translate the thoroughbass symbol into an abstract harmony and then retranslate that harmony into the notes to be played (Mitchell 1949, p. 18). But the situation was not as simple and straightforward as Mitchell and others imply. Even in the relatively simple category of 6-chords, a performer had to analyze the context to decide which rules applied to a given 6 in the bass.

Part of the reason for this complexity was that eighteenth-century writers included under chords of the sixth all the harmonies that might be intended when only 6 appears in the figures, not merely the first inversion of triads that modern musicians mean when they refer to 6-chords. Some writers subdivided what modern theory treats as a single harmony and also added different harmonies, all within the same category. Couperin, for instance, lists four types of 6-chords: 8/6/3, 3/6/3, 6/3, and 6/4/3. We

*Example 3-2. Bach 1762, Chapter 3; Mitchell 1949, Figs. 255c, 260a*

might regard the first three as different doublings of the same chord type, and the last as a separate chord. But for Couperin, each category was a separate harmony indicated by 6.

Other writers, such as C. P. E. Bach, include quite a few different categories of chords under the rubric of 6-chords: what we call first-inversion major, minor, diminished, and augmented triads; augmented-sixth chords; and various 8/6 or 6/3 simultaneities arising from nonharmonic tones. In each of these diverse chord types, different rules determine which notes are to be played, which notes can be doubled, and how the voice leading is to be arranged. Bach follows standard practice in recommending that as a rule the third or sixth over the bass be doubled in a sixth chord, and that the octave of the bass be omitted. This makes good sense when the sixth chord represents what we would call an inverted triad, especially when the bass is scale-step 3 or 7. When the sixth chord is built on scale-step 2, however, the sixth above the bass is the leading tone and cannot be doubled, and the bass may be doubled. For other sixth chords, new rules are needed for almost every example, as is shown in Example 3-2. For the first case, Bach recommends adding a fourth; for the second, he recommends doubling the bass. As it turns out, in both cases the fourth voice he recommends can be construed as the root of the chord. But since he does not discuss simultaneities in terms of roots, that mode of explanation is closed to him.

He then discusses 8/6 chords where the 8 or 6 is diminished (see Example 3-3). Once again, the harmony does not result from a first-inversion triad, the sixth cannot be doubled, and new rules are needed.

Another source of problems was the relationship between 6/3 and 6/4/3 chords. On scale-degree 2, 6 could be realized as a 6/3 or a 6/4/3 chord, whereas on scale-degree 3 or 7, 6/4/3 was not plausible when 6 alone was

*Example 3-3. Bach 1762, Chapter 3; Mitchell 1949, Figs. 257[b], 259*

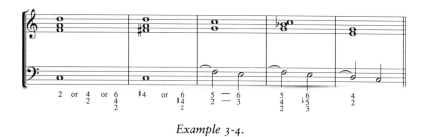

*Example 3-4.*

indicated. Since 6 sometimes implies either 6/3 or 6/4/3, many thorough-bass writers discuss 6/4/3 chords along with 6 chords. By contrast, C. P. E. Bach, despite his supposed antipathy to chord-inversion theory, reflects that theory by discussing 6/4/3 chords along with 6/4 chords (Chapter 6; Mitchell 1949, p. 229). He acknowledges that a 6/4/3 chord is sometimes intended when only 6 appears in the figuring (Chapter 7; Mitchell 1949, p. 234) and allows the fourth of a 6/4/3 chord to be omitted in a three-part accompaniment, but he does not point out the similarity between 6/3 and 6/4/3 chords (ibid.; Mitchell 1949, p. 235).

DISSONANT CHORDS

Most theorists tried to impose some rational order on dissonant chords. Heinichen 1728, for instance, begins with those dissonant chords having 2 in the signature or implying 2 (2, 5/2, 4/2, 5/4/2, 6/4/2, ♯4, 6/♯4/2), those having 3 (6/4/3, 6/♯4/3), then 4, and so forth through 9. Among the "2" chords are what we recognize as the third inversion of a seventh chord (variously labeled 2, 4/2, 6/4/2, ♯4, and 6/♯4/2), a first-inversion triad with bass suspension (5/2), a first-inversion seventh chord with bass suspension (5/4/2), and a root-position triad with a bass suspension (4/2) (see Example 3-4).

St. Lambert 1707 also orders dissonant chords numerically, but in a different manner: first all chords having only one number in the signature, then those with two numbers in the signature, those with three, and finally those indicated by numerals in succession, such as 6–5 or 9–8.

Writers from later in the century often departed from these numerical orderings and categorized dissonances according the newer harmonic theories, whether or not they were supporters of that theory. C. P. E. Bach, for instance, although he scrupulously avoids explicit discussions of Rameau-like chordal theories, nevertheless orders his chapters according to that theory: triads and 6/3 chords (including, as noted, many dissonant combinations), then dissonant triads (diminished and augmented), the dissonant 6/4 inversion of the triad, inversions of seventh chords (6/4/3,

Compositional Theory in the Eighteenth Century

6/5/3, 6/4/2), and then the remaining signatures, most of which (except the root-position seventh chord) result from one or more notes added to a triad or seventh chord. By the end of the century, the ordering of chords was closely tied to harmonic theory, as in Türk 1791, which treats the consonant triad and its inversions (5/3, 6/3, and 6/4 positions), the dissonant triads (diminished and augmented), seventh chords (7, 6/5, 4/3, and 2), ninth chords, eleventh chords, and then the addition of from one to four added notes in each of these categories in turn. In all these classification systems except that of Türk, chords of widely divergent harmonic functions are frequently discussed together and chords of quite similar function appear far apart, sometimes arising twice in different locations, with the types of problems just discussed in connection with chords of the sixth.

Changing keys could obscure parallel harmonic functions by requiring different figurings for the functionally equivalent harmony. For instance, in a piece in A major, a dominant seventh chord required only 7. But if the piece moved to E major or A minor, the equivalent dominant seventh required 7/♯. This was further complicated because various usages, especially doublings, were codified by many writers in terms of the key signature. For instance, a common rule stated that a bass note raised by a sharp should not be doubled. In most cases, this rule prohibited doubled leading tones in "first-inversion secondary dominants" ("V$^6$ of ii, iii, V, and vi" in a major key). But the rule was not infallible. If a composition began in C major and moved to E minor, the rule implied that an F♯ in the bass supporting an F♯-A-D♯ chord should not be doubled, while in any other key closely related to C major (D minor, F major, G major, and A minor, for instance) the bass would normally be doubled in a "vii$^{o6}$" chord.

Additional complications arose from the fact that signatures with one flat or sharp too few were common well into the eighteenth century. Campion 1716 presents the *règle de l'octave* for the minor mode with a Dorian signature. The body of the text in Rameau's 1722 *Traité* also uses Dorian as the model for minor (although the Supplement and all his later treatises use Aeolian). J. S. Bach's *Sonata in g for violin solo* (BWV 1001), also dating from the 1720s, uses a one-flat signature for the movements in G and in B♭, resulting in Dorian and Lydian signatures. These signatures were maintained partly by habit and partly to minimize the clutter of accidentals in the signature, especially since musicians did not yet agree on the ordering of accidentals or even whether to notate them in one or two octaves in the signature. Abbreviated key signatures appeared even into the early nineteenth century: Beethoven used only six flats in the A♭-minor *Klagender Gesang* of his opus 110 *Piano Sonata* (1821).

Musicians of the time were well aware of the complexities cited above. Decade by decade, the number of thoroughbass signatures increased, compounding the problems. Although some seventeenth-century manuals include fewer than a dozen signatures, Heinichen 1728 lists 32 "common signatures" (up from 12 in Heinichen 1711); Rameau 1726 lists 62 signatures for 30 different chords; Mattheson 1735, intending characteristically to include "all the known" signatures, lists 70, yet omits 6 found in Heinichen; and Rousseau 1768 lists 120 signatures. As a result, comprehensive thoroughbass methods often contain huge numbers of chordal types, a range of contexts into which each of these types fit, and numerous rules and exceptions. There was a continual stream of new thoroughbass manuals, each promising fewer and easier rules than its predecessors.

Another approach was to do away with explicit rules altogether and instead offer paradigmatic progressions to be learned by rote. Handel's brief manuscript of thoroughbass lessons for Princess Anne (in Mann 1987, pp. 21–32) falls into this category: the first progressions contain only 5/3 chords, later progressions add 6/3 chords, then various suspensions and pedal points. The last exercises are *partimento* fugues—fugues written on a single staff on which the opening statements of the subject are indicated, followed by a figured bass over which fugal entries can be introduced.

Jean-François Dandrieu (c. 1682–1738), "after Couperin and Rameau . . . the most celebrated French harpsichord composer of the 18th century" (Fuller 1980), published a popular method based on a similar approach that remained in print from around 1719 into the 1760s. Dandrieu offers a one-page plate for each of twenty-one chord types: the "perfect chord" (8/5/3), the "simple sixth chord" (8/6/3), the "chord of the small sixth" (6/4/3 on scale-step 2), and so on through "the diminished seventh." The brief text on each plate merely describes the chord, its location within a key, and its common figuring. Each plate appears three times: first with complete figuring (such as 8/5/3, 3/8/5, or 5/3/8 to show the proper voicing of each triad), then with the common figuring (such as only 6 for 8/6/3 chords), and lastly with no figuring.

Other methods following this approach were based on the *règle de l'octave,* an ascending and descending bass scale with a fixed harmony over each scale degree. Many such methods, referred to collectively as *partimenti,* were published throughout the eighteenth century, concentrated mostly in Italy but appearing to some extent in most regions of Europe (discussed in Christensen 1992b). The pupil learned voice-leading patterns that could be applied to realizing figured basses as well as to improvising.

Some methods contain little explanatory text, making it difficult to assess the types of discussions that might have taken place between teacher and student. It may well be that teachers who used these methods simply stressed rote memorization of voice-leading patterns. Or it may be that teachers adopting these methods commented on the exercises using the language of more explanatory works. Whatever the case, writers of all types of methods stressed how important it was to develop automatic voice-leading habits from one figuring. Even Rameau, surely the most verbal explainer of the century, repeatedly stresses in each of his accompaniment methods (published in 1722, 1732, and 1761) the need for the fingers and hearing to develop ingrained habits: "knowledge, the ear, and the fingers contribute equally to judging, feeling, and immediately executing a piece of music" (Rameau 1761, p. 24).

## Dissonance Treatment

Because thoroughbass performers played right-hand chords along with most bass notes on the beat, it was essential to avoid clashes between an accented dissonant note somewhere in the texture and the simultaneous resolution of that dissonance in the continuo. Hence, when thoroughbass methods treat dissonances, they are primarily concerned with dissonances played along with a bass note; it matters little whether they form what we call chord sevenths, dissonant fourths in second-inversion chords, or suspensions and appoggiaturas. All these dissonances were deemed part of the chord and were to be indicated in the figures. Dissonances occurring after the beat—passing tones, neighbors, anticipations, and the like—would not create such articulated clashes and were generally ignored in thoroughbass figures. They concerned melody, not harmony.

### IDENTIFICATION OF DISSONANCES

In most dissonant chords, at least one dissonant note forms a second, fourth, seventh, ninth, or an augmented or diminished interval clashing with the bass, allowing easy identification of the dissonance via the thoroughbass figures. Often, a simple rule explained proper resolution of the identified dissonance and appropriately coordinated motions in the other voices.

Some dissonances required further elucidation. When the dissonance is a step above the bass, either the upper voice must resolve (such as a D-C suspension over a C in the bass), or the bass itself must resolve (such as a bass C under a D-triad). A notational convention generally differentiates these two situations: an upper-voice note that resolves is indicated by 9 (as in 9–8) and a bass note that must resolve is indicated by 2. Also, 2 is preferred over bass pedals (Arnold 1931, pp. 674–675, 874–877). Delair 1690 expresses the convention in what seems an elliptical manner, but

Example 3-5.

one that contains the required information: "when made on the first part of a [bass] note it is called a ninth, when made on the second part of a note it is called a second" (p. 24): a ninth is an upper-part dissonance, hence prepared before a new bass note and appearing over the beginning of a bass note; a bass suspension, chord seventh, or dissonant chord over a bass pedal would occur only after the bass note has already been present, hence 2 appears only as the second numeral over a bass note.

The use of 2 and 9 in figures is one of the last remnants of some seventeenth-century practices that indicated intervals in more than one octave. Penna 1684 still uses numbers as high as 22. Bach 1762 uses numbers up to 12 to clarify certain voice leadings (Chapter 1; Mitchell 1949, p. 183), but fewer than a half-dozen times in the entire treatise. Otherwise, thoroughbass figuring is universally octave-equivalent (Arnold 1931, pp. 35–65, 874–879).

Some combinations of intervals are dissonant yet contain only consonances against the bass, such as a sixth with a fifth. Writers who did not utilize a theory of seventh chords and their inversions explained that in a 6/5 chord "the fifth is treated as a dissonance" (Bach 1762, Chapter 8; Mitchell 1949, p. 244). Gasparini 1708 offers a more general rule: upper parts can be "linked with one another by dissonances of a second or seventh. In relation to one another, they resolve regularly, but are always consonant with the bass" (Chapter 7).

The issue was thornier with 4/3 chords. C. P. E. Bach notes "the exceptional features of the chord are that the third is treated as a dissonance and the fourth enjoys more freedom than usual" (Chapter 7; Mitchell 1949, p. 233). The third had to resolve downward, but the fourth could either remain (Example 3-5a) or even ascend (Example 3-5b). Because of the different resolutions of the fourth, Heinichen regarded these two usages as entirely separate harmonies even though both harmonies had the same figuring (Arnold 1931, p. 262). Because the fourth in 4/3 chords did not have to be prepared in a preceding chord and did not resolve by stepwise descent, it came to be known as the "irregular fourth" (Muffat 1699, Heinichen 1728). Some theorists ban such unresolved fourths altogether (Werckmeister 1698, p. 16). Systematic explanations of 6/5 or 4/3 chords were beyond thoroughbass methods.

*Example 3-6.* Bach 1762, Chapter 1 (Mitchell 1949, Fig. 206a)

## THE STRUCTURAL FRAME FOR DISSONANCES

The resolution of one dissonance into another usually merited a special discussion, as in Bach 1762, Chapter 1 (Mitchell 1949, pp. 192–193) (see Example 3-6). Bach writes: "A moving bass often causes dissonances to resolve to dissonances . . . Eventually, however, there must be a resolution to a consonance. Such a relationship is called *retardatio*." Bach means that the fourth C over the first downbeat resolves to a second dissonance, the tritone B, and that a consonant chord over the bass does not appear until the 6 chord. This explanation fails to show how the B satisfactorily resolves the C to the third of a G$^7$ chord, a resolution that is simultaneous with but conceptually separate from introduction of the F in the bass that gives rise to the 4/2 chord. Rameau would have had little trouble explaining the resolution in this manner. But even if Bach did not wish to invoke Rameauian harmony here, he could have drawn on older approaches that reduced complex voice leadings to their structural basis, as Bernhard had done nearly a century earlier or as Heinichen had done in 1728.

Heinichen's explanations appear in a long chapter devoted to dissonances in the theatrical style, the equivalent of Bernhard's *Stylus luxurians* (pp. 580–720, translated in Buelow 1962). In particular, he seems to be answering those who appealed solely to the text to rationalize dissonances, as Fux had done in his discussion of recitatives in *Gradus* (1725), or as Sébastien de Brossard (1655–1730) had done in his influential *Dictionaire de musique* (1703; article "Settima"). Heinichen castigates "the ignorance of those individuals . . . who accuse the *stylus theatralis* of observing no rules and of dealing with dissonances and their beautiful resolutions without a foundation" (p. 586). He repeatedly illustrates techniques by which apparently improper dissonances resolve properly in some voice: arpeggiation before a suspension resolves, leaps to or from a dissonance prepared or resolved in another part or within a single line that contains two or more real parts, or anticipation or retardation of a dissonance, its preparation, or its resolution.

In cases akin to Example 3-6, Heinichen demonstrates how a dissonance moving to another dissonance can arise because

> the bass, rather than remaining in place until the resolution of the dissonance it carries and only then proceeding to the following dissonance, moves anticipating this latter dissonance, thereby omitting all or a portion of the

preceding note [see Example 3-7]. According to the old foundation, this would be as [shown in Example 3-8].

Whereas Bach merely notes that one dissonance can follow another, Heinichen shows how the first dissonance resolves along with the early appearance of the second one.

Because of the scope of the issues raised throughout this chapter, Heinichen often deals with matters that are not so much a part of thoroughbass

*Example 3-7.* Heinichen 1728, p. 691

*Example 3-8.* Heinichen 1728, p. 692

*Example 3-9.* Heinichen 1728, pp. 613–616

Compositional Theory in the Eighteenth Century

*Example 3-10.* Heinichen 1728, pp. 603–604

as an extempore performance technique but rather a part of composition. The excerpts in Example 3-9 dissect the polyphonic underpinning of a single melodic line and show how dissonances that seem to disappear without resolving (C over F♯ in measure 1 and B♭ over E in measure 4 in the third excerpt) are prolonged via arpeggiation of a harmony until a true resolution occurs.

Other passages demonstrate Heinichen's secure understanding of the origins of various commonly elided voice leadings. His explanations of the origin of the cadential 6/4 and conchordal sevenths are exemplary (see Example 3-10). Heinichen knew that other treatises he studied simply do not explain these usages, often rationalizing them by the motto *sic volo, sic jubeo* ("what I like, I command"). He was justifiably proud of his achievements.

## Thoroughbass and Composition

Although some musicians regarded thoroughbass solely as a performance technique, others believed that thoroughbass played an important role in the pedagogy of musical composition. J. S. Bach, in a 1727 letter, explains that one of his students had studied "Clavier, Thorough Bass, and the fundamental rules of composition based thereupon" (David and Mendel 1966, p. 111). C. P. E. Bach confirms that thoroughbass was the heart of his father's approach to composition: "His pupils had to begin their studies by learning pure four-part thorough bass . . . He particularly insisted on the writing out of the thorough bass in [four real] parts . . . The realization of a thorough bass and the introduction to chorales are without doubt the best method of studying composition, as far as harmony is concerned" (ibid., p. 279). Georg Philipp Telemann (1681–1767) explained that thoroughbass led to improvising fantasies and then to free composition (Telemann 1730, p. 185).

Title pages of numerous manuals from different countries and different stylistic orientations acknowledge the common ground shared by thoroughbass and composition. Werckmeister, a German organist interested in sacred music, links composing and extempore playing in 1702; Campion, a French theorbist, entitled his manual *Treatise of Accompaniment and Composition* in 1716; and Heinichen, active in Italian opera in Hamburg and Dresden, entitled his encyclopedic work *Thoroughbass in Composition*. For these authors, thoroughbass and composition were fully complementary: in order to play thoroughbass properly, one must understand "composition or at least simple counterpoint"; and learning thoroughbass "teaches the student the foundation of composition" (Werckmeister 1702, p. 67).

The path from learning thoroughbass to composing is described in many sources. But the one thoroughbass writer who demonstrated more completely than any other how this was to be done is Niedt.[2] The essence of Niedt's approach lies in adding variations to a straightforward thoroughbass realization. In Part 2 of his *Handleitung,* Niedt illustrates dozens of patterns to elaborate every ascending and descending interval from a second to an octave (Chapter 2). In the following chapters, he applies these elaborations to thoroughbass realizations, demonstrating how to elaborate simple bass lines and then right-hand parts in a host of meters, suggesting that still further elaborations are possible if permutations are applied to patterns of notes. As the examples get more sophisticated, Niedt even adds dynamics to some of them, suggesting echo effects of orchestral writing. In the last of the dozen chapters, he uses elaborations of a single bass to produce an entire partita of eleven dances.

The openings of some of these dances appear in Example 3-11. Niedt's diminutions encompass not only foreground embellishments such as added passing tones, neighbors, and arpeggiations, but also interpolations on a larger scale in the form of added harmonies. These harmonies are themselves capable of elaboration. Although comparison of the various diminutions with the original thoroughbass may be suggestive of Schenkerian structural levels, Niedt intended these possibilities as different foreground realizations, not as analyses of one another.

Although no other work offers a path from thoroughbass to composition as detailed as Niedt's, other publications cover some of the same material. Mattheson 1719, for instance, teaches thoroughbass via a number of "test pieces" *(Probestücke).* Because of the great variety of realizations that

2. Feil 1955 thoughtfully compares Niedt's approach to composition to Riepel's and Koch's later in the century.

*Example 3-11.* Niedt 1706, Chapter 12

Mattheson illustrates, he in effect covers in a different fashion many of the points that Niedt had included.

The contrasts between Niedt's composition method adding diminution techniques to a full-voiced harmonic structure and Fux's composition technique built from species counterpoint are quite sharp. Fux begins with simple two-voice intervallic writing; Niedt begins with complete chords and assumes that two-voice writing represents part of a full-voiced harmonic texture. Fux disdains elaborative reworking of examples; such diminutions form Niedt's method. Apart from imitative counterpoint, Fux avoids motivic repetitions; motivic repetition is a high priority for Niedt in working with a given elaborative pattern in a bass or melody. In addition, Niedt's approach contrasts with that of Fux in general outlook. Niedt, living in the Hanseatic League seaport of Hamburg, clearly felt the influence of the heady ideas of British and French science and philosophy promoting rational re-examination of traditions and a simplification of education:

> My true goal is this: just as a closer and easier path is found nowadays in all sciences and arts, so likewise I have also endeavored to find an easy path in thoroughbass by which to lead the beginner who wishes to learn. Without doubt, our dear elders have broken the path and shown us the way up in everything; but with so many digressions and tiresome labyrinths that one had to spend a long time at it before the desired goal could be attained, and most remained stuck in those labyrinths. (Niedt 1710, fol. A2$^r$)

By contrast, Fux disparaged innovations and pedagogical shortcuts.

Niedt's definition of the very term *counterpoint* underscores the contrast between his thoroughbass approach and Fuxian counterpoint: "Counterpoint is truly spelling in the musical alphabet from which I learn to place the letters together and to make syllables from them. To state this more clearly: when I wish to set a note, for example a C, and form a *complete harmony, i.e., a counterpoint,* with it, then I spell as follows: C is the foundation-key, E is the third, G is the fifth, C is the octave—I place these letters above one another" (Niedt 1717, p. 2; emphasis added). This meaning of counterpoint, denoting the formation of harmonies, existed alongside the more traditional notion of counterpoint throughout the eighteenth century.

Niedt was not alone in his espousal of a harmonic approach to composition via thoroughbass. Similarly rejecting the contrapuntal tradition, Heinichen argued that "experience teaches that the greatest and most passionate contrapuntists are in general the worst composers and also most often the greatest pedants" (in Mattheson 1722, p. 357).[3] These sharp differences made the proponents of thoroughbass and contrapuntal methods wary of each other through much of the eighteenth century. The two traditions borrowed from each other, as when thoroughbass treatises utilized Fux's four rules of voice leading and when Fux discusses chordal ideas. But the two traditions stood quite apart in underlying principles, in pedagogical method, and in general philosophical outlook.

---

3. On the other hand, J. A. Hiller reports that on his deathbed Heinichen said he wished he had composed a mass in the *stile antico* and a book on counterpoint (Hiller 1766–1770, vol. 1, pp. 224–225).

## Unfigured Basses

From the earliest days of thoroughbass, writers chastized composers and copyists for providing bass parts without any figures to guide performers. Despite perennial complaints, however, unfigured basses persisted right through the eighteenth century. Indolence may partly account for this situation. But it is hardly likely that unfigured basses would have existed at all if bass parts by themselves did not suggest predictable harmonies. The instructions many manuals give to assist performers with unfigured basses provide us with invaluable insights into the thinking of seventeenth- and eighteenth-century musicians on the nature of harmony and key.

Many writers simply ignore unfigured basses. Others explicitly decline to discuss them, believing that even a vast number of rules would be inadequate to cope with all the conceivable progressions (Bach 1762, Chapter 35; Mitchell 1949, p. 180). But a fair number of manuals, the most important being Penna 1684, St. Lambert 1707, Gasparini 1708, Heinichen 1711 and 1728, and Campion 1716, tackle unfigured basses in several different ways. Perhaps these writers realized that although unfigured basses are an annoyance to performers, they are the normal state of affairs for composers. After all, at some point in the process of composing a piece, a composer has to decide what chords go with the bass part.

There were four methods for dealing with unfigured basses. Specific chords might be placed over a given solmization syllable or an easily identified note, such as a sharped note. Specific chords might be applied to various patterns of bass intervals. Model bass lines with chords might be learned by rote to be used whenever applicable. Or specific chords might be placed over particular scale degrees. One or more approaches appeared in different manuals.

The first method appears in print as early as Praetorius 1619 (p. 134; p. 106 in the 1916 edition). Lorenzo Penna (1613–1693), among the earliest to discuss unfigured basses extensively, formulates this approach as his second and third rules of thoroughbass:

> Rule 2: Each note of the bass is accompanied by thirds and fifths or their compounds except for *mi* [the lower note of a semitone], which ordinarily uses thirds and sixths or their compounds [see Example 3-12].
> Rule 3: When the lower part has a sharp, it is generally to be accompanied by the third and sixth [Penna 1684, pp. 146–147] [see Example 3-13].[4]

The content of these rules appears in all types of works into the early eighteenth century—even in Fux's exposition of triads.

4. Penna follows the practice begun in Viadana 1602 of notating accidentals in the staff location of the note to be altered. This usage persisted at least through Martini [1756] (p. 3).

*Example 3-12.* Penna 1684, p. 147

A rationale for Penna's rules seems obvious and can be stated without recourse to later harmonic theories. When the bass is the leading tone, it needs a sixth, since there is no perfect fifth over that scale degree. When the bass is accidentally sharpened, it is generally the leading tone of the following bass note. And when the bass is the third note of the scale, it is frequently approached by step from either scale-step 2 or scale-step 4 supporting the leading tone; scale-step 3 must have a sixth so that the leading tone in the preceding chord can resolve. The leading tone and scale-step 3 in major keys fall on solmization syllable *mi* in the six-syllable solmization still common in Italy and Italian-influenced areas at the time.

Although these reasons, which translate Penna's rules to scale-step locations, may seem self-evident and are partly given in Heinichen 1728, they might well have been unintelligible to Penna. First, Penna does not discuss scales or scale steps. Second, his two rules cut across our categories. We see a common factor in bass leading tones, whether diatonic or chromatic; but Penna explains that bass leading tones receive a sixth *either* because they are *mi or* because they are sharped, not because they are leading tones. Penna's rule concerning *mi* explains both scale-steps 3 and 7, whereas our scale-step explanation gives different reasons for using sixths above scale-steps 3 and 7. In brief, Penna's rules are based on simple and what are to us arbitrary features of the musical surface. Although the rules frequently apply in major keys with few accidentals, theorists at the time already noted that they did not apply to minor keys or where there are many sharps: Speer 1697 notes the great variability in the placement of sixth chords in minor keys (p. 182), and Werckmeister 1702 notes that

*Example 3-13.* Penna 1684, p. 147

Compositional Theory in the Eighteenth Century

*Example 3-14. Gasparini 1708, Chapter 4*

placing a sixth-chord over sharps yields improper results in a piece built on F♯ (p. 45).

In addition to these rules, Penna also uses the second of the methods listed above. He lists various types of bass patterns that suggest specific figures: basses rising or falling by steps, thirds, fourths, and fifths. The result is a plethora of rules.

St. Lambert 1707 and Gasparini 1708 likewise discuss many bass patterns and the harmonies they imply. Gasparini lists many more possibilities for each pattern than did Penna, probably reflecting the increasing proliferation of voice-leading possibilities in the music of his generation. A bass ascending by a semitone generally takes a minor sixth on the first note, as shown in Example 3-14. But if the first chord has a major third above it, it is the second harmony that requires a sixth, always major (as in "V-iv⁶" in minor keys) (see Example 3-15). Gasparini then treats stepwise basses. If three ascending notes begin a composition (or, presumably, a phrase), the second note gets a major sixth, the third a natural sixth (as in "I-vii°⁶-I⁶" in major or minor keys). But if the same bass occurs a step higher, a natural sixth is required over the note that received a major sixth earlier (see Example 3-16). Gasparini proceeds to four ascending notes beginning on a downbeat, four ascending notes beginning with a rest, five ascending notes, and so forth. St. Lambert deals with unfigured basses in a similar fashion, introducing thirty-three separate rules.

*Example 3-15. Gasparini 1708, Chapter 4*

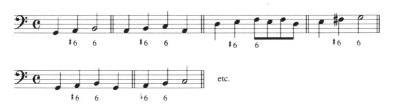

*Example 3-16. Gasparini 1708, Chapter 4*

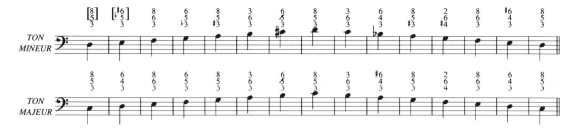

*Example 3-17.* François Campion 1716. The bracketed intervals have been added according to Campion's explanation of each chord (p. 21).

Modern musicians nod in agreement with each of Gasparini's and St. Lambert's recommendations, interpreting them (as Penna's were interpreted above) in the light of later harmonic theories. But these writers did not think in terms of modern scale-step explanations. In the absence of such explanations, the number of rules and the possibilities to which they applied must have been daunting, even for the most diligent student.

### THE *RÈGLE DE L'OCTAVE*

One way to get around these rules was to prescribe a given chord for each degree in a major or minor scale. Such patterns were dubbed the *règle de l'octave* by Campion, the French theorbist who in 1716 was the first to publish complete bass octaves in this form. Campion ascribed their invention to his predecessor at L'Académie Royale de Musique, one M. de Maltot, about whom absolutely nothing is known. Campion's model scales for major and minor are shown in Example 3-17. Although Campion was the first to publish the scales as complete octaves, similar examples appear in Gasparini 1708 and Heinichen 1711 (Example 3-18). Comparable patterns, using less tonally oriented chord progressions, may be traced well back into the seventeenth century (discussed in Brenet 1888; Mason 1981; Christensen 1992a, 1992b).

In one crucial respect, the *règle* and the closely related patterns in Heinichen and Gasparini signal a distinct change in focus from rules based on solmization syllables or bass patterns apart from any scale. In the *règle*, it is the scale-step status of each bass note that determines the harmony it supports. There is a close agreement between the type of chord and the scale degree: a root-position triad appears only over 1 and 5; a 6/4/3 chord appears over 2 and over 6 in major when descending; a 6/5/3 chord with a consonant fifth appears only over 4 ascending; a 6/♭5/3 appears only over the leading tone; and so forth. As a result, if the scale degree is known, then the chord type is known, and if the chord type is known, then the scale degree is known. Via these correspondences, the *règle* promoted recognition of the manner in which harmony expresses a key.

Compositional Theory in the Eighteenth Century

Gasparini:

Heinichen, 1711:

C *dur:*

A *moll:*

*Example 3-18.* Gasparini 1708, Chapter 8; Heinichen 1711, p. 201

The *règle* also hastened recognition that triads and seventh chords were more fundamental than any other harmonies. Whereas thoroughbass methods in general treated any figuring as a separate harmony, the *règle,* by using only one chord per scale step, necessarily omitted what we today would call chords with suspensions and appoggiaturas, leaving only triads, seventh chords, and their inversions.

Since use of the *règle* was predicated on knowing the key, manuals instructed performers how to recognize the key at each point in a piece. Campion gives the common rule: look for a sharp; this lies one semitone below the final of the key and is the "sensitive note" *(notte sensible).* Other writers also called it the lower semitone *(subsemitonium)* or simply the semitone of the mode *(semitonium modi).* Since knowledge of keys is so important to using the *règle,* it is no accident that early eighteenth-century thoroughbass manuals, including those that present the *règle,* are among the earliest published sources to list most or all of the twenty-four keys (Lester 1989, Chapter 6). Campion writes out his *octaves* in all twenty-four keys. The need to know the proper notes of the scale and to recognize locations within a scale in order to apply the *règle* and other similar patterns was probably a major incentive in the rapid codification and standardization of major and minor keys and key signatures early in the eighteenth century.

In the sense that the *règle* presents the customary or normal placement of chords within a key, the English cognate *rule of the octave* fails to give *règle de l'octave* its due. In this term, the word *règle* implies both what is customary or "regular" *(cela est de règle)* and what is arranged in order, but not what is a rule in the sense of a regulation. German writers of the eighteenth century adopted a number of locutions close to this meaning: "arrangement of the musical octaves" *(Einrichtung der musicalischen Octaven)* in Walther 1732 (article on Campion), "ordering of an octave scale" *(Ordnung eine Octaven-Leiter)* in Hahn 1751, "common bass scale" *(allgemein Bassleiter)* in Riepel 1786, and "common bass passage through an octave" *(allgemeine Octav Gang)* in Albrechtsberger c. 1791. Padre Martini (1706–1784) calls it the "table for progressions" *(Tavola per la modulazione;* Martini 1774–1775, 2, p. xxxvii). An English term that carried this meaning might be "the regularly ordered octave" in the sense of "the regular or customary chords over an octave scale." To avoid both the misleading English term *rule of the octave* and a clumsy neologism, this book always refers to the *règle* by its French name.

The *règle* appears in innumerable eighteenth-century writings. It provided a way of learning common chord successions, a way of dealing with unfigured basses, and a basis for improvisation. Löhlein 1765 and 1781, an extremely popular keyboard, harmony, and accompaniment method that appeared in numerous editions through 1848, devotes much space to the *règle* in both volumes. C. P. E. Bach opens his discussion of improvisation with the simple form of the ascending *règle*, followed by numerous realizations of increasing complexity with suspensions and chromatic tones (Chapter 41; Mitchell 1949, pp. 431–433). The *règle* also made its way into compositions: the descending bass scale that underlies the opening portion of J. S. Bach's *Prelude in C major (Well-Tempered Clavier,* 1) is in effect the descending *règle* with interpolated harmonies.

### CAMPION'S OTHER CHORDS

Despite its widespread use and general applicability, and despite Campion's extravagant claim that "a piece is an assemblage of portions of these *octaves*" (p. 8), the *règle* does not work in all circumstances. When a bass proceeds by skips, many chords in the *règle* no longer apply. For instance, a 6/4/3 chord on scale-step 2 is appropriate only when the bass moves by step to 1 or 3. In addition, numerous commonly used signatures are absent from the *règle*. To account for common chords missing from the *règle*, Campion includes two additional progressions, one in major and one in minor. As he does in the *règle*, Campion also relates these chords to specific scale steps, confirming the growing recognition of the relationship between harmonic structures and the expression of keys. Following each progression, there is an explanation of the notes in each chord and its scale-step location, some of which are presented in Example 3-19.

1. [This chord] only occurs on the first [degree] of the minor key.
2. [This chord] ordinarily occurs on the first [degree] of the key, and is almost always resolved to the semitone below.

3. [This note] carries the chord conforming to the seventh [degree].

5. [This chord] is placed on the final or dominant.

6. [This chord] is only found on the dominant of the major and minor key and on the final of the major key.

12. Here we depart [from the key], since the tritone of D is G♯, which is the leading tone in the scale [*octave*] of A . . . Here the tritone is accompanied by the sixth and the minor third [above the bass]; ordinarily it is accompanied by the sixth and the second . . . [but when it has only ♯6 and ♭3] the note that carries this chord is the ascending second degree of the minor key.

13–14. Like the first chord [meaning that it is a triad and hence a tonic chord].

15. The seventh of the key [*du ton*] descending.

16. To descend to the dominant, before the ordinary chord that is made on the sixth [degree] of the key, one often finds the seventh . . . on the first part of the note. On the second part of the note the usual chord indicated in the *octaves* occurs. On this sixth [degree] of the key, the sixth [above it] is naturally major. However, I have placed a sharp before it to raise it, and this is called the augmented sixth; it is an extraordinary chord . . . The D♯ that makes the augmented sixth is now in some sense the leading tone of E, where the harmony ends extremely well.

26. [I]nstead of the sixth, one may employ the fifth. (Campion 1716, pp. 10–15)

These examples, combined with the *octaves*, constitute a detailed catalog of chord types and their scale-step locations. But although this approach does provide significant insights into the relationship between harmonies and the expression of keys, it is by no means a theory of harmony in the

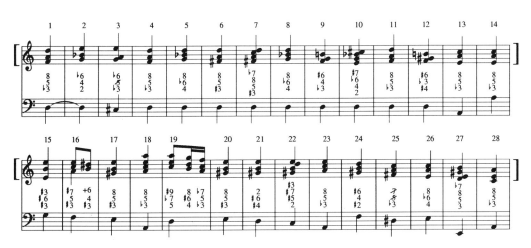

*Example 3-19.* Campion 1716, p. 10. Campion presents only the bass line and figures; the realization has been added here.

*Example 3-20.* Malcolm 1721, p. 429

Rameauian sense. Campion does recognize chordal inversions when he notes that the guitar can be more suitable than theorbo for accompaniment because on the guitar the chords need not be inverted (*renversé;* p. 19). But it would have contradicted his whole approach to apply chord inversions to the *octaves* or to his additional progressions. In his method, a performer needs to relate only a chord type and a scale degree: 6/♭5/3 occurs only on the leading tone. If he had included inversions, the whole procedure would have become much more complex, since 6/♭5/3 would be an inverted 7/5/3 chord, which could appear on scale-step 2, 4, 5, or 7.

Just five years after Campion published his *Traité,* the Scottish musician Alexander Malcolm (1685–1763) applied harmonic scale-step norms in a rather different way, adding to them the notion of harmonic context as the basis of "simple counterpoint" (Malcolm 1721, pp. 422–432). First, he lists the possible intervals that can appear in a melody over each bass scale step and then the possible bass scale steps that could harmonize a given melodic scale step. For instance, scale-step 3 in the melody is almost always supported by 1; scale-step 6 almost always by 4. Other scale steps offer various choices.

To select the best interval for a given situation, Malcolm appeals to the "great many common Places in point of Air, equally familiar to all Composers, which necessarily produce correspondent common Places in Harmony" (p. 431). He illustrates common voice leadings, such as melodic motions from scale-steps 3 to 1 and from 7 to 5, melodic phrases ending on scale-steps 7 or 2, and the like, along with their common harmonizations. He urges the reader to find such norms in the works of Corelli. Malcolm closes this discussion with one fully worked-out harmonization and reasons for his choice of each note. His reasons are eclectic, touching on the bass as a line, the contrapuntal interaction of bass and melody, and structural imitation (see Example 3-20). The first note requires C because the key is C. B or G would be possible for the second note:

> But I rather chused the latter, because having begun pretty high with the Bass, I foresaw I should want to get down to C below. [For the following bass notes, I] chused to ascend gradually with the Bass, to preserve an

Compositional Theory in the Eighteenth Century

Imitation that happens to be between the Parts, by the Bass ascending gradually to the 5th f[undamental] [scale step] from the Beginning of the second
Bar, as the Treble does from the Beginning of the first Bar . . . As to the
following Notes of the Bass I need say nothing; for the Choice of them will
appear to be from one of these Two Considerations, either that they are the
only proper Bass Notes that the Treble could admit of, or that one is chosen
rather than another to favour the contrary Movement of the Parts. (pp. 429–
430)

This may not be a fully developed theory of melodic-harmonic structure.
But with its invocation of harmonic norms combined with well-considered
voice-leading recommendations and awareness of structural motives (the
hidden "imitation" between the melody and bass), it sounds strikingly
modern. It also stands almost alone in its time in demonstrating in detail
a possibly practical working method for a beginning composer. The only
other comparable discussion of the time is Henry Purcell's explanation of
the harmonization of a melody (Purcell 1694, pp. 151–154).

The notion of harmonic norms is reflected not only in the gradually
evolving understanding of the relationship between harmony and the expression of a key, but also in the most commonplace explanations, such
as the criteria for determining the proper notes of a scale. In his 1703
*Dictionaire,* Brossard favors the form of the minor that we call harmonic
because using notes foreign to a given scale implies leaving the key: "It is
for this reason that the sixth and often even the augmented fifth are better
over the mediant of a mode [in the bass] than the perfect fifth, unless one
cadences there. For the same reason the major sixth is better than the
minor sixth over the note immediately above the final of minor modes,
and the minor third is better than the major third over the note immediately below the dominant of minor modes" (article *Modo*). By defending
a scale type in terms of harmonic norms, Brossard implicitly acknowledges
that mode or key is intimately connected with harmonic usages.

Scale-step norms also arise in simple terminology. In a discussion of
fugal subjects and answers, Werckmeister refers to scale steps not by
numbers but by placement in a significant harmony (Werckmeister 1700,
Chapter 4): scale-step 1 is the "fundamental note of the triad of the
primary cadence" *(Fundamental-Clave triadis clausulae primariae),* scale-
step 3 is the "middle note of the harmonic triad," and scale-step 7 is the
"middle note of the triad of the secondary [half] cadence." Despite the
clumsy terminology, the harmonic-functional perspective that places notes
of the scale into significant chords is clear.

HEINICHEN'S DISCUSSION OF UNFIGURED BASSES
Of all the writers who discuss unfigured basses, Heinichen as usual is the
most comprehensive, offering three strategies even in his briefer 1711

treatise. First, he demonstrates how to figure out the chords according to the intervals between the bass part and a solo part. This, the easiest technique, is not an option when the solo part has rests or is absent from the continuo part.

His second method is that used by Penna, Gasparini, and St. Lambert: rules based on characteristic bass intervals regardless of the key. Instead of presenting an endless series of rules and exceptions, as his predecessors had done, Heinichen formulates his recommendations in six General Rules in the 1711 treatise (pp. 193–195). These rules cover what to do with rising and falling semitones or thirds, sharps in the bass, and potential cross relations. As with the rules given by others, Heinichen's work often but not all of the time.

To remedy this, he turns to his third strategy: Special Rules specifying the location of various chords within keys. These are more general than Campion's recommendations and do not deal with as many harmonies as Campion covers. The first four rules explain the required notes in major and minor keys (leading tones and the minor form of scale-step 6 in minor) and that "the semitone below and the third above the tone of any key" require a 6-chord. Heinichen then introduces his formulation of the *règle* (shown in Example 3-18).

The remaining two Special Rules, 5 and 6, cover key changes. According to rule 5, a new sharp or the absence of a sharp previously present determines the semitone of the mode, thereby indicating a new key. Rule 6 lists the common goals of changes of key for major and minor: major keys move to their third, fifth, and sixth; minor keys commonly move to their third and fifth, also to their seventh and fourth, and rarely to their sixth.

Like Campion, and in contrast to both the contrapuntal theories of the seventeenth and early eighteenth centuries and earlier thoroughbass methods, Heinichen demonstrates a strong harmonic and tonal sense. As inadequate as his rules may be for explaining many usages or even for predicting the proper harmonies in a given context, they are an attempt to establish harmonic and voice-leading norms within major and minor keys and to explain how movement from one key to another affects harmony and voice leading.

Heinichen greatly expanded this section in his 1728 treatise. There are now eight General Rules (Buelow 1966a, pp. 207–210), which cover a larger number of situations in both major and minor keys. The six Special Rules are also expanded (ibid., pp. 210–218) and now cover different possibilities for ascending and descending motions: for instance, scale-step 4 may support a 5/3, 6/3, or 6/5/3 chord when ascending by step, but a 6/4/2 in a stepwise descent; scale-step 2 in major keys bears a 6 when moving stepwise, but a 5/3 when followed by skips; scale-step 6 bears a

6 when skipping to scale-step 4, but bears a 5/3 chord in other circumstances. These rules amply supplement what is contained in his revised *règle*.

Between the General Rules, the Special Rules, and the *règle,* Heinichen covers a large number of harmonic norms. But even with all this information, the inadequacies described in connection with other approaches to unfigured basses still remain, requiring numerous Special Observations whenever Heinichen approaches a given situation. This is most evident in the fascinating penultimate chapter of the 1728 treatise, where Heinichen adds figures to the bass throughout an entire solo cantata by Alessandro Scarlatti (1660–1725) and explains every choice as he goes along (English translation in Buelow 1966a, pp. 230–260).[5] This chapter of Heinichen's gives us a unique opportunity to view a composition from a contemporary musician's perspective. It merits line-by-line study in addition to the salient points covered here in connection with Example 3-21.

In general, Heinichen's chord choices are made on local criteria—the immediately preceding or following notes. He generally cites one of the Special Rules, regarding it as self-evident that a given scale degree in the given circumstance requires a certain harmony. Thus at the very opening, after ascertaining from the first two chords, which he calls a cadence, that the key is E minor (despite the signature and the opening bass note), Heinichen cites scale-step rules for the choice of chord over the first eight notes (see Example 3-21).

*Example 3-21.* Heinichen 1728; Buelow 1966a, pp. 231–232, mm. 1–3.
The realization is according to Buelow, p. 282. The comments
paraphrase Heinichen's text.

The first note implies the key of B minor; but the cadence (B to E) indicates
E minor with an incorrect signature. Conclusion: never judge the key from
the first note but rather from the first cadence.

5. Another realization of this unfigured bass according to Heinichen's instructions is in Schering 1931, pp. 378–383.

Each B, as scale-step 5, carries a major third.

The C in measure 1 carries a sixth, being the sixth degree skipping to the fourth degree.

D♯, the leading tone, carries a sixth.

G, scale-step 3, carries a sixth.

F♯, as scale-step 2, could have a major sixth. But when 2 immediately precedes a cadence, it is more beautiful to retain a seventh over it.

The Bs at the cadence could have $^5_4$-♯, $^{6\text{-}5}_{4}$-♯, or just a major third. Remember this cadence pattern because it is very common.

Scale-step harmonic norms and cadence patterns clearly play the major roles here. In some later passages, such as the opening of the recitative in Example 3-22, preparation for a cadence provides an explanation for the harmonic motion throughout an entire phrase. B, leading tone in C major, supports a first-inversion triad. The A can support a triad (as scale-step 6 in a major key), but

an experienced accompanist, however, would prefer to give this note a major 6, since the two bass notes C and B have preceded . . . In a major scale if a bass descends stepwise a fourth, the second bass note normally has the [minor] 6th and the third [note] the major sixth: C $^6_B$ $^{6+}_A$ G. Reason: This progression forms a half cadence with the fifth degree of the scale and requires the major sixth as leading tone over the third note. Even though the half cadence in our example is broken off after the $^{6+}_A$ and in place of the final G an unrelated $^{♭7}_{F♯}$ chord is taken, this [latter chord] is only an inversion of the preceding $^{6+}_A$ whose resolution to G follows.

This remarkable paragraph explains clearly that a four-measure progression with five harmonies is but an extended half cadence; that as such it implies specific harmonies to fill in the motion between the first and last chords; and that one of the connecting chords can be extended by inversion (and have an added note, since E♭ is not implied over the bass A but is in the melody over the bass F♯). Heinichen's method here is similar to his approach to complex dissonances: search for the explanation to a complex usage in a simpler underlying structure. The appearance of this approach

Sa-zio an- co- ra non sei    d'a ver-mi a- per-to il cor, fan-ciul cru-    de- le,    con mil- le e mil- le stra- li?

*Example 3-22.* Heinichen 1728; Buelow 1966a, pp. 234–235.

Compositional Theory in the Eighteenth Century

*Example 3-23.* Heinichen 1728; Buelow 1966a, p. 235

in two separate discussions suggests that it was an integral part of Heinichen's overall perspective. Perhaps the most striking feature of this discussion is that Heinichen treats the entire four measures as a passage in C major, despite the bass F♯. For in general, Heinichen, like all theorists of his time, regards almost any chromaticism as a signal of a temporary key change.

Heinichen's perspective and Niedt's diminution techniques imply that perceptive musicians using thoroughbass methods were aware of the relationship between a compositional surface and the structural foundation lying below its surface. Although Heinichen is capable of such insights in some passages, he is puzzled in connection with others, including the immediately following portion of the same recitative (see Example 3-23). Heinichen knows that the chord over the asterisked C needs a minor third (E♭) because of the minor sixth between the bass and the solo part. But try as he might, he cannot figure out the scale to which the chord belongs:

> In this case the scale seems to be so obscure that one really cannot name or distinguish it. This bass note with its minor sixth cannot belong to G minor, because the *Specie octavae* [the scale] of G minor does not include A♭ but A. Also one cannot consider it part of C minor, because otherwise the leading tone B instead of B♭ would follow [on the next bass note]. It cannot belong to A♭ major, because the *Specie octavae* for this scale does not contain a D.

On the other hand, this D appears over the B♭, and from this it becomes clear that in this case the 6♭/C chord cannot be reduced to any scale.

Heinichen's notion of extended cadential preparation, which serves him so well elsewhere, deserted him here. He fails to note that the coming cadence is on E♭, albeit E♭ minor. Probably the distant relationship perceived between parallel major and minor keys in early eighteenth century theory would not allow him to see that the A♭ chord could be part of the key of E♭, suddenly changing to minor at the cadential arrival.

## Two Eighteenth-Century Bach Analyses

The manuscript of Volume 1 of the *Well-Tempered Clavier* known as P401 contains analytic markings in an unknown hand in the *C-minor Fugue* and the *D-minor Prelude*.[6] The analyses, probably dating from Leipzig in the 1730s or 1740s, do not follow procedures mentioned in any particular thoroughbass manual. Nevertheless they reflect the thinking that underlies rules for unfigured basses as well as other aspects of thoroughbass methods, thereby confirming the prevalence of these modes of thought in the early eighteenth century (see Example 3-24).[7]

The *C-minor Fugue* contains three types of analytic notations. First, there is a series of numbers under each lowest note. They indicate scale steps, numbered 1 through 8 at first, then with nearly every 8 replaced by *f* (for *finalis*) after measure 3. These scale-step numbers frequently shift key, with the shift generally taking place underneath a new leading tone or the negation of an old leading tone. For instance, the numbers shift to G minor under the top-voice F♯ in measure 3. During the episode in measures 5 and 6, the numbers shift to C minor, then to B♭ major under the A♮, and to C minor under the B♮.

The second set of analytic markings is a separate series of numbers for each upper voice. These numbers function like thoroughbass figures, measuring intervals over the bass. The *f*s in measures 3 and 7 seem to be silly substitutions for *8*, probably made because the notes in question are both an octave over the lowest voice and also the final of the key.

The third set of analytic symbols are short lines that connect stepwise motions into scale-steps 3, 5, or 8: 7-8, 6-5, 4-5, and so forth. These lines do not appear consistently. But there is an interesting line across the skip

6. Similar analyses appear in other Bach manuscripts, including P418 (French suites).

7. Spitta 1889 erroneously believed that the analytic markings show J. S. Bach testing Rameau's harmonic theories on his own works (an error repeated in some modern writings). The markings are not in J. S. Bach's hand and they have nothing to do with Rameau. Dürr 1986 and Deppert 1987 reliably interpret the markings. Similar analyses appear in one of the manuscripts of the French suites.

*Example 3-24.* J. S. Bach, *C-minor Fugue* in P401. The key signature is Dorian (without A♭).

*Example 3-25.* J. S. Bach, *D-minor Prelude* in P401

of a seventh in measure 6, possibly to indicate that this skip of a seventh is really a conjunct 2-1 despite the registral change that gets the middle voice out of the way before the bass-voice entry.

The *D-minor Prelude* contains similar analytic markings in a different handwriting and with some additional features (Example 3-25). The thoroughbass intervals are written one above the other, confirming that the analyst saw the right hand as chordal arpeggiations. In addition, the keys are labeled: *F dur* on system 2, *B dur* and *G moll* on system 4, and so forth. Above the prelude, a series of numbers lists all the keys in the prelude as scale steps within the overall tonic. The numbers begin *F (finalis)*, 3, 6, 4, and so forth, for D minor, F major, B♭ major, and G

*Example 3-26. J. S. Bach, D-minor Prelude, mm. 13–17*

minor. The number 16 at the end is the total number of keys (an error due to one omitted key).

Some of the key changes are quite temporary, such as measure 14 of the prelude (shown in Example 3-26), where only two eighth notes are analyzed in B♭ major. Although it seems narrow-minded to cite such a brief key change, doing so confirms the practicality of the analytic method and early eighteenth-century attitudes toward keys and key changes in general. Both thoroughbass players and composers needed to know the proper chord over each and every bass note. A 6/♭5 chord appears only over the leading tone of a key; hence in measure 14, the bass A is best understood as scale-step 7. Whether thoroughbass is a real-time performance aid or a method to learn composition—and the best thoroughbass manuals claimed to be both—its notation was designed to deal with immediate issues, not long-range analytic contemplation. By contrast, the listing of keys atop the *D-minor Prelude* was probably meant for just such contemplation after the details of the piece had been ascertained. The difference between the long-range structure atop the score and the quick changes in the score helps us to understand why the notion of secondary dominant or tonicizing dominant took so long to become universal. The eighteenth-century analyst knew that the excursion to B♭ in measure 14 of the prelude is a temporary one, and that the B♭ is ultimately scale-step 6 of the overall tonic. But that did not change the fact that within measure 14, A-B♭ was best understood as scale-steps 7-8 in B♭.

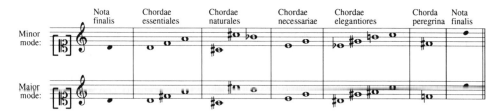

| | Nota finalis | Chordae essentiales | Chordae naturales | Chordae necessariae | Chordae elegantiores | Chorda peregrina | Nota finalis |
|---|---|---|---|---|---|---|---|

*Example 3-27.* Walther 1732, article *modus musicus*

This type of thinking continues throughout the century. In 1784, Mozart cites the key of C minor to explain the proper doubling for a B-diminished-seventh chord lasting a single eighth note within a long cadential preparation in G minor (Mozart 1784, fol. 8$^r$).

Finally, next to some chromatic notes there are letters that abbreviate terms for scale steps in several books: Mattheson 1719 (pp. 16–20) and 1735 (p. 126), Kellner 1732 (pp. 44f.), and Walther 1732 (articles *chordes belles* and *modus musicus*)[8] (see Example 3-27). For instance, in measure 16 of the *D-minor Prelude, c.e.* under the 4 means *chorda elegantior,* or scale-step ♯4. Calling the C♯ ♯4 in G rather than 7 in the key of D shows considerable sophistication on the part of the analyst. G is a better local key than D at this point because the bass Ds in the previous and following measures support ♭6/4 or 7/5/♯3, harmonies appropriate to scale-step 5 in the key of G, not to scale-step 1 in the key of D.

Despite the sophistication of such aspects of the analyses, they are not without errors. In the *C-minor Fugue,* the key of A♭ is retained throughout the subject entry in E♭ (measures 11–12) despite numerous D-naturals. And in measure 5, beat 2, of the *D-minor Prelude,* the analyst misread the bass note as F and figured 9/5/4—the resulting unresolved dissonant F in the bass should have indicated to the analyst that the bass note should be E.

The limitations of the entire analytic method are evident at the very end of the prelude. In the absence of a bass, the analyst despaired at labeling a string of diminished triads with keys, scale-step numbers, or interval numbers. Instead, only some individual notes receive labels, such as *c.e.* and *p.* (*peregrina* for the foreign form of scale-step 3).

Without a verbal text, we cannot be sure why the analysts went to such trouble. But from the written evidence, it seems likely that these analyses were done to show how scale-step norms taught by thoroughbass appear in actual compositions. The analysts possibly compared the intervals above the bass to the scale-step norms expressed in the *règle* and in rules for

8. Mattheson, who first proposed such names in Germany, probably modeled them on a briefer list in Brossard 1703 (article *modo*).

*Example 3-28.* Frère 1706, p. 10

unfigured basses. To make such a comparison between these pieces and the norms, the analysts had to know the key, the scale step of each bass note, and the intervals set against those scale steps—precisely the information contained in the analyses. For instance, in measure 3 of the *C-minor Fugue,* the analyst probably noted that the intervals over scale steps 7, 2, *f,* 6, and 4 are parts of the chords prescribed for those degrees in the *règle* or in scale-step norms described in Heinichen's or another author's treatise. The augmented second over scale-step 6 and the fourth over scale-step 5 toward the end of the measure might have then been ascribed to the idiosyncrasy of the experienced composer.

The lines showing conjunct connections to scale-steps 3, 5, and 8 were probably inserted to show how notes within a phrase always seem to return to the members of the tonic triad. Many published works of the time explored such an attitude. Frère 1706, for instance, illustrates how the notes of the triad built on the final form "the basis of melodic structure" (*la baze de la Modulation,* p. 5) (see Example 3-28).

By applying information found in many thoroughbass and composition manuals of the period in a manner not appearing in any published works, these analyses help to fill that ever-present gap between the way ideas appear in treatises and the way materials might have been used pedagogically. It is a confirmation of the vitality and flexibility of the one-on-one teacher-student pedagogy of the time that these analyses do not imitate any particular published work. The analysis of the *C-minor Fugue* seems to be written in a more experienced hand than the analysis of the *D-minor Prelude* (judging from the imaginary straight line under the numbers below the bass in the *C-minor Fugue,* the similar size of all the numerals, and the absence of mistakes as basic as that in measure 5 of the *D-minor Prelude*). Perhaps the *C-minor* analysis was done by the unknown teacher as a demonstration, and the *D-minor* analysis as an exercise by the unknown student.

## Summary

In many ways, thoroughbass is merely a system of simultaneity classification designed to train performers, largely by rote repetition, to realize the harmonies and voice leadings specified by the figures or suggested by the structure of the bass. With the capacity to label any simultaneity according to the intervals above the bass, thoroughbass can name and discuss the behavior of any verticality conceivable in tonal music. But this universal applicability of thoroughbass figures is also its primary limitation. The neutrality of thoroughbass figures, which can be applied equally to any simultaneity, precludes any functional hierarchization of harmonies—a triad and a sonority with multiple suspensions are both simply chords. In addition, classifying harmonies according to their figuring implies that chords figured similarly are close in function and that chords figured differently are different in function. Assuming that the bass voice is the sole point against which to measure intervals works against recognizing that intervals consonant with the bass may be better understood structurally as dissonances against another essential note of the harmony. Without a comprehensive explanation of the way pitches interact with one another, the methods introduce huge numbers of rules and exceptions that apply to some contexts but need amendments for many others. All this excludes from thoroughbass the differentiations between chord types and chord functions—nonharmonic versus chord tones, and structural chords versus passing chords—that are central to modern theories of harmony. And all these factors work against turning thoroughbass into an explanation of the harmonic framework of a passage.

Nonetheless, thoroughbass methods bring to the fore aspects of musical structure absent from many of the contrapuntal theories of the time. With its ability to convert any combination of notes into figures and place them into a context—even if an adequate explanation of that simultaneity or its context were not forthcoming—thoroughbass oversteps the bounds of a species approach or any other manner of presenting *prima pratica* counterpoint. This may be the source of J. S. Bach's supposed dissatisfaction with "the dry species of counterpoint that are given in Fux and others." While contrapuntal theory required a structurally reductive process like Bernhard's in order to deal with contemporary practices, thoroughbass could immediately incorporate any contemporary practice merely by including the harmony and voice leading in the figuring.

The whole notion of key structure, which was bypassed entirely or treated in terms of modes in contrapuntal approaches, came to the fore in thoroughbass approaches. The need to know the key at every point spurred the codification of major and minor keys, the growing standardization of key signatures, the explanation of how to recognize keys, and the establishment of standard progressions in each key, whether by means of the *règle* or various verbal explanations of common practices. And the inclusion of only triads and seventh chords in the *règle* and in various rules for unfigured basses promoted the sense that these harmonies were more fundamental than what we view today as chords with added nonharmonic tones. Furthermore, as we have seen in various discussions by

Heinichen, Niedt, C. P. E. Bach, and others, perceptive comments about musical structure were often generated by the desire to explain various practices.

Thoroughbass approaches, at least in the hands of the more perceptive theorists, thus contained a wealth of knowledge about musical structure. But the multitude of rules and exceptions and the ever-growing number of chords and signatures called attention to the need for a more systematic way of explaining all these interactions. Mizler—perhaps facetiously, perhaps in desperation—suggested "one single rule":

> The intervals of the harmonic triad (the octave, fifth, and third) can ascend as well as descend to all possible intervals, and all possible intervals can once again be resolved by ascent as well as descent to each interval of the harmonic triad, and each dissonant interval, before being resolved into the harmonic triad, can first proceed several times to all possible dissonant intervals, depending upon the circumstances. All this must always happen so that no nonharmonic relationship occurs and no fifths and octaves follow one another immediately, be they direct or hidden, unless they are so covered by many other intervals that the ear does not take note of them. (Mizler 1736–1754, Vol. 1, Part 5, p. 66)

It was to address this situation that Rameau published the first comprehensive attempt at an explanation in 1722. Within a generation his influence changed forever the context of discussions of musical structure.

# Rameau's Early Works

*Music is a science which should have definite rules; these rules should be drawn from an evident principle; and this principle cannot really be known to us without the aid of mathematics. Notwithstanding all the experience I may have acquired in music from being associated with it for so long, I must confess that only with the aid of mathematics did my ideas become clear and did light replace a certain obscurity of which I was unaware before.*

*Rameau 1722, preface*

## Rameau as a Theorist of Harmony

Harmony joins counterpoint and thoroughbass as the third theoretical tradition inherited by the early eighteenth century. It too traces its lineage back to the sixteenth century. But it was the least developed of the three before the *Traité de l'harmonie* by Jean-Philippe Rameau (1683–1764) appeared in 1722. This is because counterpoint and thoroughbass had immediately practical applications in the seventeenth century. Counterpoint codified voice interactions for instruction in composition, both in the *stile antico* and in more modern styles, and thoroughbass taught patterns of simultaneity successions for performers who needed to realize figured and unfigured basses and for composers who assembled these patterns into new compositions.

The study of harmony, although it had been the medium for important theoretical breakthroughs in the late sixteenth and early seventeenth centuries, had no comparable pedagogical application. Many of the theoretical tenets that Rameau drew together in his theories—chord inversion, harmonic scale-step norms, basic harmonic progressions (especially cadences), dissonance resolutions, and cadential evasion—were recognized before he was born. But they had remained isolated bits of information and rules of thumb. Rameau built a perspective on musical structure from these tenets, thereby transforming them from peripheral information to the center of musical knowledge.

By re-examining musical knowledge and reorganizing it according to what he regarded as more consistent principles, Rameau brought to music theory the intellectual revolution that transformed Western thought in the seventeenth and early eighteenth centuries. René Descartes (1596–1650) had both reflected changed attitudes in thinking and also propelled these changes with new energy and direction. Facts were no longer valid because they stood the test of time; now they would have to pass the test of reason as well. "At best an argument from what has been, to what should of right be, has no force" (John Locke, *Second Treatise on Government* 1689, par. 103).

Furthermore, facts were not to be accepted simply because they existed: their significance was to be deduced according to first principles, which gave them a place in the cosmos of ideas. Copying Descartes, who sought to place all knowledge on a solid methodological foundation built on the principles of mathematics, Rameau sought basic principles that would place musical knowledge on a sound footing and replace the myriad rules and exceptions of thoroughbass and counterpoint—a disorganized mass of individual facts and opinions that had arisen from unconsidered experience.

But Rameau was not merely a deductive systematizer who followed his reasoning wherever it led him and disregarded musical realities. He was a practical musician, a major organist, and one of the great composers of the century. He would have no part of the theorizing of musical amateurs and lesser musicians who, caught up in the investigative spirit of the age, attempted to systematize musical knowledge without knowing music well, who rejected common chords or progressions that had did not fit into some deductive system, and who proposed musical practices that bore little resemblance to common reality.

For Rameau, the deductive process, which exalts reason over experience, did not necessarily denigrate the practical, living knowledge yielded by experience. Practical skills were not only useful, since "a musician can excel in the practice of his art without knowing theory" (Rameau 1726, title to Chapter 21)—they were absolutely necessary: "Only by means of keyboard accompaniment can one promptly acquire a sensibility to harmony" (ibid., title to Chapter 22). Throughout his life he addressed practical concerns: Books 3 and 4 of his *Traité* (1722) treat composition and accompaniment, the latter reading in many places like a thoroughbass manual; his *Dissertation* of 1732 defends a new method of accompaniment; the longest chapter in his *Generation* of 1737 deals with composition; and the *Code* of 1761 is largely a method teaching composition and accompaniment.

No matter how important experience was, Rameau argued as a Cartesian that knowledge and skills gained thereby were unreliable without understanding their foundation. Reasoned knowledge together with skills attained through experience would complement one another. The mediating factor was talent—a gift of Nature. Reasoned knowledge, experienced skills, and talent had to work together. Even "persons with mature taste" and a "natural gift" might "stray from the truth unless this gift is sustained by knowledge, though knowledge cannot suffice for perfection unless good taste comes to its aid" (Rameau 1722, Book 3, Chapter 41).

Talent is crucial for Rameau because "music is doubtless natural to us" (Rameau 1726, p. 90). Nature allows a naive singer to discover the intervals and structure of the major scale merely by singing what comes naturally (ibid., Chapter 9). And, as Rameau urges his readers to prove by experiment, Nature bestows on "anyone sensitive to harmony, even children of 8 or 9," the ability to sing the fundamental bass (what we call the root) of a cadential chord without even knowing what they are doing (ibid., Chapter 10). The full title of the *Traité,* "Treatise on Harmony reduced to its natural principles," reflects both Rameau's Cartesian search for first principles and his belief that music has a natural basis. In arguing from Nature, Rameau shared common roots with many diverse traditions of musical thought in the eighteenth century. As the German musical scholar Lorenz Mizler (1711–1778) wrote in 1737, "'orderly' and 'natural' are one and the same in music, for Nature itself orders the tones . . . [F]rom this natural ordering of tones arise all other truths in music" (Mizler 1736–1754, Vol. 4, p. 60).

Because Rameau both searched for the basic principles underlying music and also addressed practical concerns, his works often present two seemingly separate explanations for a given phenomenon. As speculative theorist he will offer an explanation, while as practical theorist he will concentrate on the results. When a speculative perspective is prominent in one work and a practical perspective predominates in others, it has seemed to many scholars that Rameau changed his opinions on the issue. But often, Rameau held similar views in both works, although he may have spoken speculatively in one and practically in another.

Rameau's ideas continued to evolve throughout his lifetime. Many of these changes took place in the speculative side of his theories. Consider the minor triad, a perennial source of trouble for Rameau the speculative theorist. For reasons to be discussed below, Rameau repeatedly proposed new methods of deriving the minor triad, once even offering two derivations within the same treatise (Rameau 1750). But whatever his justification for the minor triad in any given work, Rameau the practical musician always recognized that the minor triad was just as firm a foundation of musical structure as the major triad. As a result, many theoretical battles that have been cast as pro-Rameau versus anti-Rameau from the eighteenth century to the present day are also battles within Rameau's own works: Rameau the speculative theorist versus Rameau the practical theorist, or Rameau the speculative theorist in one work versus Rameau the speculative theorist in another.

Thus the charge that Rameau "pronounced a *theory,* whereas thoroughbass was essentially a practice" (Mitchell 1949, p. 17) is ultimately a criticism largely directed against the speculative side of his writings. Both the speculative and practical sides of Rameau might have argued against this statement by noting that the ultimate value of reason lies not in abstractions but in practical applications. For him, the innumerable rules and exceptions of traditional theory of thoroughbass and counterpoint-composition were the impractical side of music theory.

Because Rameau built much of his new perspective from existing tenets and verifiable musical facts, many of his ideas spread throughout the musical world quite rapidly. Within a decade after the appearance of Rameau's *Traité* in 1722, many of its premises had been adopted by an anonymous French musician arguing with Rameau in the pages of the prestigious Parisian journal *Mercure de France* over *how* to apply some of his ideas, not *whether* to apply them. Rameau's *Traité* is probably the source for the discussion of inversions in Heinichen's 1728 thoroughbass treatise; David Kellner's formulation of chordal inversions in his extremely popular thoroughbass manual of 1732 is even closer to Rameau's than is Heinichen's. During the 1730s and 1740s English, French, and German publications on thoroughbass and composition are based on Rameau's theories. Beginning in the 1750s, students of J. S. Bach who claimed to deal with their teacher's composition method were analyzing the master's compositions with Rameau's theories (Nichelmann and Kirnberger). And musicians avowing to be opponents of Rameau claimed that they or their own predecessors had discovered tenets of his theory.

Rameau's ideas on harmony rapidly transformed counterpoint and thoroughbass. By the last third of the century, counterpoint was more often than not presented as the activation of a harmonic structure (in Kirnberger 1771–1779 and Koch 1782–1793), and species counterpoint was understood in terms of chords and their inversions, even when Fuxian methods were used (in Mozart 1784 and Albrechtsberger 1790). Thoroughbass came to be taught in terms of triads, seventh chords, and their inversions, much as Rameau had recommended in 1722 (as in Türk 1791). Even the composition method of Johann Philipp Kirnberger (1721–1783), published in the 1770s, in which Kirnberger claimed to follow the instructional method of his teacher J. S. Bach, is largely based on Rameau's theories; this despite the fact that it was supposedly to support Kirnberger's treatise that C. P. E. Bach penned his famous remark "you can loudly declare that my principles and those of my late father are anti-Rameau" (Kirnberger 1771–1779, Vol. 2, p. 188). The study of harmony long remained the heart of tonal music theory.

Unlike the traditions of counterpoint and thoroughbass, which derive from the works of numerous writers, harmonic theory first rose to prominence in the eighteenth century because of works published by a single theorist over several decades. Since much of what happened in theory later in the century was dependent on understandings and misunderstandings of the tenets and attitudes enunciated by Rameau, a full appreciation of later theory is possible only via knowledge of Rameau's ideas and their manner of presentation.

## Rameau's Works

Rameau was a mature musician when he began producing the works that made him famous as a theorist and composer. When his first treatise, the *Traité de l'harmonie,* appeared in 1722, he was already thirty-nine and still relatively obscure, describing himself, in a country where Paris was by far the most important musical center, as "Organist of the Cathedral of Clermont in Auvergne." Likewise, he was fifty when his first opera premiered in 1733. With untiring energy, he became one of the most prolific music theorists of any age, publishing several lengthy treatises and numerous shorter works during the four decades after 1722. At age eighty, Rameau poignantly described how he treasured the few hours of daylight during which his failing eyesight still allowed him to put his ideas to paper (Rameau CTW 6, p. xli–xlii).

Rameau published several treatises, smaller independent items, and many letters and articles in various journals. Additional items remained in manuscript, some only recently rediscovered, some still unpublished, others apparently lost. With the great number of his writings, there are minor discrepancies in the contents of the four comprehensive lists of his published and unpublished writings (Rameau CTW 6, pp. lxix–lxxi; Girdlestone 1969, pp. 581–582; Cyr 1980; Damschroder-Williams 1990). All the published works appear in facsimile in *Jean-Philippe Rameau, Complete Theoretical Writings* (Rameau CTW below), along with many contemporaneous secondary sources. Erwin Jacobi's meticulous introductory essays in each of the six volumes constitute the single most comprehensive study to date of the circumstances surrounding Rameau's writings, critical reception of his works, and people connected with his theories.[1]

1. In addition to secondary literature cited in connection with specific points, the most comprehensive surveys of Rameau's theories in English are Shirlaw 1917 and Ferris 1959, which concentrate on Rameau's speculative ideas; Keane 1961, which offers a broad survey; and Christensen 1993, which places Rameau in the intellectual world of his time.

Rameau's major works, all published in Paris, are the following (the Bibliography contains information on facsimiles and translations):[2]

*Traité de l'harmonie reduite à ses principes naturels* (1722)

*Nouveau système de musique theorique . . . pour servir d'introduction au Traité de l'harmonie* (1726)

*Dissertation sur les différentes métodes d'accompagnement . . . avec le plan d'une nouvelle métode* (1732)

*Generation harmonique, ou Traité de musique théorique et pratique* (1737)

*Démonstration du principe de l'harmonie, servant de base à tout l'art musical théorique & pratique* (1750)

*Observations sur notre instinct pour la musique, et sur son principe* (1754)

*Code de musique pratique . . . avec de nouvelles réflexions sur le principe sonore* [1761]

*Origine des sciences* (1762)

Rameau addressed his works to a wide range of audiences. Some works are dense speculative tracts, some are practical. Some are philosophical musings on musical and nonmusical topics. Some are addressed to musicians. Others are for musical amateurs, among them the *Dissertation,* whose title page explains that his new accompaniment method can be used "even by those who do not know how to read music," and the *Code: methods to learn music, even by the blind.*

Rameau republished none of his works and seems never to have contemplated preparing a definitive edition (as Zarlino did in 1589), whether because he feared difficulty finding a publisher due to the hostility between himself and the Encyclopedists in his later years (Rameau CTW 1, pp. xiii–xiv), or, more probably, because he was still searching for new solutions to problematic areas in his theories. He was an inveterate reviser of his writings. Even after the *Traité* had been printed, Rameau had substitute pages printed and inserted in the book, and then issued a Supplement along with it containing numerous other changes of substance and of details (Gossett 1971, pp. vii–xii).

The *Traité* of 1722, although it does not contain a number of Rameau's most significant theoretical ideas, was the work that first introduced his ideas to the musical world. This chapter covers Rameau's ideas as pre-

2. Manuscript treatises date from before, during, and after the period of these publications. Suaudeau 1958 and 1960, though brief and relatively uninformative, are the only sources for now-lost manuscripts dating from 1716–1722. Christensen 1987a and 1990a discuss an important manuscript composition treatise probably written between 1737 and 1744 and published in modified form as Gianotti 1759. Schneider 1986 includes Rameau's last treatise (1763–1764).

sented fully in this first treatise. Chapter 5 treats his ideas as they developed in his later works, including aspects of his theory that appear in the *Traité* but are much more fully developed later.

## Chords and Inversions

Rameau believed that triads and seventh chords, along with their inversions and other derivatives, accounted for all the structurally meaningful harmonies in tonal music. He also seems to have believed he was the first to relate different chords as inversions of one another: "why is it that until the *Traité de l'harmonie* it was not known that a certain number of chords could join together in one?" The footnote to this passage is "See, on this subject, all treatises on music" (Rameau 1732, p. 14; Hayes 1974a, p. 19).

In the absence of thorough studies of earlier theory, this assertion was accepted by those who supported Rameau and wished to make him the sole discoverer of chordal inversion and by those who attacked Rameau and wished to blame him for the same discovery. When Hugo Riemann cited ambiguous statements hinting at knowledge of chord inversions in thoroughbass manuals around 1700 by Werckmeister and Keller, Matthew Shirlaw vigorously defended Rameau's priority (Riemann 1898, pp. 431–433; Mickelsen 1977, pp. 160–161; Shirlaw 1917, pp. xii–xiii, 8–12, 25–26). Schenker, probably also responding to Riemann, would hear nothing about Germans preceding Rameau in harmonic theory. He branded chordal inversion a "French innovation" and compared its results to the French Revolution: "'Below is above and above is below,' screamed the French Below . . . But what is born above remains above, just as what is below always keeps its place, and all the murder and pillage . . . trying to overturn this natural order remained ineffectual" (Schenker 1930, p. 14). So much for polemic pro and con in the absence of facts.

### TRIADIC INVERSIONS BEFORE RAMEAU

It is now clear that several German theorists fully grasped the unity of the triad before the end of the sixteenth century, and that by 1610 two German theorists had stated a theory of triadic inversion, explaining the root-position form as the origin of the two inversions. The German theorist Johannes Avianius (?–1617) describes *perfect* (5/3), *imperfect* (6/3), and *absurd* (6/4) chords in his brief *Isagoge* of 1581 (in Rivera 1978). Unlike Zarlino, who considered chords as composites of intervals, Avianius deems chords three-pitch units even if only two different pitches are present. Thus, he treats a chord containing only C# and A as an imperfect harmony with a missing E.

Other German theorists of the time also treat harmonies as units (dis-

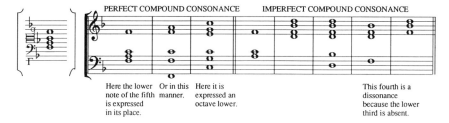

*Example 4-1.* Harnish 1608, p. 54

cussed in more detail in Lester 1989, pp. 28–41). Joachim Burmeister (1564–1629) begins his discussion of composition with four-part harmony, offering charts with four types of chords: those with a perfect fifth and a minor third, those with a perfect fifth and a major third, those with minor thirds and sixths, and those with major thirds and sixths (Burmeister 1599 and 1606). Neither Avianius nor Burmeister relates different inversions to one another.

Shortly thereafter, Otto Siegfried Harnish (c. 1568–1623) differentiates the *basis* or fundamental note from the "lowest note of the harmony" *(inferior vox concordantiae)* and recognizes the inversional relationship among different forms of the triad (Harnish 1608) (see Example 4-1).

Two years later, Johannes Lippius (1585–1612) dubs all forms of this chord the "harmonic triad" *(trias harmonica)* because, like the Holy Trinity, it is a unity born of three separate parts—three pitches and three intervals (Lippius 1610 and 1612). He explains inversions, takes note of the "root" *(radix)* of both intervals and triads, differentiates major and minor forms of the triad, and differentiates modes according to the quality of the triad built on the final. Lippius also offers a compositional method based on the triad, explaining how "all the melodies must so join together that in their combination there will be no consonant portion that does not rest on that unitrisonic harmonic root." Smooth voice leading over a skipping bass line will create "various kinds of triads more elegantly, more easily, and more wonderfully mixed, combined, and arranged in proper order" (Lippius 1612, fols. G4ᵛ-G7ʳ; Rivera 1977, pp. 46–47).

Lippius recommends composing the bass first and placing dots to indicate the notes of a triad over each bass pitch (see Example 4-2). The other voices are to be composed by connecting those dots, as shown in Example 4-3. If one starts composing from the tenor or discant, the bass should be added first, with the remaining voices built from the bass. Ornaments of rhythm (unequal note values or syncopations), volume, or pitch (running notes and suspensions) turn such structures into actual compositions. Thus, the basis for an elaborative method of composition building on a

*Example* 4-2. Lippius 1612, fol. H1ʳ; Rivera 1977, p. 48, with minor errors emended

chordal texture—not unlike that presented a century later by Niedt—had appeared in print by 1612.

Many of Lippius' ideas were not unique to him or to German theorists. The English poet, composer, and theorist Thomas Campion (1567–1620), like his German contemporaries, recognizes the difference between the sounding "Base" of a chord and its "true Base" in the mid-1610s: when a sixth is used over the bass, "such Bases are not true Bases, for where a sixt is to be taken, either in F sharpe, or in E sharpe [that is, E natural], or in B or in A the true Base is a third lower, F sharpe in D, E in C, B in G, A in F" (Campion [c. 1613], p. 204).

Discussions of inversions and chord roots appeared through the early eighteenth century. Werckmeister 1702, in addition to showing how knowledge of the proper root *(Wurtzel)* explains the doubling in a chord of the sixth (as discussed in Chapter 3), also speaks directly of "the inversion of the triad [*Die Versetzung der Triadum*] . . . such as E-G-C or G-C-E" (p. 6). Discussions akin to Lippius in terminology appear in two early eighteenth-century manuscript treatises by young musicians who later became major writers: Walther 1708 (p. 101) and Scheibe c.1730 (Chapters 2 and 5). Fux too explains root-position and first-inversion triads in *Gradus* (as discussed in Chapter 2). Mizler, who seems to have been unaware of Rameau's works, treats rearrangement *(Verwechselung)* of notes in a chord as everyday knowledge (Mizler 1736–1754, Vol. 1, Part 5, p. 65; Vol. 2, p. 117). Even Mattheson, who was hostile to Rameau, speaks of triadic arpeggiation (Mattheson 1739, Part 3, Chapter 12).

Inversional thinking entirely independent of this late-sixteenth-century and early-seventeenth-century chordal theory arose because of playing

*Example* 4-3. Lippius 1612, fol. H1ʳ; Rivera 1977, p. 48

*Example 4-4.* Open strings on a theorbo

*Example 4-5.* An A-5/3 chord on the theorbo

techniques on plucked and strummed instruments.[3] In contrast to plucked lute playing, which emulated the contrapuntal texture of vocal polyphony, Iberian guitar players beginning in the late sixteenth century popularized *rasgueado* or strummed chords. To strum all the strings, players grasped chords in a fingering they could maintain for the length of a harmony. Some of these positions created triadic inversions, used interchangeably with the root-position form. *Rasgueado* technique on the guitar spread to Italy (renamed *battente*) and France by the 1620s, and to England later in the century.

Triadic inversions arose for another reason on the theorbo, a lute-like instrument used in thoroughbass accompaniments. The theorbo's upper strings were tuned like the lute in descending fourths with a single major third, but the top two strings were an octave lower than their place in the fourth-cycle (see Example 4-4). In thoroughbass realizations, the written bass would be played on a middle or lower string, while the chord was strummed across the remaining upper strings. Thus a 5/3 chord built on the top-line A in bass clef would be played as follows: the bass A would be fingered a whole step above string number 4, C would be fingered a half step above string number 3, and strings 1 and 2 would be strummed as open strings (see Example 4-5). The result is a 6/4 chord, recognized by theorbists as an inversion *(renversement)* of the proposed harmony. To preserve the integrity of the bass line in theorbo realizations, Denis Delair insists that "the bass must always precede the chord; it does not matter which [of the other notes] is sounded first or last after the bass" (Delair 1690, fol. C^v). François Campion (c. 1686–1748) supports using the guitar instead of the theorbo in accompaniments in part because "the accompanimental parts are not inverted [*renversées*]" (Campion 1716, p. 19). Various collections of theorbo tablatures also refer to inverted chords: Fleury 1660, Bartolomi 1669, and Grenerin [c. 1670].

3. For information in addition to that in the following discussion, see Christensen 1992a and Mason 1981.

In contrast to the older belief that Rameau invented triadic inversions, or the more recent argument that German early-seventeenth-century inversional theory was soon forgotten or even "suppressed" until Rameau rediscovered inversions (Dahlhaus 1984, p. 123; Dahlhaus 1989, p. 75), it is clear that knowledge of triadic inversion was widespread during the century before Rameau's *Traité*. Some theorists did not refer to the concept, and others may have been unsure about the exact relationship between different positions of a chord (as discussed in connection with Heinichen in Chapter 3). But it is clear that Rameau did not invent or reinvent the notion of triadic inversion.

So what did Rameau mean by his claim that "until the *Traité de l'harmonie* it was not known that a certain number of chords could join together in one"? What did he accomplish in this area that no one before him had done? And why if knowledge of triadic inversions was so widespread did it seem so marginal? First, Rameau extended inversional thinking to all chord-types, not just triads—to seventh chords, and, via his theory of subposition (discussed below), to suspensions. Second, and more important, he was the first to realize that the notion of chord roots could be the basis of a powerful explanation of harmonic progression. When he claimed that no one before him had shown how several chords were really rearrangements of a single harmony, he probably referred to his theories in this larger sense.

RAMEAU'S BASIC CHORD TYPES

Rameau built his theory of harmony on the belief that there are basically only two types of chords: the perfect chord (*accord parfait;* Rameau never uses the term *triad*) or consonant harmony, and the seventh chord or dissonant harmony. Every harmony for him is a perfect chord, a seventh chord, an inversion of these, or a derivative of a seventh chord (the added-sixth chord and chords by *subposition,* both discussed below).

By treating these types of simultaneities, and ignoring what we nowadays call nonharmonic tones other than suspensions and appoggiaturas (passing tones, neighbors, anticipations, and the like), Rameau attempted to explain the harmonies recognized by thoroughbass (though thoroughbass writers before Rameau did not of course categorize chords in his manner). Thoroughbass deals with the simultaneities that need to be figured for the performer. It generally disregards post-chordal nonharmonic tones because as a rule they do not affect what a continuo player performs and are omitted from thoroughbass figuring. Throughout his works, Rameau deals primarily with the chords that appear in French thoroughbass methods of the period. What we call post-chordal nonharmonic tones are

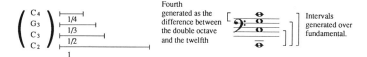

*Example 4-6.*

for Rameau "Ornamented Melody or Supposition"[4] (Rameau 1722, Book 3, Chapter 39), or, in his later works, "grace notes" *(notes de goût)*. They belong to melody, not to harmony.

### THE SOURCE OF CHORDAL INVERSION

To place his theory of chordal inversion on a solid foundation, Rameau needed a reliable way to determine the primary form of each chord type. For instance, 6/5 chords have the same notes as 7 chords whose bass is a third lower. If Rameau could only demonstrate that each was a rearrangement of the other, he could not show whether the 6/5 form or the 7 form was primary. Pre-Rameau theorists might well have chosen the 6/5 form, since it was implausible that a dissonant 7 chord might be the source of the 6/5 chord, which contained only consonances over the bass. Rameau needed to explain that certain intervals (and, hence, certain forms of a chord) were the source of others. To do this, he generates the individual consonances so that within each complementary pair of consonances (fourth-fifth and third-sixth) one is original and the other derived from it.

To accomplish this he turns in the *Traité* to the age-old technique of dividing a string. He dubs the note which sounds when an entire string vibrates the *fundamental*. From half a string, the octave of the fundamental arises. The next integral division of the string, into thirds, yields a twelfth (a compound fifth) over the fundamental. The difference between this fifth and the next octave yields the fourth. The origin of the fourth, however, is entirely unlike that of the octave and the fifth: "Only the octave and the fifth are directly generated by the fundamental sound. The fourth is merely a result of the octave, since it arises from the difference between this octave and the fifth" (Book 1, Chapter 3, Article 4) (see Example 4-6).

By distinguishing the fourth from the fifth and octave, Rameau takes a route different from most earlier theorists. Zarlino, and, indeed, theorists going back to Pythagoras, knew that string-ratio 2:1 represents the octave, 3:2 the perfect fifth, and 4:3 the perfect fourth. But for these theorists,

---

4. Cohen 1971 traces this meaning of the term *supposition* from the late sixteenth through the mid-eighteenth century.

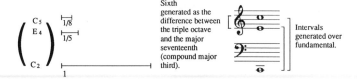

*Example 4-7.*

the fifth and the fourth are equally original intervals. For Rameau, the fourth is not an original interval, but, as Descartes had described it, only "the shadow of the fifth" (Descartes 1618; Robert 1961, p. 24) because it merely filled in the difference between the fifth and the octave but did not itself arise over the fundamental. Thus, Rameau shows how the octave, the fifth, and the fourth in Example 4-6 all have the same fundamental sound. With the fundamental fifth and its derived fourth Rameau can now explain why a 6/4 chord with a fourth over the bass is a derivative of a perfect chord with a fifth over the bass.

To show that 6/3 chords are inversions of 5/3 chords, Rameau has to demonstrate that sixths are similarly "shadows" of thirds. Rameau divides the string into five parts, yielding a compound major third (a seventeenth). The minor sixth is its complement. Thus the major third is the fundamental interval and the minor sixth the derived interval (Book 1, Chapter 3, Article 5). This enables him to explain that a 6/3 perfect chord with a minor sixth over the bass is a derivative of a 5/3 chord with a major third over the bass (see Example 4-7).

So far, so good. Rameau has shown how the perfect fifth and the major third appear over the fundamental, and how the perfect fourth and the minor sixth are merely complements of these two fundamental intervals. To complete his theory of triadic inversions, Rameau need only demonstrate the same relationship between the minor third and the major sixth. But this last step cannot be accomplished in this manner. Put simply, the minor third does not occur over the fundamental in any integral division of the whole string. Rameau desperately wants it to occur there: "Since all intervals are generated by the octave and begin and end there, so *should* [!] the minor third. It should not be found indirectly, between the major third and the fifth, but related directly to the fundamental sound or its octave" (Book 1, Chapter 3, Article 5). If Rameau as speculative theorist cannot demonstrate that the minor third occurs over the fundamental, he cannot demonstrate that minor triads are basic chords akin to major triads, which he as a practical musician knows to be true. Through the contorted and unconvincing reasoning that follows, Rameau insists that thirds cannot arise simultaneously when a fifth is divided; they must arise separately, and therefore can arise in either order. (Lewin 1978 comments on this passage.) It need hardly be pointed out that this explanation is inadequate.

The derivation of the minor third was to bedevil Rameau throughout his life. With his belief that music was Natural and with his Cartesian belief in the explanatory power of numbers, Rameau never abandoned the search for an origin of the minor third. He was not alone in this search—theorists from antiquity to the present have sought the sources of their musical system in divisions of a string or, later, in harmonic resonance which is numerically the same as divisions of a string. Ultimately, the reason a solution has never been found is the fallacious basis of the search: an ethnocentric belief that music, a cultural phenomenon, is a Natural phenomenon. As Pascal put it, "What are our natural principles if not our acccustomed principles? . . . a different custom will yield other natural principles" (Pascal c.1658, p. 514). Divisions of a string certainly measure intervals. But several arbitrary assumptions (or, to be kinder, several axioms) are needed if intervals and roots are to arise in an appropriate manner.

First, one must assume octave equivalence; that is, that all the string divisions that are powers of 2 (halves, fourths, eighths, sixteenths, etc.) are merely duplications of the fundamental, but that string divisions of all other powers (of 3, for instance) are different pitches. Without octave equivalence, for instance, the twelfth and its compounds, which do arise from string divisions, could not be the source of the perfect fifth. For Rameau the musician, octave equivalence seemed obvious. But in his dispute with the eminent mathematician Leonhard Euler in the 1750s, he could not disprove Euler's assertion that octave duplications were not equivalent to the fundamental (Rameau 1752; discussed in Shirlaw 1917, pp. 274–275).

Second, one must assume that the simple numerical ratios of string divisions do in fact represent musical intervals which are rendered in practice in various systems of temperament (or that are frequently rendered "out-of-tune"). Rameau argues in later works that this problem is not serious because the small alterations arising from temperament are nearly imperceptible. But this answer denies the very premise of the investigation. The whole point of deriving intervals from small numbers is to demonstrate that the consonances can be represented by small-number ratios. If small-number ratios are perceptually equivalent to the irrational-number ratios that arise from temperament, then there is no rationale for using small-number ratios in the first place. For this argument insists that $3/2$, the ratio of the pure perfect fifth, is equivalent to the seventh power of the twelfth root of 2, the ratio of the perfect fifth in equal temperament (which Rameau supports beginning in 1737).

Third, one must exclude division of the string into sevenths. Division

minor 3 and 6     major 3 and 6     minor thirds and sixths     major thirds and sixths

*Example 4-8.*

into eighths is necessary if the minor sixth (8:5) is to be included among the consonances. But sevenths of the string create intervals that do not agree with Western diatonic music. Zarlino had already encountered this problem when he exalted the *senario* (the numbers 1–6), but allowed 8 in order to include the minor sixth. Put briefly, one can find a rationale for what one wants in the divisions of a string, but only by manipulating the numbers until the desired results appear.

Despite his lifelong preoccupation with deriving intervals and chords systematically from divisions of a string, or, later, from harmonic resonance which is numerically equivalent to divisions of the string, Rameau was never able to come up with a derivation of the minor third that was comparable to that of the major third. Nor was he able to come up with a derivation of the fourth degree of the scale, which likewise does not appear in harmonic resonance, that was comparable to the derivation of the fifth degree of the scale. And no later theorist has solved these problems using Rameau's or similar procedures. His attempts to do so are part of the history of ideas of the eighteenth century, with its assumptions that Nature is the source of music and that the proper numerical ratios constitute a valid explanation. This aspect of Rameau's speculative theory is covered in exhaustive detail in Shirlaw 1917. Other than commenting on his use of such reasoning, the present study will not explore further the means Rameau used to give a speculative foundation to his musical ideas or the adequacy of those means. It will concentrate instead on the application of his ideas to musical situations.

Whatever the systematic shortcomings of Rameau's derivation of the minor third, what is important to musical practice is that Rameau sorted out the consonances into fundamental ones (the perfect fifth and both sorts of thirds) and their derived forms. This was a change in perspective from Zarlino, who had derived sixths from the addition of a third to the perfect fourth. According to this traditional method, minor thirds are related to minor sixths and major thirds to major sixths: a fourth plus a minor third equals a minor sixth; a fourth plus a major third equals a major sixth. This shows how consonant 6/3 chords have a unified sound (because the thirds and sixths are of like quality), and how the 5/3–6/3 alternation of fifth and sixth gives rise to closely related chords (see Example 4-8). But as already noted in Chapter 1, this approach precludes

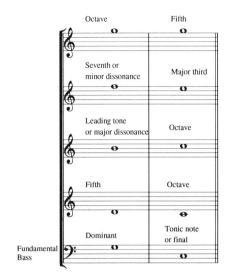

*Example 4-9.* Rameau 1722, Book 2, Chapter 5

a theory of chord inversions. Lippius derives sixths as inversions of thirds in his study of harmonic intervals, allowing him to present a theory of triadic inversion. But his study of melodic intervals retains a traditional derivation of sixths. Rameau was the first theorist to use a fully harmonic perspective on intervallic generation for all purposes.

## THE PERFECT CHORD AND ITS FUNDAMENTAL BASS

Rameau distinguishes two different basses for a perfect chord: the actual sounding bass or the *basso continuo,* and the *fundamental bass* or *fundamental note (basse-fondamentale, son-fondamental)*—what we call the root. Rameau's first example of a fundamental bass (shown in Example 4-9) illustrates not an isolated chord, but the perfect cadence, an important chord progression:[5] "If the fundamental bass is removed [from the bottom voice] and one of the other parts is put in its place, all the resulting chords will be inversions [*renversements*] of the original chords. The harmony will remain good, for even when the fundamental bass is removed, it is always implied" (Book 2, Chapter 5).

Here and elsewhere, Rameau combines two conceptually separate aspects of fundamental bass (discussed in Keiler 1981): it can be an actual voice in the texture, and it is a structural foundation explaining the other parts. As a voice in the texture, it can appear in any register; as an explanation for the other parts, it is implicitly the underlying source. As

5. Rameau uses multiple staffs to show the voice leading of each part. To facilitate legibility, these examples also appear here in a two-staff version in brackets.

a sounding part, it obeys voice-leading rules; as an explanation of the other parts, it is not part of the voice leading. Rameau's use of musical notation for these two separate aspects is akin to Schenker's use of single noteheads in a graph to denote both pitches in a score and their role in the underlying structure.

Nowadays we use Roman numerals to identify the chords, thereby separating notationally the progression of chord roots from any actual voice in the texture. Placing numbers next to a score to label the chord roots was published as early as 1766, but the practice was not widely adopted until well into the nineteenth century.

It is easy to view Roman numerals as a substitute notation for Rameau's fundamental bass notated on a separate staff. But translating Rameauian fundamental bass into Roman numerals actually marks a significant shift in perspective. A Roman numeral immediately identifies the scale-step of a chord root, but requires some calculation to identify the interval between two consecutive chord roots. That is, we must already know what the key is before we can assign Roman numerals to a chord in a given passage. But it takes some calculation in a mod-7 system to realize that the progression iii-vi may be expressed as a descending fifth just like V-I. In short, when chord roots are labelled by numbers, one begins by knowing the key and then can calculate the interval of root progression.

It is quite the reverse when the fundamental bass is notated as Rameau did. The intervallic relations among chord roots are easy to see. But to figure out the scale-step one must first decide on the key, and then figure out the interval between the chord root and the tonic of that key. As discussed below, when Rameau dealt with chord progressions, he was primarily concerned with the intervallic relationship among chord roots. Only after studying interval successions in the fundamental bass and the types of chords occurring over these intervallic successions would he decide on the key. For this reason (and others to be discussed later), many of the issues Rameau dealt with cannot easily be translated into Roman numeral notation.

## THE SEVENTH CHORD AND DISSONANCE

Rameau offers two possible methods to generate the perfect chord: he divides a fifth into major and minor thirds (his "official" generation discussed above), and he stacks two thirds to add up to a perfect fifth. He applies only the second of these methods to generate the seventh chord, adding a third above a perfect chord. Such stacking of thirds is a most problematic generation in that it omits all the care that Rameau exercised in finding the root intervals over the fundamental when he generated the perfect chord.

Whatever the problems with his speculative generation of seventh chords, Rameau's extension of the process of inversion to seventh chords solved a number of major problems concerning dissonance treatment. By treating 6/5/3, 6/4/3, and 6/4/2 chords as inversions of the seventh chord, Rameau greatly simplified explanations of how to identify and resolve several dissonances. For him the chord seventh is always a seventh against the fundamental, no matter what the inversion. In a 6/5 chord, for instance, the fifth over the bass is only an apparent consonance; its role in the chord is dissonant seventh against the fundamental. In the 4/3 chord, the third is not a consonance but the dissonant chord seventh; the fourth is not a dissonance needing resolution, but the fundamental note of the chord—the "irregular fourth" of thoroughbass theory is no longer irregular.

The seventh chord always contains at least one dissonance, the chord seventh which resolves by descending. When a seventh chord has a major third (when it is what we call a "dominant-seventh chord"), there is a second dissonance: the diminished fifth between the third and seventh of the chord. Because both the chord seventh and the leading tone create dissonances against other members of the chord, and because they both must resolve in restricted ways, Rameau calls both of them dissonances. The chord seventh is the *minor dissonance* because it arises from a *minor* third above the perfect chord and it resolves downwards. The leading tone *(notte sensible)* is the *major dissonance* because it is a *major* third and resolves upwards.

With this terminology, Rameau turns triumphantly to Zarlino's problematic recommendation that major intervals should ascend and minor intervals should descend (Part 2, Chapter 5). Rameau interprets Zarlino's statement to refer to the major and minor dissonances, no matter the actual interval over the bass. Thus, even when the minor dissonance appears as a major second (in a 6/4/2 chord) or as a diminished fifth (in some 6/5 chords), it remains a minor seventh that descends to resolve. As noted in Chapter 1 of this study, Zarlino's remark had been repeated by many seventeenth-century theorists, who invariably explained that the rule was unreliable. By finding an interpretation in which it always applied, Rameau had the best of two worlds: in an almost medieval way he had taken a puzzling dictum of a revered authority and unraveled its true meaning; and at the same time he was a true man of the Enlightenment, using reason to cut through a complex of dissonance rules and enunciate a single principle.

TONICS AND DOMINANTS

Because the two chord-types (perfect chords and seventh chords) occur primarily on specific scale degrees, Rameau frequently refers to them by scale-step location rather than by chord quality. Perfect chords are *tonic* chords because they occur on the tonic. And seventh chords are *dominant* chords. A *dominant* (a seventh chord) with a major third and a minor seventh (what we call a dominant-seventh chord) is a *dominant-tonic* chord (dominant of the tonic). All other seventh chords are *simple dominants*. There is no equivalent for this terminology in modern harmonic theory, and it makes many of Rameau's ideas difficult to translate into Roman-numeral equivalents. In quoted passages and other discussions in this and the next chapter, whenever there might be a question of Rameau's terminology, a modern equivalent is placed in parentheses (as was done in this paragraph).

CHORDS BY SUBPOSITION

By introducing the seventh chord as a fundamental harmony and extending to it the principle of chord inversion, Rameau explains the resolution of thoroughbass figurings 7/5/3, 6/5/3, 6/4/3, and 6/4/2 in terms of a single chord-type. Numerous other dissonant thoroughbass figurings still awaited an explanation. Rameau probably had observed similarities between the resolutions of these dissonances and the two types of dissonances in a seventh chord. While most suspensions resolve downward, resembling a minor dissonance or chord seventh, other suspensions resolve upward, resembling a major dissonance or leading tone. If Rameau could explain all descending suspensions as minor dissonances (chord sevenths) and all ascending suspensions as major dissonances (leading tones), the seventh chord would become the source of all conchordal dissonances.

To turn suspensions into chord sevenths or leading tones, Rameau placed a new bass a third or a fifth below the fundamental bass of a seventh chord, generating ninth chords and eleventh chords. A third below a seventh chord created a ninth chord; a fifth below a seventh chord created an eleventh chord. Example 4-10 includes four such chords on the downbeats of measures 2–5. The next-to-lowest staff is the sounding bass. The lowest staff contains the fundamental bass (the chord roots).

The crucial suspensions resolve as if they were chord sevenths or leading tones in a seventh chord. In measure 2, the top-voice A-G is a 9–8 suspension over the bass G. Rameau explains that the soprano A resolves as a seventh over B♭, with the bass G below that B♭. In measures 3 and 4 both the top-voice G and the inner-voice C♯ resolve normally as chord seventh and leading tone of an $A^7$ chord despite the fact that the bass in measure 3 is a third below A and the bass in measure 4 is a fifth below A. In the penultimate measure, the inner-voice D resolves as if it were a chord seventh against E. Rameau achieves precisely what he set out to do. Several different figurings (9/♭, 5♯, 7♯, 4-♯) are all shown to be seventh chords resolving just as they should. The same process can be extended to other figurings.

Rameau referred to this process by the French term *supposition*. This

*Example 4-10.* Rameau 1722, Book 2, Chapter 10

was a new meaning of the term. It is a direct derivation from the Latin origin of the word: the prefix *sub-* (meaning *below*) and *positio* (participle of the verb *ponere, to place*), with double *p* replacing *bp*. In the sense that Rameau uses the term, it quite literally means "to place below," a meaning obsolete in the modern English word *supposition*. Hence, Rameau's meaning is rendered here by *subposition*.[6]

In a chord by subposition, the seventh chord explains the dissonance while the subposed bass remains separate. The portion of a subposed chord that is a seventh chord (the upper four notes of a ninth or eleventh

6. Some writers in English retain *supposition* (Shirlaw 1917), some use *sub-position* (Ferris 1959, Wason 1985), and others use *subposition* (Baker 1988, which presents on p. 27 n. 45 reasoning similar to that given here).

chord) can be inverted or rearranged in any manner, just like any seventh chord. This rearrangement is possible because no matter where the dissonances occur, they will resolve in the same manner. By contrast, the subposed bass cannot participate in any such rearrangements because, quite simply, it is not a part of the seventh chord. If it were to participate in inversions, the resulting chord could end up looking like a scalar collection rather than a harmony; for instance, a C-eleventh chord (C/G-B-D-F) could be voiced as B-C-D-F-G. These are the reasons for Rameau's seemingly arbitrary assertion that since subposed chords exceed the span of an octave (in his terminology, they are *supernumerary*), they cannot be inverted.

Rameau's delight over his discovery that all descending dissonances could be explained as chord sevenths and that all ascending dissonances could be explained as leading tones is understandable. For by extending seventh chords to chords by subposition, Rameau was now able to explain the voice leading of nearly every thoroughbass figuring in terms of a perfect chord or a seventh chord. The few exceptions are the diminished seventh chord (discussed below) and occasional other chords. It is easy nowadays to pass over this achievement and see only the problematic areas and troubling influences of subposed chords. For two centuries now, we have been sorting out the harmonies of tonal compositions into chords and nonharmonic tones. But no one had done that before Rameau.

In his enthusiasm, Rameau neglected to state in a prominent position in the *Traité* that subposition is essentially a way to explain suspensions. He does include that information, but only after repeated explanations of what notes to include in ninth and eleventh chords and why the subposed bass does not participate in inversions (Book 1, Chapters 6–7; Book 2, Chapters 10–11; Book 3, Chapters 29–32). Not until the very end of Book 3, Chapter 31, does Rameau remark that eleventh chords yield "pleasant suspensions," and that "Chords by subposition serve only to suspend [that is, delay] sounds which should be heard naturally." Similar remarks appear in Book 3, Chapter 32, where Rameau explains that, as shown in Example 4-11, "the sounds labeled *A* suspend [that is, delay] the sounds labeled *B,* and the lines designate the natural progression of the sounds labeled *A* [that is, the lines show how the notes labeled *A* follow their 'natural' paths and resolve as members of a seventh chord]."[7]

Rameau's later works more explicitly relate subposition and suspensions. Chapter 16 of his *Generation* (1737), on the "Origin of Subposition

7. "*Les Sons A, suspendent les Sons B . . .*" Rameau uses the verb *suspendre* in a meaning that its cognate lacks in English. When we say A suspends B we mean that A holds onto B longer than B would otherwise last. Rameau means exactly the opposite: that A lasts longer (is suspended) and delays B. The meaning Rameau imparts to the verb *suspendre* was used by other French theorists of the period (Campion 1716, p. 11).

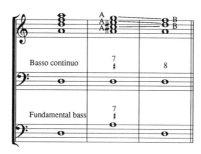

*Example* 4-11. Rameau 1722, Book 3, Chapter 32

and Suspension," begins by noting that suspension "is but a consequence" of subposition. In that chapter and elsewhere, his text explains notes as suspensions while his fundamental bass illustrates chords by subposition (Rameau 1737, Chapter 18, Article 1, Part 1; Hayes 1974b, p. 119). *Le Guide du Compositeur,* a treatise by Rameau pupil Pietro Gianotti (?–1765) that is closely based on Rameau's own unpublished manuscript of c.1740 (Christensen 1990a), is even more specific about the role of subposition: "the suspension has no fundamental bass, and if one gives it one, it is most frequently done only to see that the suspension takes its origin from subposition. But since that knowledge serves no purpose in practice, it is better, upon recognizing the suspended note, to omit it from consideration and to give to it the fundamental bass that the suspended consonance [the delayed consonance] should have" (p. 271). Rameau's last practical work, the *Code* of 1761, likewise notes that "the fundamental is only given to satisfy those who are curious about the source of the harmony" (Rameau [1761], p. 60).

Some historians have argued that in the *Traité,* Rameau considered suspensions as isolated verticalities and modified this position to recognize the melodic role of suspensions only in later works (Ferris 1959, pp. 232 and 238–239; Cohen 1980, p. 569). But the examples and citations just introduced make it clear that he always recognized that subposition was a way of providing a speculative theoretical explanation for the linear motion of suspensions (Christensen 1987a, pp. 28–32).

Possibly because Rameau did not articulate more clearly the purpose of subposed chords, many later theorists included absurd collections of stacked thirds as isolated verticalities, believing they were following Rameau in doing so. By presenting such isolated verticalities, however, these theorists went against Rameau's whole purpose in developing his theory of subposition—to place suspension patterns in a linear context and show how the suspensions had to resolve.

All this is not to say that Rameau's theory of subposition is without its problems. First, if the aim of the fundamental bass is to represent root

*Example* 4-12. Delair 1690, fol. D<sup>v</sup>

progressions, how is it that measures 3 and 4 of Example 4-10, in which an entire chord must resolve, are akin to measure 5, in which just one note has to resolve? All three measures are fifth-progressions in Rameau's fundamental bass.

A second problem is more critical. Are the subposed chord and the chord of resolution two separate harmonies, or do they represent a single harmony? If the latter is the case, does the bass of the subposed chord anticipate the following harmony, or does it represent the arrival on the second harmony with the upper voices delayed? In measure 3 of Example 4-10, for instance, does the bass F represent an F harmony, or is F part of the following D harmony? If the latter is the case, does F anticipate the D harmony, or does F announce the arrival of the D harmony, stated with suspensions that resolve into the D harmony?

Although Rameau does not address these questions, evidence points to contradictory answers. By notating the subposed chord and the chord of resolution with two separate fundamental basses, he implies they are two separate harmonies. If this is so, then Rameau was thinking in terms of thoroughbass, in which a suspension chord and its resolution had separate figurings. For instance, in an example of suspended notes, Delair makes no distinction between what modern theory calls a seventh chord (at A), which requires a change of harmony to resolve, and what modern theory treats as a single note resolving into a chord already present (at B)—in each case, there is a "chord of the second" followed by another chord on another bass pitch (see Example 4-12). Fuxian species counterpoint offers quite a different perspective, explaining suspensions as delays of a note within a single harmony. But because of the restraints of the contrapuntal species, seventh chords hardly ever arise, so Fux does not have to deal with them.

Other passages in the *Traité* suggest that Rameau thought of the subposed chord and the chord of resolution as a single harmony. When he explains that subposed chords "serve only to suspend sounds which should be heard naturally," he implies that the subposed bass represents the arrival on a harmony, and that the upper parts delay their motion into the remaining notes of that harmony. If that is the case, then Rameau agrees

*Example 4-13.* Rameau 1722, Book 3, Chapter 30, mm. 9–10

with Fux's notion of suspensions and the modern view of suspensions. In this stance, he differs with C. P. E. Bach, who regards the voices simultaneous with a suspension as *anticipations* of the following harmony (Bach 1762, Chapter 1; Mitchell 1949, p. 193).

If Rameau intends the main harmonic arrival to occur on the downbeat, then in effect the subposed bass and the fundamental bass have switched roles. The fundamental bass, whose purpose it is to explain the underlying harmony, only shows an elaborating harmony. And the subposed bass, which Rameau explains as an note added to the chord, shows the essential harmony.

The point of arrival of the essential harmony is further complicated because Rameau generally forbids harmonic syncopation in a fundamental bass (a harmony beginning on a relatively weak metric position and continuing through the next strong beat; Book 3, Chapter 40).[8] If a subposed chord would create syncopated harmonic rhythm, Rameau simply figures a suspension over the fundamental bass in the manner of a thoroughbass (see Example 4-13). In the last measure, Rameau analyzes the suspension as 4–3 over a single chord. To have explained it as a subposed bass would have given rise to harmonic syncopation in the fundamental bass.

The chord in the last measure is the same harmony labeled as a subposed chord in measure 5 of Example 4-10. Ironically, it is in Example 4-13 that explanation as a chord by subposition would make more sense, for there the preceding harmony actually establishes the D as a dissonant seventh against E, which dissonance then remains until it resolves on the second half of the following measure. These two explanations of the same progression raise the question of where the dominant arrives: on the second

8. Rameau only rarely allows harmonic syncopation in a fundamental bass (Rameau 1722, Book 2, Chapter 17, Article 6; Rameau [1761], p. 5 of examples, "2nd N," mm. 1–2).

half of the measure (as in m. 5 of Example 4-10) or on the downbeat (as in m. 2 of Example 4-13)? Rameau does not address the issue.

Despite their problems, these two interpretations demonstrate Rameau's desire to have his examples make sense to him as a musician. He opts for using the thoroughbass notation that he believes is a less satisfactory theoretical explanation (Example 4-13) to avoid a harmonic syncopation that is more problematic. (Two other such analyses of 4–3 suspensions occur in the last example of Book 3, Chapter 38, mm. 14 and 25.) As Rameau applies it, subposition requires the theorist to study the context of a suspension to decide how to render it in the fundamental bass. Chord analysis is not a mechanical task of lining up the vertical notes and stacking them in thirds to find the root, as it became for some later musicians.

In sum, Rameau's theory of subposition has many problematic aspects that Rameau neither answers nor, in some cases, even addresses. But for him it was an attempt at a single explanation for resolution of all suspended notes, and it did allow him to explain almost all thoroughbass chords as perfect chords, seventh chords, or their derivatives.

Within a generation, harmonic theorists proposed what has remained the modern approach to suspensions by distinguishing two fundamentally different types of suspended notes: chord sevenths that require a change of root to resolve and suspensions that can resolve into a chord already present. First suggested by the German theorist Georg Andreas Sorge (1703–1778) around the middle of the century, the distinction was formalized by Kirnberger in the 1770s with the labels *essential* and *incidental* dissonances. This distinction would have been inconceivable without Rameau's notions of seventh chords and of chord roots.

## FOURTHS VS. ELEVENTHS

Just as thoroughbass theory had differentiated the second and ninth by their resolutions, Rameau believed that fourths should be differentiated from elevenths (Book 1, Chapter 6; Book 2, Chapter 11; Book 3, Chapter 15). Rameau insists that the fourth is the inversion of a fifth and is a consonant interval; the eleventh, however, is always a dissonance, a seventh over the fundamental bass in a subposed eleventh chord. However, when he notates 4–3 suspensions, he uses the standard numbering and not 11–10.

## THE DIMINISHED SEVENTH CHORD

Rameau explains that the diminished seventh chord arises *by borrowing (par emprunt)* when the sixth scale degree in minor replaces the root of a dominant seventh chord (F-G♯-B-D instead of E-G♯-B-D; Book 1, Chapter 8, Article 7; Book 2, Chapter 12; Book 3, Chapter 33). He calls it the chord of the augmented second, not a type of "diminished chord," reflecting the fact that E, not G♯, is the fundamental bass. By deriving the diminished seventh from the dominant seventh, Rameau formalized observations other theorists had made about the interchangeability of these chords in many cases (Campion 1716, p. 11; cited here in Ex. 3-19, note 12).

In later works, Rameau is ambivalent about the fundamental bass of the diminished seventh chord, but he always recognizes it as a harmony parallel in function to the dominant seventh. In his last discussion, he explains that in "the chord of minor thirds" (*l'accord de petites tierces*) the leading tone is an "implied [*censée*] fundamental . . . and the rules given regarding that note as well as its chord [the "leading tone chord" or *l'accord sensible,* synonymous with the "dominant-tonic"] do not vary in the slightest; it is always the leading-tone chord, that which carries the dominant-tonic, in which its [the dominant's] upper semitone is substituted" (Rameau [1761], p. 65).

## Chord Successions

Having established that two fundamental chord-types, the perfect chord and the seventh chord, were the basis of all harmonies, Rameau was now able for the very first time to consider the nature of harmonic succession. The issues he dealt with go to the heart of musical structure and have remained the focus of much music theory since his time. What is the nature of chord successions, both local and long-range? What different kinds of harmonic connections are there? Are all chords in a progression of equal harmonic weight? How do we know when a progression comes to an end? And how does the vertical dimension (the structure of simultaneities) in music relate to the horizontal (the progression of simultaneities)?

CHORD-TO-CHORD SUCCESSIONS
For Rameau, the nature of harmonic successions depends on the intervals in the fundamental bass. Rameau posits a close relationship between the structure of harmonies and their connection from one to another, arguing that the very intervals contained in chords connect one chord to another (Book 2, Chapter 1; discussed in Lewin 1978). Thus the fundamental bass should move by perfect fifths and thirds, the two intervals in the perfect chord. In his later works, Rameau attempted to demonstrate that all fundamental-bass successions were by fifths or thirds. But in the *Traité,* he notes that dissonances and license (a concept he uses when his theory becomes too restrictive) allow the fundamental bass to move by second. As a result, the fundamental bass can move by any interval.

*Example 4-14.* Rameau 1722, Book 2, Chapter 7

CADENCES

Not all these successions are of equal structural import. Most important are *cadences* (Book 2, Chapters 5–9), a term Rameau uses to denote a type of harmonic progression, not just the concluding motion of a phrase. Rameau is not as explicit about this definition as is his pupil Jean Laurent de Béthizy (1709–1781): "cadence in general signifies the passage from one note to another note which is over a different fundamental than that to which the first note belongs" (Béthizy 1754, p. 173).

There are two basic types of cadences, each with its own characteristic dissonance. The *perfect cadence* is a motion down by fifth (from dominant to tonic) in which the first harmony is a seventh chord whose urge to resolve propels the progression. The *irregular cadence* is a motion up by fifth (from tonic to dominant, or from the fourth scale step to the tonic).[9] The first harmony in an irregular cadence contains a special dissonance— an added sixth—whose urge to resolve propels the progression (see Example 4-14). This added-sixth chord is equivalent in pitch to a D-minor seventh chord. But Rameau explains that the fundamental bass of this chord is F. The D is a dissonance added to the perfect chord, a type of major dissonance that must rise to resolve.

Rameau uses his added-sixth chord to explain a progression from the 1699 composition treatise of Charles Masson (?-?). Masson used the example (4-15) to illustrate the use of the tritone approaching a cadence. Rameau omits the bracketed portion of Masson's example. Since Rameau views the 6/4 chord as a tonic chord, he cannot regard the alto G as a

9. In later works, Rameau also uses the term *imperfect cadence* to refer to progressions up a fifth (Rameau 1737, Chapter 6, Article 7). The modern term *plagal cadence* appeared around the turn of the nineteenth century (Catel 1802, p. 34).

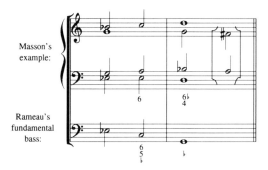

Example 4-15. Masson 1699, p. 99; Rameau 1722, Book 2, Chapter 7.
Rameau omits the bracketed portion of Masson's example.

chord seventh because it does not resolve as a seventh. If the G is not a chord seventh, the A must be the added note, a sixth above the fundamental bass. On his terms, Rameau is consistent. But in terms of the entire progression, his interpretation is clearly problematic. In his later works, beginning with the manuscript treatise *L'art de la basse fondamentale* (c. 1740), Rameau changed his mind, and henceforth viewed the cadential 6/4 as a pair of suspensions over the dominant (Rameau [1761], p. 54).

Though the example of an added sixth that he uses comes from Masson 1699, Rameau may have gotten the idea for this chord from Delair 1690, which he deemed the most praiseworthy thoroughbass method (Rameau CTW 1, p. 19; Rameau 1732, p. 5; Hayes 1974a, p. 7). Delair recommends that when perfect chords descend by a fifth the player should add a seventh after the first chord, and when perfect chords rise by a fifth, the player should add a sixth after the first chord (fol. H$^r$) (see Example 4-16). Delair offered this as a suggestion. But Rameau developed these added dissonances into a general principle of harmonic progression.

A FUNCTIONAL ROLE FOR DISSONANCES AND A THEORY OF HARMONIC CONTINUITY

By using the characteristic dissonances of each cadence as part of the explanation for the harmonic drive of the progression, Rameau takes an

Example 4-16. Delair 1690, fol. H$^r$

old idea and gives it a wider application. The notion of moving from imperfection to perfection had long figured in explanations of cadences (dissonances and imperfect consonances to a perfect consonance). Indeed, Tinctoris and others called cadences *perfections*. Rameau extended this notion to all chord progressions within a phrase. If two notes of the fundamental bass both "bore a perfect chord, the mind, not desiring anything more after such a chord, would be uncertain upon which of these two sounds to rest. Dissonance seems needed here in order that its harshness should make the listener desire the rest which follows" (Book 2, Chapter 2). "Far from dissonance being an embarrassment in composition, it facilitates its course" (Book 3, Chapter 7; extended discussion in Rameau 1726, Chapter 11). For Rameau, a chord with a consonance is a tonic; only dissonances can disturb its implication of a point of repose. In later writings, Rameau expanded this functional role of dissonance into a comprehensive explanation for chordal connections and the placement of chords within a key. Even if the dissonances were not actually present, Rameau argued that they were implied. Since Rameau developed these ideas much more fully in later works, they are discussed in Chapter 5.

With perfect and irregular cadences and their characteristic dissonances as models for directed harmonic motion leading to a conclusion, Rameau asks why it is that harmonic motion does not continually halt every time the fundamental bass falls or rises by a fifth. To answer this question, he turns to Zarlino's notion of cadential evasion as a means of extending the span of musical motion. This tenet recurs in numerous seventeenth and early eighteenth-century writings (Werckmeister 1702, pp. 50–51; Brossard 1703, article *motivo*). Rameau reworks the idea from his harmonic perspective.

Complete cadences can be evaded by inverting one or both chords in a progression (Book 2, Chapter 8), by adding a dissonance to a consonant chord of arrival, thereby requiring the new dissonance to resolve, or by making the third of a dominant-tonic chord (a dominant-seventh chord) minor so that the chord lacks the power of making the next chord into a tonic (Book 2, Chapter 9). Or a perfect cadence can be avoided entirely by having the dominant resolve up a step to form a *broken cadence (cadence rompuë)*, what we call a deceptive cadence (Book 2, Chapter 6).

Taken together, Rameau's notion of characteristic dissonances on all chords that are not tonic chords and his notion of harmonic successions as a series of continually evaded cadences is the first attempt to explain the sense of continuing motion created by harmonic successions. But it is inadequate for three reasons. First, it assumes a one-to-one relation between consonance and tonal stability. In effect, Rameau argues that a consonant chord is a tonic and therefore if we know it is not a conclusive tonic, it must be because we hear a dissonance (a chord seventh or added

*Example* 4-17. Rameau 1722, Book 2, Chapter 17, Article 2

sixth), whether actual or implied. Surely there are factors other than consonance that make a chord a convincing tonic.

Second, Rameau's explanation is a point-to-point approach. It assumes that we hear a continuous phrase as a series of short motions that are continually prevented from coming to a conclusion by an added dissonance or an irregular voice leading.

Third, Rameau's cadence-oriented harmonic progressions are incapable of dealing with progressions where the root movement does not at all resemble a cadence. In Example 4-17 the contorted fundamental bass under a series of stepwise sixth chords speaks for itself. Basically, since this progression is not modeled on root progressions by fifth, Rameau cannot explain its origin. He does not condemn the progression; he just cannot fit it into his cadence-oriented notion of harmony. When he referred to this progression in 1737, he virtually admitted that he could not explain it: "the sole exception to our general rules [of harmonic succession] . . . is the ability to have several tonics [perfect chords] immediately following one another where there is no connection among them; this is only done in inversion" (Rameau 1737, p. 189). It seems never to have occurred to him that harmonies could relate to one another in meaningful ways other than in terms of cadential progressions or their imitation.

LARGE-SCALE HARMONIC PROGRESSIONS WITHIN A KEY

As in contemporary counterpoint or thoroughbass manuals, most discussions in the *Traité* concern connections between consecutive harmonies or even within a single harmony (as with suspensions explained by subposed chords). Only occasionally does Rameau study a larger context, as when he recasts into his own terms a common rule for unfigured basses. Instead of stating that the bass should carry a 6/3 chord when moving by third to or from a perfect chord, Rameau extends the rule to refer to longer-range motions involving these notes, not only to local skips by a third: "All notes found a third above or below the tonic or the dominant [these being

*Example 4-18.* Rameau 1722, Book 3, Chapter 11. The symbols * and +
replace Rameau's clumsy letter-identifications.

*Example 4-19.* Rameau 1722, Book 3, Chapter 41, mm. 1–4

the only scale steps that Rameau believes merit perfect chords] should
bear sixth chords, when the progression of the bass *leads to* one of these
two notes" (Book 3, Chapter 11; emphasis added) (see Example 4-18).[10]
Rameau explains that the asterisked notes require a triad and are goals,
so that those chords with + use sixth chords. By implication, the remaining
harmonies "lead to" these notes.

Another discussion involving larger contexts occurs in Book 3, Chapter
41, "How to Compose a Basso Continuo below a Treble." His example,
one of the few resembling an actual composition, opens with the phrase
shown in Example 4-19.

"In the first and second measures of the fundamental bass, there are
two equal progressions [tonic to dominant]. I reserve the progression most
closely related to the cadence [that is, the progression in root position] for
the second measure, because this is where the cadence occurs normally
[that is, on a downbeat]; notice that the cadence is irregular here and
perfect in the fourth measure." This discussion touches on the roles of
various types of harmonic progressions within phrases: when to use root-

10. On the downbeat of measure 3, Rameau has E in the upper voice; this is emended
to agree with the figuring. Rameau does not mention the parallel fifths between measures
3 and 4.

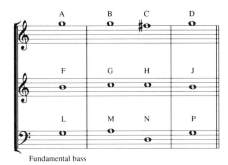

Fundamental bass

*Example 4-20.* Rameau 1726, p. 68

position chords versus inverted chords, and when to use irregular versus perfect cadences.

But Rameau never addresses this issue comprehensively as some theorists later in the century were to do (especially Koch). His primary interest is in the local function of harmonies and the way those local movements add up to a larger phrase. Consider his explanation of the progression in Example 4-20, from the *Nouveau système:*

> Suppose that the *key of G* is announced at *L* [because a perfect chord appears there] and that one wished to continue [in that key]; the *A* (note *M*), as a fundamental, should support the *seventh* in its harmony, and then the same *dissonance* should exist in all the chords until that of the *principal sound* [or tonic]. The *connection* begins from *A* to *B* where the *seventh B* is *prepared* by *A;* then this *seventh* is *resolved* at *C* so that the *connection* is evident in the three successive chords which include *A, B,* and *C;* and *C* as the *leading tone* creates the desire for *D.* While on the one hand the *connection* ends at *C,* there begins another at *G* which *prepares* the *seventh H,* which *seventh* then *resolves* at *J.*
>
> Accordingly, the keys of *fundamental sounds M* and *N* can never seem permanent *keys,* and the key of *L* or *P* is always present. (p. 69, Rameau's emphases)

Despite his emphasis on chord-to-chord successions here, Rameau does deal with how a key is expressed, how consonance and dissonance contribute to this, and how various voice-leading patterns interlock until the cadence of this "harmonic phrase of the octave" (as Clement 1758, p. 9, refers to this pattern). His discussion predicates the concepts of interval-roots and chord-roots for triads and seventh chords, the notion of a discrete number of chord-types, the functional placement of those harmonies on different scale degrees, the key-defining roles of consonance and dissonance, and the notion of harmonies fulfilling their roles between key-defining chords—all theoretical issues introduced by Rameau. No other school of early eighteenth-century theory was even aware of most of these issues.

## Practical Applications

As Rameau notes in his preface, Books 3 and 4 of the *Traité* (on composition and accompaniment) are more practical than Books 1 and 2. Both owe much to thoroughbass. Like that approach, Rameau starts instruction with four-voice writing, and is always more concerned with the structure of the bass and the chords built upon the bass than with the melodic construction of the upper voices. Unlike contemporaneous thoroughbass methods, Rameau's theory is based on perfect chords, seventh chords, and their interaction. Book 3 recapitulates much of the material in Books 1 and 2, but without the speculative (mathematical) bases and many of the arguments. It begins with the fundamental bass, triads, seventh chords, and chord progressions, applying these materials to compositional situations. In explaining which chords belong on which scale steps, for instance, Rameau does not simply list the figuring of those chords, as Heinichen or any of the other thoroughbass theorists dealing with unfigured basses do. Instead, he discusses the chords and their inversions (Book 3, Chapter 9), drawing parallels between different progressions that share fundamental-bass motions. He draws one such comparison between what we call ii$^6_5$-V and V$^6_5$-I, showing that in both cases the fundamental bass descends a fifth and the first chord moves to a triadic goal (see Example 4-21). This leads to his explanation of a secondary-dominant function:

> The composer is thus free to make the bass proceed by a tone or by a semitone, even if he should be in a key in which the semitone is not appropriate; for since the dominant can be treated as a tonic note [in that it can support a perfect chord], it may be approached using all those sounds which naturally precede a tonic note . . . It is by means of the difference between the progression of a tone and a semitone ascending to the note bearing the perfect chord that we differentiate a dominant and a tonic note . . . [But]

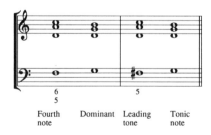

*Example 4-21.* Rameau 1722, Book 3, Chapter 11

even if this progression of a semitone is used, thus giving a dominant all the attributes of a tonic note, we may still continue after this dominant (which would then appear to be a tonic note) in the original key. (Book 3, Chapter 11)

Practical concerns notwithstanding, Rameau's discussion of composition in much of Book 3 remains largely theoretical. Not until Chapter 35 is there an example of "real" music, as opposed to a schematic representation of a harmonic progression in whole notes.

The situation is similar in Book 4 on accompaniment (thoroughbass). Rameau covers most of the materials found in the more complete thoroughbass manuals, but in a new ordering, and with new emphases. He begins with the perfect chord and seventh chord and their inversions and repeatedly relates all figurings to those basic harmonies and their progressions.

## Harmony vs. Melody

One of the major controversies surrounding Rameau's approach to music concerns his belief that harmony is the source of melody. Since Johann Mattheson (1681–1764) in the 1730s, Rameau's opponents have read this as a slogan denying the melodic element in music. Indeed, nearly every eighteenth-century writer had something to say on the primacy of melody vs. harmony. From the beginning, much of the controversy concerning Rameau's stance has been over statements taken out of context and outright misunderstandings. It may well be that Mattheson, for instance, misread Rameau, and thought that Rameau was promoting the *stile antico* and denigrating *galant* melody (Rameau CTW 3, xxxi–xxxiv). As composer and theorist Rameau was fully aware of the importance of melody. Just like Fux, Rameau urges that in a successful piece "each part should have a flowing and graceful melody" (Rameau 1722, Book 3, Chapter 43). Also like Fux in *Gradus* (and unlike authors of thoroughbass manuals), Rameau frequently writes his musical examples on multiple staffs, emphasizing the propriety of each voice. In practical discussions, Rameau repeatedly suggests that one might begin composing by writing a melody (Rameau 1722, Book 2, Chapter 28, and Book 3, Chapter 40; Rameau 1737, Chapter 18; Rameau [1761], Chapter 8). In recurring discussions of chord progressions, Rameau explains how the propriety of various types of harmonic motions depends upon their placement within a well-constructed phrase.

But for Rameau these are all practical considerations, none of which are capable of indicating to him that melody is supreme. From his theoretical perspective, musicians are wrong when they believe that harmony arises from melody since the melodies produced by each voice come together to form the harmony. It is first necessary, however, to find a course for each voice which will permit them all to harmonize well together. No matter what melodic progression is used for each individual part, the voices will join together to form a good harmony only with great difficulty, if indeed at all, unless the progressions are dictated by the rules of harmony. (Rameau 1722, Book 2, Chapter 19)

Read in this context, Rameau's reasoning is akin to Fux's explanation of how the melodies in a multi-part counterpoint exercise interact to connect the notes of one triad to another.

Rameau also came to believe that the source of melodic expression lay not in a melody, but in the underlying harmonic progressions. As proof, he illustrates seventy-nine different harmonic progressions supporting the ascending melodic fourth G-C, arguing that each imparts a different affect to the melodic interval (Rameau 1726, Chapter 8). In the *Traité*, Rameau had not been so entirely convinced that expression was so dependent upon harmony: "Melody has no less expressive force than harmony, but giving definite rules for its use is almost impossible, since good taste plays a greater part in this than anything else. We shall leave to privileged geniuses the pleasure of distinguishing themselves in this domain on which depends almost all the strength of sentiment" (Rameau 1722, Book 2, Chapter 20).

Some of the heated polemic over the primacy of harmony and melody died down by the end of the century. Heinrich Christoph Koch (1749–1816), the most important theorist of the last two decades of the century, probably summed it up the best by insisting that both melody and harmony were fully complementary. For him, the best melody was "melody conceived harmonically."

## Rameau's Achievements in the *Traité*

In his *Traité*, Rameau introduced a harmonic theory capable of explaining simultaneities and voice leading in contemporary music. Though he was an innovator and not a theorist contributing to a long tradition (like Fux and Heinichen, for instance), his works were taken under consideration throughout Europe even during the 1720s. In France, Père Louis Bertrand Castel (1688–1757), at that time Rameau's friend, wrote about the influence of the *Traité* in 1728: "Its success surpassed the hopes of the author . . . The public has ratified the new system . . . It is uncommon to see a somewhat superior system, when it is still new, overcome old prejudice and routine in such a short time" (Castel 1728, pp. 472–473). Castel took note of some resistance to his ideas—but certainly Rameau was not being ignored. In Germany, Christoph Gottlob Schröter (1699–1782) reports that he studied the *Traité* in Jena in 1724 with his teacher Johann Nicolaus

*Example* 4-22. Kellner 1732, p. 86, ex. 1

Bach (1669–1753), one of Johann Sebastian's cousins (Schröter 1772, p. x). Heinichen's *Der Generalbass* (1728) cites Rameau in several passages, and it is likely that he derived his ideas on triadic and seventh-chord inversions from the *Traité*. Considering that references to the *Traité* all occur in late additions to this book, it is significant that Heinichen cites Rameau's new work almost as much as any other work on thoroughbass. In Sweden, two dissertations at the University of Uppsala in 1727 and 1728 acknowledged the *Traité* (Westbladh 1727 and Löfgrön 1728, neither of which is musically sophisticated).

An indication of the extent to which Rameau's understanding of chords, inversions, and progressions were rapidly incorporated into common understanding is found in the 1732 thoroughbass manual of David Kellner (c. 1670–1748), probably the best-seller among such works for the remainder of the century with numerous reprints and translations. It is a relatively short work, explaining matters simply, borrowing freely though without acknowledgement from Heinichen's voluminous work of 1728. The subject of inversions comes up in the seventh and last chapter, which deals with dissonances in a traditional thoroughbass manner. At the end of the chapter, Kellner treats situations where dissonances succeed one another. Following Heinichen, and adopting two of his three examples,[11] Kellner explains that such situations often involve an inversion or rearrangement *(Umwendung)* of the dissonant harmony (see Example 4-22). "In the first example is D with 6/4+/2; then, in the notes over the following G♯, the dissonance is only rearranged; and because after the first D the resolution should be C-E-A, this very harmony then follows over the third note, for the chord A-C-E is only a rearrangement of C-E-A" (p. 86). Kellner then notes that such situations usually involve four types of seventh chords, each of which can occur in three inversions (see Example 4-23). This is introduced with no fanfare or any suggestion (as with Heinichen's explanation of inversions) that this is a new or experimental idea. It is significant that Kellner lists the root-position chord first. Heinichen had begun his listing of inversions with different forms: from the chord of the second (D-E-G♯-B), the chord of the diminished fifth (E-C-G-Bb), and the

11. The first two examples on p. 86 (1732 edition) in Kellner are derived from Heinichen 1728, pp. 625 (first example) and 627 (first example).

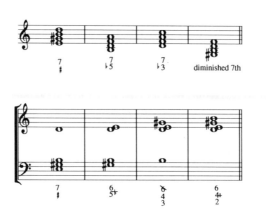

*Example* 4-23. Kellner 1732, pp. 86–87; scored from tablature, with minor errors emended

chord of the diminished seventh (G♯-B-D-F) (Heinichen 1728, pp. 624–625).

Kellner's presentation offers seventh chords and their inversions as basic harmonies and the notion that the progression from one harmony to another is essentially the same no matter what position the chords appear in. In this manner, Rameau's ideas began to permeate general musical discourse. They answered a need among musicians for a new way of organizing and explaining harmonies and their successions. Fuxian counterpoint was capable of dealing with some aspects of musical structure, but Fux's own inability to deal with relatively simple harmonies in the recitative cited in Example 2-7 demonstrate the inadequacy of that approach in explaining modern harmony. Musicians also sought respite from the burgeoning harmonies, rules, and exceptions of contemporary thoroughbass manuals. By reducing all harmonies to triads and seventh chords with or without added notes, and by explaining all successions among these harmonies in terms of fundamental-bass progressions, Rameau pointed the way out of the difficulties of counterpoint and thoroughbass. The theoretical battles involving Rameau and others later in the century generally took place not over whether to accept the inversions of triads and seventh chords, the notion of chord roots, and the concept of harmonic progressions, but how best to explain these concepts and put them into use.

# CHAPTER FIVE

# Rameau's Later Works and Controversies

*Music is a physico-mathematical science; sound is its physical object, and the ratios found between different sounds constitute its mathematical object.*

*Rameau 1737, Chapter 2*

## Rameau as Scientist

The ink had hardly dried on the *Traité* when Rameau became aware of a powerful idea that was to shape his speculative theories for the remainder of his life. In an extended review of the *Traité,* Père Louis Bertrand Castel (1688–1757) cited acoustical research by the Jesuit philosopher, mathematician, and scientist Ignace Gaston Pardies (1636–1673) and the physicist Joseph Sauveur (1653–1716) proving that the very consonances Rameau had painstakingly demonstrated by string divisions to arise over the fundamental—the octave, twelfth, and major seventeenth (compound major third)—were audible in the resonance of a vibrating string. It appeared, as Castel put it, that "Nature gives us the same system that M. Rameau discovered in numbers" (Castel 1722, pp. 1733–1734).

It is difficult for us in the twentieth century to imagine the effect of this revelation on Rameau. In 1722, the foundation of science was not a relatively ancient history of accepted facts, as it is to us. Descartes (1596–1650), who had elevated rational examination over accepted authority, was still a living memory during Rameau's youth. And Isaac Newton (1642–1727) was the towering giant of recent science—as Voltaire said of Newton, "We are all his disciples now." The perspectives opened by Descartes and Newton were yielding new discoveries at an ever-increasing pace. And unlike much modern science in which it is difficult for a layman even to follow the latest advances, many educated persons in the eighteenth century could and often did contribute to the advance of science because of the fundamental nature of many of the new discoveries.

In the *Traité*, Rameau had been the Descartes of music, searching for first principles and deducing the place of musical knowledge in an orderly system. Now, living in Paris, one of the capitals of the new scientific age, Rameau also became the Newton of music. He continued to insist that rules must be based on first principles. But now those principles had to be based on empirical fact. His foundation is no longer string divisions, but the resonating string—the *corps sonore (sonorous body)*. The basic intervals are no longer merely related to a fundamental note, they are actually generated by that fundamental because they physically sound along with it.[1]

Even the titles of Rameau's next works reflect his changed perspective. *Nouveau Système* (1726), which acknowledges many new aspects of his scientific approach, pays homage to the 1701 report on Sauveur's acoustical ideas to the French Royal Academy of Sciences: "Sur un nouveau système de musique" (Fontenelle 1707). The treatise that fully sets forth Rameau's new perspective is entitled *Harmonic Generation* (*Generation harmonique*, 1737; foreshadowed by Chapter 3 in Rameau 1726: "On the generation of chords and all intervals"). Rameau confidently dismisses traditional discussions of string divisions and mathematical operations, replacing them with a series of scientific experiments demonstrating matters of acoustics and even the physiology of hearing (Rameau 1737, preface and Chapter 1). Proposition 12, for instance, deals with the construction of the cochlea and the manner in which it transmits sounds to the brain. In short, Rameau separated *musica teorica* from its ancient mathematical basis and made the physical properties of sound the basis of speculative music theory.

The *corps sonore* gave Rameau an unchanging physical source to replace the manipulable numbers arising from string divisions. But it did not solve the problems he had earlier, such as the origin of the minor third. In fact, it made these problems more serious. No longer able to juggle numbers to generate the minor third, Rameau now had to face its absence over the fundamental as a physical fact of harmonic resonance. But this did not stop him from proposing new generations, some of which were based on acoustical errors.

For instance, one experiment in the *Generation* deals with sympathetic vibration. Rameau correctly notes that a vibrating string causes other strings tuned a twelfth and a major seventeenth lower to vibrate sympa-

---

1. Duchez 1986 and Christensen 1987a, 1987b, and 1993 discuss Rameau and science in greater detail.

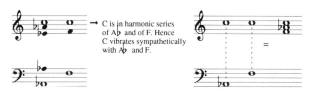

*Example 5-1.*

thetically. But he mistakenly believed that these lower strings vibrated in their entire lengths, not in thirds and fifths, respectively. This error led him to posit an origin for the minor perfect chord out of the resonances of these lower strings (see Example 5-1). Rameau recognized his acoustic error in the *Démonstration* (1750), but still insisted on this downward generation of the minor perfect chord, conceding only that it was merely "indicated by nature" instead of being actually present (Rameau 1750, pp. 24, 63). Had Rameau tuned sympathetically vibrating strings to other intervals, he could have shown just as easily that many any other combinations of tones were likewise "indicated by nature."

Such logical or factual lapses are less important than Rameau's failure to address the implications of downward generation of the minor triad. He certainly does not want to argue that the upper note of the minor triad is its generator or root with all the absurdities that entails (as in Riemann 1893). In fact, Rameau had previously rejected Zarlino's downward explanation of the minor triad in part because of such difficulties (Rameau 1722, Book 1, Chapter 4). Rameau also does not want F minor to be the relative minor of C major. So later in the *Démonstration,* he came up with yet another generation of minor, arguing that the chord A-C-E has two generators: A-E yields the perfect fifth and C-E the major third (Rameau 1750, pp. 69ff.). This implies that the minor perfect chord has two roots, its fundamental bass (A, root of the fifth A-E) and its third (C, root of the third C-E). Rameau neither recognizes that implication nor explains why the minor chord, functionally equivalent to the major chord, should have such a different generation.

Chapter 4 has already taken note of the fallacies of attempting to find any particular system of music in mathematics or natural resonance. It merits repetition here that none of the problems Rameau has in generating the minor perfect chord affect how he explains its use. No matter which generation he uses in a given work, the minor perfect chord, like major, is a single harmonic unit with its lowest tone the fundamental bass.

Other acoustical errors in Chapter 1 of the *Generation* do not affect the practical side of his theorizing but do illuminate his powerful desire to find in Nature via the *corps sonore* a model for his view of music. For instance, in order to find only consonances in the resonance of a string, he plaintively suggests that the note created by one-seventh of a string is so weak "that it could not conceivably be heard if it were not pointed out; thus perhaps it will always escape you" (Rameau 1737, Chapter 1, Experiment 3). In fact, the relative loudness of any harmonic depends on the construction of the vibrating string and on how and where it is set in motion. Despite Rameau's hope, it may not in fact "always escape you." He also insists that harmonic resonance exists "in the resonance of every sonorous body, such as a sound of our voice, of a string, of a tube, of a bell, and so forth" (Rameau 1754, p. 2). In fact, only physical systems vibrating with one degree of freedom, such as air columns and strings, regularly yield the harmonic series.

To judge from surviving anecdotes, Rameau must have been somewhat exasperating with his insistence on the *corps sonore* as a universal phenomenon. The Encyclopedist Denis Diderot (1713–1784) has the protagonist in his novel *Rameau's Nephew* describe how the theorist stalked the streets of Paris listening for harmonic resonance in church bells. And one M. Boisgelow reportedly took Rameau to a pond full of croaking frogs to point out that "this is in nature as much as is your system of fundamental bass" (Choron-Fayolle 1810–1811, Vol. 2, p. 197; Keane 1961, p. 49).

Modern scholars, viewing Rameau's acoustic errors and changing opinions on acoustic facts, often portray him as a scientific dilettante who desperately searched for validation of his speculative ideas. But according to Christensen 1987b, the first study to correlate Rameau's acoustic assertions with the rapidly evolving science of the time, Rameau in fact "accurately reported much of the most progressive scientific research of his day" (p. 24). It took a long time for scientists and mathematicians to show how it was possible for multiple sounds to arise in a single vibrating column and to explain how sound waves traveled through the air and how we perceive them.

As a result, some of the polemic in which Rameau engaged concerned disputes over what we regard as scientific fact, but what the eighteenth century saw as questionable conclusions of a new science. For instance, Rameau's adversary in 1729–1731 argues that "a vibrating body . . . only causes the three different sounds of the perfect chord to be heard *by accident,* as, for example, *when it has been overly forced [trop-forcé]*" (Rameau 1729–1731, p. 2370; original emphases). Furthermore, many prominent musicians remained unaware of the implications of harmonic resonance. As learned a musical scholar as Johann Gottfried Walther (1684–1748), for instance, did not mention resonance in the article on Sauveur in his 1732 *Lexicon*.

Regardless of the speculative or scientific problems Rameau encountered, what is of greatest significance is that he (and many later musicians) now believed that the harmonic series, hitherto deemed primarily the abstract result of string divisions and numerology, was in fact audible in sound. To use one of the catchwords of the eighteenth century, these intervals occur in Nature, and Nature gives us the ability to perceive them.

## Innovations in Harmonic Theory

Apparently at the suggestion of Castel (Rameau CTW 3, p. xxv), Rameau published in 1726 the second of his treatises "to serve as an introduction to the *Traité de l'harmonie*" (title page). Some of the chapters in the *Nouveau système* are indeed glosses on ideas in the *Traité*. But in this work and his *Dissertation* of 1732, which deals mostly with accompaniment, there are also important innovations, as well as analyses of classic compositions of the time. He analyzes a monologue from Lully's *Armide* (Rameau 1726, Chapter 20).[2] He also discusses the figuring of the bass part in Corelli's opus 5 sonatas (Rameau 1726, Chapter 23; English translation in Appendix 2) and presents his tablature of an accompaniment to one movement of these sonatas (Rameau 1732; discussion and a realization in Hayes 1974c).[3] Yet neither the *Nouveau système* nor the *Dissertation* was designed as a comprehensive picture of his new perspectives.

To present his new ideas in a work comparable to the *Traité*, he published the *Generation harmonique* in 1737. This work marks the end of the development of Rameau's practical theories in most matters concerning harmony and composition. Although he published more than half his writings on music theory after 1737, discussed some of his practical ideas with more clarity within his later works, continued to change various aspects of his speculative ideas, and engaged in seemingly endless polemic over many of his ideas, most of his practical ideas appear in the *Generation* in their final formulation.

Much of the practical foundation laid out in the *Traité* remains in the *Generation* and later works. The major and minor perfect chords are the source of consonant harmony; the seventh chord is the source of dissonant harmony (including chords by subposition and added-sixth chords). Cadences are the models for chord progressions, and imitated and evaded cadences explain harmonic continuity. Many of the new tenets added to this foundation had already appeared in some form in the *Traité*, but without a clear vocabulary or else without explicit discussion.

2. Rameau re-analyzed this recitative in a different manner in Rameau 1754. Verba 1973 discusses both analyses insightfully.

3. The fundamental bass in this realization is by Hayes.

## THE SUBDOMINANT

The most important innovation is the added prominence accorded the fourth scale degree and the more comprehensive approach to chord progressions resulting from this. In the *Traité*, Rameau recognizes two principal cadences as models for all chord progressions: the perfect cadence or fundamental-bass motion down by a fifth, and the irregular cadence (also called the *imperfect cadence* in the *Generation*) or fundamental-bass motion up by a fifth. In each, a dissonant chord (seventh chord or added-sixth chord) progresses to a perfect chord. Rameau highlights the status of the two chords in the perfect cadence by using the terms *dominant* and *tonic* to refer not only to the scale degrees on which the chords are built but also to the quality of the chords themselves. *Dominant* had been used in French theory to refer to the fifth scale degree since the early seventeenth century, and *tonic* had appeared in print for the first time in St. Lambert 1707 as a synonym for the final of the mode. Rameau has no such name for scale-step 4 or its dissonant chord in the imperfect cadence.

In the *Nouveau systême*, Rameau adopts the name *subdominant* (*sous-dominante;* apparently coined as *soudominante* in Dandrieu c. 1719) to refer to scale-step 4 as well as the added-sixth chord built there. Whereas Jean-Françios Dandrieu (c. 1682–1738) probably intended the prefix *sub-* to refer to the note below the dominant, Rameau denotes by that prefix that scale-step 4 lay a fifth below the tonic, complementing the dominant a fifth above the tonic. Just like the dominant, the subdominant supports a dissonant first chord of a cadence.

With the subdominant now a formal member of the key, Rameau sought a way to generate it from the fundamental or tonic in a manner comparable to the generation of the dominant, which appears as the second pitch over the fundamental in the *corps sonore*. Unfortunately for Rameau, the perfect fourth does not appear above the fundamental any more than the minor third does. In *Generation*, Rameau proposes an origin for the subdominant akin to his derivation of the minor third, locating the interval below the fundamental rather than above it. In relation to C, he finds F a twelfth (or compound fifth) below, complementing G a twelfth above. Reduced to simple fifths, the three principal notes of the key supporting the three principal types of chords appear as a series of fifths, F-C-G. Rameau calls this the *triple proportion* because each tone is the third harmonic of the previous one and thus each term is triple the previous one. If F equals 1, then F, C, and G are 1:3:9 (Chapter 4; and Rameau 1726, Chapter 4).

Downward generation of the subdominant is just as problematic as downward generation of the minor third. Since F does not exist in the resonance of C, all Rameau has done is explain that C exists in the resonance of F. That would imply that F was the source of the key of C, which of course Rameau does not intend. Shirlaw 1917 and Ferris 1959 cover this speculative issue in more detail, including Rameau's later attempts to find a source for the subdominant. As with his search for the generation of the minor third, these speculative issues do not affect his practical application of the subdominant.

Each of the three scale degrees participating in cadences now had a name and a characteristic chord. Occasionally in some works, and routinely in the *Code,* his last practical work, Rameau uses the terms *tonic, subdominant,* and *dominant* to refer both to a scale-step and to the characteristic chord type it supports. *Tonic* means both scale-step 1 and a perfect chord—any perfect chord is simply a *tonic. Dominant* means scale-step 5 and a seventh chord. If a seventh chord has a major third, it is a *dominant-tonic*—a dominant of the tonic. Otherwise it is a *simple dominant,* imitating the dominant-tonic in a perfect cadence. And an added-sixth chord, often referred to as an *added* chord, is a *subdominant.* When the notes of this subdominant are rearranged to form a seventh chord on scale-step 2, Rameau calls it the *chord of the second (degree),* or more simply, a *second* chord. Although the terms *tonic, subdominant,* and *dominant* have remained in use, these special connotations linking chord type to scale degree were not widely adopted by musicians other than Rameau's own proteges, and they faded from use by the latter part of the century (Rousseau 1768, article *dominante;* Scheibe 1773, p. 187).

## THE SUBDOMINANT AND DOUBLE EMPLOYMENT OF THE DISSONANCE

With the subdominant more firmly established, Rameau returns with renewed vigor to his assertion that the fundamental bass should progress from one harmony to the next only by the fundamental consonances—fifths and thirds. He proposes this in the *Traité* but also admits that because of compositional license the fundamental bass can progress by step. In the *Dissertation,* he mentions a process called *double employment of the dissonance (double emploi;* Rameau 1732, p. 33; Hayes 1974a, pp. 47–48), referring the reader to chapters in the *Nouveau système* that explain the difference between a simple dominant chord and an added-sixth chord—that is, whether the combination C-E-G-A is a simple dominant (an A-minor seventh chord) or a subdominant (a C-chord with an added sixth). But a full explanation does not appear until the *Generation.*

*Double emploi* refers to a change of harmonic function within a single harmony that arises because the minor seventh chord on the second degree (A-C-E-G in G major) has the same notes as the added-sixth chord on the subdominant (as C-E-G-A). An instance of this chord can be a simple dominant (a seventh chord) with the seventh resolving down as the fundamental bass descends a fifth, or it can be a subdominant (an added-

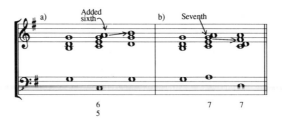

*Example 5-2.*

*Example 5-3.* Rameau 1737, Chapter 11; Hayes 1974b, p. 80

sixth chord) with the added sixth resolving up as the fundamental bass ascends a fifth (see Example 5-2).

With two possible fundamental basses (roots) for this chord, the fundamental bass can progress by a fifth no matter how it resolves. In Example 5-2a the goal is a tonic, so the fundamental bass ascends a fifth in an imperfect cadence. In Example 5-2b the goal is a dominant-tonic, so the fundamental bass descends a fifth, imitating a perfect cadence.

In Example 5-2b, there is a fundamental-bass progression by step between the first two chords. It is this situation that Rameau addresses with *double emploi* (see Example 5-3). A single chord changes its functional meaning so that the chord and its dissonance function in two different manners, or are "doubly employed":

> [At the asterisked chord] our ear takes the new fundamental sound as representing the subdominant [as an added-sixth chord] . . . There originates in the ear the impression of a new possible succession for the harmony . . . Let me explain. The order of the harmony above the new fundamental sound, being like that of the dominant [arranged as a seventh chord], especially between the two sounds from which the impression of dissonance originates, causes this new fundamental sound to be adopted as a dominant, and from then on causes its descent by a fifth—as required in passing from the dominant to the principal sound [the tonic]—to be desired, so that it satisfies the ear by complying with this succession. (Rameau 1737, Chapter 9; Hayes, p. 71)[4]

4. Example 5-3 appears in Chapter 11 of Rameau 1737; the explanation of *double emploi* appears in Chapter 9, referring to the progression illustrated in Example 5-3, but without musical notation.

With *double emploi,* Rameau can explain that fundamental-bass motions appearing to rise a second really fall a fifth. Hence he succeeds in showing how virtually all fundamental-bass successions occur by the consonances contained within the perfect chord as it appears in the *corps sonore.*

*Double emploi,* although fully explained for the first time in the *Generation,* is another of the tenets implicitly present in the *Traité,* where several examples apply two fundamental basses to a single chord in order to avoid a succession by a second (Book 3, Chapter 41, quoted as Ex. 4-19, m. 2; and examples of the *règle de l'octave* in Book 4, Chapter 6).

### DOUBLE EMPLOI AND CHORDAL CONTEXT

If thought of in terms of the single chord under which the fundamental bass changes, *double emploi* seems arbitrary. How could we possibly know that the fundamental bass was changing during a sustained sonority? But fundamental-bass progressions for Rameau concern movement between chords, not individual harmonies. The extensive discussions in all his works about fundamental-bass progressions are predicated on his belief that chords occur in a context. *Double emploi,* like cadences and chords by subposition, forces one to decide about the context of a chord before being able to assign a fundamental bass. In Example 5-3, the motion leading to the asterisked chord imitates a perfect cadence (G-C, with the C-chord having an added sixth to prevent it from being conclusive). The motion between this chord and the next one also imitates a perfect cadence (A-D, with the first chord being a simple dominant instead of a dominant-tonic, and with the second chord being a dominant-tonic instead of a perfect chord), but only after reinterpreting the fundamental bass of the asterisked chord. The chord changes its meaning and hence its implied goal because of *double emploi.*

As a result, later harmonic theorists who agree with Rameau that chordal identity depends on context (many of Rameau's French protégés, Padre Martini, and J. S. Bach pupils Nichelmann and Kirnberger) incorporate *double emploi* or similar concepts in their writings, whether or not they use the term itself. Other theorists who disagree with Rameau and treat chordal identity mostly in terms of vertical structure (Marpurg, Koch, Türk, and W. A. Mozart) do not include *double emploi* or related ideas.

### CHORD PROGRESSIONS, KEYS, AND IMPLIED DISSONANCES

In Rameau's harmonic theory, chords may be tonics (perfect chords), dominants (seventh chords), or subdominants (added-sixth chords). The quality of a specific chord is determined by the nature of the progression in which it participates—a real or imitated cadence. Thus when the fundamental bass moves up or down by fifths, the first chord in each pair is either a dominant (some sort of seventh chord) or a subdominant (an added-sixth chord), and the second chord in each pair is a tonic (a perfect chord). That tonic, unless it is the final chord of a phrase, becomes the first member of the next pair of chords. To assume that role, the tonic takes on the dissonance (seventh or added sixth) characteristic of the first member of the next progression.

For instance, in a chain of simple dominants (minor seventh chords proceeding by descending fifths), such as the progression E-minor$^7$ to A-minor$^7$ to D-minor$^7$, each pair of chords imitates but does not present a perfect cadence. The first chord in each pair has a minor third (not a leading tone to make it a dominant-tonic), and the second chord in each pair is a seventh chord (not a perfect chord). From Rameau's perspective, these chords relate primarily to one another and only indirectly to a tonic. Only when one of the simple dominants moves to a dominant-tonic (a dominant-seventh chord) can a key be specified by a leading tone (whether or not that dominant-tonic actually resolves to a tonic chord). If the chords following this chain of dominants are a G$^7$ chord and a C perfect chord, there is a real cadence on C.

The result is a sense of key in which there often is a "floating tonic" (not a term Rameau uses; Dahlhaus 1986b adds further thoughts). A tonic when played may add a sixth and become a subdominant, then rising a fifth. Or a tonic may add a seventh and become a simple dominant, then falling a fifth. When the fundamental bass moves by thirds, the resulting progression is a succession of tonics (perfect chords), since the first chord in the pair can be neither a dominant nor a subdominant because its dissonance would not resolve.

Rameau thus posits a ternary relationship between chord quality, type of progression, and sense of key. The quality of a chord suggests where that chord may move, while its actual movement in turn determines what its quality should be. The chord qualities and the progression determine the temporary tonic.

At bottom, this perspective is based on a simplistic dichotomy between consonant tonics that are goals and dissonant chords that are mobile. Rameau the practical theorist and composer knew that actual music can go on for long periods of time without any dissonances being present and still sound like it is not continually coming to a halt. Certainly his own written compositions are not packed with continuous dissonances. In order to explain how consonant chords do not imply continuous halts, Rameau the speculative theorist explains that even when a chord in the score looks consonant and carries no figuring, it may still imply a dissonance. If the dissonance is missing from the score, he asks, "Do the eyes suffice in music? There must be ears, and above all impartial judgement, if reason is not to be blinded" (Rameau 1754, pp. 86–87).

Thus when Rameau in the *Nouveau système* adds a fundamental bass

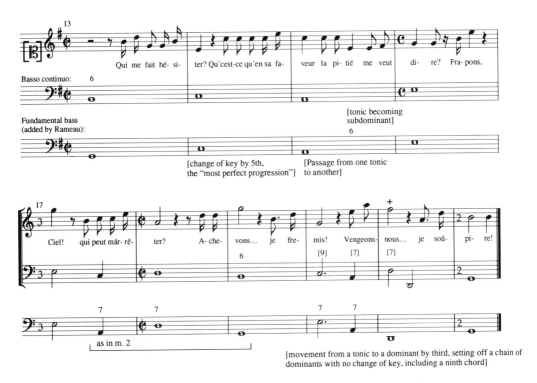

*Example* 5-4. Rameau 1726, pp. 82–84. Basso continuo figures in brackets absent
in Lully's 1686 edition (facsimile in Verba 1973, p. 74). Remarks below
the fundamental bass paraphrase Rameau.

to a monologue from Lully's *Armide,* he adds implied dissonances wherever necessary to explain the progression (see Example 5-4). The excerpt
begins and ends in G major (within the E-minor monologue). There are
no accidentals in the melody, bass, or figuring. But because of his harmonic
norms, Rameau analyzes temporary changes of key to C major (m. 14),
A minor (m. 15), E minor (m. 16), A minor (m. 17), D major (m. 18),
and G major (m. 19). The progression ends with a chain of dominants
within the key of G major to confirm the cadence in measure 22. Rameau
adds implied dissonances in measure 15 (added sixth turning the tonic of
A into the subdominant of E), measure 17 (avoiding stepwise motion in
the fundamental bass into m. 18), and measures 18 and 20 (changing
tonics into simple dominants or dominant-tonics).

In a later analysis of the same passage in his *Observations* (1754),
Rameau extends the notion of implication even further via chromaticism
to strengthen the changes of key. He marks a 5♭ over the bass in measures
13 and 19 to confirm the move to C major, and a ♯ over the bass A in
measure 20 to project a brief change to D major before the cadence in G
(Rameau 1754, pp. 91, 98). To be sure, Rameau's assertion of local key

changes in this later analysis was partly motivated by his desire to answer a critique of the monologue made by Jean Jacques Rousseau (1712–1778). As part of the critique of French music in his *Lettre sur la musique française* (1753), Rousseau, himself a composer of some note,[5] singles out this excerpt precisely because Rameau praised it in 1726 as an exemplar of French music. Rousseau charges that Lully's setting fails to portray Armide's hesitancy and then her resolve to act because the monologue ends in the same key in which it begins and has too many perfect cadences. Rameau seeks to demonstrate that changing harmonic functions do in fact mirror Armide's hesitancy. If the implied key changes in his 1754 analysis are understandable to answer Rousseau, there is no such motivation for the implied dissonances in the 1726 analysis.[6]

Rameau's focus seems deplorably short-ranged, even though he understands that the temporary tonics are not established as keys because they are not preceded by cadences and that a ruling key *(ton régnant)* encompasses the quick tonal shifts. In his defense, it should be pointed out that although some theorists, including Rameau himself in the *Traité*, occasionally note that local chromaticism can occur without effecting a change of key, most theorists until well into the nineteenth century call even a single chromatic leading tone evidence of a key change. But Lully's monologue contains no chromaticism.

The issue of dissonances not indicated by a composer arises again in Rameau's critique of the figured basses in Corelli's opus 5 sonatas (Rameau 1726, Chapter 23). As shown in the annotated translation of this critique in Appendix 1, Rameau felt quite strongly that the omission of crucial dissonances in Corelli's figures makes the sense of key or of harmonic direction insecure. Although he was trying to explain how the harmonies function both locally (in terms of dissonance treatment and chord-to-chord progression) and in the large (creating a key, changing a key), some of Rameau's emendations replace Corelli's simple triads with preposterous strings of complex dissonances and subposed chords.

Was Rameau speaking as a speculative theorist in adding these dissonances and chromatics, simply trying to explain the directionality of harmony? In other words, was he arguing that when we hear a triad that sounds mobile, its mobility is the result of dissonances that we add mentally because we know that the chord is not restful? Or did he mean that these dissonances should be played? Various evidence points to the latter.

---

5. Rousseau's *opéra comique Le Devin du village* (1752) remained in active repertoire for some sixty years. The personal enmity between Rameau and Rousseau may have arisen from Rameau's criticism of a performance of Rousseau's ballet opera *Les muses galantes* in 1745 (Girdlestone 1969, pp. 478–479).

6. Verba 1973 comprehensively discusses Rameau's and Rousseau's dispute over this monologue.

At the end of the *Dissertation,* Rameau realized a thoroughbass from Corelli's opus 5 in a tablature proposed to replace thoroughbass notation (Hayes 1974c).[7] This tablature, clearly meant to be performed, includes many implied dissonances.

Earlier, Rameau's adversary in the dispute of 1729–1731 complained that Rameau's accompaniments are "almost always full of dissonances, and consequently hard on the ear; quite often this is contrary to the composer's intentions." Part of the dispute focuses on a measure containing a sustained bass D in a one-flat signature with the figuring $\frac{5\ 6\ 5}{3\text{-}4\text{-}3}$ (no musical illustration is provided). Rameau's adversary explains that this progression is merely "to vary the tonic chord." But Rameau repeatedly insists that playing the figures as written "amounts to entering the key of G by a cadential progression without having placed a major third on the first note, which is its dominant, and to going from the minor third to the octave [i.e., from F-to-G over D-to-G]; it offends the ear and good sense. Zarlino prohibited it. It amounts to making a cadence without having a major third on the dominant . . . The foundation of harmony teaches us that the perfect chord of G announces the G-mode, which is not at all in question here." Rameau ridicules his adversary's claims to have merely followed the composer's intention: "If it is on the figuring that he bases the composer's intention, as is abundantly clear, that's another matter. Following this reasoning, if the figures are wrong, be it by the negligence of the composer, the copyist, or the publisher, of course it's necessary to play a wrong chord" (Rameau 1729–1731, pp. 1286–1288, 2376).

It seems clear that Rameau failed to see that factors other than local consonance and dissonance could affect the potential finality of a harmony within a progression. His reasoning is similar to that of Arnold Schoenberg, who for many years avoided octave doublings in his atonal compositions because "to double is to emphasize, and an emphasized tone could be interpreted as a root, or even as a tonic; the consequences of such an interpretation must be avoided" (Schoenberg 1950, p. 219). Surely it takes more than an octave doubling (as Schoenberg feared) or a consonant chord (as Rameau feared) to establish a key.

A separate issue involving harmonic scale-step norms and implied key changes concerns the possible chords that can represent the dominant at a cadence. When a cadence on the dominant ends on a perfect chord, not a seventh chord, does that mean that scale-step 5 is really a tonic, even if temporarily? Rameau continually wavered on this issue, sometimes ex-

7. This is only one of several notational reforms proposed by Rameau. In the *Traité,* he suggests a new way of notating key signatures, meter, and tempo (Book 2, Chapters 24–25). In keeping with the spirit of the Enlightenment, there were countless suggestions for notational reform from all quarters.

*Example 5-5*. Rameau [1761], Lesson K

plaining that the dominant could have a perfect chord and yet still be a dominant (Rameau 1722, Book 3, Chapter 9), and elsewhere suggesting that when it supports a perfect chord, scale-step 5 is temporarily a tonic, and the original tonic its subdominant (Rameau 1737, Chapter 18). This ambiguity remains in his last published thoughts on the topic: "Each phrase-ending concludes in the fundamental bass exclusively on the tonic, or on its dominant, [which is] therefore an implied tonic [*censée tonique*]" (Rameau [1761], p. 84; discussed in Caplin 1981, pp. 42–45).

SUBPOSITION AND SUSPENSION

Throughout his works, Rameau continues to insist that subposition is the proper theoretical explanation for suspended notes. But in the *Code* he backs away from several former positions, no longer insisting, for instance, that a suspended fourth need be called an eleventh.

Rameau also extends the notion of suspension to include the cadential 6/4, which as a triad does not arise from subposition. Whereas in the *Traité*, he explains a cadential 6/4 as a tonic chord (illustrated in Example 4-15), now it is a "suspension that consists of retaining the entire perfect chord of a fundamental note when one rises a fifth." These suspensions "are quite frequent immediately before a perfect cadence; they willingly announce that cadence since they simply suspend [i.e., delay] the harmony of the dominant that in fact announces the cadence; and often the fourth then suspends [delays] the third of the tonic which concludes that same cadence" (Rameau [1761], p. 54) (see Example 5-5).

Rameau explains the cadential 6/4 similarly in an earlier manuscript treatise (Rameau c. 1740; Christensen 1987a, p. 30). Around the same time, Charles Levens (1689–1764), a Bordeaux musician who appropriated some of Rameau's ideas although he probably never studied with Rameau, explains the cadential 6/4 in a similar fashion when he notes that on the arrival of a cadential dominant, suspensions and trills "cause the chord of the principal note [the tonic chord] to be heard by means of the suspension" (Levens 1743, p. 18).

Compositional Theory in the Eighteenth Century

## Rameau on Accompaniment

Before establishing himself in Paris as a theorist and opera composer, Rameau had spent the better part of two decades working primarily as an organist and teacher. He continued actively teaching for decades thereafter. It is therefore no surprise that he published his thoughts on accompaniment several times. Book 4 of the *Traité* applies his newfound harmonic perspective to thoroughbass. A decade later, the *Dissertation on Different Methods of Accompaniment and Plan of a New Method* contains a critique of traditional thoroughbass and a new tablature for indicating harmonies. Finally, an extended chapter in the *Code* lays out a pedagogy of accompaniment based on his harmonic theories (Chapter 5, pp. 24–78).

This last method is as close as Rameau ever got in print to a truly practical work. Despite its frequently turgid prose, it provides a good summary of his mature harmonic theories. Each of the thirty-two separate lessons presents a single topic. Most lessons are illustrated by exercises. Both the ordering and content of Rameau's lessons highlight the differences between his approach and thoroughbass methods.

After the first lesson, which briefly defines accompaniment, Rameau lists the notes in a perfect chord and a seventh chord (Lesson 2), inversions (3), how to finger these chords in the right hand (4), the scale (5), the difference between basso continuo and the fundamental bass, and the three types of chords (tonics, subdominants, dominants; Lesson 6). Then he teaches how to play all sorts of progressions from the simplest to the most complex. Each progression is to be learned in the right hand alone: chains of dominants (7), the dominant-tonic chord (8), finding these chords in different keys (9), relative major and minor keys (10), cadences (11), keys and key signatures (12), relations between the *ton régnant* and other keys (13), changing keys via cadences (14), which chords can follow a tonic (15), *double emploi* (16), moving between keys via a chain of dominants (17), a chain of irregular cadences (18), suspensions common at cadences (19), chords common to several keys (pivot chords; Lesson 20), subposition and suspension (21), mixing subpositions with perfect chords (22), deceptive and otherwise evaded cadences (23), sixth chords connected by step (24), the diminished seventh chord (25), chromaticism (26), and enharmonic changes involving diminished seventh chords (27).

Rameau repeatedly insists that before moving on to the next lesson, the student practice each exercise until it can be played automatically, without even thinking. Only in this way will the student learn finger technique and how to hear these progressions even before they are played. For as he explains at the very beginning, "The principles of composition and accompaniment are the same, but in exactly the opposite order." If students have diligently learned all the progressions through Lesson 27, they are now ready to add the basso continuo to these right-hand progressions (Lesson 28). The remaining lessons cover syncopation (29), the preparation and resolution of dissonances in general (30; earlier he had taught this by rote), some matters of fingering (31), and how to figure a bass part (32).

Rameau presents much of the material found in comprehensive thoroughbass methods as well as matters such as changing key by using harmonic pivots and enharmonic changes of diminished seventh chords. But his orientation is the opposite of thoroughbass methods. Where thoroughbass manuals teach how to play according to what is in the bass part, Rameau teaches how to play all sorts of chord progressions and only then explains how to recognize which progression belongs over a given basso continuo. To defend his approach, he argues that a given fundamental-bass progression yields the same right-hand chords no matter what inversions appear in the bass. Decades earlier, he had even argued that since "harmony alone is of concern in accompaniment, and if I furnish a way to render it always complete and regular without the help of the bass, then the bass part [on the keyboard] will no longer be anything but an extra part . . . Except for the case where there are no other instruments, I do not see that there is any constraint against dispensing with the bass in accompaniment on the harpsichord" (Rameau 1732, pp. 17–18; Hayes 1974a, pp. 24–25). Where thoroughbass methods taught voice leading based on the type of verticality over the continuo, Rameau taught voice leading based on the type of progression in the fundamental bass.

Both methods teach the player voice-leading patterns that can then be used as the basis of composition. But the application of these patterns to composition would be quite different. In the thoroughbass composition method detailed by Niedt, the composer learns to build the texture from the bass and then vary it. If Rameau's accompaniment method were used to compose, the progressions would appear, but the actual bass line would have to be chosen from the possible bass notes in each chord.

It might seem that Niedt's thoroughbass approach was ideal for early eighteenth-century styles, heavily dependent on the bass voice for support, and that Rameau's approach was more amenable to the newer styles appearing after the middle of the century, where the emphasis was on inventing articulated melodies and then harmonizing them. But Rameau's approach was in fact adopted by adherents of the older as well as the newer styles. J. S. Bach pupil Christoph Nichelmann (1717–1762) used a Rameauian approach in his 1755 treatise to compose and analyze numerous examples in the older style (discussed in Chapter 8). And in the 1780s W. A. Mozart used both thoroughbass and Rameauian fundamental bass in his teaching (discussed in Chapter 7). He used thoroughbass exercises to add the inner voices to existing outer-voice structures in a string-quartet format. This teaches voice leading, not the creation of a texture over a basso continuo. By contrast, he teaches melodic harmonization in a Rameauian manner. His student works out a fundamental bass to a melody, then composes an actual bass line from the notes in the fundamental-bass chords.

This change in compositional focus and pedagogy did not occur as a rapid switch to an alternate perspective. Rather it was a gradual process that evolved during much of the century—an evolution discussed in the remaining chapters in this study.

## Rameau as Publicist and *Philosophe*

From the time of his first publications, Rameau himself as well as reviewers both friendly and hostile bemoaned the density of his prose and the poor organization of his ideas. In the preface to the *Traité* (1722), Rameau included not only a common disclaimer about "the feebleness of my intellect," but also a more heartfelt apology for "my long discourses and repetitions." Castel concurred, complaining about the *Traité*'s "overly profound and learned style" (Castel 1728), as did Diderot, who in a 1748 essay on the science of sound expressed the wish "that someone would bring [Rameau's system] out from the obscurities enveloping it and put it within everyone's reach" (Rameau CTW 3, p. xl).

Aware that his writing was a potential obstacle to the spread of his ideas, Rameau repeatedly solicited supporters to review his works so that they could summarize his ideas in more accessible prose. Even when he was virtually unknown in Paris in 1722, Rameau had his recent acquaintance Castel publish a sixty-six-page review of the *Traité* in the Jesuit *Journal de Trévoux* only shortly after the *Traité* itself appeared. This was no scholarly critique by an outsider, but the work of a knowledgeable enthusiast who had discussed the work with its author (Girdlestone 1969, pp. 486–489; Rameau CTW, 1, pp. l–li; 2, p. xxii). The review clearly lays out the main ideas of the *Traité*—as Rameau later wrote to him, "I can only say the things, but you are able to give them life and color" (Rameau 1736, p. 1698; Rameau CTW 3, pp. xxxix–xl). Castel, prominent in intellectual circles and interested in music theory, invented the *clavecin oculaire,* a keyboard instrument capable of producing both notes and colors, and wrote a treatise proposing color-music (an idea enunciated by Newton). Castel later reviewed the *Nouveau système* (Castel 1728), a work whose inception he claimed to have inspired (Rameau CTW 3, p. xxv), and the *Generation* (Castel 1737), the latter unfavorably after a rift with Rameau. Extracts of Castel's *Traité* review appeared in the Leipzig-based *Neuer Zeitungen von Gelehrten Sachen* in 1723, giving his ideas a forum in Germany.

A similarly sponsored review of the *Generation* (1737) was written by Thérèse Deshayes, Rameau's pupil and the bride of Rameau's patron, La Pouplinière (Deshayes 1737; Rameau CTW 3, pp. xxi–xxii). To be sure, there were also reviews of Rameau's works that were produced without his participation; no less than five French journals printed discussions or extracts of the *Generation,* and his later works received similar notice.

At the end of the 1720s, Rameau engaged in a public controversy with an anonymous musician, sometimes assumed to be Michel Pignolet de Montéclair, well-known author of a comprehensive and elegantly engraved tutor published in 1709 (which contains, among other topics, an extensive discussion of rhythm and meter including an illustrated discussion of conducting patterns). In eight articles, Rameau and his adversary discussed various aspects of fundamental bass, acoustics, and the practice of accompaniment (Rameau 1729–1731). The appearance of these articles in *Mercure de France,* a leading journal, shows the stature Rameau's theories had gained in France even before he was known as an opera composer. Also of interest is the origin of the controversy: "two quite renowned musicians met on Sunday, May 8 in a house where the daughter is skilled on the clavecin in order to confer about various issues of harmony." Rameau was already cultivating the intellectual world of Paris. Within not too many years, he was close to the leading figures of the age, among them Voltaire (1694–1778), Rousseau, Diderot, and Jean le Rond D'Alembert (1717–1783).

Rameau took Diderot up on his 1748 wish for a more organized presentation of Rameau's ideas and enlisted the philosophe's help in preparing the *Démonstration* (1750), a work generally agreed to be his best organized (Rameau CTW 3, p. xxxix–xli).

Further publicity for Rameau's theories, this time a rather mixed blessing, came in D'Alembert's *Elemens de musique . . . suivant les principes de M. Rameau* (1752). D'Alembert, one of the leading mathematicians of the day and a prime mover behind the *Encyclopédie,* presented what he viewed as Rameau's essential ideas in refreshingly lucid prose. The *Elemens* became quite a popular work, remaining in print through 1779, appearing in partial English translation as the article on music in the second and third *Encyclopaedia Britannica* (1784 and 1797, the latter edition also published in New York), and becoming the primary reference work on Rameau's theories in German via a 1757 translation by the German musician, critic, and theorist Friedrich Wilhelm Marpurg (1718–1795).

Unfortunately for Rameau's ideas, although the *Generation* and *Démonstration* are the basis of much of *Elemens,* D'Alembert's exposition often agrees only superficially with Rameau's theories.[8] Rameau broke

8. Christensen 1989 skillfully covers the intellectual background of D'Alembert's *Elemens.*

publicly with D'Alembert not long after and the two quickly became bitter enemies. The dispute first centered on D'Alembert's defense of the *Encyclopédie* (1751–1765) from Rameau's attacks on the music articles. In the 1740s, Rameau had been asked to write the articles on music but had declined, requesting instead to review them before publication. Rousseau wrote many of the articles, generally following Rameau's theories but differing with him on many points. Rameau published increasingly bitter denunciations of the articles on music as the volumes appeared. D'Alembert's initial defense may well have been motivated by his desire to deflect criticism of the politically sensitive project as a whole. But it soon became an argument between opposing views on many issues, heightened by Rameau's renewed close relationship with the Jesuits as his friendship with the Encyclopedists waned (Rameau CTW 3, pp. xlvi–xlviii, lxi, and 4, pp. xiii–xviii, xli). In 1762, D'Alembert revised the *Elemens* and departed further from Rameau's formulations.

D'Alembert was a dedicated amateur musician, but an amateur nonetheless. He became acquainted with Rameau's ideas when Rameau submitted a draft of his *Démonstration* to the Royal Academy of Sciences in 1749. He apparently did not even know how to read music before encountering this work, but nonetheless wrote a knowledgeable and glowing report. As Thomas Christensen argues, D'Alembert was primarily interested in publicizing Rameau's ideas as a purely deductive system, casting his title in homage to both Voltaire's *Eléments de la philosophie de Neuton* (Amsterdam, 1738) and Euclid's *Elements of Geometry*. He had little interest in practical matters, declaring with almost medieval zeal that "a physical scientist worthy of the name has no more need of experiment in order to demonstrate the laws of movement and statics than a good geometer [the eighteenth-century title for a mathematician] needs ruler and compass to verify that he has correctly resolved a difficult problem" (D'Alembert-Diderot 1751–1765, article *Expérimental*). This deductive stance is clear from the preface to the *Elemens*, where D'Alembert explains that he "is unconcerned here with physical principles of resonating bodies, and even less concerned with the metaphysical principle of the sentiment of harmony . . . the sole issue here is making known how one can deduce from a single experimental principle the laws of harmony that artists have only found, so to speak, gropingly" (pp. v–vi). He thereby greatly limits application of the *corps sonore* and the effects of harmony, the most important underpinnings of, respectively, Rameau's speculative and practical theories.

Throughout, D'Alembert deals with musical matters as only an amateur could. His treatment of chord sevenths is characteristic. For Rameau, the resolution of chord sevenths is a crucial element in the system of harmony. It is a prime reason for using chord inversions, and a major motivation for using cadences as models for chord progressions and for introducing subposed chords. D'Alembert, by contrast, finds nothing special about the resolution of chord sevenths. He explains that in the progression G$^7$ to C, F must resolve to E simply because in the four-voice setting he shows it has nowhere else to go (pp. 78–79). Nowhere does he mention the term or concept "minor dissonance."

While various examples are far-fetched (such as the progression from C-E-G to E-G#-B-C# illustrating an ascent of a third in the fundamental bass, p. 115), essentials such as the difference between fundamental bass and basso continuo are relegated to a digression at the very end of Part 1 (p. 95). Without this distinction, the whole topic of chord inversions plays only a minor role in the book.

In the absence of German translations of any of Rameau's works, it was Marpurg's 1757 rendering of D'Alembert and Marpurg's own works claiming to be based on Rameau that many Germans in the later eighteenth century assumed to be Rameau's theories. As a result, in the various German debates over Rameau's theories later in the century both sides often misunderstood Rameau's positions, Marpurg claiming to represent Rameau but often differing from him in the most fundamental ways, and his opponents upholding ideas similar to Rameau's but attacking Rameau's name because they believed that Marpurg's position was Rameau's (Marpurg vs. Sorge, Marpurg vs. Kirnberger, C. P. E. Bach's proclamation, and so forth; discussed in Chapters 8 and 9). Many of the misconceptions about Rameau's theories that arose at that time have remained in modern scholarship.

RAMEAU AND THE SCIENTIFIC COMMUNITY

As Rameau's speculative theorizing became more involved with acoustics and natural resonance in the 1730s, he came to believe that his achievements merited recognition not only among musicians but among scientists and mathematicians as well. The spirit of the Enlightenment encouraged musical amateurs to believe that with study they could discourse knowledgeably on music theory. After all, D'Alembert wrote the *Elemens* and some of the musical articles in the *Encyclopédie,* Diderot assisted Rameau on the *Démonstration* and later either assisted Anton Bemetzrieder (c. 1743-c. 1817) or wrote the *Leçons de clavecin* published in 1771 under Bemetzrieder's name,[9] and various musical amateurs confidently sparred with Rameau on musical issues. So Rameau quite confidently believed he

9. Bemetzrieder was a prolific writer on music, mathematics, and philosophy first in Paris and then in London after 1781. The *Leçons* was one of twenty-two separate works on music, many of which appeared in several editions. The extent of Diderot's contribution to the *Leçons* remains uncertain, most recently surveyed in Gribenski 1980, which catalogs Bemetzrieder's works. In any event, the *Leçons* are at best useful for an amateur, full of preposterous voice leadings.

could discourse on science and philosophy. Rameau had already received favorable reviews of his first two treatises from Castel, a figure better known as a mathematician than a musician. And by the time he had published the *Generation* in 1737, the fifty-four-year old Rameau was no longer a relatively unknown current or former "Organist of the Cathedral of Clermont in Auvergne" as he announced himself on the title pages of the *Traité* and *Nouveau système,* but a renowned figure recognizable simply as "M. Rameau" on the title page of all his remaining works. As an opera composer, he was deemed successor to the legendary Jean-Baptiste Lully (1632–1687), sparking the debates of the 1730s between the *lullistes* and the *ramistes,* even though Rameau deplored the attacks on Lully's music, which he esteemed (surveyed in Girdlestone 1969, pp. 481–483). In short, as a theorist, composer, organist, conductor, and teacher, he had become a central figure in the musical-cultural-intellectual world of mid-century Paris.

He now strove for recognition from the scientific community for himself and for the music theory he believed he had placed on a more scientific basis. One avenue to such recognition lay in the scientific academies. He dedicated the *Generation* to the *Académie royale des sciences* (the first dedication of any of his works, including his compositions). The *Académie* responded with a favorable review by three eminent scholars, portions of which Rameau appended to the work. A dozen years later, Rameau submitted a draft of the *Démonstration* (1750) to the *Académie.* But despite a second favorable report, this time by D'Alembert, there was still no offer of membership (Cohen 1981, pp. 82–85, details Rameau's relationship with the *Académie royale*). Later in the 1750s, Rameau turned his attention abroad, submitting an early draft of the *Nouvelles réflexions* (1760) to the prestigious *Accademia delle Scienze dell' Istituto di Bologna* (of which D'Alembert was a member), resulting not in the offer Rameau had hoped for, but in a review of all of Rameau's works by Padre Martini (1706–1784), himself a member of the *Accademia* since 1758 (Rameau CTW 4, pp. xxxii–xxxix; Jacobi 1964). He also submitted both the *Generation* and the *Démonstration* to the Royal Society of London (Cohen 1981, p. 84). In addition, Rameau corresponded with a number of prominent mathematicians, among them Leonhard Euler (1707–1783), himself the author of a treatise on music (Euler 1739), with whom Rameau then entered into a polemic when Euler questioned octave equivalence (Rameau 1752; Rameau CTW 5, pp. xxxii–xxxiv), and Jean Bernoulli (1710–1790) (Rameau CTW 3, p. lviii; Girdlestone 1969, pp. 490–491).

For various reasons none of these applications got Rameau the scientific recognition he believed he merited. A major one is that Rameau was too experienced a musician to eliminate musical practices from his theory that were irreconcilable with rigorous deductive or inductive methods. As

Pierre-Joseph Roussier (c. 1716–1792), one of Rameau's followers and systematizers, put it, the "Founder of Harmony . . . sometimes forgot this principle [Roussier's interpretation of fundamental bass] in his writings, substituting concepts of practice and routine from which he was unable to completely free himself, as they had been unfortunately inculcated into him since early childhood" (Roussier 1765, pp. 37–38; Gessele 1989, p. 170).[10]

Rameau's arguments with scientists reveals how much he was a musician, not a scientist. When Euler pointed out that octave duplications were not identical with the unison, a reality that creates problems for the generation and inversion of chords, Rameau responded with an acoustical error (arguing, among other points, that the octave was inaudible in harmonic resonance) and a music-functional, not a scientific or mathematical rebuttal (that when men and women sing together in octaves, they think they are singing in unison).

Additional reasons for rejections of Rameau's applications for membership apply to different circumstances. Concerning the Bologna *Accademia*, for instance, Martini's lack of support for Rameau's application probably had little to do with theoretical matters. According to a letter of 1750, Martini apparently thought Rameau's system applied only to profane and theatrical music (Schnoebelen 1979, letter 476). Even in the 1770s, when Martini was fully applying Rameau's harmonic theory to sixteenth- and seventeenth-century sacred music (including chordal inversions, added-sixth chords, *double emploi,* and subposition to explain suspensions), Martini chastised Rameau for only applying his ideas to "the modern style of music for the theater and for pure pleasure . . . But the purpose of music is much more noble, and its use far more important when it is created, even by the confession of the same M. Rameau, to sing the praise of God" (Martini [1774], p. vi).

Rameau in his later years made increasingly grandiose claims for the role of music theory and his own discoveries of the *corps sonore*. He came to believe that "nature seems to impart to us via music the physical principle of those first purely mathematical notions from which devolve all the sciences—I mean the harmonic, arithmetic, and geometric proportions" (Rameau 1750, p. vi). He even contended that not only mathematics and the sciences, but religion itself was revealed to man via the *corps sonore*. This brought Rameau to a position commonly held by many devout theorists before him: "The entire basis of harmony consists of numbers and proportions, for GOd has set the measure and importance of everything in numbers because he himself is a GOd of order. What

10. Osborne 1966 and Gessele 1989 contain the most complete surveys of Roussier's theories.

GOd and Nature order, man must willingly imitate . . . When we consider the musical proportional numbers, they are nothing other than a proper order set by GOd and Nature" (Werckmeister 1697, p. 2).

A part of Rameau's scientific stance may have been the result not only of the age but also of the French penchant for public debate over every development in the arts and sciences. No significant innovation in eighteenth-century France avoided being subjected to a war of words. Rameau as composer was involved in the *lulliste-ramiste* battle of the 1730s and the *Querelle des Bouffons* of the 1750s (Girdlestone 1969, pp. 482–484, 493–494, and 500–507). So it was only natural for him to seek recognition as a theorist in the public arena.

As more than one historian has noted, the wars of words in midcentury France, even those on nonpolitical issues, were in many ways proxy battles over allegiances to entirely different world views—battles that led to the Revolution after all the principals in the debates had departed from the scene (Paul 1971). In the highly polarized political-religious-cultural-intellectual world of eighteenth-century France, alliances with one or another party often led to disastrous relations with the others. It is no coincidence that the warm reviews that Castel, a Jesuit, gave to the *Traité* and the *Nouveau système* in the 1720s gave way to a hostile reception of the *Generation* as Rameau considered collaborating with Voltaire on stage works in 1733 and actually did so in 1745, courted the *Académie,* and was called an *artiste philosophique* by D'Alembert in the preface to the *Encyclopédie.* Likewise, those who supported the *lullistes* against Rameau in the 1730s, when Rameau was friendly with the *philosophes,* once again became ardent *ramistes* in the 1750s, when the *Querelle* made Rameau's music a symbol of the French establishment and culture. In fact, even Rousseau's famous attack on the very existence of French music in 1753 may have had more of a political than a musical motivation. Only three years earlier, Rousseau had supported French music over Italian music (Strunk 1950, p. 654). And just the previous year, Rousseau's own *Devin du village,* in French of course, had opened for one of the longest runs in the history of musical theater. In the 1750s, when the *Querelle* and Rameau's criticism of the music articles in the *Encyclopédie* made it clear that he was no longer the darling of the *philosophes,* the Jesuit *Journal de Trévoux* once again begin to publish enthusiastic reviews of his works.

One reading this polemic nowadays easily gets the feeling that Rameau was in over his head and was used as a pawn by both sides. For instance, Erwin Jacobi suggests not only that the rift between Rameau and Castel may have originated over issues other than music-theoretical but that the fires were stoked by writers other than the two principals, Voltaire among them (Rameau CTW 3, pp. xxvii–xxviii, xlvi–xlviii). Rameau's primary interests were music and music theory, not the political and social contexts of these disputes. When he tried as a musician to support Lully at the time of the *lulliste-ramiste* battles of the 1730s (in the preface to his *Les Indes galantes* of 1735), he seems not to have understood the motivation of the *ramistes*.

At the same time, his allegiances within French politics affected his reputation outside France. The German composer, theorist, and critic Johann Mattheson (1681–1764) waged a campaign against Rameau's ideas, never once dealing substantively with any of the major theoretical issues, but repeatedly invoking religious and nationalistic animosity. He links Rameau, "one of the most famous music teachers in France, . . . with his Jesuit devotees (who, unfortunately!, are now in power)," he refers to "M. Rameau and those of his rabble," and he disparages "the Jesuits [who] now turn him into a miracle" (Rameau CTW 3, pp. xxxi–xxxiv). Later in the century, nationalistic sentiments against the inordinate French influence in the court of Frederick the Great influenced many to reject Rameau's name while they supported ideas that came directly from his works. Similar nationalistic arguments even appear in the twentieth century (Schenker 1930; in more muted forms elsewhere).

## The Transmission of Rameau's Ideas

Considering the difficulty of Rameau's writing style, the novelty of his overall perspective, the continual evolution of his ideas on some topics, the lack of any single definitive treatise that presents his theory in a unified fashion, and some problematic concepts, what is perhaps most surprising is that his ideas became as widespread as they did in a relatively short time. Some basic tenets—reduction of harmonies to triads and seventh chords, inversion of these chords, and root motions as a way of understanding musical continuity and tonal identity—must have answered a need among musicians for a new mode of explaining harmony and voice-leading, for these tenets spread rapidly and became a part of common musical parlance, even among musicians who claimed ignorance of Rameau's writings.

Probably only a few musicians read his treatises from cover to cover. Even Marpurg, who saw himself as Rameau's publicist in Germany, seems to have been unfamiliar with much of Rameau's writings. Most of Rameau's ideas probably spread more via reviews of his works and by word of mouth than by his works themselves. Sorge, for instance, who apparently did not read French (Marpurg 1759–1763, 10, p. 79), claimed that he found out that Rameau derived all dissonances from the seventh chord via a critical remark in Mattheson 1735 (Sorge 1760, Chapter 12, pars. 3–4). In sum, a few musicians studied his writings, but most knew only a few slogans or superficial features.

*Example 5-6.* Lampe 1737, Plate 2, Ex. 3

As a result, there are not that many works before the 1750s (three decades after the *Traité*) that cite Rameau directly. This is especially true in Germany, where as widely read a commentator as Lorenz Mizler (1711–1787) seems to have remained virtually unaware of Rameau as a theorist. In 1747, he included Rameau "formerly [25 years formerly!] of Clermont" among a list of organists copied from Mattheson 1739 (Mizler 1736–1754, Vol. 3, p. 531). And in 1754, Mizler merely cited D'Alembert's 1752 *Elemens* among "recent and noteworthy works" (ibid., Vol. 4, pp. 181–182). The similarly widely read Jacob Adlung (1699–1762) seems to have been aware in 1758 only of the existence of Rameau's *Traité,* but not its ideas. Yet Joseph Riepel (1709–1782), living in Regensburg, not a main musical-intellectual center in Germany, cites the *Démonstration* (1750) only two years after its publication (Riepel 1752, p. 75).

The absence of Rameau's name (except in sloganeering such as Mattheson's) does not indicate, however, that his ideas were not entering common musical parlance. The German-born John Frederick Lampe (c. 1703–1751), who arrived in London around 1725 as a bassoonist and remained as a prolific opera composer, introduced many of Rameau's basic ideas to England in a 1737 thoroughbass manual "after the most rational manner," although Lampe does not credit Rameau by name and departs from Rameau's terminology. The work is amply illustrated, with ninety-three plates for only forty-five pages of text. Lampe presents his material with a clarity of organization, language, and graphic illustration that Rameau's works so signally lacked. For instance, to explain chordal inversions, Lampe differentiates the *Natural Bass* of a chord from its *Thorough Bass:* "the latter sounds any Part or Note of a Cord as a Bass, but the Former keeps its place as Ground-Note of the Cord" (p. 18) (see Example 5-6). The illustration of inversions of a seventh chord are even more striking (see Example 5-7).

Lampe's presentation of the key system is similar to what Rameau offered in the *Generation* of the same year, but without Rameau's termi-

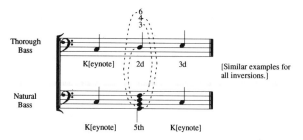

*Example 5-7.* Lampe 1737, Plate 6, Ex. 16

nology, suggesting that Lampe may have received this conception from another musician who had studied with Rameau: "Any Ground Note of a Cord may be made a Key Note," but only C major and A minor serve as models for keys "because they have the nearest related Harmonies for their principal Cords, viz. the Cord of the fourth and fifth note to the Key Note, and the Third Note of either Cord having the same Relation to the third Note in the Cord of the key" (pp. 22–24) (see Example 5-8). He thus recognizes the tonic, subdominant, and dominant as the "principal Cords," but without using the term subdominant.

In this work, as well as his composition manual published three years later, Lampe seems to disavow any knowledge of Rameau's works when he claims that his method is "something peculiar from the Way Masters have generally taught Thorough Bass" (Lampe 1737, p. vi; Lampe 1740, p. 17). But in the later work he quotes from Rameau's *Traité* (p. 46).

Another work from the 1730s, a thoroughbass treatise by the Dutch musician Quirinus van Blankenburg (1654–1739), borrows several ideas from Rameau, including the *sousdominante* (Plate dd) and subposed chords. "If in the indicated chord on C the fifth is changed to a sixth, the root-tone [*Hoofdtoon*] becomes A; furthermore if one sets the fifth and fourth together, the chord has two roots, namely F and C. Similarly, if a seventh is added there are then two root-tones C and E" (p. 178) (see Example 5-9).

The most comprehensive early work borrowing Rameau's ideas is Levens' 1743 treatise on harmony and composition. This work, praised in

*Example 5-8.* Lampe 1737, Plate 4, Ex. 9

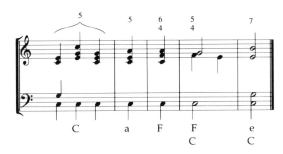

*Example 5-9.* Blankenburg 1739, Plate cc.

Gerber 1790 for its "considerable insight and practical knowledge," organizes the materials of harmony according to Rameau's approach, but departs from Rameau on some matters, uses its own terminology, and includes some interpretations of chords that do not appear in Rameau's publications until after 1743 (Krehbiel 1964 discusses speculative aspects of Levens' ideas). This suggests that Levens, whose spent his life in Marseilles, Aix-en-Provence, Vannes, and Bordeaux, but who seems never to have been around Paris, probably learned about Rameau's ideas both from his earlier publications and from other musicians who had studied with him.[11]

Rameau's influence is apparent in the categorization of chords and in the use of *basse fondamentale* to explain chord progressions. Consonant chords are either *direct* (the *accord parfait*) or *indirect* (6 and 6/4 chords), which "represent the perfect chord in their progressions [*modulation*] . . . [and] differ from the perfect chord in that they do not have the principal note in the bass" (pp. 13–14). There are three types of dissonant chords: small *(petit),* including all seventh chords (Rameau's dominants); medium *(moyen),* including the added-sixth chord (Rameau's subdominant); and large *(grand),* including ninth and eleventh chords (Rameau's subposed chords).

Chord progressions are discussed in terms of the *basse fondamentale* (Chapters 10–12), the characteristic dissonances of a seventh on dominants and an added sixth on subdominants (Chapter 6), major and minor dissonances (Chapter 6), and cadences (Chapter 17). Levens does not use *double emploi* but does differentiate the added-sixth chord on scale-step

11. The copy of the *Abregé* in the New York Public Library is bound together with an eight-page manuscript of music paper entitled, on its second leaf, "principes de compositions de Mr Rameau." The topics covered are intervals and their inversion, chord types, fundamental bass, rules of fundamental-bass progression, inversions, cadences, licenses, and various progressions in numerous keys (through D♯ major!). Although it summarizes Rameau's ideas, the manuscript uses Levens' terminology (*petits* and *moyens* dissonances on fol. 1ʳ).

4 progressing to the tonic from the same notes progressing to the dominant as a seventh chord (pp. 17–18).

An interesting practical application of fundamental bass rules appears in Chapter 12 on "more extended rules of composition." Levens treats each scale step in turn, discussing each chord type that could occur and how that chord would function in a fundamental-bass progression. Scale-step 1, for instance, can support nine possible harmonies:

1. A perfect chord, moving as the fundamental bass permits.
2. A seventh chord, if the fundamental bass permits resolution of the seventh.
3. An added-sixth chord, if the fundamental bass permits resolution of the sixth.
4. A 6/4 chord, as a subdominant chord .
5. A 7/4/2 chord, as a dominant over the tonic bass between two tonic chords.
6. A 6/4/2 chord, as a subdominant over the tonic bass between two tonic chords.
7. A 9/4 chord, as a suspension between a dominant and its tonic resolution.
8. A 5/4 chord, a suspension after a subdominant or dominant.
9. A 6/4/2 chord, a suspension after a tonic and before a dominant. Note that Levens differentiates this chord from number 6. Number 6 functions as an added-sixth chord, while number 9 functions as a seventh chord.

This is a discussion comparable to that in many later harmony texts. There is nothing quite so well organized in any of Rameau's published works.

Another work that indicates Rameau's influence, although it contains no material derived from Rameau's works, was published in Paris a year before Levens' treatise. *La musique pratique et theorique, réduite à ses principes naturels* (1742) by Charles Antoine Vion is a primer in musical rudiments that does not progress to the study of harmony. Near the end, Vion recommends that students interested in further study consult the "excellent *Traité de l'Harmonie,* composed by M. Rameau, which will not be difficult for them . . . [and] which will serve them as an inexhaustible source of everything that pleases the ear and the eye" (p. 58). Vion recommends only one other book, Brossard's 1703 *Dictionnaire,* in which students will find "advanced and curious instructions" (ibid.).

A further French work of the 1740s citing Rameau is the *Harmonie theorico-pratique* (1746) by Charles Blainville (c. 1710–c. 1777). Part 1 of Blainville's work is a brief but thorough summary of Rameau's ideas, citing triads, seventh chords, and their inversions as the sole chord types, and explaining fundamental bass, the various types of cadences, and chords by subposition. The remaining parts of the work form a traditional presentation of counterpoint, proceeding from simple intervals in two parts through added figurations, fugues, key changes, and even enharmonic changes of diminished sevenths and other chords. Despite his promise "to reconcile the modern theory of M. Rameau with the old and common practice" (p. ii), Blainville makes no further reference to Rameau in the later parts of the manual. Less than a decade later, he published a criticism of Rameau's theories and compositions, claiming that traditional counterpoint produced better compositions than Rameau's theory.

These works and others published in the 1740s and early 1750s (Sorge 1745–1747 and Hahn 1751, discussed in Chapter 6) show the extent to which Rameau's ideas had spread beyond his works and his direct influence, even before D'Alembert's and Marpurg's popularizations. As shown in Chapters 6 through 9, many of Rameau's ideas were so widely known and accepted by the 1750s that musicians no longer associated them with Rameau. They were simply common musical knowledge.

## Summary

Rameau took the study of harmony, the least prominent of the three theoretical traditions inherited from the seventeenth century, and placed it at the center of music-theoretic discourse, where it has remained to the present time. Rameau's harmonic perspective provided solutions to problems of dissonance treatment that Fux despaired of explaining and that thoroughbass theorists dealt with only by inventing rule after rule and exception after exception.

Likewise, Rameau changed chord classification forever. For him there are two types of chords: the triad and the seventh chord (which by subposition generates the ninth and eleventh chords, and by reinterpretation generates the added-sixth chord). Every harmony is either an arrangement of one of these or contains melodic ornamentation. Generations of theorists continued to argue over how many chord types there are, whether the added-sixth chord is a separate chord type, and even whether the seventh chord is a harmonic entity. But Rameau's types remained the point of departure. No theorist since Rameau's death has argued for a return to the seventy or more different chord types listed in thoroughbass manuals. And no theorist has argued that chordal inversions were not related to one another.

Some theorists believed that Rameau had simply demonstrated that harmonic units were to be constructed in thirds and proceeded to enumerate all sorts of ninth, eleventh, and thirteenth chords. By doing so, they forgot that Rameau's motivation for subposed ninth and eleventh chords is to provide a speculative explanation for all dissonance resolutions alongside the linear understanding of suspensions. Certainly the most absurd application of a rule connected to Rameau's suposed chords occurred around 1900, when a Viennese society, refusing to premiere Arnold Schoenberg's *Verklärte Nacht* (1899), explained that they could not present the work because it contains an inverted ninth chord—quite an impossibility according to the censor's perspective (Schoenberg 1946, p. 131).

In addition to clarifying dissonance resolutions and altering chord classifications, Rameau's harmonic perspective raises issues that had been considered only peripherally, if at all, by earlier theory. Primary among these is what is to be considered the expression of a single harmony. In thoroughbass theory, as soon as the figures change, theorists generally spoke of a new harmony. In some cases, Rameau maintains a thoroughbass perspective, arguing that what modern theory considers a single harmony is in fact more than one harmony (a suspension and its resolution when treated as a subposed chord and a chord of resolution). Yet in other instances, he explains how what others call two or more harmonies is really only one (such as a cadential 6/4 resolving to a dominant seventh as an expression only of the dominant). His recommendation that the basso continuo generally be conjunct during a phrase before literally following the fundamental bass at the cadence, his treatment of separate levels of key change, and his long search for a basis for harmonic progressions—these and other aspects of his thinking raise questions that have been recast in the twentieth century in the terminology of scale-step (*Stufe*) and prolongation.

With his new harmonic perspective, Rameau articulated new questions concerning musical continuity. For Rameau, harmonic motion continues until reaching a tonic—since dissonance creates the need for resolution, Rameau equates nontonic status with dissonance, arguing that nontonics must carry real or implied dissonances. This dichotomy (consonant tonic versus dissonant nontonic) is certainly too simplistic to stand up to much scrutiny—indeed, Rameau's unconvincing insistence that all nontonic harmonies have either actual or implied dissonances or chromaticism is all that is needed to demolish his argument. But he was the first to raise the issue at all.

The speculative side of Rameau's theories also had its consequences. Rameau removed music theory from mathematical manipulation and made its focus the scientific study of sound, its propagation, and its reception by humans. His own attempts to explain tonal harmonic practices via scientific investigation did not lead to widely accepted answers—they were largely ignored by practical musicians and were deemed an extravagant and ultimately futile endeavor by scientists. But his attempts prompted others, amateur musicians and professionals alike, to seek in the relationship between musical phenomena and acoustics the models for the musical syntax they preferred. None of these theorists has come up with a satisfactory origin of the minor triad, of the seventh chord, of harmonic progression, or of a host of other issues. Nowadays, following the demise of common-practice tonality as the sole recognized musical language, all such naturalistic investigations seem suspect, having been replaced by psychological modeling, information theory, and other approaches. But Rameau's interest in this topic was not at all out of line with other speculative theorists of the past. And his invocation of the major triad as a "chord of nature" is reflected in many an eighteenth-century and nineteenth-century piece, Beethoven's *Pastorale Symphony* being one obvious example.

In sum, Rameau's ideas were the single greatest influence on harmony theory for following generations. Just as much of late-sixteenth-century and seventeenth-century theory can be understood only in terms of Zarlino, Rameau's theories dominate both his own century and the following ones. There is hardly an idea in later eighteenth-century, nineteenth-century, or much twentieth-century harmonic theory that does not have its origin in Rameau's works. And not until Schenker does a theorist articulate a significantly different musical perspective.

# CHAPTER SIX

# Mattheson and the Study
# of Melody

*It is not enough to avoid what is bad; one must also bring forth what is good, expressive, and beautiful. Not everything in composition is accomplished by means of tidiness and correctness . . . In sum, more should always be judged by an expressive melody than by the artistic harmony that is obedient to it.*

*Mattheson 1725, pp. 54–55*

## Johann Mattheson as Theorist

The preceding chapters survey the origins of eighteenth-century concepts and three principal theoretical traditions of the first half of the century: species counterpoint, thoroughbass, and the theory of harmony. These may be three distinct approaches to musical structure, but they are by no means the only ones of the time. Many composition treatises, both manuscript (Walther 1708, Scheibe c. 1730) and published (Masson 1699), do not hew to a single approach. Instead, they utilize elements of several approaches: some counterpoint (interval successions, dissonance resolution), some harmony (triads and other chord types), some thoroughbass (especially the content of rules for unfigured basses), imitation and fugue, and other topics. What these manuals may lack in theoretical consistency they often offset by presenting practical experience accumulated over generations.

Consider one instance in the manuscript composition treatise that the composer and music-lexicographer Johann Gottfried Walther (1684–1748) wrote in 1708. As he introduces their notation, Walther cites five important uses for rests: "1. To allow singers to breathe; and to allow instrumentalists, especially wind players, to rest. 2. To differentiate the text. 3. To form fugues [presumably because rests in some voices allow a fugal exposition to occur]. 4. To avoid forbidden intervals. 5. To arouse the attention of the listener" (p. 28). This list is a paradigm of systematic inconsistency in that each item belongs to an entirely different domain of musical knowledge. Yet each illuminates a great deal of practical information. One can easily imagine a composition teacher using any one of them to launch a detailed discussion of a crucial aspect of compositional craft: instrumentation and timbral variety, the relation of textual structure to what we call musical form, textural variety, the rules of counterpoint, and the relation between music and rhetoric. Some of these topics hardly appear in works more singlemindedly devoted to any one of the three main traditions.

Of all the writers on music during the first half of the eighteenth century, the one whose works best exemplify this type of presentation that eschews the metholodogies of the three traditions of counterpoint, thoroughbass, and harmony is Johann Mattheson (1681–1764), theorist and composer in Hamburg. He was one of the most prolific writers on music in the eighteenth century, publishing treatises, manuals, journals, and biographies from the 1710s through the 1750s.

Despite his wide-ranging publications, Mattheson is not a significant figure in species counterpoint, thoroughbass, or harmonic theory. He thought well of Fux's *Gradus* but does not include anything resembling species counterpoint in his encyclopedic *Der vollkommene Capellmeister* (1739)—instead he borrows Christoph Bernhard's atomistic treatment of simple counterpoint. Although he published two thoroughbass manuals (Mattheson 1719/1731 and 1735), he regarded thoroughbass mostly as a mechanical task for performers. His efforts do not add anything substantial to thoroughbass theory, and his examples have been criticized for their "extraordinarily slovenly and incorrect" voice leadings (Arnold 1931, p. 281). Finally, though he knew Rameau's *Traité*, he had little interest in harmonic theory. His lifelong polemic against Rameau ignores almost all the features of Rameau's theories, instead railing repeatedly against Rameau's statement that harmony is the source of melody and criticizing Rameau for his links to the Jesuits.

In fact, on the topics that lie at the heart of these three theoretical traditions, Mattheson's discussions are sometimes only barely respectable. His remarks on voice leading and harmony contain a host of peculiar and extravagant statements. He argues that changing the size of an interval does not affect its status as a consonance and proceeds to include augmented and diminished thirds, fifths, sixths, and octaves among the consonances. With typical bombast and lack of explanation, he asserts that the diminished fifth "does far more consonant service for harmony than the perfect fifth" (Mattheson 1739, Part 3, Chapter 3, par. 4). And since the perfect fifth can be treated as a suspension in a 6/5 chord, he argues

*Example 6-1.* Mattheson 1739, Part 3, Chapter 7, par. 28

that it is therefore equivalent to the diminished fifth in quality (Part 3, Chapter 6). He includes an example of the diminished sixth, noting that "one treats it almost exactly the same as the ordinary minor one when a fifth follows" (see Example 6-1).

Concerning dissonances, Mattheson opposes the position held by virtually every other theorist of his and earlier ages. He rejects the notion that in a dissonant configuration one or more parts create dissonance against a consonant substructure, asserting instead that both parts are dissonant (Part 3, Chapter 10). With such a perspective, he has great difficulty specifying systematically which note should resolve and how that resolution must take place. He has problems explaining other resolutions as well, offering Example 6-2 to show how a seventh "resolves" to a diminished fourth. He also notes that the C is an accented passing tone *(Note Cambiate),* failing to realize that this implies either a resolution of D to B or an unresolved D.

To be sure, there are other instances where Mattheson shows a solid understanding of voice leading. In Example 6-3, for instance, he demonstrates that a succession of a seventh to an augmented fourth can arise as an elaboration of 7–6.

His writings concerning harmony and voice leading also suffer from confusing combinations of different materials within a single discussion. For instance, when he discusses how to use perfect and imperfect consonances, he cites various authorities, among them Fux's four rules (Mattheson 1739, Part 3, Chapter 3, par. 21). But he also allows occasional parallel fifths and octaves and recommends parallel octaves when cello and bass

*Example 6-2.* Mattheson 1739, Part 3, Chapter 13, par. 8

Compositional Theory in the Eighteenth Century

*Example 6-3.* Mattheson 1739, Part 3, Chapter 13, par. 11

play together or when flutes double a melody (par. 35). In another passage, he gives the good advice to use more imperfect than perfect consonances and to avoid frequent unisons and octaves in writing for few voices. He then argues that the second harmonization in Example 6-4 is better than the first despite the opening octave.

Surely a reader to whom this material was new would be confused. Fux's four rules apply to independent parts, while doubling basses or melodies concerns instrumentation. Occasional parallels between voices may be excusable when relatively covered, but that advice hardly belongs in a discussion of elementary counterpoint. And an adequate explanation of the superiority of the second alternative in Example 6-4 would deal with its expression of the basic harmonies of the key, not how it uses perfect or imperfect consonances.

## The Study of Melody

If Mattheson is somewhat less than authoritative on harmony and voice leading, he is nevertheless an important theorist because his works include the first serious acknowledgement of the central role of melody in the newer musical styles emerging in the 1720s and 1730s. Melody was a central concern to him throughout his life. Even before he was irritated

*Example 6-4.* Mattheson 1739, Part 3, Chapter 3, par. 43

by Rameau's assertion that the source of melody resides in harmony, he complained:

> As a rule, we pay far too little attention to the science of melody, and mix almost everything together under the science of harmony. Similarly, we consider it unimportant that those who wish to compose must be thoroughly acquainted with the melodic science as the first part of composition: thus, we always regard the melodic science as something unimportant or totally worthless, and thus do not know, understand, or consider that this noblest and most pre-eminent part [of music] is not only the true basis of all the others, but is also certainly and truthfully the only solid essence by which the emotions can be moved . . . It truly requires more knowledge to construct a single monody that will force its way into one's heart than to concoct a thousand canons. But thus far no books or precepts have taught this knowledge. (Mattheson 1722, pp. 261–262)

The word *monody* in the penultimate sentence refers not to the *seconda pratica* but to a formulation of the German theorist Wolfgang Caspar Printz (1641–1717). Printz had suggested two ways to compose: the *monodic* method in which one wrote a single part and then added others to it, and the *polyodic* method in which all the parts were worked out simultaneously. Printz's distinction is a late reflection of the shift from successive composition of voices to simultaneous composition during the fifteenth and sixteenth centuries. Eighteenth-century musicians reinterpreted Printz's terms so that the monodic method meant composing the main melodic part first, and the polyodic method meant working out the entire texture at once, as in the approach to composing via thoroughbass offered by Friderich Erhard Niedt (c. 1674–1708). Mattheson must have been torn between the two methods. He penned this lament over the absence of a text on melody only shortly after having edited and overseen the posthumous publication of Niedt's thoroughbass method, which is the epitome of a polyodic approach to composition.

Mattheson's most comprehensive discussion of melody appears in Part 2 of *Der vollkommene Capellmeister*, in large part a reworking of materials in his *Kern melodischer Wissenschaft* (1737). There are partial discussions and occasional remarks in works by earlier theorists that cover similar materials. But the scope of Mattheson's presentation is unprecedented.

He argues against teaching beginners to compose via either counterpoint or thoroughbass, instead insisting that students should begin their studies by composing complete melodies, first vocal, then instrumental. Only after melodic writing is mastered should the beginner tackle harmonic issues in two-voiced pieces (Part 1, Chapter 1).

In Part 2, Chapter 4, Mattheson deals with melodic invention, essentially what we refer to as *motives*. To stimulate the invention of motives, he suggests elaborating a chorale (par. 10) or using melodic patterns from other compositions (par. 15). The bulk of the chapter explains how to manipulate these motives via rhythmic changes, permutation, inversion, repetition, and transposition.

The whole approach is based on the premise that melodic motives need not be invented anew for every composition. For Mattheson and many of his contemporaries, a new composition will always contain something old and something new. (Ratner 1980, Part 1, discusses this issue as an attribute of the Classic style in general.) Some writers called such motives common to many pieces "figures" *(figurae)* or "manners" *(Manieren)*. Long lists of them were common in seventeenth-century works, especially those dealing with vocal improvisation (such as Herbst 1642 and 1653). The patterns included trills, mordents, and simple dissonances (passing tones and neighbors) as well as more elaborate passages, formulas for recitatives (as in Fux 1725), and so forth. Patterns introduced by one author for one purpose often ended up in another works being applied quite differently. For instance, many of Bernhard's complex dissonant figures explaining the basis of *seconda pratica* dissonances turn up in the *Trifolium musicale* (1691) of Johann Christoph Stierlein (?–1693) in a discussion of vocal improvisation. It was from Stierlein's presentation that Walther borrowed some of these figures for his *Lexicon* (Lester 1990). Theorists throughout the eighteenth century continued to explain melodic construction according to figures (as in Albrechtsberger 1790, p. 18; the use of figures in the melodic theories of Riepel and Koch is discussed in Chapters 10 and 11).

Having introduced motives and their manipulation, Mattheson in Chapter 5 berates Rameau for saying "it is almost impossible to give definite rules for the use of melody" (Rameau 1722, Book 2, Chapter 20). Mattheson enumerates four features that contribute to a good melody: facility, clarity, flow, and charm. To possess *facility*, a melody must have something with which almost everyone is familiar. It follows nature and avoids forced progressions and great artifice or else hides these features well. *Clarity* results from projecting a single passion, following the accent of the words (if present), avoiding too much embellishment, and, in general, noble simplicity. *Flow* arises when there are no interruptions. And *charm* arises from using more steps than large skips, and so forth. Variety too is important, and Mattheson urges avoiding too many successive semitones, steps, thirds of one kind, and the like. The remainder of this long chapter offers numerous examples of each point. Mattheson urges composers to keep a collection of good and poor melodies by others so they will know what to emulate and what to avoid (much as schoolboys studying rhetoric at the time were urged to keep collections of topics, cogent phrases, and the like).

Chapter 6 deals with melodic rhythm. Mattheson adopts the approach outlined in Niedt 1706 (which Mattheson revised for a second edition in 1721). Niedt applies variations to a thoroughbass realization, turning it into various types of dances. Mattheson applies this method to melody alone, using a simple chorale-like melody as the basis of his variants. He cites twenty-four types of poetic feet, beginning with those containing two syllables: the spondee (− − or two half notes), the pyrrhic (⏑⏑ or two eighth notes), the iamb (⏑ − or quarter-half or eighth-quarter), and the trochee (− ⏑ or half-quarter). He illustrates melodies with one pattern and with several patterns. Then he adds poetic feet with three and four syllables.

All these discussions are organized in the manner of contemporaneous compositional manuals. Much as thoroughbass and counterpoint manuals offer innumerable voice leadings patterns, Mattheson suggests many possibilities but gives little if any advice on how to use them. There are no general rules. But much as a comprehensive thoroughbass manual suggests a vast range of voice-leading possibilities for exploration, doubtless Mattheson's extensive discussions and copious examples awakened many readers' imaginations.

Having explained the properties of melodies, Mattheson turns to phrasing in Chapter 9. He compares music to language. Just as language has paragraphs subdivided into phrases and subphrases, musical rhetoric features sentences or their subdivisions that add up to a whole structure (par. 5). The end of a musical paragraph requires a full close; the end of a sentence a lesser but still affirmative close (par. 14), and so forth. Much of this discussion concerns vocal music, and Mattheson frequently refers to the text for guidance in composition: commas in the text may be set as longer notes but without a cadential articulation (pars. 28 and 29); a semicolon in the text frequently implies separate thoughts, which can be expressed by a change to a related key, such as A minor to C major; greater textual contrasts require motion to more distant keys.

Although Mattheson's discussions are more comprehensive than any others of the time, he was not the first to treat some of these topics. Among his predecessors are Printz, who discusses extensively the cadential orientation of phrases (Printz 1676, Part 1, Chapter 8), Fux, who suggests various possibilities for setting a variety of punctuations in recitatives (translation in Lester 1989, pp. 205–209), and Niedt (1717, Chapter 6).

Mattheson applies notions associated with language and rhetoric to explain many of these points: the use of figures, the discussion of rhythm via poetic feet, the modeling of cadences on punctuation, and the suggestion to use punctuation in a text to determine the cadences. Mattheson also invokes rhetoric to describe the creative process in general, likening the various stages of composing to the *Dispositio, Elaboratio,* and *Decoratio* of an oration (Part 2, Chapter 14, par. 1).

Finally, he relates the parts of a completed composition to those of an oration: the *exordium* (introduction), *narratio* (report), *propositio* (discourse), *confirmatio* (corroboration by others), *confutatio* (refutation of opposing points of view), and *peroratio* (conclusion) (par. 4). To illustrate this, he applies these labels to an aria by Benedetto Marcello (1686–1739) (pars. 14–22; discussed in Dahlhaus 1989, pp. 224–226). Mattheson's application of these labels suggests contrasting attitudes toward the roles of themes in what we refer to as musical form. When he calls a contrasting theme a *confutatio* and a thematic return a *confirmatio,* he suggest a defining role for thematic statement and contrast. But elsewhere, his labels seem to defy such a role. He calls the opening ritornello the *exordium* and the opening vocal statement the *narratio,* which implies that they relate as prelude and statement. This contradicts the thematic content, which suggests that the ritornello, which is heard first, is the source of the motives developed at the vocal entry. On the other hand, these labels support the sense that the ritornello merely prepares for the important music when the voice enters. What is perhaps most interesting about his analysis is that Mattheson does not refer to the text—in effect, he treats the aria as if it were an instrumental piece with a featured solo part.

Mattheson's subdivision of a musical work according to the sections of an argumentative oration—like a much earlier analysis by Joachim Burmeister (1564–1629) that applies the sections of an oration as well as rhetorical figures to a motet by Lassus (Burmeister 1606, English translation and commentary in Palisca 1972b)—seems more Procrustean than illuminating to many modern scholars. But it may well be that such rhetorical parsings were more meaningful to earlier musicians than they are to us. In the eighteenth century, familiarity with classical rhetoric was as much a part of an educated person's background as arithmetic is today. Among other early-eighteenth-century musicians who make use of rhetorical devices is Heinichen when he advises composers on how to invent musical figures (Buelow 1966b; general discussion of rhetoric in Buelow 1980a).

Mattheson also uses rhetoric to impart sound musical advice in more traditional terms, as when he notes "the clever advice of the orators in offering the strongest points first; then the weaker ones in the middle; and, finally, convincing conclusions. That certainly seems to be the sort of trick which a musician can use" (par. 25). Similarly practical advice to composers also appears elsewhere. He urges the frequent use of imitation to enliven the texture of a piece because "a discourse pretty soon induces sleepiness," whereas imitation is akin to friendly controversy, debate, objections, and responses (Part 3, Chapter 15, par. 3). Yet Mattheson is concerned that use of imitation might detract from the quality of the melody. Even imitative textures should express a specific passion, maintain a variety of rhythms, and contain good melodies (Chapter 16).

He draws on all this advice in a demonstration of how to compose a

*Example 6-5.* Mattheson 1739, Part 3, Chapter 16, par. 5

*Example 6-6.* Mattheson, 1739, Part 3, Chapter 16, par. 6

two-voiced piece (Part 3, Chapter 16). A novice might borrow a bass from a composition and set a new melody to it, as in Example 6-5. Although not specified here, Mattheson's earlier advice on imperfect consonances, on transposition of motives, on repetitions of rhythms, and on maintaining variety are evident. Mattheson complains that this version lacks a specific character and suggests that imitation might provide a remedy (see Example 6-6). The reason that the imitation is so easily accomplished here is that the opening motive in the right hand in Example 6-5 is a diminution of the opening of the bass part—Mattheson does not make this point in connection with this example, but a careful reader would have noted this after previous discussions of how to draw motives out of chorale melodies.

In essence, such examples and their discussion illustrate the role played by rhythmic and motivic activity in creating successful musical continuity—aspects of musical structure that had gone unnoted by most earlier writers. Mattheson returns to this topic in Chapter 23 on double fugue (fugue with a recurring countersubject), noting that in a successful fugue there must be rhythmic variety and that the beginnings and endings of melodic and rhythmic segments in different voices must be kept separate from one another. He comments on fugues by Johann Kuhnau (1660–1722), who was Heinichen's teacher, J. S. Bach's predecessor at the Thomaskirche in Leipzig, and the author of a manuscript treatise on composition (described in Hahn 1957). He begins with a hypothetical exposition by a novice on a subject by Kuhnau (see Example 6-7). Among the problems Mattheson cites are the asterisked rest, the "absurd break at the end of measure 4," and the rhythmic similarity of the voices. These are emended as shown in Example 6-8. Problems remain: there is still no

Compositional Theory in the Eighteenth Century

"sense of cohesion" at the end of measure 2, there are too many thirds and no contrary motion, the rhythmic uniformity is boring, the line lacks direction, and there are no prominent dissonances. Kuhnau's version is in Example 6-9. Mattheson praises the interchange of thirds and sixths and contrary motion in measure 3, the suspensions in measures 4 and 5, the avoided cadence in measure 5, and the rhythmic variety both within and between voices. There is no other comparably extensive discussion of textural, contrapuntal, melodic, and rhythmic issues in any earlier work (not even in the study of fugue in Fux's *Gradus*).

Although *Der vollkommene Capellmeister* was too comprehensive to be a practical text for beginners, its sheer volume and valuable perspectives made it useful for experienced musicians. Haydn apparently worked on it with the same diligence he applied to Fux's *Gradus* (Pohl 1875, 1, p. 175). And Beethoven owned the treatise, on several occasions copied out ex-

*Example 6-7.* Mattheson 1739, Part 3, Chapter 23, par. 40

*Example 6-8.* Mattheson, 1739, Part 3, Chapter 23, par. 42

*Example 6-9.* Mattheson 1739, Part 3, Chapter 23, par. 44. In Mattheson 1739, the opening subject appears erroneously in the soprano, not the alto part.

amples of particular problems and worked on them, and discussed the work in later years (Kramer 1975, pp. 92–99).

The emphasis Mattheson places on melodic structure, phrasing, and cadential articulations became ever more important to theorists in the latter part of the eighteenth century. Joseph Riepel (1709–1782), who published the first part of a composition treatise stressing melody thirteen years after Mattheson's *Vollkommene Capellmeister,* acknowledged Mattheson's contribution to the study of melody. But Mattheson was not entirely alone in emphasizing these aspects in the 1730s. For instance, Walther's 1732 *Lexicon* occasionally raises issues of melodic structure, most prominently when he specifies some of the necessary characteristics of various dances. The gavotte is "a dance and dance-song [*Tanz-Lied*] consisting of two reprises [sections bounded by repeat signs] of which the first has 4 measures, the second however commonly eight measures in common time . . . The first reprise should not end in the key in which the gavotte begins but should conclude on the third or fifth."

Johann Adolph Scheibe (1708–1776) applies similar terms to larger constructions. An overture, for instance, has three parts. The first part ends on the dominant (or on the third degree in minor). The fugal second part, in which the phrases flow into one another, may end on the tonic. But it is even more effective when the final cadence has some striking effect, such as a strong dissonance. The last part is like the first but only has cadences in the tonic (Scheibe 1737–1740, pp. 667–674).


## Mattheson as Publicist

In addition to being the first theorist to attempt a comprehensive approach to melody and texture, Mattheson is also important for propagating newer musical ideas and in general acting as a commentator on numerous musical topics. Like his Age of Enlightenment colleagues, Mattheson believed that the inherited musical knowledge of his age was very much in need of a thorough housecleaning (to use his metaphor). His earlier works, especially "The Newly-Published *Orchestre*" (*Das neu-eröffnete Orchestre*) of 1713, its two sequels published in 1717 and 1721 to respond to critics, and the journal *Critica musica* (collected volumes in 1722 and 1725), are marked by provocative presentations of new ideas along with harsh criticisms of traditional notions. These pioneering efforts, especially his journal, were a model for several later writers: the *Musikalische Bibliothek* (issued irregularly from 1736–1754) by Lorenz Mizler (1711–1778), *Der critische Musicus* (1737–1740) by Scheibe, and the several journals of the 1740s-1770s published by Friedrich Wilhelm Marpurg (1718–1795), as well as the more permanent journals and other one-editor publications later in the century.

Mattheson's prose style is often quite abrasive and even crass. In a letter exchange with Fux, he was enraged at Fux's denigrating remark that "Hamburg is not the entire musical world" and retorted, "People also live behind the mountains [Alps]. Here and there in Germany as well as in England (not to mention France) a small but rich and solid musical culture emerges far and wide, which 'the wicked crowd of the Tuscan Street' [a Horatian haunt of prostitutes and their customers] has never been able to find on the map of Castrato-Land" (Lester 1977, p. 55). Elsewhere he refers to Glarean as "a learned buffoon [*Pickelhering*] from Glaris, more skilled at riding a jackass into the lecture hall and playing other tricks than at writing something of excellence on music" (Mattheson 1739, Part 1, Chapter 9, par. 31). (In this context, his rebukes of Rameau seem mild indeed.) Such extravagant remarks often miss the mark as reasoned arguments. But they certainly lend his writings an exuberance largely absent from more modern music theory and scholarly disputes. And they provoked those whose views he criticized to publish rebuttals, bringing into print various controversies that might otherwise have remained unpublished. Besides being informative for modern scholars, these disputes probably brought alternative ideas to many German musicians who might not otherwise have been confronted with them.

For instance, in the *Neu-eröffnete Orchestre* Mattheson urges numerous reforms, among them replacing the modes with the twenty-four major and minor keys—he was only the second German musician (after Heinichen 1711) to publish all twenty-four—and doing away with six-syllable solmization involving hexachordal mutation. The Erfurt organist Johann Heinrich Buttstett (1666–1727) was sufficiently outraged to respond with *Ut mi sol, re fa la, Tota Musica et harmonia aeterna* (c. 1715). Buttstett favored the church modes over the major-minor keys, supported six-syllable solmization, and rejected other modern notions, citing ancient authorities like Boethius and Guido D'Arezzo to support his opinions on a host of matters.

Mattheson's response in "The *Orchestre* Defended" (1717) is as spirited as its subtitle: "*Todte (nicht tota) Musica*" ("Dead music, not all music"). Secretary to the British ambassador in Hamburg and a devotee of the British legal system, Mattheson dedicated his response to a jury of thirteen musicians who were to judge the issue. He published the letters he received from the dedicatees in 1725 under the heading "The *Orchestre*-Chancellery, or testimonies, letters, declarations, investigations, etc., by the former judges in the *Orchestre* trial" (pp. 179–288). Among the respondants was Fux, the only one to decline the honor of the dedication. Like Buttstett, Fux rejected major-minor keys and favored six-syllable solmization, showing that such tenets were held in the Catholic, Italian-oriented musical culture of the south as well as in the Lutheran north.

A full history of the transition from modal thinking and terminology to major-minor is complex, affecting the seventeenth century more than the eighteenth. But aspects of modal thinking persisted well past 1700, especially in German-speaking areas. Besides those writers like Buttstett and Fux, who reject major and minor keys outright, others, including Andreas Werckmeister (1645–1706) and Walther, worry that abandoning the modes might entail losing valuable terminology and concepts. Modal theories in their many forms had at one time or another encompassed not only the recognition of the final of a piece and its attendant scale, but also such apparently unrelated notions as modulatory possibilities (via lists of the cadence points appropriate to each mode) and spacing of voices in a polyphonic texture (by using plagal and authentic modes in adjacent voices). Lutheran Protestant musicians also express concern that without the modes, chorales might be debased. As late as the 1770s, Johann Kirnberger (1721–1783) is troubled by the growing ignorance of modal harmony and the resulting trivial treatment of chorale melodies in major-minor harmonizations (Kirnberger 1771–1779, Vol. 2, p. 47).

In addition to lingering modal thinking among these theorists, even those writers who present twenty-four keys around the turn of the eighteenth century sometimes tend to treat them in ways that reflect modal categorizations as much as the modern sense of major and minor. For instance, the French mathematician Ozanam (1640–1717), apparently the first to list all twenty-four keys in musical notation (Ozanam 1691, p. 660), differentiates the twenty-four keys into three categories according to the old hexachords: the "natural modes" containing only white notes and B♭, the "chromatic natural modes" built on white notes or B♭ with black notes in their scales, and the "transposed modes" built on black notes. Mattheson in 1713 still divides the twenty-four keys into three groups of eight, the first of which are a traditional listing of keys evolved from the church modes (pp. 60–62), although other theorists had presented all twenty-four keys as equally original (Janowka 1701, Brossard 1703, Frère 1706, and Heinichen 1711).

Early-eighteenth-century writers who accept major and minor keys also disagree on the proper scale and signature of the minor mode. The A-mode, the D-mode, what we call the melodic minor scale, and what we call the harmonic minor scale were all proposed. Janowka 1701 argues for the A-mode because using the D-mode requires many extra accidentals during a piece (pp. 290–293). Campion 1716 recognizes what we call the separate ascending and descending forms of the melodic minor scale (p. 13), which causes him to advocate D-mode signatures because he sees just as little reason to incorporate the lowered sixth degree into the signature as to incorporate the raised seventh. And Brossard 1703 advocates what we call the harmonic minor scale because he regards the raised

*Example 6-10.* Albrechtsberger 1790, p. 1

seventh and lowered sixth degrees as the primary components of chords (article *Modo*).

The maintenance of many aspects of modal theory, especially in Germany, through much of the eighteenth century is the subject of *Between Modes and Keys: German Theory 1592–1802* by the present author. The reader is urged to consult that work (Lester 1989) for a more thorough consideration of eighteenth-century modal theory.

The ideas expressed by Buttstett and Fux, as well as those of Franz Xaver Anton Murschhauser (1663–1738), author of a 1721 treatise designed "to bring a little more light to the excellent Herr Mattheson," and others need not be viewed solely as outmoded notions on their way to extinction. These and other tenets help give us a more rounded picture of the musical ideas circulating at the time. For instance, many German-speaking eighteenth-century musicians quite probably learned their musical ABCs while they were choirboys, using *Lateinschul* manuals whose contents had remained relatively unchanged since the mid-sixteenth century. The last extant edition of one of these works, the *Breviarium musicum* by Johann Quirsfeld (1642–1686), was published in Dresden in 1717, where Heinichen had just arrived. Quirsfeld's work is quite similar in content to the 1548 *Compendiolum musicae pro incipientibus* by Heinrich Faber (?–1552), teaching the basics of pitch notation, mensural notation, solmization, and the church modes (absent from Faber 1548, but included in many derivative works).[1] It bears repeating here that Haydn, as a choirboy in St. Stephens in Vienna while Fux was still its musical director, quite probably learned six-syllable solmization with hexachordal mutation.

Six-syllable solmization persisted at least through the 1790 composition manual by Johann Georg Albrechtsberger (1736–1809), which presents the major and minor scales on its opening page with syllables as shown in Example 6-10. In both major-scale syllabifications, the tonic appears as *do* and *fa*; and in the upper syllabification, *do* denotes both the tonic and the dominant. In the minor scale, *re* is used for both the tonic and the raised form of scale-step 6. It gives one pause to realize that Beethoven,

1. The most complete studies of these *Lateinschul* manuals are Preussner 1924 and Allerup 1931. Lester 1989, pp. 68–76, surveys their discussions of modes.

who worked from this text when he studied with Albrechtsberger only a couple of years later, was familiar with a solmization system in which the tonic of a key could appear with more than one syllable, and in which the syllable denoting the tonic could also denote another scale degree. Modern, seven-syllable solmization methods, whether based on fixed or movable *do,* always link the tonic with a single syllable in a passage within a single key.

In evaluating the role of such tenets in the conceptual world of the time it is important to remember that their absence from other works may not necessarily indicate their absence from common musical parlance. When Mattheson challenged the strength of Fux's advocacy of six-syllable solmization, asking why Fux had never written about it, Fux responded: "I have never had any reason to doubt the usefulness of this invention, and have never thought to write about it" (Lester 1977, p. 51).

## Nature, Mathematics, and Science

Like his Enlightenment colleagues elsewhere, Mattheson exalts Nature and often uses mathematics and reason to defend his positions. There are both similarities and differences in the way he applies these concepts and the way Rameau applies them. Like Rameau, Mattheson is aware of the intervals that arise on a natural horn (Mattheson 1739, Part 1, Chapter 7, par. 72) and recommends reading the works of Sauveur (Part 1, Chapter 3, par. 27). But he does not mention harmonic resonance. Also like Rameau, Mattheson is convinced that since music is natural, the hearing of the musically uneducated can serve as proof for his arguments. For instance, he argues that scalar differences between the Mixolydian and Ionian modes are unessential because a hypothetical Thuringian peasant would not be able to hear the difference between the lowered and raised forms of scale-step 7 (Mattheson 1717, p. 82). But consistency is not his strongest suit; elsewhere he argues that barely audible microtonal variants in tuning are important in differentiating one key from another (Lester 1977, pp. 48–49 and 60).

Unlike Rameau, Mattheson will have nothing to do with systematization that proceeds from first principles such as resonance or Nature to create a harmonic theory. He recognizes that "Nature (the force present in every thing which, on God's command, produces and sustains every thing) produces sound and all its proportions." These proportions are indispensible, for mathematics is a "diligent, industrious aid, and a useful, indefatigable, and noble servant." But mathematics is not the "heart and soul of music." "Music draws its water from the spring of nature and not from the puddles of arithmetic" (Mattheson 1739, Foreword, section 6).

Like some of his contemporaries, Mattheson is fascinated by one aspect of mathematics: permutations (discussed in Ratner 1970). He uses permutations to generate broken-chord figurations (Mattheson 1739, Part 3, Chapter 18) and rhythmic patterns, noting that if each of twenty-four different rhythmic patterns appeared once in a melody, 62,044,840,173,323,943,936,030 possibilities would arise, although he does not explain his calculation (Part 2, Chapter 6, par. 52). He rejects the proposition that the supply of novel melodies might someday be exhausted since their number is so huge, introducing as one example the number of possible melodies using each note in the chromatic octave only once (twelve-tone rows!): 479,001,600 or 12! (Mattheson 1725, pp. 6–7).

## Two Oddities

No survey of theoretical works published through the mid-eighteenth century would be complete without mention of two unique approaches to composition published in England just after the middle of the century, one apparently serious, the other humorous. The first is the *Guida armonica, o dizionario armonico* (c. 1754[2]) of Francesco Geminiani (1687–1762), the Italian violinist-composer who lived in England after 1714. As he explains in the preface, Geminiani was distressed by the lack of novelty in compositions, particularly the fact that so many pieces are based on the same harmonic progressions. To promote variety, he offers his glossary containing hundreds of figured bass progressions between two and five notes in length for novices to use. Each progression is followed by an annotation directing the reader to continue his piece by turning to specified other pages and selecting any of the progressions there, continuing this process until a progression ends with a some sort of cadence (indicated by a fermata or a double fermata). Subsequent phrases are constructed in the same manner. At the very end of the work, Geminiani notes that "by observing the foregoing Directions it is impossible for the most ignorant to err. But the good Effect of the Melody and Harmony will be greater or less, according to the Choice of the Passages"—quite an understatement! Apparently readers found the work confusing, for Geminiani soon provided *A Supplement to the Guida Armonica, with Examples*. Here he works out a number of examples from the *Guida* and realizes them in different numbers of voices and various meters.

A more curious work by the English organist and composer William

2. The frontispiece, which includes an image of the *Guida*, is dated 1741. But evidence in McArtor 1951 points to a date around 1754 (Ladewig 1980). In addition, Serre 1753 announces that Geminiani "will soon publish" the *Guida*, "whose title is already known" (fol. 1ᵛ).

Hayes (1708–1777) is a satire on instruction manuals for amateurs. *The Art of Composing Music by a Method entirely New, suited to the meanest capacity* (London, 1751; summarized in Deutsch 1952) suggests that one acquire a small brush or *Spruzzarino* and follow these directions:

> Take a Gallipot [a small jar], put therein Ink of what Colour you please; lay a Sheet of ruled Paper on your Harpsichord or Table; then dip the Spruzzarino into the Gallipot; when you take it out again shake off the superfluous Liquid; then take the fibrous or hairy Part betwixt the Fore-finger and Thumb of your Left hand, pressing them close together, and hold it to the Lines and Spaces you intend to sprinkle; then draw the Fore-finger of your Right-hand gently over the Ends thereof, and you will see a Multiplicity of Spots on the Paper; this repeat as often as you have occasion . . . This done . . . take your Pen and proceed to the placing of the Cliffs or Keys at the Beginning, marking the Bars, and forming the Spots into Crotchets, Quavers, &c. as your Fancy shall prompt you . . . this done, season it with Flats and Sharps to your Taste. (pp. 29–30)

Hayes directed the satire to his compatriot Barnabas Gunn (?–1753), who apparently took the joke in stride, publishing *Twelve English Songs . . . Set to Musick by the New-Invented Method of Composing with the Spruzzarino* (London, 1752). Mid-twentieth-century avant-garde composers experimenting with similar aleatoric processes probably had no idea that their technique had been so thoroughly discussed and utilized two centuries earlier.

CHAPTER SEVEN

# Harmonic Perspectives
# on Counterpoint

THE PRECEDING CHAPTERS show how a chordal perspective on voice leading and harmony went from being a peripheral area of compositional theory early in the eighteenth century to become a central concern by mid-century. Beginning with the 1750s, chord-inversion and root-progression thinking is an organizing force in virtually every music-theory document: in speculative treatises on harmony as well as practical counterpoint or thoroughbass manuals, in discussions of melody and style as well as composition treatises, in works designed for professionals as well as those for amateurs, in musical dictionaries as well as keyboard primers, in works published in all regions of Europe, and in records of private instruction (such as W. A. Mozart's teaching).

Indeed, the differences among these categories are not always what seems obvious to us. In particular, the distinction between publications designed for amateurs and those aimed at professionals was not as sharply drawn in the eighteenth century as it is today. A major premise of the Enlightenment was that with diligence and reason, an educated person could learn much about any topic. Popularizations of music theory were no less prevalent than popularizations of Newtonian mechanics. In music theory, to be sure, many insubstantial publications for or by amateurs would have had little if any use to a professional musician. But weightier works were often intended for musically literate amateurs as well as professionals. No less a figure than Johann Nicolaus Forkel (1749–1818), the "founder of modern musicology" (Duckles 1980), argued cogently in 1777 that every educated person should know music theory. Numerous title pages announced works intended for "beginners and those with experience" (Marpurg 1755–1762). Other works as well imply such multiple use, even substantial tomes like the 1790 *Gründliche Anweisung zur Com-*

*position* "for self-instruction" by the Viennese pedagogue Johann Georg Albrechtsberger (1736–1809). Some theorists known for serious tomes also wrote for amateurs. For instance, Johann Philipp Kirnberger (1721–1783), one of the most important theorists of the second half of the century, published two parlor-game pamphlets: a 1757 dice game for composing menuets and polonaises and a 1783 method for "tossing off sonatas." And C. P. E. Bach (1714–1788) published in 1757 a dice game for composing invertible counterpoint "without knowing the rules." The thinking behind these apparent trifles can sometimes illuminate the more serious works by these theorists.

Likewise, works whose principal subject matter we might be inclined to place under one theoretical category often deal with other topics as well. As happened earlier in the century, discussions of composition turned up in thoroughbass methods (C. P. E. Bach 1762 and Marpurg 1755–1762), counterpoint treatises (Albrechtsberger 1790), and harmony treatises (Rameau [1761] and Kirnberger 1771–1779). C. P. E. Bach's keyboard manual had a companion volume on thoroughbass and applications to composition (just like other keyboard manuals earlier in the century), serving as model for popular works of similar structure by Georg Simon Löhlein (1725–1781) in editions from 1765–1848 and by Michael Johann Friedrich Wideburg (1720–1800) in 1765–1775. In his 1755 keyboard manual, Friedrich Wilhelm Marpurg (1718–1795) includes a substantial discussion of nonharmonic tones within a section on ornamentation.

It is not surprising, therefore, that the same perspective that informs discussions of harmony per se is also evident in other aspects of music theory. The various manifestations of chordal thinking in all these genres after the middle of the century are the subject of this and the next two chapters. The present chapter deals with documents involving counterpoint during the second half of the eighteenth century. The next two chapters survey other works of this period and describe the general agreement of much of the musical community on viewing most matters from a harmonic perspective, despite doctrinal differences.

As with any generality, there are exceptions to the prevailing harmonic viewpoint in the later eighteenth century. A number of thoroughbass methods that remained in print into the nineteenth century avoid any explicit mention of Rameauian perspectives on chord structures, chord inversions, and chord progressions (including Pasquali 1757, appearing in English as well as a French translation through the early nineteenth century, and a method first appearing in the 1790s under Albrechtsberger's name), especially *partimento* thoroughbass instructors that simply offer patterns for rote memorization. Two more substantial works falling into this category are C. P. E. Bach's 1762 thoroughbass manual and the publications on melody by Joseph Riepel (1709–1782) (discussed in Chapter 10). But even these works tacitly acknowledge chordal thinking. As already noted in Chapter 3, C. P. E. Bach orders his chapters according to Rameau's chordal theories: triads and their inversions, most seventh chords, and then what Rameau would have included under chords by subposition. No pre-Rameau thoroughbass writer organized harmonies in this manner. Riepel's works, which also do not discuss chordal theory, nevertheless build the essence of musical structure from what Heinrich Christoph Koch (1749–1816) in the 1780s called "melody conceived harmonically."

Some recent theorists and historians believe that although theories reflecting Rameau's harmonic perspective were widespread during the later eighteenth century, the truly musical approach of educated musicians and of the great composers of the time is represented by other evidence of the period: C. P. E. Bach's thoroughbass treatise, Albrechtsberger's composition manual of 1790, Fuxian counterpoint as in the records of Haydn's and Mozart's teachings, the *stile antico* studies of Padre Martini, and linear aspects in Kirnberger's treatises. Scholars espousing this perspective envision a composition method in which linear species counterpoint and thoroughbass, uninhibited by and even ignoring chordal and root-progression considerations, leads directly to free composition. To these historians, the famous theoretical squabble in Berlin between Marpurg and Kirnberger in the 1770s was a battle between chordal and linear thinking, and resulted in the rejection of a chordal perspective in favor of a linear voice-leading approach.

As shown in this and the next two chapters, this perspective is based in large part on imposing twentieth-century theoretical schisms onto eighteenth-century evidence and misreading some eighteenth-century evidence. In fact, there was a remarkable degree of conceptual unity among the various schools of late eighteenth-century theory concerning the basic nature of musical structure. Theorists and practicing musicians were comfortably at home mixing what we might consider the separate perspectives of linear and harmonic thinking. Nowhere is the basic unity underlying different perspectives more apparent than in the contrapuntal theory and practice surveyed in this chapter. Species counterpoint exercises and counterpoint in the *stile antico* may seem to us evidence of linear instruction from a perspective uninfluenced by invertible chords and root progressions. But in the eighteenth century, major theorists and teachers including Albrechtsberger, Martini, and Mozart explicitly explain counterpoint from a chordal point of view. To them, teaching the principles of good lines and good interaction among lines went hand in hand with teaching harmonic structures and harmonic progressions.

# Padre Martini

Giovanni Battista Martini (1706–1784), Bolognese composer, theorist, teacher, and scholar, was one of the major musical authorities of the age. He collected a library of over 17,000 treatises and scores, and was consulted by many of the important musicians of the time. His major publications are *Storia della musica* (1757–1781), a three-volume history of music through Greek antiquity, and *Esemplare o sia saggio fondamentale pratico di contrappunto sopra il canto fermo* [1774–1775], a huge collection of annotated musical scores mostly from the sixteenth and seventeenth centuries. The first volume contains nonfugal works, the second fugal works.

The *Esemplare* stands as a monument to the eternal verities of the *stile antico*. Though it spells out the basic rules of counterpoint in Volume 1 (pp. xix–xxviii), Martini's work is not a counterpoint text in the usual sense. Rather it is a collection of scores with annotations presumably reflecting the topics Martini taught: imitation, voice leading, motives, texture, text setting, and harmony. Martini cites numerous theorists from the Renaissance through the eighteenth century.

Because of Martini's interest in the *stile antico* and his failure to support Rameau's application for membership in the Bologna *Accademia delle scienze,* some modern scholars have viewed Martini as the last major figure in the line of Italian-tradition contrapuntists relatively uninfluenced by harmonic theory—in the line stretching from Zarlino and Artusi through the seventeenth century and Fux. But numerous aspects of the *Esemplare* itself and of Martini's overall musical activity make it clear that although he felt it important to show young composers that styles other than modern theatrical music existed (p. xiii), his perspective on this music was that of a harmony-oriented theorist of the eighteenth century. As already noted in Chapter 5, Martini's principal complaint against Rameau may have had less to do with theoretical matters than with what he perceived as Rameau's exaltation of hedonistic theatrical music.

Despite these philosophical differences with Rameau, Martini places Rameau's perspective at the core of his notion of counterpoint, wedding harmonic theory and traditional rules of the *stile antico*. His very first rule of counterpoint, for instance, is the ancient prescription to begin and end a piece with perfect consonances (p. xix).[1] Martini recasts the rule in terms of harmonic theory: beginnings and endings "should form the perfect harmony." A footnote directs the reader to p. 177, where Martini explains that the perfect harmony is the major triad, source of all consonances,

---

1. Tinctoris 1477, Book 3, Chapter 1, first rule: "All counterpoint ought to begin and end with a perfect concord"; likewise in Gafori 1496, Book 3, Chapter 3, rules 1 and 8.

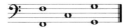

*Example 7-1.* Martini [1774–1775], I, p. 227

including 6/3 and 6/4 chords, which are inversions against the "funda-mental note" *(nota fondamentale).*

Martini likewise interprets harmonic progressions in his musical ex-amples according to Rameauian harmonic theory. Pages 224–228, for instance, discuss which scale degrees merit 5/3 and which merit 6/3 chords. Writing in a vein reminiscent of Rameau, Martini raises the problematic harmonic relationship of root progressions by step; his solution invokes parts of Rameau's theory of *double emploi* in all but the term itself:

> We can avoid [root progression by step] in two ways: first by going through an intermediate tone between the two indicated notes, and this happens by ascending or descending a fifth or fourth [see Example 7-1]. . . . However, the leading masters do this only occasionally; every day the masters of our age use another means to avoid the displeasure that the ear receives from the immediate progression of two adjacent tones accompanied by a fifth [root progression by step]. This consists in accompanying the first note with a fifth and then changing the accompaniment of the fifth to a sixth above the same note, thereby removing that annoyance that the ear receives as follows [see Example 7-2]. By this means the problem is removed according to all the laws of voice leading [*Modulazione*] described above. What makes that progression agreeable is that with the double accompaniment of the fifth and sixth on the first note, the progression becomes an ascending fourth or descending fifth, as [in Example 7-3].

The importance of this issue to Martini is clear when he repeats it within the rules for fugue that open the second volume. His *règle de l'octave* (called *Table for Progressions; Tavola per la modulazione*) contains 5/3 chords on scale-steps 4 and 5. But he warns that "even though the fourth

*Example 7-2.* Martini [1774–1775], I, p. 227

*Example 7-3.* Martini [1774–1775], I, p. 228

Harmonic Perspectives on Counterpoint    

of the key is adjacent to the fifth, one should still not progress [*far passaggio*] immediately from one to the other, but should instead observe what is prescribed in the first volume on pages 226–227" (p. xxxvii, fold-out).

Martini also writes out fundamental basses to a number of examples, explaining that such an *analisi* will demonstrate that

> all the notes can be reduced to the direct accompaniment of third and fifth, with the addition of the seventh, and sometimes even the ninth. Such an added bass only serves to demonstrate to young composers how the succession of harmonies [*Modulazione*], in order that it be natural and not offend the ear, reduces to ordinary progressions [*Modulazione*], for it proceeds almost always by ascending or descending a fourth or fifth except, as just mentioned, in progressing from one tone to another quite foreign tone. (Vol. 2, pp. 114–115)

Martini applies such fundamental basses to a seventeenth-century antiphon by Francesco Foggia (1604–1688) (Vol. 2, p. 55) and an *Adoramus te* by Antonio Pacchioni (1654–1738) (pp. 112–115). Martini's fundamental bass and accompanying commentary for the latter excerpt (in Example 7-4) cite a $C^7$ chord at the end of m. 1 (not indicated in Pacchioni's thoroughbass) that avoids the stepwise root progression from G to F. Martini uses an interpolated bass between measures 2 and 3 to avoid another stepwise progression, a chord progression to explain suspensions (mm. 2, 5, 7, 10, 11), a dominant ninth to explain diminished-seventh chords (mm. 4, 8), and a dominant seventh to explain a diminished triad (mm. 6, 10). Among items of particular interest are Martini's analysis of the suspension patterns in measures 5, 7, and 11, which ignore the decorated resolution of the suspension and introduce syncopated harmonic rhythm into the fundamental bass; his assertion of A as the fundamental bass in m. 8; and an explanation for the last chord in the first measure that contains a cross-reference to the discussion of 5–6 motions from volume 1, p. 227 (translated above).

These discussions and many other passages in the *Esemplare* make it clear that however Martini felt about the importance of knowing and respecting the *stile antico,* however much one could learn in that style about voice leading, texture, motives, imitation, and the like, and however important it was to be able to base modern practices on the foundation of the *stile antico,* his interpretation of that music was not divorced from the harmonically directed root-progression considerations of his own time. Similarly, Martini's own compositions in the newer styles are primarily homophonic, exhibiting little of even the rudimentary polyphony of his compatriot Giovanni Battista Sammartini (c. 1700–1775) (Brofsky 1980).

Confirming this interpretation of Martini's views on the *stile antico* and

*Example 7-4.* Martini [1774–1775], 2, pp. 112–115. Text omitted. Some notations
modernized. The first flat in the continuo is not a key signature, but an archaic
thoroughbass notation indicating the minor third above G in the opening chord.
It is unclear whether 5/3 in the thoroughbass in mm. 5 and 7, and 6/4 in m. 6,
should appear on the second or third quarter

contemporaneous harmonic theory is the presence of the same features in
a similar collection of scores that Martini had his pupil Giuseppe Paolucci
(1726–1776) prepare just a few years earlier: *Arte pratica di contrappunto
dimostrata con esempi di vari autori e con osservazioni* (3 volumes: Venice,
1765, 1766, 1772). Similar to Martini's *Esemplare* in layout, size (over
800 pages), and content, and prefaced by Martini's recommendation, the
*Arte pratica* contains examples in two and more parts from an even wider
range of styles and periods than Martini's *Esemplare*. Paolucci even includes *stile antico* pieces by Martini. The commentary, apparently based
on Martini's teaching (Mann 1965b, p. 60), deals with motives, counterpoint, harmony, and so forth. Like Martini, Paolucci draws on authorities
ranging from Gafori through Rameau and applies a root-progression perspective when issues of harmony and voice leading arise. He shows how

a diminished fifth over the bass is really the seventh of a dominant-seventh chord (Vol. 1, p. 25), he shows how to invert chords (p. 74), and he notes that tonic, subdominant *(sottodominante),* and dominant are the principal notes of the key (p. 171). The Italian theorist Francesco Antonio Vallotti (1697–1780), maestro di cappella from 1730–1780 in Padua, also contributed a recommendation to Paolucci's preface. In his own treatise, most of which remained in manuscript until the twentieth century, Vallotti stresses the structural importance of the fundamental bass: "because it should always be present in the mind of the composer, I state that the other parts should be regulated and distributed above that bass" (Vallotti 1950, Part 3, p. 335).

## Mozart as Composition Teacher

Wolfgang Amadeus Mozart (1756–1791) left no formal work in any area of music theory.[2] However, the extant records of his activity as a composition teacher are among the most important documents we possess concerning composition instruction in the later eighteenth century (Lester 1993). Two published sets of such exercises with Mozart's corrections are particularly relevant here: (1) studies from 1784 that circumstantial evidence strongly suggests were by Barbara Ployer (1765-after 1811), a piano student of Mozart to whom he dedicated the piano concertos K.449 and K.453 (Mozart 1784); and (2) studies from 1785–1786 by Thomas Attwood (1765–1838), an English composer and organist (Mozart 1785–1786).

The Attwood studies are considerably more extensive, possibly because the Ployer studies as they now exist may be incomplete. But both sets contain the same types of exercises, except for melodic harmonization, a task Mozart gave to Ployer as well as to an earlier Parisian pupil (Anderson 1966, letter of May 14, 1778) but not to Attwood. There are extensive species counterpoint exercises in varying numbers of voices (especially in the Attwood studies), bass parts or bass-soprano frames with or without thoroughbass figures to fill in, fugal and canonic studies, and free composition, mostly in the form of minuets.

Interestingly, despite the fact that Mozart and both of his students were keyboard players, many harmony and composition exercises are laid out in string quartet format (two treble clefs, alto clef, and bass clef), even where the exercise merely involves filling in harmonies over a figured bass part. This is a distinct change from thoroughbass approaches to compositional instruction earlier in the century where working with keyboard

2. A thoroughbass manual that has appeared under his name in several editions since the nineteenth century is clearly not his (Federhofer 1971–1972, p. 100).

texture was the norm. Thoroughbass here is used primarily for practicing voice leading, not for extempore realization or as a model to be elaborated to become a composition, as is the case earlier in the century.

The extensive sets of counterpoint exercises, the use of string quartet texture for thoroughbass realizations, and the ubiquitous emphasis on writing good lines show the paramount importance Mozart paid to linear aspects of music. In one species counterpoint exercise Mozart acknowledges that a note is technically correct, but still complains that "clearly it is only present to avoid going from one perfect consonance to another in direct motion—just like poor poets often write something idiotic to please the rhyme scheme" (Mozart 1784, fol. 11$^r$).

However, just as in Martini's *Esemplare* and Paolucci's *Arte Pratica*, Mozart's emphasis on linear aspects of music in no way prevents him from understanding the resulting chords in terms of root progressions. He was fully conversant with chord inversions and fundamental bass. In the Attwood studies there are examples illustrating inversions of triads (p. 30, in Mozart's hand) and seventh chords (p. 22), fundamental-bass explanations (p. 38, in both Mozart's and Attwood's hands), and fundamental-bass analyses (pp. 167–173).

Fundamental bass is even more prominent in the Ployer studies, where it is central to melodic harmonization. Mozart provided several melodies. Either he or Ployer worked out a fundamental-bass analysis of the melody—a fundamental bass to one melody is in Ployer's hand (fol. 1$^r$) and for another in Mozart's hand (fol. 3$^r$). Ployer then composed a bass part using notes largely from the chords in the fundamental bass. Example 7-5 is the opening of the first such harmonization. Staff 1 shows the melody, staff 2 Ployer's fundamental bass analysis, staff 3 her first bass line, staff 4 its revision, presumably after Mozart made corrections, and staff 5 Mozart's own bass using similar root progressions. All the versions appear here one under the other to facilitate comparison. In the original, they appear separately.

As in most records of compositional instruction, only the successive versions survive, not the conversations that took place between teacher and pupil to evaluate the earlier versions. According to the written evidence, Mozart probably notated the melody and asked Ployer to work out the fundamental bass and first harmonization on her own. The D-minor and F-major chords in measure 6 confirm that Ployer completed this without Mozart's assistance. In fact, the editor of the *Neue Mozart Ausgabe* finds the F chord so preposterous that he changes the fundamental-bass F to F♯ without even indicating an editorial emendation(!). Nevertheless, Ployer clearly intended F♮. F♯ is not possible in the fundamental bass, since it indicates a diminished triad, which is not a fundamental chord-type. And Ployer continues in the key of C in the next measure, deceptively

Mozart's melody:

Student's first bass part:

Student's second bass:

Mozart's bass:

*Example 7-5.* Mozart 1784, fol. 1ʳ

resolving a G⁷ to an A-minor triad in the fundamental bass. (That she does not utilize this progression in her actual bass line confirms that the fundamental bass was worked out before the actual bass part.)

How could Ployer have composed a harmonization that so clearly goes against the grain of the melody? Quite simply, she diligently followed standard eighteenth-century teaching and regarded each sharp in the melody as a chromatic leading tone, part of what we call a secondary dominant. Her error is that she assumed the F♯ (m. 5) and C♯ (m. 6) are temporary leading tones and she kept the phrase within C major. Mozart probably explained that the F♯ in measure 5 and the coming cadence on G signal a more significant key change, for Ployer corrected this in the next version. Mozart probably also suggested a more conjunct bass, for her next solution is better in this respect. But if he mentioned the unresolved leading tone in measure 4 or the peculiar 6/4 chords in measures 1, 3, 5, and elsewhere, Ployer did not understand how to correct these problems.

Mozart finally provided his own bass, generally retaining the chords in Ployer's second version. In explaining the superiority of his harmonization, he probably talked to her about using chords belonging to the key, avoiding improper 6/4 chords, resolving leading tones and chord sevenths, and watching contour, thereby repeating advice found in many contemporaneous treatises. But beyond those technical matters, Mozart's bass expresses structural features that seem to have been beyond his ability to explain verbally. For instance, in measures 1–5 the melody moves to or through scale step 3 three times, each time in a progressively stronger metric position. Mozart supports all three Es with a root-position tonic chord. In measures 2 and 4, the motion to the tonic in the melody is harmonized with a voice exchange. His bass then highlights the E on measure 5, the pivot in the modulation to the dominant, by the extraordinarily graceful rest and change of register—as if to say that having finally reached the main melodic note on a metric strong point its support could be delayed for an instant, thereby separating the end of the antecedent from the consequent that contains the change of key. Similarly strategic choices of harmonic support, rhythm, and contour characterize all of Mozart's solutions.

But Ployer never caught on. Although Mozart sometimes helped her choose good chords by writing out the fundamental bass himself (or perhaps writing it down as he worked it out with her), each of her later harmonizations yields clumsy bass lines. Mozart could compose a beautiful bass line, but he most likely could explain his choices only in terms of a smooth bass and avoiding problematic resolutions and progressions. Otherwise his method of teaching harmonization was probably that suggested by Rameau's theory: work out a good fundamental-bass progression and choose well among the alternatives it suggests—a method still used by many harmony texts. For him, attending to point-to-point harmonic thinking in this manner while keeping the large-scale linear and structural aspects of the music in mind was not a problem. But he seems to have had no way to communicate this.[3]

3. Helmut Federhofer, Daniel Heartz, and Alfred Mann evaluate Mozart's use of fundamental bass quite differently than argued here. In their commentary on the Ployer studies in the *Neue Mozart Ausgabe,* Federhofer and Mann suggest that Mozart had Ployer abandon the fundamental bass after her very first harmonization. Federhofer also agrees with Heartz's assertion that Mozart used fundamental bass "merely as a teaching tool by which the student would have before his eyes the root of all inverted chords" (Federhofer 1978–1979, p. 173; same citation in *Neue Mozart Ausgabe* X,30,2, p. xi). But the maintenance of the same chords from version to version (after the problematic modulation was corrected) and the fact that Mozart himself furnished the fundamental bass for Ployer in the next two harmonizations suggest instead that the fundamental bass was not written anew under each version of each harmonization simply because it was already present from the first harmonization.

Elsewhere, Mann argues by contrast that Mozart's teaching, based on Rameau and Marpurg, probably reflects the training he himself received (Mann 1978–1979, p. 198). Mozart's use of fundamental bass is indeed like Marpurg's in that Mozart, like Marpurg, sees no problems with step progressions in the fundamental bass. But in that Mozart explains cadential 6/4 chords both with a tonic fundamental bass (Ployer studies, fol. 1$^r$; and even on fol. 9$^v$ where this creates syncopated harmonic rhythm) and also as suspensions over the dominant (fol. 3$^r$, m. 4), he was more likely following no particular theorist closely. Cecil Oldman thus errs on p. x of the preface to the Attwood studies when he writes that

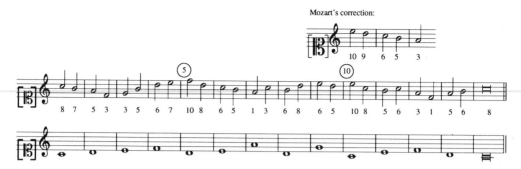

*Example 7-6.* Mozart 1784, fol. 11[r]

An even more striking instance of Mozart's harmonic perspective occurs in the species counterpoint exercises in the Ployer studies. Although most exercises are corrected without any written comments, some pages do include explanations of the reasons for errors, possibly because Mozart corrected these exercises between formal lessons. One such page includes the two-voiced exercise in second species shown in Example 7-6. Mozart comments about the B in the eighth measure: "The sixth cannot be used here, for each measure must begin with a perfect chord—with the octave, fifth, third; or with a sixth that has a perfect chord as its basis. Here, however, the perfect chord would be B with the false [diminished] fifth which cannot exist." Mozart clearly believed that intervals in two-voiced species counterpoint were not to be evaluated as intervals, but as parts of a consonant root-position or first-inversion triad.

Although there seems to be no other explicit discussion of the voice leading that Mozart censures (B-D over a D in two-part writing in second species or in a comparable rhythmic position in any other species) in any eighteenth-century counterpoint manual, the voice leading does not in fact appear in any counterpoint manual of the time (in Fux's *Gradus*, Mozart's Ployer and Attwood studies, or Albrechtsberger 1790). A sixth representing a diminished triad can only arise in the white-note scale when B appears over D. (Every other white-note sixth forms the root and third of a major or minor triad.) Mozart does not cite B over D in second species (even in the immediately preceding exercise) when the B is followed by a conjunct motion to A. Apparently he believed that only the skip from B to D caused the sense of a diminished triad being prolonged. (Only a skip from B to D will create this problem; from B no other note consonant with D is within reach by an allowable skip.)

---

Mozart follows Kirnberger's approach to fundamental bass. Mozart may well have learned fundamental bass from a variety of sources, since as shown in Chapter 8, its widespread acceptance in German theory antedates both Marpurg's and Kirnberger's writings.

Mozart's insistence that species counterpoint was to be worked out thinking of chords agrees fully with Albrechtsberger's instructions for species counterpoint, published only six years later. Albrechtsberger tells the student to figure out the proper triad to which each note of a cantus firmus belongs before beginning to write a two-part species counterpoint (discussed below). Since Mozart may well have learned strict-style species counterpoint from his contacts with Haydn (Mann 1978–1979, p. 198; Federhofer 1971–1972, p. 96), it is possible that Haydn too thought of species counterpoint via chords and inversions, although the manuals that Haydn drew up for his counterpoint students are condensations of Fux's *Gradus* (Mann 1973) and are silent on this issue.

## Albrechtsberger's Composition Method

By the end of the eighteenth century Johann Georg Albrechtsberger (1736–1809) had earned the plaudits of Haydn ("the best teacher of composition among all present-day Viennese masters") and Mozart (who considered him the standard by which other organists were to be judged) and counted the young Beethoven among his pupils (in 1794–1795). In 1793 he assumed the post of Capellmeister at St. Stephen's in Vienna, the post that Fux had held more than half a century earlier. Much like Fux, he published just one major work, his *Gründliche Anweisung zur Composition*, a comprehensive practical treatise (440 pp.) comparable in scope to Fux's *Gradus*.[4]

Like Fux's classic text, Albrechtsberger's work is clearly the product of a teacher with long practical experience (Fux was 65, Albrechtsberger 59). It is decidedly nonspeculative, eschewing even the mathematical explanations of intervals that open *Gradus*. After a brief resume of intervals (which Albrechtsberger implies on p. 1 that the reader should already know from studying thoroughbass), chords, and rules of voice leading, the bulk of the book deals with species counterpoint in 2–4 parts (pp. 19–160) and imitation and fugue (pp. 161–362). The remainder of the treatise, like the end of *Gradus,* covers various topics: rules for five-part writing, different styles, and an extraordinarily extensive list of instruments (including even the glass harmonica, invented by "D. Franklin").

Also like Fux's *Gradus,* the *Gründliche Anweisung* is a decidedly conservative work for its time. Although he was well aware of the newer styles of his time, Albrechtsberger, like Fux and Martini, believed that the path to learning these newer styles lay in mastering the strict style. Like

---

4. As discussed in Appendix 2, there are reasons to question whether thoroughbass manuals appearing under Albrechtsberger's name beginning in the 1790s are actually by him.

*Example 7-7.* Albrechtsberger 1790, p. 24

Fux, he maintained the use of six-syllable solmization with mutation of hexachords (substituting *do* for the traditional *ut;* p. 1). He even calls flats and sharps "*fa*-tones" and "*mi*-tones" (*Fa-Töne* and *Mi-Töne*, p. 18). But the passage of over six decades between *Gradus* and the *Gründliche Anweisung* led to many changes of focus. The church modes of Fux's species counterpoint are replaced by *cantus firmi* in major and minor keys. And there is a decidedly harmonic focus to the *Gründliche Anweisung.*[5]

This harmonic focus is apparent right from page 1 via the explanation of chords as well as the invocation of thoroughbass knowledge. Whereas Fux had taught two-part species counterpoint as intervals between voices, Albrechtsberger assumes that intervals are always part of proper chords and assumes that readers understand chords and inversions just as they understand the basics of thoroughbass. On pp. 4–5, for instance, discussing whether the fourth is consonant or dissonant, he says "some teachers count the perfect fourth, accompanied by the minor or major sixth and perfect octave, among the consonances, because it arises from the second inversion of a perfect chord . . . You can call it as you wish! In my ears it always remains a dissonance. There is more than one reason to maintain this." On p. 120, he explains that a 6/4/3 chord is "the second inversion of the essential seventh." These passages, like innumerable others throughout the work, show Albrechtsberger's practical attitude. He assumes knowledge of inversions without explaining it because his purpose is not to engage in polemic but to teach counterpoint and composition. Likewise he understands the reasons that some theorists deem 6/4 chords consonant, but he will not join the heated polemic over this issue, noting that he has reasons for his opinion, but does not care to state them.

Also included in the introductory chapters are explanations of the *règle de l'octave* and the use of its chords (a discussion based largely on rules for unfigured basses), enharmonic modulations (even from G-minor to D♭-major!), and the like.

Albrechtsberger's harmonic perspective also affects his explanation of how to write a two-part counterpoint in first species. He offers a *cantus firmus* and explains its structure (see Example 7-7):

5. Benary [1961], p. 130, and Dahlhaus 1989, pp. 66–67, also discuss the harmonic underpinnings of Albrechtsberger's approach to counterpoint.

Compositional Theory in the Eighteenth Century

*Example 7-8.* Nottebohm 1873, p. 47

The first and last notes stand properly in the C chord if they are accompanied. The second and third are derived from G major, the fourth and fifth are again from C major; the sixth and seventh belong to the A-minor chord. The eighth and ninth taken together belong to E minor. The tenth derives from A minor; the eleventh from D minor, or both taken together from F major. The twelfth can be regarded as the octave of G major, or as the fifth of the C-major chord. The thirteenth can be taken as the tonic or for the third of A minor or for the sixth above E if the counterpoint is below. The fourteenth must be considered as the upper fifth of G major; that G ought to appear in the penultimate measure in compositions of three and more voices. In two-part writing, only B is added to it; for in the fifth species *a due* our two cadences are 6 8 and ♭3 1—only half cadences [cadences that are lacking some essential parts]. Now the following chords can be placed over and under this chorale. (p. 25)

This detailed discussion of harmonic possibilities suggests that Albrechtsberger, like Mozart, had similar attitudes toward species counterpoint, although only a single remark about a problematic sixth remains to illuminate Mozart's thinking.

In addition to this explanation, Albrechtsberger's harmonic approach to species counterpoint is confirmed by other evidence. For instance, there are various annotations that Albrechtsberger made on counterpoint exercises the young Beethoven completed for him, such as the one shown in Example 7-8. In another passage in the *Anweisung,* Albrechtsberger explains a D-B verticality as an inverted G-major triad, even though no G is present (p. 32). And finally, he discusses harmonic rhythm in third species counterpoint in two voices: "The best two-, three- and multi-voiced counterpoints in this species are those in which each measure has only a single chord; because it is more manly and serious . . . In any case, it is not prohibited to have a different chord on each beat provided that the first chord and the last are perfect [consonant]" (p. 53).

In sum, like Martini and Mozart, Albrechtsberger knew that compositional craft was strengthened by work in counterpoint. But all three of these musicians saw no conflict between such appreciation of the linear aspects of musical structure and harmonic thinking.

## Harmonic Theory and Linearity

The complementarity of harmonic foundations and linear counterpoint is evident in writings from numerous other quarters during the latter half of the eighteenth century. For instance, Johann Philipp Kirnberger (1721–1783), whose harmonic theories are discussed in Chapter 9, explains simple counterpoint as follows: "complete harmony is in four parts . . . Therefore it is impossible to judge with certainty what must be omitted from the harmony in the various situations that arise [in fewer parts] until one has a thorough knowledge of four-part composition. Consequently, this [simple] counterpoint should be considered as a succession of complete chords" (Kirnberger 1771–1779, Vol. 1, p. 142; Beach-Thym 1982, p. 159). With this argument, Kirnberger was merely continuing the long-standing practice of deriving a contrapuntal texture from an implied full-voiced texture, as Rameau had stated was always the case, as Niedt and other thoroughbass writers had practiced much earlier in the century in teaching composition from thoroughbass, and as Lippius had suggested should be practiced as a composition method as early as the first decade of the seventeenth century.[6]

It is clear that figures as diverse as Albrechtsberger, Kirnberger, Martini, Mozart, Rameau, and Vallotti all agree that counterpoint, stressing the linear relationships between voices, is based on chordal harmony. But this does not deny that counterpoint methods also taught aspects of musical structure not covered by harmonic theory per se. The issues that Mattheson discusses in 1739—melodic contour, melodic rhythm, melodic motives and their manipulation, and the creation of an interesting texture via the interaction of multiple melodies and their contours, rhythms, and motives—are the issues that come to the fore in Martini's *analisi* of music in the *stile antico* as well as in Albrechtsberger's commentaries on music in more recent styles. These are also the issues that come to the fore in Martini's corrections of a piece that the fourteen-year-old W. A. Mozart wrote as his admission test to the Bologna *Accademia dei Filarmonici* (discussed in Mann 1987, pp. 49–51, 55–56). And they are the issues that come to the fore in Albrechtsberger's emendations of exercises that Bee-

---

6. David Beach therefore errs when he explains that "during the latter half of the eighteenth century, counterpoint instruction normally meant the study of species counterpoint as codified by Johann Fux in his *Gradus ad parnassum*. This approach, which begins with two-part writing, is primarily linear in conception. The vertical dimension is controlled exclusively by intervallic considerations. Thus in recommending that the study of counterpoint begin with four parts to accommodate harmonic considerations, Kirnberger was going against the prevailing practice of treating harmony and counterpoint as separate disciplines" (Beach and Thym 1982, p. xvii).

thoven wrote when he studied with him in the early 1790s (discussed in Mann 1965b, pp. 213–220).

These are also the issues that come to the fore in eighteenth-century fugal studies in Fux's *Gradus* (1725), in Marpurg's *Abhandlung von der Fuge* (1753–1754), and in Albrechtsberger's *Anweisung* (1790). Much of fugal theory during the eighteenth century deals with mechanics—the structure of a proper fugal subject, working out an appropriate fugal answer, writing a countersubject, and various fugal devices such as stretto, inversion, and double or invertible counterpoint. During the century, fugal theory changed its focus from modal, nonchordal explanations of many of these features in Fux's presentation, to tonal and chordal explanations by Rameau (1722, 3, Chapter 44) and Marpurg. This change from a modal-nonchordal to a tonal-chordal perspective is surveyed in Horsley 1966 (especially Chapter 4) and Mann 1965b (Part 1, Chapters 3–4).

Because these aspects of fugal structure involve so many details, they occupy much space in the fugal treatises of the time. But they should not be confused with the underlying purpose of studying fugue—to learn to control texture in any style. Thus fugal theory raises many of the same issues as Mattheson's discussions of melody. These features of contrapuntal theory are relevant to every eighteenth-century musical style. Fux and Martini composed some of their works in the *stile antico,* while Mattheson spoke vehemently against "contrapuntists" and wrote exclusively in the *galant* style. Yet all three theorists discuss in their own terms various techniques of motivic development, imitation, and rhythmic activation of individual voices and of texture as a whole. As a result, Haydn could have learned about the techniques of textural and motivic activation that so characterize his music from his study of either Fux's *Gradus* or Mattheson's *vollkommene Capellmeister.*

Basically, these motivic and contrapuntal techniques are conceptually independent of any approach to the harmonic dimension, whether intervallic counterpoint, chordal counterpoint, thoroughbass, or Rameauian harmony. Therefore discussions of line, of motives, or of the interactions among voices in a polyphonic texture can and do appear in works independent of Rameauian influence (such as those by Fux and Mattheson) as well as works fully adopting Rameau's harmonic theories (such as that by Martini). As a result, the dichotomy that some twentieth-century scholars propose in order to separate eighteenth-century harmonic theory from linear aspects of tonal music is mostly irrelevant to the eighteenth century. By and large, after the middle of the century, almost all theorists explicitly used at least some portions of Rameauian harmonic theory. But this did not prevent them from discussing in a meaningful manner many of the linear aspects of the music of their time.

This is not to say that in the hands of imperceptive musicians, the adoption of a harmonic approach to counterpoint did not result in absurdities. One example is the brief *Traité du Contrepoint par P. Signoretti dédié a Mrs. les amateurs* (Rennes, 1777), a work that seems to have had a rather limited circulation (the examples are entered by hand on printed staffs, as in the author's violin method, published in The Hague, 1777). Signoretti presents a unique mixture of Fuxian species and Rameau's notions of triads, seventh chords, and inversions, treating all chordal inversions as equivalent, and even beginning three-part exercises in first species with 6/4 chords. But in the hands of the masters discussed earlier in this chapter, formulating traditional counterpoint on a chordal basis allowed them to treat simultaneously both harmonic direction and linear continuity as complementary aspects of musical structure.

# CHAPTER EIGHT

# Changing Aspects
# of Harmonic Theory

*In working out a composition, one must always keep in mind the har-*
*monic triad, because not only all the rules of harmony but also the*
*invention of melody itself must in part be referred to it, and in part flow*
*from it . . . The harmonic triad . . . is therefore like the soul of the*
*entire composition; it must be investigated intensively and taken into*
*consideration most painstakingly.*

*Scheibe 1773, p. 81*

THE PREVIOUS CHAPTER shows how even those areas of music theory
most concerned with linearity were strongly influenced by harmonic thinking after the middle of the eighteenth century. This and the next chapter
survey various facets of harmonic theory itself during that period.

## Novel Approaches to Chord Generation

While many theorists did not bother justifying the origins of intervals and
chords, and those who did generally borrowed one or another of Rameau's
explanations, others continued to propose new derivations based on mathematics or acoustical phenomena. Two such musicians are Sorge and
Tartini.

### SORGE

Georg Andreas Sorge (1703–1778), a prolific theorist in Lobenstein, published treatises on harmony, thoroughbass, composition, tuning, and organ
construction and left other writings in manuscript. His three works on
harmonic theory and composition are the *Vorgemach der musicalischen*
*Composition, oder . . . Anweisung zum General-Bass* (Sorge [1745–

1747]), the *Compendium harmonicum, oder . . . Lehre von der Harmonie* (Sorge [1760]), and the *Anleitung zur Fantasie* (Sorge [1767]).

Like Rameau, some of whose ideas he knew but whose works he apparently never read, Sorge sought mathematical and scientific bases for chords and intervals, changing his ideas from one work to another. But whereas Rameau was inspired by a search for Cartesian first principles and by scientific discoveries, Sorge also reflects the theism of his German predecessors such as Andreas Werckmeister (1645–1706) and contemporaries such as Christoph Gottlieb Schröter (1699–1782). Sorge first derives intervals and chords from string divisions but differs from many others by invoking the ratio 1:7 as the origin of the minor seventh (Sorge [1745–1747], Vol. 3, Chapter 4). This exemplifies for him how music reflects God: the chord seventh must resolve because false intervals like 1:7 represent depravity in need of redemption (ibid., Chapter 22). Such arguments were not deterred by scientific discoveries. Writing around the same time as Sorge, Schröter recognizes the presence of the triad in instrumental resonance, explaining that we respond to the triad because God implanted it both there and in the human soul to represent the Trinity (Schröter 1772, probably completed by 1754, pp. 7–8).

In the *Compendium*, Sorge changed his model from string divisions to harmonic resonance. He was aware of resonance in his earlier work but did not use it in interval or chord generation. He now finds all intervals and chords among the first thirty-two partials of a natural horn (Chapter 1). An unfortunate implication of this approach is that the fundamental tone is the basis of each interval and chord located among its upper partials. Although Sorge did not draw this conclusion, the French theorist Ballière de Laisement (1729–1800), working independently of Sorge, did. He argued, for instance, that since a D-F-A chord arises between the partials 27, 33, and 39 over C, C is therefore the root *(base)* of the chord (C . . . D-F-A as 3:27:33:39; Laisement 1764, p. 100)! Other than Jamard 1769, no writers followed Ballière's approach to locating chordal roots. In other matters, Ballière generally follows Rameau or D'Alembert.

In his *Anleitung zur Fantasie*, Sorge again changed his mind, using the harmonic series primarily to justify the major triad and deriving some other chords by joining major triads. An A-minor triad, for instance, arises from two joined major triads on F and C: f-A-C-E-g. Elsewhere in this work, though, he uses multiples of the seventh and ninth partials to derive various chords.

Sorge is important not so much for these speculative ideas but for his own formulations of various slogans associated with Rameau's ideas. He apparently did not read French (according to Marpurg 1759–1763 10, p. 79) and claimed ignorance of any work based on Rameau prior to Marpurg's 1757 translation of D'Alembert's *Elemens* (Sorge [1760], Chapter 12, pars. 3–4; Sorge [1745–1747], 3, Chapter 23, fn. to par. 24). But he asserts that harmony is the generator of music, that triads and seventh chords are the basis of all harmonies, and that the seventh is the source of dissonance. He construes each tenet differently than Rameau had done. Concerning harmony as the source of melody, he adds the qualification that melody is what makes each piece distinctive (Sorge [1745–1747], 2, Chapter 2).

Concerning triads, Rameau recognizes two types of triads (major and minor) and calls the triad the source of consonant harmony. Sorge counts five types, adding diminished, augmented, and "defective" (*manca* for B-D♯-F)—inversions of the defective triad are his source for augmented sixth chords (Sorge [1745–1747], 1, Chapters 6–10). Thus for him the triad is not a source of consonant harmony.

Sorge's expanded number of basic types of triads and his use of combinations of triads to explain dissonances were adopted by theorists seeking to list chord types as in thoroughbass, though using the language of harmonic theory. Johann Adolph Scheibe (1708–1776), for instance, adds triads such as C-E♭-G♯ to Sorge's five types, thereby deriving all sorts of consonant and dissonant chords (Scheibe 1773, Chapter 2, and p. 363, where Scheibe states that a dozen major and minor triads stacked one upon the other produce all possible intervals).[1] Others ridiculed Sorge's five types of triads. Citing Sorge's description of major and minor triads as male and female, Friedrich Wilhelm Marpurg (1718–1795) wonders whether the three other types might be labeled "castrati and hermaphrodites" (Marpurg 1759–1763, pp. 74–75).

Concerning seventh chords as the source of dissonant harmony, Rameau made this claim based on chordal inversions and chords by subposition. Sorge learned the slogan "seventh as the source of dissonant harmony" from Mattheson's critique of this notion (Sorge [1760], Chapter 12, pars. 3–4) and formulated it idiosyncratically. Alongside Rameau's seventh chords, Sorge adds a variety of dissonant suspensions arranged so that they produce a seventh over the bass. For instance, a 7–6 suspension is fundamental because of the seventh over the bass—Sorge then inverts this pattern as if it were a fundamental chord (ibid., 3, Chapter 16)—once again, Sorge reveals thoroughbass thinking in the language of harmonic theory. He contradicts these harmonic derivations elsewhere, explaining seventh chords and augmented sixth chords as phenomena arising from passing motions (ibid., 3, Chapter 7, par. 13–16 and 18–20).

1. Around the same time, Friedrich Wilhelm Riedt (1710–1783) announced his intention to calculate the total number of possible chords, listing 27 different types of triads and 108 types of seventh chords, including absurdities like a triad with triply diminished fifth and doubly diminished third (B♯-D♭-F♭) (Riedt 1756).

More important in the long run than Sorge's adaptations of Rameauian slogans is his establishment of three categories of chords: basic chords *(Stammaccorde)*, inversions *(abstammende Accorde)*, and mixed *(vermischte)* chords requiring resolution (Sorge [1767], pp. 32–33). The last category includes what we would call chords with suspensions. This anticipates a similar categorization of harmonies appearing just four years later in the *Kunst des reinen Satzes* of Johann Philipp Kirnberger (1721–1783). But like many of Sorge's discussions, his presentation lacks the clarity of Kirnberger's. Kirnberger makes this differentiation the starting point of his discussion of harmony, while Sorge buries his categorization amid other material. Immediately before this classification, Sorge differentiates chords into nine categories: major, minor, anomalous (other), tonic, dominant, other functions, root-position, inverted, and mixed (pp. 31–32). Sorge also anticipates another tenet often credited to Kirnberger, distinguishing among different types of 6/4 chords. But because Sorge uses 6/4 chords rather freely as consonant chords in many examples, this distinction too loses the power and clarity it has for Kirnberger.

Sorge's ideas influenced several writers, including Georg Simon Löhlein (1725–1781), author of a popular *Clavier-Schule* in print from 1765 through 1848. In his first edition, Löhlein extols Sorge's system "because it appears to be the most natural" (preface), referring readers desiring more information to both Sorge's *Compendium* and Marpurg's *Handbuch*. Löhlein soon realized that these authors were hostile to one another and replaced Sorge's name with Rameau's in this citation without altering any of the contents. Sorge's harmonic ideas are also apparent in a brief, not terribly well written English thoroughbass manual published around 1760 by John Jasper Heck (c. 1740–1791), who was probably the translator of Fux 1725, Mattheson 1735, and Quantz 1752 into English (Kassler 1980).

Sorge, influential in his own right, gains added historical significance through an extended theoretical battle with Marpurg around 1760 (unraveled in Bernard 1989). The polemic forms a part of Marpurg's extensive campaign to promote in Germany what he believed were Rameau's theories. Marpurg's theories as a reflection of Rameau's ideas are discussed in Chapter 9; the present discussion covers Marpurg's interaction with Sorge.

Marpurg, who inspired polemical writing much as Mattheson had done earlier in the century, was disturbed by the free interpretation of Rameauian ideas in Sorge's *Vorgemach*. He encouraged Sorge to write his 1760 *Compendium*, urging Sorge to use the opportunity to express his displeasure over ideas in Marpurg's 1757 translation of D'Alembert's *Elemens*. Shortly after Sorge's *Compendium* appeared, Marpurg published his own highly critical, annotated edition (Marpurg 1760). Copying Mattheson, who dedicated his 1717 critique of Buttstett to a "jury" of

thirteen prominent musicians and published their replies, Marpurg dedicated his critique to fifty-two "famous German composers," including W.
F. and C. P. E. Bach, both Bendas, Graun, Kirnberger, Mattheson, L.
Mozart, Quantz, Riepel, and Scheibe, and published some replies and
additional polemic in 1761 (Marpurg 1754–1778 5:110 [labeled 100]–
20, 131–220, 263–284). He also discussed Sorge's theories in a separate
extensive discussion (Marpurg 1759–1763, Nos. 8, 10, 18).

The dispute generated unusual animosity on both sides, including the
usual nationalistic and religious barbs, such as Marpurg's comment that
a particular resolution "is not recognized in Germany; it can be used only
in countries where reindeer or rhinoceros live" (Marpurg 1760, p. 150)
and Sorge's reference to 'Mr. Marpourg' (Sorge [1767], dedication). Sorge
likens Marpurg to the devil (Sorge [1767], p. 56), while Marpurg includes
a mock prayer punning on the German word Sorge (care, sorrow): "Ora
pro Sorgio nostro, Sancta Caecilia!" ("Pray for our Sorge/sorrow, Sancta
Caecilia!"). When Sorge realized that the recently deceased Mattheson,
whose writings Sorge had cited frequently in the Vorgemach, sided with
some of Marpurg's positions, Sorge damned him too: "Now [Mattheson]
awaits his own Judge. He ill-considered the adage 'Do not damn others,
lest thou be damned thyself. Do not judge others, lest thou be judged
thyself.' May GOd bless him!" (Sorge [1767], p. 76). More heat than
light, perhaps, but more entertaining reading than more sober disputes.

Sorge and Marpurg clashed over speculative issues (including the number of basic chord-types, whether to derive only the triad or all chords
from harmonic partials, and the utility of subposed chords) and practical
ones (including Sorge's free use of 6/4 chords in many examples). As in
all of Marpurg's disputes, Rameau's name frequently enters, often associated with ideas that were Marpurg's but not Rameau's. Sorge, who had
not read Rameau's works, believed that Marpurg's 1757 translation of
D'Alembert's Elemens and Marpurg's Handbuch bey dem Generalbass
represented Rameau's thinking. Marpurg said nothing to dispel this
impression. And Sorge came to despise every idea associated (however
erroneously) with Rameau.

TARTINI

Another speculative approach to chord derivation was proposed by the
Italian violinist, composer, and theorist Giuseppe Tartini (1692–1770). In
addition to works on violin playing and ornamentation, he wrote several
speculative and practical theoretical treatises, many of which remained in
manuscript.[2] Like Rameau, Tartini sought to give his theories a scientific

---

2. Capri 1945 contains a complete bibliography of his writings. The best critique of
Tartini's theories in English is Planchart 1960; additional information appears in Krehbiel
1964.

*Example 8-1*. Tartini 1754, p. 14

and methodological aura. He drew on his violinistic experience with the acoustic phenomenon of combination tones to build a harmonic system. A *third sound (terzo souno),* as Tartini called it, is heard when two tones are played sufficiently loud. Although it is hard to believe they were unknown to string players, since they are a reliable means of checking intonation, combination tones were not mentioned in print prior to Sorge 1745 and an apparently independent report to the Royal Academy of Sciences in Paris published in 1752 by Jean-Baptiste Romieu (1723–1766) (Cohen 1981, pp. 91–92).

Tartini heard what are now called first-order difference tones: the result of subtracting the frequency of the lower pitch of an interval from that of the upper pitch. The first chapter of his principal treatise, the *Trattato di musica secondo la vera scienza dell' armonia* (1754), treats this "Harmonic Phenomenon, Its Nature and Significance." Although Tartini's system was viewed by some as comparable in standing to that of Rameau as a path to understanding the origin and use of musical elements, its coherence is marred by Tartini's mistaken perception of the combination tone of many intervals, his assertion of two roots for many chords, and numerous mathematical errors.

Example 8-1 is Tartini's illustration of the third sounds he heard for some consonances. (He believed that unisons and multiple octaves had no third sounds and that the third sound of the perfect fifth was the lower note of the interval.) The third sounds for the first three intervals are an octave too high, which does not alter the root of the interval. The error for the minor sixth is more serious: the third sound is D, not G.

Tartini believed that chord roots should be determined by combination tones. In progressions of root-position major triads voiced so as to avoid minor sixths, the third sounds of all the intervals do indeed give plausible harmonic roots, as is shown in Example 8-2. But when minor triads are present, multiple "roots" arise, as in Example 8-3.

His problems with dominant-seventh chords are more serious. If the upper third of the chord is a pure minor third (6:5), its third sound is a minor third above the chord root, clashing with the leading tone. To prevent this, Tartini asserts that the top third is actually 7:6, making the third sound the root of the chord. Unfortunately, for this to be so, scale-step 4 would have to change pitch significantly if sustained from a preceding chord.

third sound

*Example 8-2.* Tartini 1754, p. 68

Tartini also derives various musical phenomena by drawing analogies with properties of a circle, not always correctly explained (Chapter 2). These arguments, like other eighteenth-century attempts to argue from extramusical premises to musical elements and practice, are properly assessed in a 1771 commentary on Tartini's theories by Benjamin Stillingfleet (1702–1771):

> The circle has bewitched many a sober man . . . I have no doubt but if Tartini had been as well acquainted with the hyperbola as with the circle, and had the hyperbola been as easy to draw, he would have fought for his system rather there . . . But I must observe, that coincidences are often merely accidental; and therefore are no proof that we have found the true explication of any thing. (Stillingfleet 1771, p. 19)

Stillingfleet's critique of Tartini's theories was inspired by an apparently similar critique of Rameau's *Démonstration* by Robert Price (?–1761), now lost. Such documents demonstrate the interest in music theory of scientifically oriented musical amateurs. They were convinced that by the diligent application of reason they could master complex disciplines and compensate for the fact that "artists who are most accomplished in their

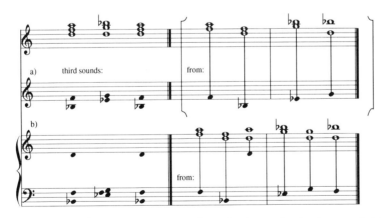

*Example 8-3.* Tartini 1754, p. 67. (a) Tartini's third sounds; (b) the actual third sounds

Changing Aspects of Harmonic Theory 199

art are ill-suited or little disposed to give the public a true theory" (Serre 1753, *Avertissement*). However well such theorists may point out faults in the works of musicians, their frequently absurd solutions reveal their lack of professional-level musical experience, whether they are philosophes like Diderot and D'Alembert, a mathematician like Euler, or a painter and scientist like the Swiss theorist Jean-Adam Serre (1704–1788).

Serre published critiques of D'Alembert, Euler, Geminiani, Rameau, Tartini, and others in 1753 and 1763, also proposing an "absolutely fundamental" bass *(basse essentiellement fondamental)* drawn from harmonic resonance.[3] Serre's method yields multiple roots for many chords, often including notes absent from the chords themselves. He posits F and C as roots of an A-minor seventh chord. And for the progression "ii$^7$-V$^7$" in C major, he posits F and G as double roots for both chords, implying that there is no harmonic progression! Regardless of our contemporary opinions about such absurdities in these works by musical amateurs, eighteenth-century musician-theorists took them quite seriously. Much as Rameau felt it important to defend his theories against Euler and D'Alembert, Tartini responded to Serre in 1767.

## Harmonic Reformulations of Thoroughbass

An indication of the extent to which harmonic theories took a central position even in the absence of a direct influence from Rameau's works is the recasting of thoroughbass practice into Rameauian harmonic terms by the German lutenist, composer, and theorist Johann Friedrich Daube (c. 1730–1797).[4] Daube denied having known Rameau's works before he wrote his "Thoroughbass in Three Chords" (1756), based on the *tonic chord (Grundtonaccord)* or triad on scale-step 1, the *fourth chord (4ten Accord)* or added-sixth chord on scale-step 4, and the *fifth chord (5ten Accord)* or seventh chord on scale-step 5. According to Daube, all the harmonies in music arise from these three chords, their inversions *(Umwendungen)*, anticipations and suspensions of notes of these chords, or imitation of these chords.

On numerous other matters as well, Daube follows Rameau closely. Scale-step 5 should carry a seventh chord, since with a triad it would be indistinguishable from scale-step 1 (Chapter 3, par. 5). Seventh chords on degrees other than 5 are imitations of the *fifth chord* (Chapter 4, par. 10). Key changes take place by changing the dissonances in a chord, such as

3. The most complete study of Serre is Jacobi 1958.

4. The most comprehensive discussions of Daube in English are in Snook 1978 and Wallace 1983.

adding a sixth to turn a *tonic chord* into a *fourth chord* in the key of scale-step 5 (Chapter 5, par. 2). And progressions other than those among the three primary chords are evaded or passing cadences (*cadenze sfuggite* or *entweichende, durchgehende, wegfliehende* cadences; Chapter 7, par. 3).

On other matters, however, Daube is independent of Rameau. For instance, the *fourth chord* normally progresses directly to the *fifth chord*—Daube shows no sign of Rameau's sensitivity to step progressions and does not use *double emploi*. By contrast, Daube proscribes moving from the *fourth chord* to the *tonic*, explaining that when this progression occurs, the *fourth chord* is a *tonic* and the *tonic chord* its *fifth chord* (Chapter 3, par. 9).

Daube's treatise is first and foremost a practical work, primarily on thoroughbass. There are numerous examples of all sorts of progressions, including interactions among the basic chords, changing keys, multiple resolutions of diminished seventh chords, progressions to be used in improvising preludes, and so forth. Much of the material is applicable to composition, of course, but specific discussions on composition occur mostly toward the end, such as how to elaborate progressions by arpeggiating chords and adding connecting notes, and how to set chords to a given melody. Yet despite his practical stance, Daube also recommends that treatises should explore the theoretical foundations of musical practices and not merely follow those practices (Chapter 5, par. 13).

The extent of Daube's direct knowledge of Rameau remains uncertain. Marpurg harshly criticized Daube for plagiarizing and misrepresenting Rameau's ideas (Marpurg 1754–1778 2:325–366, 464–477, 542–547). Daube replied that he had only seen Rameau's *Démonstration* for "a couple of hours" no earlier than the summer of 1754, by which time his treatise was already in publication (Marpurg 1754–1778 3:69–70). This could explain the passing reference to Rameau in Daube's preface, dated 1754, where he commends the accomplishments of various earlier theorists: Mattheson for his rules on melody, Fux for his four rules of voice leading, and Heinichen, along with Gasparini and Rameau, for discovering the natural progressions of chords in a key. From this passage, Daube seems to regard Rameau as a thoroughbass writer, not the progenitor of a new discipline of harmony.

Most historians believe that Daube did indeed plagiarize Rameau. Barbara Wallace disagrees, arguing that Daube could have come up with the idea of the added-sixth chord on scale-step 4 from Gasparini 1708, which frequently uses this chord (Wallace 1983, pp. 14–15). But it is a far cry from including this ubiquitous harmony to developing a theory with so many tenets in common with Rameau. Still, plagiarism is not the only plausible explanation for Daube's borrowings. It is far more likely that Rameauian ideas had already entered common musical discourse and Daube, like many other musicians, was unaware of their source.

Supporting this hypothesis is a 1751 thoroughbass manual by Georg Joachim Joseph Hahn (c. 1690-after 1769) that anticipates Daube's approach. Like Daube, Hahn cites three principal chords (*Haupt-Accorden* or *Haupt-Klänge*) on 1, 4, and 5, whose original form or inversion (*Veränderung* or *Verwechselung*) ordinarily appears over each bass note (for instance, "the second degree uses an inversion of the fifth of the mode;" Chapters 7 and 16). Hahn does not announce this harmonic approach as a novelty, but simply places it alongside traditional thoroughbass material. Chapters 8 through 15, for instance, treat in order chords with 2, with 3, with 4 in the signature, and so forth. And Hahn includes one of the last presentations of the archaic system of "church keys" alongside the twenty-four major and minor keys (Lester 1989, pp. 77–82). As with Daube, it is unlikely that Hahn knew his harmonic ideas came from Rameau, since he freely acknowledges borrowings from thoroughbass treatises by Gasparini and Telemann, but does not mention Rameau. Instead, Hahn's approach, published when he was around sixty years old, appears to be like many other comparable works—the result of years of teaching this material with what seems to us a free mixture of newer and older approaches. Most likely, Hahn simply understood the three principal chords in each key as common knowledge, as is also quite possible with Daube.

Daube spent the earlier portion of his life in several German cities. In 1769 he settled in Vienna, where he remained. Shortly after arriving, he published the contents of his thoroughbass manual in a serialization, then as the first part of *Der musikalische Dilettant* (1771), and again in Chapter 1 of the second part, his treatise on composition (1773). The chapter headings in this composition manual might suggest an approach similar to Fux's *Gradus:* after a first chapter on Harmony in General, Daube treats Voice Motions, Writing for Two Voices, Writing for Three Voices, Writing for Four Voices, Writing for Five and More Voices, Variation, Imitation, Canon, Simple Fugue, Double Counterpoint, and Double Fugue. But the discussions throughout are based on harmonic progressions. As Daube explains in the foreword, thoroughbass, by which he means his own formulation based on the three principal chords,

> can properly be called the guide to composition. The reason is this: thorough-bass consists of knowledge of chords and their succession. Composition, on the contrary, teaches how these chords are to be combined skilfully with melody so that expression or the depiction of the affects arises from this alliance. Furthermore, each melody is composed of tones which are borrowed intervals from chords.

*Example 8-4.* Daube 1773, p. 11

Daube repeatedly discusses the chordal foundation of voice leadings, as in the illustration of contrary motion shown in Example 8-4. He now calls the three principal chords in the key the *first chord* or *ruling chord,* the *second chord* (on scale-step 4), and the *third chord* (on scale-step 5).

> The example begins with the diminished seventh; the resolution takes place as usual to the *first chord* [the tonic chord on beat 2]. Then the *third chord* [the chord on scale step 5] follows, and once again the *first chord.* After this the *third chord* appears yet again, but its resolution takes place not to the *first chord,* but to a chord similar to the *first chord,* namely the *third chord* of D minor [on the last beat of measure 2]. This harmony again proceeds to a harmony similar to its *first chord,* namely the compound seventh chord of G major. The following harmonizing tones have the same resolution as the first two measures, but a tone lower. (Daube 1773, p. 12)

For Daube, each interval expresses a chord, even on the third beats of measures 1 and 2, where he cites dominant-seventh chords although the root and leading tone are absent. He recognizes the downbeat of measure 3, which presents F♯ and E, as a leading-tone chord from G major that is nonetheless similar to and can substitute for the expected arrival on a tonic chord in D.

In two-part writing, Daube distinguishes writing for two upper parts from writing that represents the bass and a melody. If the lower part is the bass, he suggests that the composer create a progression from the three principal chords, first placing the root (*Grundton*) in the bass and then elaborating the chords. This is similar to the harmonization method used by Barbara Ployer when she studied with Mozart a decade later: work out a fundamental bass of root-position chords, and then compose the actual bass from the notes in those chords.

Daube expresses in harmonic terms the standard explanation for changing key by introducing a new leading tone: "the harmony of the foreign *third chord* [the chord on the new scale-step 5] must always precede the appearance of the foreign *first chord* [the new tonic chord]" (p. 29). He discusses at length how to choose basic progressions, when to invert harmonies, how to use chromatic tones that do not imply a change of key, how to place a cadence at the end of a passage, and so forth. As he proceeds to more voices, he adds discussions on imitation, on the proper use of melodic writing versus passage-work (*Singbaren* versus *Brillanten*), on scoring, on dynamics, on fast movements, on slow movements, and so forth, leading eventually to symphonic scores. In short, he systematically builds from his three principal chords in thoroughbass up to the composition of symphonic passages.

Daube published a third volume to the *Musikalische Dilettant* in 1797, but quite likely he wrote it in the early 1770s (Snook 1978, pp. 458 and 469). This third part deals mostly with the invention of melody. Since its subject matter does not so directly concern harmony, Robert Wason interprets the work as representing a retreat from "the radical traits of the *Generalbass in drey Accorden*" (Wason 1985, p. 11), part of his argument that such harmonic thinking was out of line with Viennese publications of the period. But Daube did not abandon his harmonic thinking—harmonic thinking pervades Daube's notion of voice leading and melody. In addition, the likelihood that Daube completed the *Anleitung* in the 1770s along with the *Dilettant* and, if so, had probably been using it as a teaching resource for the quarter-century prior to its publication speaks against any retreat from a harmonic theory that was in any case by no means "radical" in Vienna at the time, as evidenced by Mozart's harmonic perspective on counterpoint and use of fundamental bass to teach harmonization, Albrechtsberger's harmonic approach to counterpoint, and Beethoven's citation of subposed chords in teaching materials.

Although Daube's presentation of melodic construction and of the structure of phrases and larger musical constructions is not as systematically organized as the comparable discussions by Heinrich Christoph Koch (1749–1816) in the 1780s and 1790s, his discussions of texture, dynamics, and scoring are virtually unique in the late eighteenth century and remain an invaluable resource on *galant* music.

## Chord Inversions and Chordal Functions

In several areas, changes in chordal nomenclature reflect changes in underlying thinking. These include replacing older names for various chords with numbering of inversions and gradually shifting toward naming all harmonies in relation to the tonic of the key.

NAMING INVERSIONS
Rameau continued to refer to inverted chords by their traditional thoroughbass names (such as 6-chords, "chord of the little sixth" for 6/4/3 chords, and "chord of the large sixth" for 6/5/3 chords), rather than as

inversions of triads or seventh chords. Starting around the midcentury, the modern system of numbering inversions became widespread. In Germany, Sorge, Marpurg, and Löhlein number the chordal *Versetzung* or *Umkehrung* (Sorge [1745–1747], 3, Chapter 7; Marpurg 1755–1762 1, p. 36; Löhlein 1765, p. 96). In France, Rameau's pupil [Pietro] Gianotti (?–1765) numbers the *renversement* in his treatise based on Rameau's manuscript on fundamental bass (Gianotti 1759). And in Italy, Giuseppe Paolucci (1726–1776) numbers the *rovescio* (Paolucci 1765–1772, 1, p. 74).

### INTERCHANGEABILITY OF INVERSIONS

For some theorists, even some sophisticated ones, the fact that various inversions were all based on the same root-position form meant that these inversions might be relatively interchangeable with one another. For instance, Mozart's pupil Barbara Ployer seems not to have learned to use second-inversion chords properly, whatever Mozart's explanation might have been. But with the exception of the Signoretti treatise cited at the end of Chapter 7, no theorist went so far as to open and close examples without regard to the position of the bass.

Rameau and those who followed him closely (including, for instance, Kirnberger) regarded chord progressions as imitations of cadences. For them, using chord positions other than those in a formal cadence required some sort of rationale (such as desiring to continue motion within a phrase). Other theorists who simply treated chords as a vocabulary from which to create progressions allowed a much freer interchange of inversions. This group includes theorists associated with Rameau as well as theorists independent of him. For instance, Anton Bemetzrieder (1743 or 1748–c. 1817), author of several popular books published in France and later in England, freely mixes chord positions within phrases in his 1771 keyboard and harmony primer, a work apparently written with some participation by Bemetzrieder's patron Denis Diderot.

Sorge also includes many examples in his *Compendium* in which 6/4 chords are approached and left by skip in the bass.[5] One is shown in Example 8-5, criticized by Marpurg. Marpurg, who recognizes the different roles played by the three positions of a triad (Marpurg 1755–1762, 1, p. 35), explains that the bass should not skip in and out of 6/4 chords as it can with 6/3 chords except amid certain arpeggiation patterns (see Example 8-6).

In accord with the freedom with which he uses 6/4-chords, Sorge argues that a fourth over the bass is a consonance (Sorge [1745–1747], 2, Part

---

5. Sorge's free use of 6/4 chords may result from his belief that a major 6/4 chord is more consonant than a minor 6/3 chord (Sorge [1745–1747], 2, Chapter 1). Although his reasoning is the same as Zarlino, Sorge does not cite Zarlino.

*Example 8-5.* Marpurg 1760, Fig. 71

2, Chapter 1). Yet he also anticipates Kirnberger's later distinction between consonant and dissonant 6/4 chords by suggesting that whereas some 6/4 chords are separate harmonies, 6/4 chords at a cadence yield to 5/3 chords (ibid., par. 10). But even in the case of the cadential 6/4, Sorge considers that the tonic, not the dominant, is the basis (ibid., Table 14, Figure 4). Löhlein's distinction between 6/4 chords that are *passing (in transitu)* and those that resolve to 5/3 (Löhlein 1765, p. 102), also preceding Kirnberger's published theories, probably derives from this passage of Sorge's.

CHORDAL FUNCTIONS

Inversional thinking and recognition of root progressions led to a marked shift in conceptualizing the nature of chord relationships during the later eighteenth century. Rameau had proposed three chordal functions: tonic, dominant, and subdominant. They were the pillars of the key and also the models for all chord progressions. As discussed earlier, these functions were not quite equivalent to our modern notions of I, IV, and V chords. For Rameau, any seventh chord (or even any chord that operated like a seventh chord, such as diminished sevenths and most chords by subposi-

*Example 8-6.* Marpurg 1760, Figs. 69a, 69e, 69f

Compositional Theory in the Eighteenth Century

tion) was simply a *dominant*. He made no further distinctions among what we would call ii7, iii7, and vi7 in a major key—they were *simple dominants* that progressed in imitated cadences, to be distinguished from the *dominant-tonic* that had a leading tone and was capable of forming a conclusive cadence. Likewise, any perfect chord (triad) was a *tonic,* and any chord that moved up by fifth, especially if it had an added sixth, was a subdominant. Outside of these chordal functions, Rameau did not differentiate chordal functions within a key or generally specify the location of the remaining chords in relation to a tonic. This aspect of Rameau's theories led him to his notions of implied dissonances (to specify the role of every nontriad as a dominant or subdominant), implied chromaticism, and even to the notion of a reigning tonic as opposed to local tonics (any unadorned triads). Most of his pupils and others who followed his ideas retained many of these ideas, including Kirnberger, who maintains the term *dominant* for any seventh chord (1771–1779, 1, p. 64; Beach-Thym 1982, p. 83).

Rameau's approach postulates a one-to-one relationship between chordal structure and chordal function. A triad is a tonic, no matter how temporary; a seventh chord is a dominant. Modern harmonic theories generally separate chordal structure from chordal function. Triads and seventh chords are chord-types that can occur on many different scale steps, and chordal functions are measured both by the position of the root in relation to the tonic of the key, and by the nature of the progression. The change from Rameau's conception to our modern notion began to appear in print beginning in the 1750s and 1760s. Jean Laurent de Béthizy (1709–1781), for instance, argues that perfect chords that are not preceded by progressions that would make them true tonics were only "implied tonics" (*censée-toniques;* Béthizy 1754, p. 153).[6] This removes the necessity of considering all chords as tonics (triads), dominants (seventh chords), or subdominants (with added sixths), thereby loosening the identity that Rameau had postulated between chord structure and chord function.

Other theorists created a terminology that led toward placing chords on scale degrees rather than arguing that a specific chord-type implied a given scale degree. Sorge, for instance, names chords according to their scale degree; a *Sextharmonie* refers to a chord on scale-step 6, as opposed to *Sextaccorde*, which he retains as the traditional term for a 6/3 chord (Sorge 1760, Chapter 12, par. 20).

A further step toward positioning all chords in terms of the tonic was taken by the Irish theorist John Trydell (c. 1715–1776), who bases his *Two Essays on the Theory and Practice of Music* (Dublin, 1766) on Rameau's theories, probably via an English writer such as Lampe. Over

---

6. The only substantial study of Béthizy's theories is Earhart 1985.

[K = keynote]

*Example 8-7.* Trydell 1766, p. 46

half a century before Gottfried Weber (1779–1839) began using Roman numerals systematically to label chords, and a decade before Abbé Vogler (1749–1814) used Roman numerals to label some cadences and seventh chords (Vogler 1776, p. 82; Vogler [1778], Table xxi, Fig. 5), Trydell introduces what he calls "harmonical figures" over chord progressions, calling them "an obvious Invention" (Dedication, p. xi) (see Example 8-7). In later examples, Trydell uses these "harmonical Figures" to compare progressions with different bass lines (p. 49). Many examples containing these figures also label all the intervals over the bass part, just as in Fux's counterpoint exercises.

Because of its appearance in such a remote geographical location in a work intended to encourage Irish composers, Trydell's notation would be a historical oddity of little larger significance but for the fact that his entire book was adopted as the article *Music* in the first *Encyclopaedia Britannica* (Edinburgh, 1771). Although this venture was quite a bit more amateurish than its momentous French model,[7] the work circulated widely and may well have suggested the use of chord numbers to continental readers.

Trydell's chord numbering is altogether separate from Kirnberger's suggestion to replace thoroughbass notation with chord root-names (article *Bezifferung* in Sulzer 1771–1774). Kirnberger's suggestion is in fact remarkably similar to Rameau's proposals of 1732 to replace thoroughbass notation with a tablature including chord roots in letters. John Holden (?–c. 1771), in his 1770 *Essay Towards a Rational System of Music,* writes the pitch names of chord roots below the score (p. 102).

A further step away from Rameauian ideas and toward nineteenth-century harmonic theory appears in the early works of Abbé Vogler. Many of the most striking ideas of this eccentric theorist, composer, and pioneering ethnomusicologist do not appear in print until the early years of the nineteenth century and therefore fall outside the present study.[8] But even his earlier works, *Tonwissenschaft and Tonsezkunst* (1776), which reap-

7. The editors' apologies for delays (in the preface to the third volume) are ample explanation of the nature of this venture.

8. The only comprehensive study of Vogler in English is Grave 1987.

pears as the first part of his *Kuhrpfälzische Tonschule* ([1778]), sanctioned as the official composition text for The Palatinate, contain a number of important innovations. Vogler studied briefly with Padre Martini and knew the works of Rameau, Tartini, Kirnberger, Vallotti, and other theorists of the age. He adopts many of the tenets of Rameau and his followers, including the three basic chords in a key, cadences as chord progressions in themselves and models for other progressions, and the fundamental bass as a representation of chordal roots. But Vogler was not at all troubled by the concerns of Rameau and other theorists about the types of chords appropriate to given scale degrees or the types of progressions allowable in the fundamental bass. Vogler establishes several types of chords on each step of the scale, even on the leading tone. This completes the separation of scale step and chord type, in that any chord type can now appear on any step within the key.

## Chord Tones and Nonharmonic Tones

Nowadays, we use a collective term such as *nonharmonic tone* or *foreign tone* to denote all pitches not belonging to chords, and we categorize the patterns that such notes form as passing tones, neighbors, suspensions, anticipations, appoggiaturas, escape tones, and so forth. The foundation of this distinction was laid during the second half of the eighteenth century. But no single theorist formulated the concept with a collective term for all notes not part of triads and seventh chords.

To an early-eighteenth-century musician, the modern distinction between chord tone and nonharmonic tone was not at all obvious. Earlier theory viewed intervals in terms of consonances versus dissonances and suspended dissonances versus passing dissonances—dichotomies not directly transferable to chord tones vs. nonharmonic tones. Some dissonances are nonharmonic tones and can resolve into a stationary harmony. Other dissonances are chord tones, such as chord sevenths (generally suspended or passing dissonances) or fourths over the bass in second-inversion chords (not treated as suspended or passing dissonances), and therefore resolve only when a harmony changes (though in the case of passing second-inversion chords, the fourth did not seem to resolve at all). Some consonances are nonharmonic tones in need of resolution, such as 6–5 over a root-position triad. Some consonances that are chord tones nevertheless resolve as dissonances, such as the fifth over the bass in a 6/5 chord. And some chord sevenths are suspended dissonances, while other chord sevenths arise as neighbors or passing tones either on or after the beat.

Conventions of thoroughbass figuring placed further obstacles in the way of the modern distinction. First, figuring commonly included only those dissonances a performer had to play to avoid unfortunate clashes—mostly suspensions and appoggiaturas. Other notes (passing tones, neighbors, escape tones, anticipations) were "notes of taste" or "*suppositions*," often simply learned by rote as part of patterns (*Figuren* or *Manieren*). Since these tones were not often played by a thoroughbass realizer, they were not deemed part of the harmony and were largely bypassed by thoroughbass theorists and harmonic theorists like Rameau. Indeed, for some theorists the term dissonance signified only conchordal dissonances included in thoroughbass figurings. Second, each verticality received its own figuring. There was no easy way to distinguish a dissonance whose resolution indicated a new harmony from a dissonance that resolved into the existing harmony, since in both cases the dissonant verticality and the chord of resolution had separate figurings. For instance, a seventh over G could resolve to E as a 7–6 suspension within an E-minor chord (in which case 7/3 resolves to 6/3) or to E in a progression to a C-major chord (in which case 7/5/3 resolves to 5/3).

Recognizing that there were only two basic types of chords—triads and seventh chords—was the first step toward the modern differentiation between chord tones and nonharmonic tones. But even those accepting this differentiation did not agree on how to understand other notes in terms of these chords. Some theorists dealt more readily with conchordal dissonances, while others dealt with notes added to already existing chords.

### SUSPENSIONS AND APPOGGIATURAS

Rameau's approach to conchordal dissonances accepts the premise of thoroughbass that such dissonances are part of the harmony. Via subposed chords, he explains all conchordal dissonances as parts of seventh chords. Explaining all conchordal dissonances as parts of chords is directly counter to the modern position, which treats some conchordal dissonances as nonharmonic tones.

Although his notion of subposed chords is one of the more problematic aspects of his theory, it was adopted in some form by many of his French protégés as well as by Marpurg, who was then the source of subposition for several German works, including keyboard and thoroughbass methods by Löhlein in 1765 and Daniel Gottlob Türk (1756–1813) in 1791, and Koch's composition treatise. As late as the 1810s, Beethoven taught his composition students Türk's subposed chords as one way of explaining suspensions (Nottebohm 1872, p. 170).

Each theorist interpreted subposition in his own way. A few, like Rameau, explain that suspended notes have a melodic origin but their resolution is best analyzed via subposition (Roussier 1764, pp. 94–95, 98), while most are silent on this issue. Some, like Rameau, use subposed chords only up to the eleventh, while others extend chords up to the

*Example 8-8.* Sorge 1767, Table 6, Figs. 3, 4

thirteenth (Béthizy 1754; Marpurg). Some theorists, like Rameau, use subposition only when it does not create syncopated harmonic rhythm in the fundamental bass (Béthizy 1754), whereas others are unconcerned by this (Clement 1758; Marpurg).

Even some theorists who argue against Rameau's formulation of sub-position came up with their own notions of chords with more notes than seventh chords. Francesco Antonio Vallotti (1697–1780), for instance, calls Rameau's attempt to explain all dissonances as sevenths via subposed chords "a mistake of the greatest consequence throwing the doctrine and use of dissonances into chaos" (Vallotti 1779, p. xxv). Yet Vallotti, in the third book of his manuscript treatise (probably written around 1770 but not published until 1950), proposes his own form of chords with up to seven different notes, each occurring in several inversions, creating virtual tone clusters. For instance, Vallotti illustrates a triad with a ninth, eleventh, thirteenth and also a suspended fourteenth (G-B-D-A-C-E-F), along with all its inversions (Vallotti 1950, Book 3, Chapter 18).[9]

Subposition was a major issue in Marpurg's disputes with Sorge in the 1760s as well as those with Kirnberger in the 1770s. Sorge argues that Marpurg's subposed chords often place the dissonance in the wrong chord. In Example 8-8, Sorge argues convincingly that "to introduce this ninth, D is needed as fifth of the dominant chord G-B-D, not as seventh of the seventh chord E-G-B-D . . . How absurd would that ninth chord be if the seventh chord E-G-B-D had to precede it" (Sorge 1767, pp. 54–55). In general, Sorge argues that "all tied dissonances . . . arise from the mixture of two chords" (p. 53). Just four years later, Kirnberger picked up on suggestions in Sorge's works and presented the modern formulation of suspended dissonances, differentiating clearly between chordal sevenths

9. Vallotti's treatise is replete with a variety of absurdities. He repeatedly contradicts himself, as when he forbids root progressions from scale-step 4 to 5 (Book 2, Chapter 24, p. 273) only four pages after using this progression in a cadence. He often misreads Rameau, insisting, for instance, that for Rameau only a chord with a major third has a true *basso fondamentale* (Vallotti 1779, p. xvi) and that Rameau introduced the term *sospensione* to music theory (p. xxv).

that require a change of harmony in order to resolve and suspensions that resolve in a harmony already present (discussed in Chapter 9).

## PASSING DISSONANCES

Whereas suspended nonharmonic tones continued to be thought of in many ways past the end of the eighteenth century, much of the modern attitude toward unsuspended nonharmonic tones appeared in Marpurg's writings during the 1750s. But terminology prevented a clear distinction from becoming universal. Traditional terminology differentiated notes according to their placement on the beat (*Hauptnoten* or principal notes) or after the beat (*durchgehende Noten* or passing notes), ignoring whether the pitches are chord tones or nonchord tones, consonant or dissonant. Such locutions reflect the assumptions of an earlier era when unsuspended notes on the beat were normally consonant and notes after the beat were regarded primarily as connections to the next beat. This terminology endured through the end of the century. For instance, Mozart uses the term *passing notes (durchgehenden Noten)* when speaking of unisons on a weak beat (Mozart 1784, fol. 11ʳ). Marpurg sometimes uses this terminology, but also treats notes in terms of their harmonic status.

Marpurg discusses nonharmonic tones in the second volume of his *Handbuch* (Marpurg 1755–1762, 2, pp. 81ff.), in the *Anleitung zur Musik überhaupt* (Marpurg 1763, Chapter 17 on *Passagen*), and in the *Anleitung zum Clavierspielen* (Marpurg 1755, pp. 36–60 on *Manierung*). His presentation is basically the same in all three, but with some differences in terminology.

In the *Anleitung zum Clavierspielen,* he uses the term *subsidiary notes (Nebennoten),* not *passing notes,* to refer to notes occurring after a beat. *Nebennoten* denotes the metric status of a note, not its harmonic status. If a piece contained only principal notes *(Hauptnoten),* it would be merely a succession of mostly consonant whole notes. Therefore, the single principal note necessary to the harmony in a given voice is frequently divided into subsidiary notes. Such embellishments *(Manieren)* are either composed into the piece *(Setzmanieren)* or added by the performer *(Spielmanieren).* Subsidiary notes can belong to the harmony as repetitions or arpeggiations *(harmonischer Nebennoten),* or can be *passing (durchgehende) notes* or *changing notes (Wechselnoten).* The term *changing note* to refer to passing tones on the beat, which remains in modern German, is another relic of the *stile antico.* Passing dissonances were viewed as occurring after the beat. When a passing dissonance occurred on the beat, it was assumed that the dissonance had changed places with a consonance. (This meaning of *changing note* is entirely separate from Fux's *nota cambiata,* which refers to a particular melodic pattern.)

*Example 8-9.* Marpurg 1755–1762, 2, Table 3, Fig. 16

In the *Anleitung zur Musik überhaupt,* Marpurg is even more explicit about the distinction between a note's metric and harmonic status. But he confuses the issue by using the term *principal note* in two separate meanings: "With changing notes it can happen that the last of two notes is at the same time both a principal [*Haupt-*] and a passing [*durchgehende*] note; the former with respect to the harmony, the latter with respect to the meter [*Tacteintheilung*]" (p. 146). Only after a generic term such as *nonharmonic* or *foreign* tone appeared in the nineteenth century would such infelicitous constructions disappear.

Even with this inadequate terminology, Marpurg does specify the difference between chord tone and nonharmonic tone and separates this dichotomy from consonance-dissonance and accented-unaccented. But he does this only with regard to nonsuspensions. In the *Anleitung zur Musik überhaupt,* he comes close to including all nonharmonic tones, differentiating those subsidiary tones that arise via diminution *(Verkleinerung)* or division of a long note from those that arise via extension of a note *(Haltung* or *Zusammenziehung;* pp. 144–145). All subsidiary tones are, therefore, either harmonic *(harmonische)* or melodic *(melodische).* This is close to the modern distinction between all nonharmonic tones and all chord tones. But his insistence on treating suspended notes as subpositions vitiates this attempt.

In the realm of nonsuspensions, Marpurg's distinctions allow him to parse examples and label each note much as a modern theorist would. This is especially clear in passages containing several nonharmonic tones, where previous theorists had trouble making these distinctions. Here is his explanation of why the suspension in Example 8-9 does not resolve to the first A: "For who is there who knows harmony and cannot see that in this example the resolution of the seventh is figuratively delayed via the inversion of the harmony, and that this [resolution] happens not at the indicated eighth but only on the last half-note A?" (p. 85). Nearly two decades later, as accomplished a contrapuntist as Padre Martini still had trouble distinguishing embellished suspensions from true resolutions (in Example 7-4).

*Example 8-10.* Marpurg 1755–1762, 2, Table 3, Fig. 24

Marpurg is able to construct a viable substructure even in complex interactions, such as the passage in Example 8-10 "by a certain good old harmonist":[10]

How will one explain this? I see no other manner than to represent the principal notes of the piece as at *b;* and if one wished to augment this with nothing but passing notes, it would appear as at *c.* But instead of executing this progression with this particular motion, the dots at *a* are removed, from which, by a harmonic freedom, this special sequence of harmonies necessarily arises. (pp. 85–86)

## Key Changes and Chromaticism

Although a harmonic perspective affected notions of key changes and chromaticism, in many ways thinking in these areas remained close to its formulation in earlier thoroughbass theory. Other than using chordal terminology to refer to keys, few theorists before Schenker related larger harmonic and tonal motions to the processes by which they understood local voice leading and harmonic progression. The occasional remarks in the works of Joseph Riepel (1709–1782) and Koch that imply such comparisons are discussed in Chapters 10 and 11.

Theorists continued to view the function of key changes much as Zarlino had viewed the use of dissonance—to add variety. Perhaps Marpurg stated it best when he notes that the "rule of unity" demands one key for a whole piece, while the "rule of variety" requires the presence of other keys (Marpurg 1755–1762, p. 24). From this perspective, theorists needed to explain how separate keys relate to one another and how progressions can be led from one key to another.

10. The conclusion of this discussion refers to such progressions in the works of J. S. Bach.

Theorists as early as Zarlino explained that regular cadential points occur on the notes of the perfect chord built on the modal final—on 1, 3, and 5. By the early eighteenth century, theorists recognized that although the dominant is a common goal of key changes, the mediant, at least in major keys, does not often play that role. They found various ways of explaining that the closely related keys are those whose tonic triads exist in the original key. In a major key, close changes are to 2, 3, 4, 5, and 6, while in a minor key, the goals are 3, 4, 5, 6, and 7.

These are the keys closest to the tonic in circular chord progressions of rising or descending thirds proposed by Werckmeister: C-e-G-b-D . . . and C-a-F-d-B♭ . . . (Werckmeister 1698, pp. 20–22). They are also the keys closest to the tonic on Heinichen's musical circle (Heinichen 1711, p. 261) and on Mattheson's "improved" circle of 1735. All these schemes incorporate both major and minor keys into a single progression, which Heinichen asserts is an improvement over earlier circular modulatory schemes by fourths and fifths that pass through only major or minor keys (as in Penna 1684, 3, Chapters 9–13; and as Heinichen relates that his teacher Johann Kuhnau [1660–1722] taught; Heinichen 1728, pp. 840–841). Michael Johann Friedrich Wideburg (1720–1800) illustrated several of these schemes in a single multitiered circle in the third volume of his immense (over 1600-page) keyboard method (1765–1775). Reading from the outside, the tiers show show Heinichen's and Mattheson's circle of keys, circles by fourths and fifths, and the common key signatures of relative major and minor keys (see Example 8-11). From at least Penna onward, manuals urged students to practice circular progressions, whether by playing the single chords one after the other, or playing a brief progression in each key before moving on to the next. Such exercises were intended to instill familiarity with all the keys and to serve as models for improvisation.

More fanciful, but just as indicative of the multiple possibilities of key relationships, is Riepel's likening of related keys to the residents of a feudal estate. In C major, for instance, C is the landowner (Meyer), G is the field hand (Knecht), A minor the head maid (Obermagd), E minor her assistant (Untermagd), F major a day laborer (Taglöhner), and D minor a maid (Unterläufferin; Riepel 1755, pp. 65ff.).

Various writers later in the century began to include keys related by major-minor mixture in the orbit of diatonically related keys. Marpurg explains that "in the galant style a short phrase [Rhytmus] in a major key may, on its repeat on the same scale step, be transformed into a minor key, upon which one returns to the major key" (Marpurg 1755–1762, 1, p. 25). Riepel illustrated this around the same time (Riepel 1755, p. 71).

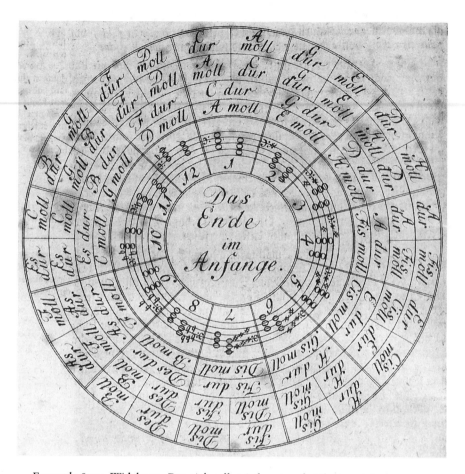

*Example 8-11.* Wideburg, *Der sich selbst informirende Clavierspieler* 3, p. 192 (Music Division, The New York Public Library for the Performing Arts, Astor, Lenox and Tilden Foundations)

Sorge goes further by noting that the common interchange of parallel major and minor keys brings the related keys of C major and A minor close to the related keys of C minor and E♭ major (Sorge 1767, p. 38).

THE PROCESS OF CHANGING KEYS

Many theorists maintained the traditional thoroughbass explanation of moving to a new key by introducing its leading tone. Some changed the terminology to urge introducing the new dominant chord. Some followed Rameau, invoking change in chordal function to explain moving from one key to another, such as turning a tonic chord into a subdominant or a dominant to change the key by a fifth (Gianotti 1759, p. 47; Daube 1756, Chapter 5, par. 2). Finally, there were widespread discussions, many trace-

Compositional Theory in the Eighteenth Century

able to Rameau's influence, of enharmonic change of diminished seventh chords allowing quick changes to distant keys.

Several theorists offer brief examples modulating from a given key to various closely and more distantly related keys. Among those offering such listings, which began the genre of *Modulationslehren* that lasted into the twentieth century, are Sorge [1753], Soler 1762, Kirnberger 1771–1779, 1, pp. 113ff. (Beach-Thym 1982, pp. 131ff.), Vogler 1778–1781 (which illustrates modulations to all other keys from each of the twenty-four keys), and Albrechtsberger 1790, p. 10.

CHROMATICISM WITHIN A KEY

As discussed in Chapter 3, there are solid practical reasons that thorough-bass theorists explained most chromaticism, no matter how brief, as a change in the local key. Even musicians of the stature of W. A. Mozart would cite a key change for a single brief chord (Mozart 1784, Fol. 8$^r$).

Nonetheless, thoroughbass theorists in occasional remarks and harmonic theorists from Rameau onward suggest that brief instances of chromaticism can also be viewed as a temporary digression within the prevailing key. Sorge notes that sharps can occasionally appear without an actual change to another key (Sorge [1745–1747], 1, Chapter 13, par. 20). Kirnberger and Koch came yet closer to specifying the difference between such local progressions and an actual change of key (discussed in Chapters 9 and 11). But as with nonharmonic tones, until terms such as secondary dominant, applied dominant, borrowed chord, or auxiliary dominant, became common, most such discussions remained isolated and did not become universal.

CONTINUOUS CHROMATICISM

Although occasional discussions arise from Rameau onward illustrating enharmonic changes, especially those involving diminished seventh chords, Vogler's 1778 suggestion for a type of constantly modulating chromaticism is unparalleled in the eighteenth century and was probably quite suggestive to many nineteenth-century composers. After illustrating numerous increasingly chromatic changes of key *(Ausweichungen)*, he offers the circular progression in Example 8-12 that some modern theorists refer to as the *omnibus* (Wason 1985, pp. 15–19). Vogler recognizes the special nature of this progression:

> It must be noted that these changes of key are based more on the position [voice leading?] than on the harmony [*mehr auf die Lage als Harmonie*]; for no dissonance is resolved and the unity of key is not observed to the least degree, since one can never know what the principal key of the piece is . . . One begins most appropriately on C with 5/3 [sic]. The following C♯ with

*Example 8-12.* Vogler 1778, Tab. xxx, Fig 2

the diminished seventh is the seventh tone of D-minor. D with the 6/4 is an inversion lying on the fifth degree of G minor. E♭ with the suspended seventh is the fifth degree of both keys of A♭ . . . (Vogler 1778, pp. 176–177)

## Use of Fundamental Bass

After the midcentury, Rameauian fundamental bass, notated on a separate staff below a score, became quite widespread throughout Europe. Appearances of this notation with little or no explanation of its meaning and purpose imply that authors expected their readers to be familiar with it, much as modern theorists assume that musically literate persons understand Roman numerals. Chapter 7 illustrates Martini's and Mozart's use of fundamental bass to explain harmonic progressions in the 1770s and 1780s. About the same time, Vogler published numerous fundamental-bass analyses of complete compositions in the three volumes of his *Betrachtungen der Mannheimer Tonschule* (1778–1781). The writings surveyed here are somewhat earlier.

### NICHELMANN

One work applying fundamental bass extensively is *Die Melodie nach ihrem Wesen sowohl, als nach ihren Eigenschaften* (1755) by Christoph Nichelmann (1717–1762).[11] Nichelmann, cembalist and composer in the royal chapel of Frederick the Great since 1745, had been a choirboy under J. S. Bach, and had studied composition with W. F. Bach, Keiser, G. P. Telemann, Mattheson, Quantz, and Graun. Despite its title, *Die Melodie* is primarily about style and harmonic theory. Nichelmann wrote it in response to a dispute between the Berlin theorists Marpurg and Johann Friedrich Agricola (1720–1774) over a favorite topic of the eighteenth century: the relative merits of Italian and French music (in Marpurg 1749–1750). Nichelmann believed that this dispute, like so many others of its

11. Christensen 1990b is the sole study of Nichelmann's music theory. Discussions of Nichelmann's aesthetics appear in the informative *MGG* article by Thomas Langner, Helm 1960 (pp. 175 and 228–235), Goldschmidt 1915 (p. 141), and Fellerer 1962.

kind, missed the point. A good composition, he argues, is one in which expression derives from proper harmony, not simply from a melody composed without concern for the underlying harmony: "The more dependent a song [*Gesang*] is on the harmonies [*Zusammenstimmung*] the more it is melody [*Melodie*]" (p. 44). If one writes considering only the main melody, or if one does not consider the proper harmonic context, as Nichelmann believes many modern composers do, then arbitrary harmonies will result, and the result will lack expressive power (p. 56). Nichelmann characterizes these opposing positions with his adaptation of Wolfgang Caspar Printz's terms *monodic* and *polyodic,* originally introduced to differentiate two methods of composition: *monodic,* in which one writes a single line and then adds the remaining parts, and *polyodic,* in which the composer conceives of all the parts together (*Die Melodie,* p. 14; Printz 1676–1796, 3, Chapters 11 and 18).

Unfortunately, as one historian has noted, Nichelmann "lacks a clear head" (Goldschmidt 1915, p. 141). He does not clearly explain how to differentiate monodic from polyodic music. But this does not stop him from laying out a number of detailed analyses almost without parallel in the eighteenth century: works by Agricola, J. S. and C. P. E. Bach, C. H. Graun, Hasse, Lambert, Lully, Telemann, and others. Almost invariably, these analyses consist of a fundamental bass and a recomposition of problematic passages to demonstrate that a proper composition is essentially polyodic. Although he argues that monodic and polyodic supersede stylistic differentiations of the time and that it is possible to compose polyodically in any style, he consistently criticizes *galant* features such as slow harmonic rhythm, purely homophonic textures, rhythmicized repetitions of bass notes *(Trommelbass),* and the scalework and passagework characteristic of Italian-style music. Clearly his predilections lay with the music of J. S. and W. F. Bach, although even the music of J. S. Bach is not immune from his criticism. Whatever his limitations in digesting many German, French, and English writings on aesthetics, Nichelmann illuminates for us the state of knowledge of fundamental bass theory in Germany before Marpurg published his translation of D'Alembert's *Elemens* in 1757.

A typical recomposition of Nichelmann's appears in Example 8-13. The extended harmonies in the monodic realization stand in stark contrast to the prolonged harmonies (virtually in the Schenkerian sense of the term) in the polyodic version. Although he never discusses the issue directly, the latter realization implies that Nichelmann understood how basic harmonies could be prolonged not only by inversion (as in nearly every measure), but also via neighboring chords (the C-chord in m. 2 and the B♭-chord in m. 7) and repetition (the repeated tonicizations of F in mm. 4–8).

Several idiosyncratic features of Nichelmann's fundamental basses are

*Example 8-13.* Nichelmann 1755, Exs. 8, 9, 10

evident here. Like Rameau, he is sensitive to root progressions by step, but he does not invoke Rameau's *double emploi* to explain them. Instead, Nichelmann treats step progressions as two fifths with the middle chord omitted. He notates the omitted chord as an interpolated sixteenth note that does not reflect a chord in the music (mm. 2, 4, and 5). Some root progressions up a fifth are analyzed as added-sixth chords like Rameau's

*Example 8-14.* Nichelmann 1755, Exs. 14, 15

subdominant (m. 7), but others are not (the progression leading to the cadential 6/4 in measure 8). The fundamental bass to the polyodic realization incorporates the grace notes (11–10 in mm. 2 and 3; cadential 6/4 in measure 8).

Nichelmann delays an explanation of fundamental-bass notation until after several such examples: "The fundamental tones [*Fundamental-Klänge*] . . . only make apparent all the more clearly the progression of the root-tones [*Grund-Töne*] which serve us in hearing music like a guide or compass, whereby the connections of the tones are led back to the very source from which they arise" (p. 40). He fails to explain his Rameauian sensitivity to step progressions or the special notation he uses to explain them. And he fails to explain his Rameauian use of implied dissonances to prevent any sense of closure (as in the A chord in m. 2 and the E chord in m. 3 of Example 8-14).

The first example Nichelmann treats is a composition for which he has nothing but praise: the opening of the sarabande from J. S. Bach's *French Suite in E major.* Nichelmann's extensive description of the harmonic progressions and their propriety to the expressive purposes of the piece is the earliest such harmonic-aesthetic analysis of a Bach composition and merits full quotation here (see Example 8-14):[12]

The progression of the tonic to its upper third with the chord of the major third, upon which this [first] connection of different chords is based, is of such strenuous force that a diminution of that force can be obtained only by the following cadence on the sixth of the tonic, which prevents the soul from becoming excessively sad. The following progression of the tonic [C♯ as a

12. This and Nichelmann's other commentaries on J. S. Bach compositions are reprinted in Schulze 1972, pp. 96–103, and discussed in Schulze 1984, pp. 135–145.

triadic cadential goal] to the fourth of the key is pleasing not only because of the good relationship which it has with the preceding chord as well as with the prevailing tonic; but also because it serves as an introduction to the following chord of the fifth of the key, in which the root of the first chord [the A-chord] becomes the seventh. Precisely this harmony, the fifth of the key, was the best means to lead to the tonic chord, and via the implied chord of the fifth of the key, to the fifth of that fifth, and therefore to the harmony of the second of the key taken with the major third, thereby securing the cadence on the fifth of the key. This connection among different chords is perfectly designed to satisfy our natural hunger for a varied harmony. It is also perfectly suited to the special design of the composer.

The character of a sarabande obliges the composer to create just such a connection of various chords, which can elevate the soul so much and place it in a state of wonderment and reverence.

Now, the different chords are perfectly suited to make us gradually perceive this state. They are, considering their connection, extraordinary and new. Their development, i.e., their tempo and movement, the unevenness of the various durations used here, the noted relationships—in a word, the rhythm of these different chords is therefore created so that the attention, the seriousness, the awe, in brief, the depicted passion can thereby give rise to similar feelings. (pp. 59–60)

Nichelmann then muses whether these good effects arose by genius or by long and hard work. Begging the question, he concludes that the composer, "before he created this piece, must have been affected by the impression of the different harmonies that are appropriate for the indicated purposes. For no continuous piece can be considered without the preceding impression of various continuous chords." Considering that Nichelmann had known J. S. Bach and that he learned his compositional craft originally from W. F. Bach, is it possible that this analysis and explanation of a possible compositional process was his impression of J. S. Bach's compositional process? And is it possible that this analysis represents the sorts of discussions that took place between composition teacher and pupil during this period, but that do not appear in print elsewhere?

Nichelmann's treatise stirred up quite a tempest in the royal court in Berlin. It was read, probably correctly, as an attack on the musical style of several members of the court, particularly C. P. E. Bach, exacerbating longstanding hostility between the two (Helm 1960, p. 175). Agricola, who like Nichelmann had studied with J. S. Bach, noted in a letter dated 1771 that Nichelmann supported "the composition style of the older Italians, the non-Italianized French, and the older Germans such as Telemann and Handel . . . but Nichelmann certainly went too far" (Agricola 1786, p. 817).

*Die Melodie* sparked several critiques and a response by Nichelmann. Ernst Gottlieb Baron (1696–1760), a lutenist and composer in Berlin, quickly penned a twelve-page attack (Baron 1756) countering Nichelmann's basic premise with the *galant* position on melody already enunciated by Mattheson in the 1730s and by Riepel in 1752: "If one wished to establish the harmonic triad as the main source and derive the melody from it, one would be putting the cart before the horse, for a hundred passages could be drawn out of frequent inversion of a chord, but never a melody, which must have an orderly sequence" (Baron 1756, pp. 11–12).

Another sixteen-page pamphlet also appeared shortly under the pseudonym Caspar Dünkelfeind (Enemy of Darkness). This work is often attributed to C. P. E. Bach, but comments on p. 15 in defense of Rameau (namely that Rameau believed that melody and harmony both contributed to melodiousness), the self-description of the author as "an amateur" (*Liebhaber*, title page), the writing style, and various philosophical positions cast some doubt on this. But if Bach did not write this critique, he probably encouraged this harsh attack, which mocks Nichelmann as an incompetent plagiarist, criticizes many of his ideas, and defends some of the C. P. E. Bach works Nichelmann had attacked.

Nichelmann's extensive use of fundamental bass with such little explanation of either its nature or the details of his own approach implies that even before Marpurg's 1757 translation of D'Alembert's *Elemens*, German musicians were familiar with fundamental bass. None of Nichelmann's critics even cites his use of fundamental bass, not to mention his interpretation of step progressions, his use of implied dissonances, the fact that Nichelmann does not explain any of this, or his analyses themselves. If Nichelmann had been arguing his case with an unfamiliar analytic notation or theoretical method, it is likely that at least one of his critics would have commented on it.

In addition, the casual presence of fundamental bass, of omitted chords as a structural explanation, and of analytical activity in the Berlin circle in the 1750s sheds light on the origins of theories commonly associated with Kirnberger in the 1770s. Kirnberger espouses many concepts first raised by Nichelmann. He supports a polyodic approach to composition when he urges that all the parts be of interest to avoid a texture where the entire "affection and true expression of the piece" is "concentrated solely in a single voice" (Kirnberger 1771–1779, I, p. 159; Beach-Thym 1982, p. 174). And, like Nichelmann, he uses the notion of omitted chords to explain various progressions, although not the step progressions that Nichelmann explains by an interpolated bass. Nichelmann and Kirnberger had common roots in the Bach circle in Leipzig, but Nichelmann was older than Kirnberger and had left Leipzig before Kirnberger arrived. The two theorists knew each other in Berlin. Kirnberger devotes three columns in the article *Melodie* in Johann Georg Sulzer's *Allgemeine Theorie der*

*Schönen Künste* to listing each chapter heading of Nichelmann's book and briefly summarizing their contents.

There remains the question of where Nichelmann learned about fundamental bass. Among his teachers, Mattheson, Quantz, and Telemann could hardly have been the source. Mattheson was no supporter of Rameau's. Quantz, to judge from his 1752 flute method (Quantz 1752) and his reply to Marpurg's 1760 critique of Sorge (Marpurg 1754–1778, 5 [1761], pp. 113–114), seems to have had a lifelong disinterest in what he considered speculative theory. And Telemann's published theoretical materials from the 1730s show no familiarity with Rameau's theories. Since Nichelmann differs with Rameau and Marpurg on crucial points, neither Rameau's published works nor Marpurg's as-yet unpublished works could have been the sole source. Did Nichelmann learn fundamental bass entirely on his own? Did he learn it from musicians in the Bach circle in Leipzig or at the Berlin court? Did he simply pick up ideas that were in common circulation? At this time, a definitive answer is not possible.

OTHER THEORISTS

Within Germany, Löhlein's *Clavier-Schule* of 1765 also includes an extended example with fundamental-bass notation in his discussion of how to work out a *fantasie*. A composition with annotations runs from pp. 181–186, accompanied throughout by its fundamental bass. Löhlein explains that this "harmonic skeleton [*harmonische Skelet*] under the bass" shows how to elaborate "fundamental harmonies." Again, there is no further explanation of the notation, implying he expected readers to be familiar with it. In addition, the fact that each German writer of this period who used fundamental bass referred to it with a different name implies an oral tradition, not a borrowing from a single published source, whether German or foreign. Löhlein's popular work also shows the extent to which a traditional approach to thoroughbass was becoming increasingly outdated after the midcentury. As he explains in the 1781 edition, even many teachers could not deal with the subject any more: "I have found that the easiest and surest path is to build the foundation upon the two principal harmonies, namely the triad [*Hauptaccord*] and the seventh-chord; the student must not be led further until he has clearly grasped these foundations."

Another theorist using fundamental bass idiosyncratically is Giorgio Antoniotto (c. 1692–1776), an Italian living in London. His substantial 1760 treatise *L'Arte Armonica or A Treatise on the Composition of Musick* boasts luminaries like Avison, Burney, and Hawkins among its many subscribers. Antoniotto derives lines for counterpoint from fundamental-bass progressions such as descending fifths (the "Skip of Cadence"), ascending fifths, and motions by thirds. Each such derived set of

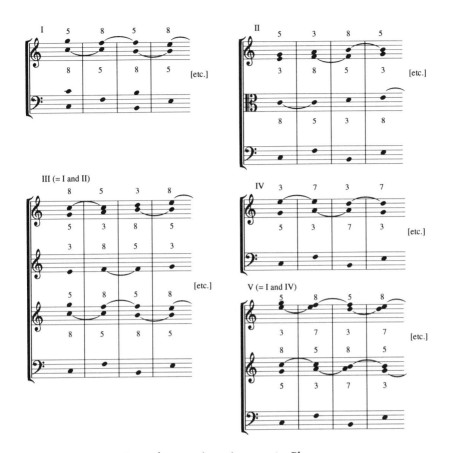

*Example 8-15.* Antoniotto 1760, Plate 17

lines is a "canon" in the sense of a law. Book 1 (pp. 1–62) presents forty-five canons dealing with diatonic progressions, Book 2 extends these progressions to the chromatic octave, and Book 3 elaborates these progressions with inversions of the harmonies, suspensions, and so forth.

Example 8-15, an illustration of the openings of the first five canons for a diatonic progression by descending fifths, gives an idea of his method. Antoniotto offers eighteen such canons in up to sixteen voices for this one progression.

The centerpiece of the treatise (pp. 88ff.) is his demonstration that these canons provide the basis for Corelli's *Violin Sonata,* opus 5, number 1. He presents Corelli's melody-bass framework with the underlying harmonic derivation of the voice leading below (see Example 8-16). As in Nichelmann's treatise, the explanatory staff system offers complete chords, and the fundamental bass adds chords to explain what would otherwise have been root progressions by step. Unlike Nichelmann, Antoniotto uses Rameau's *double emploi* to explain these step progressions.

*Example 8-16.* Antoniotto 1760, Plate 54

Another Italian, this one living in Italy, who used fundamental bass to teach harmonization is Vincenzo Manfredini. Part 2 of his *Regole armon-iche* (1775) describes "a new system of learning bass accompaniment." The result is quite similar to what Mozart used to teach Barbara Ployer in the next decade. A fundamental bass is worked out, from which the actual bass *(basso continuo)* is drawn. Other aspects of Manfredini's work are in the *partimento* tradition.

## Permutation

One aspect of eighteenth-century theory sometimes regarded as more diverting than serious is permutation *(ars combinatoria)*. Although some theorists were more absorbed than others in such mathematics, it permeates a rather wide range of music theory, and its presence often highlights important aspects of musical structure (Ratner 1970). Even theorists who disparaged using mathematics to justify harmonic progressions were themselves addicted to permutations. In 1757, C. P. E. Bach published a way to generate 429,536,481 examples of invertible counterpoint "without knowing the rules" (Helm 1966). And Riepel, who ridicules Rameau's use of mathematics (Riepel 1755, p. 53), is perhaps the century's most eager advocate of permutations: "The unique art of permutations, by which one can uncover in a single day far more than 99 themes, is at least 99 times healthier for composition than the calculation of ratios" (Riepel 1755, p. 25). Riepel calculates permutations that yield numbers as high as $10^{66}$ (ibid., p. 26) and demonstrates applications on all sorts of musical elements: melodic pitches, rhythms, bowings, even harmonies.

One of his most interesting applications is to harmony (Riepel 1757).

Compositional Theory in the Eighteenth Century

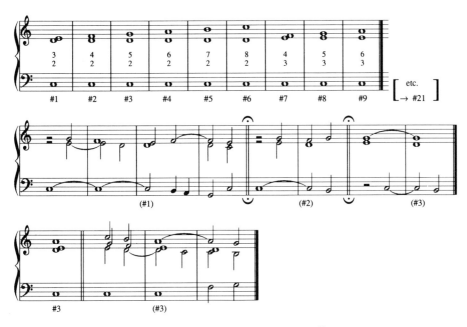

*Example 8-17.* Riepel 1757, pp. 57ff

He considers all the possible three-note and four-note combinations of diatonic scale steps over a given bass, rejects those four-note simultaneities with three consecutive scale steps (such as 4/3/2, 5/4/3, 6/5/4) as "cater-wauling," and demonstrates that many others are quite usable in harmony (see Example 8-17). This whole procedure may strike some as downright silly, but Riepel actually sheds some light on an aspect of tonal structure that has received virtually no attention at all from theorists—simultaneity structure of harmonies regardless of their functional role (chord versus nonharmonic tone, consonance versus dissonance). He is well aware that these chords have different uses: "They could be divided into good, me-dium, and poor. The good ones are in daily use and are known everywhere. As for the poor ones, one might use perhaps only one or two all year in an adagio if, for example, the text called for it" (p. 64). But his examples show how a composer can exploit these harmonies with care. For instance, the first excerpt builds up to his "triad number 1," which contains two seconds (C-D; D-E), by presenting two simultaneities with a single second each (E-F, then C-D, then C-D-E). Likewise, tetrad number 3, which contains two steps (C-D-E), follows a simultaneity with two steps (B-C, C-D) and precedes another simultaneity with one step (C-D in the super-tonic chord).

Looking at tonal music from this perspective brings out unexpected relationships. For instance, in the much-discussed variations theme that

*Example 8-18.* Mozart, *Piano Sonata,* K.331, first movement

opens Mozart's *Piano Sonata,* K. 331, virtually every simultaneity is either a major triad (labeled *T* in the following example), a minor-third-plus-whole-step (labeled *X*), or a combination of one of these (*T+X*) (see Example 8-18). The almost exclusive use of these two simultaneities is part of what gives this theme its special sonority. And since Mozart seems to have been familiar with Riepel's writings (Anderson, 1966, letter of September 15, 1773), he may well have been consciously aware of these structural relationships.[13]

Another theorist who generally avoids using mathematics to back up his harmonic theories but who used permutations for various purposes is Kirnberger. His invocation of possible arpeggiation patterns is similar to Riepel (Kirnberger 1771–1779, 1, pp. 211–213; Beach-Thym 1982, p. 224). But other applications are idiosyncratic. One concerns the traditional topic of invertible counterpoint, the subject matter of about one half of his composition treatise (ibid., 2, Parts 2 and 3).

A further application of permutations is in a spate of dice games that began in 1757 with Kirnberger's *Ever-Ready Polonaise and Menuet Composer* and continued well into the next century. Kirnberger offers six melodic possibilities for each measure of each dance type and asks the "composer" to cast a die for each measure to decide which melody to play. The harmonic structure of each resulting dance remains the same, but the number of possible melodies is immense. Marpurg tutted that not every connection would actually yield a sensible melody—but who's counting? (Marpurg 1754–1778, 3, p. 145). Most later dice games are by otherwise insignificant musicians, though one is questionably attributed to C. P. E. Bach (a c. 1790 dice game producing waltzes) and another to Haydn (*Gioco filarmonico* published in Naples c. 1793 and 1812).[14]

These lighthearted works reflect in their own way the rationalistic me-

13. Lester 1978 and Lewin 1979 pursue the issue of simultaneities apart from tonal function.

14. Gerigk 1934 surveys the genre. Feil 1955 offers provocative insights into the significance of dice games (Chapter 4).

chanistic spirit of the age. Just as the French philosophes believed that the proper application of reason could teach them the basics of musical composition without a traditional apprenticeship, the writers of these pamphlets believed that reason could produce a mechanical method of composing acceptable pieces. Many a bourgeois host probably found it both easier and cheaper to procure one of these methods and produce his own dance music than to have to continually purchase the latest sheet music.

Despite the apparent emphasis on melodic line in these games, they actually illuminate the continuing dominance of bass motions and harmonic progressions in determining the coherence of a composition. As with popular music of many eras, seemingly innumerable melodic possibilities occur over a small number of harmonic progressions. By offering innumerable melodies to go with the same bass patterns, these methods are part of the tradition of teaching composition by rhythmicizing thoroughbass realizations (Niedt) or drawing the actual voice leading of a piece from the underlying harmonic progressions (as in Lippius, Rameau, Nichelmann, or Antoniotto). As Marpurg explained, C. P. E. Bach's permutational game for producing invertible counterpoint could only be put together by maintaining the same root progression in each possible solution—showing that Bach understood the nature of root progressions, whether or not he chose to include that concept in his thoroughbass manual.

## "The Genealogical Tree of Harmony"

No survey of harmonic thinking in the eighteenth century would be complete without resurrecting at least one of the imaginative didactic publications of the time: the three-page folio-sized *Arbre Généalogique de l'harmonie* (c. 1767) by François-Guillaume Vial (c. 1730–?), nephew of the violinist and composer Jean-Marie Leclair (1697–1764) (Fétis 1833–1844). Example 8-19 is the imaginatively engraved frontispiece. Instructions explain how to use the compass *(boussole)* by fifths to learn key names, key signatures, the three principal notes in a key (tonic, subdominant, dominant), the order of sharps and flats, and the location of the semitones in each scale. The compass by thirds is useful for accompanying or composing because it shows how to make perfect chords, seventh chords, added-sixth chords, diminished seventh chords, all their inversions, and also how to construct chords by subposition. According to Vial, the tree itself is helpful in fingering and voice leading by showing common tones, in creating melodies from the voice leading that connects chords, in finding the fundamental bass, in preparing and resolving dissonances, in learning the cadences and their role in the Rule of the Octave, and in modulating by showing keys related in various ways.

*Example 8-19.* Vial [c. 1767], frontispiece (Music Division, The New York Public Library for the Performing Arts, Astor, Lenox and Tilden Foundations)

# CHAPTER NINE

# The Marpurg-Kirnberger
# Disputes

*People speak the worse [of fundamental bass] in direct proportion to
their ignorance of it.*

*Gianotti 1759, p. xi*

THE MOST SIGNIFICANT dispute concerning harmonic theory in the
second half of the eighteenth century is that between Friedrich Wilhelm
Marpurg (1718–1795) and Johann Philipp Kirnberger (1721–1783). Each
man had been associated with the Bach circle in Leipzig. And each was
an important and prolific author in Berlin, the city that Charles Burney
described in 1772 as "the capital of a prince . . . where both the theory
and practice of music had been more profoundly treated than elsewhere,
by professors of great and acknowledged abilities, who are still living; and
who have published the result of their long experience and superior skill
in treatises which are regarded throughout Germany as classical" (Scholes
1959, p. 159).

Marpurg viewed himself as Mattheson's successor in the role of musical
critic at large. During the late 1750s and 1760s he took on Sorge, Daube,
and others who challenged his conception of music theory. But as interesting as those writers are, neither is of Kirnberger's stature. And in no
other polemic do the issues seem as clear as in his dispute with Kirnberger.

Marpurg and Kirnberger sparred on a number of issues in the late 1750s
and again in the 1770s. Most historical interest has centered on their later
dispute. Marpurg, insisting he was Rameau's advocate, attacked the application of fundamental bass and the interpretation of suspensions in
Kirnberger's composition text *Die Kunst des reinen Satzes* (1771–1779)
and a companion work, *Die wahren Grundsätze zum Gebrauch der Har-*

*monie* (1773). In an often cited passage, Marpurg states his notion of Rameau's fundamental bass and explains why it differs from Kirnberger's:

> Rameau designated by the word fundamental bass a bass which contains nothing more than the simple fundamental chords . . . without the slightest connection among them. I say without the slightest connection because in laying out the fundamental chords no consideration whatever is given to the type of progression; rather each individual chord of the fundamental bass is merely reduced to its root form. (Marpurg 1776, p. 232)

This seems to draw the line between a vertical conception of harmony as isolated chords and a more linear conception of harmony and voice leading in which the nature of the progression determines a proper analysis of chordal structure.

The same perspectives seem to underlie their views on suspensions. Marpurg utilizes the theory of subposed chords, extending subposition to create chords of the thirteenth and even the fifteenth. Kirnberger, by contrast, views some suspended dissonances as chord sevenths, while others are linear suspensions temporarily delaying chord tones.

As in his earlier dispute with Sorge, Marpurg appealed to his compatriots, claiming that his position represents the true German tradition of J. S. Bach and others. Kirnberger countered that by rejecting French theory he stood in the true German Bach tradition. C. P. E. Bach seemed to settle the matter in a letter from which Kirnberger quoted a few sentences: "You can proclaim loudly that my foundations and those of my late father are anti-Rameau" (Kirnberger 1771–1779, 2, p. 188).

Taking this polemic at face value, many historians have characterized the dispute as a confrontation between a Rameau-Marpurg view of harmony consisting of isolated vertical chords and a Kirnberger-Bach view of harmony as a more linear phenomenon derived from thoroughbass thinking. But when placed in context, Marpurg's and Kirnberger's positions cannot be characterized in that manner. On most of the issues they debated, Kirnberger's positions are actually very close to Rameau's theories (though Kirnberger may not have been aware of that), and Marpurg's positions are not only directly opposed to Rameau's theories, but often reflect a thoroughbass perspective.

As a result, despite its clear wording, C. P. E. Bach's statement simply cannot be read as a condemnation of the contents of Rameau's theories. If Bach meant to defend Kirnberger in his dispute with Marpurg—and without the context of the sentences that Kirnberger quotes, it is not clear just what Bach's statement refers to—Bach was in fact defending much of Rameau's conception of music! What comes through clearly from Kirnberger's anti-Rameau polemic and C. P. E. Bach's retort is that although Rameau's writings themselves may have remained unread in many circles, quite a few Rameauian tenets had become so widespread and so pervasive that prominent musicians believed them to be the ideas of German musical traditions and not relatively recent and foreign discoveries.

This chapter explores the writings of Marpurg and Kirnberger to place their disputes into the context of theoretical issues explored in the preceding chapters.

## Marpurg as Theorist

### LIFE AND PUBLICATIONS

Little is known about Marpurg's early life (Serwer 1980 surveys what is known). He apparently traveled widely through the mid-1740s, living in Paris in 1746. But he probably neither met nor studied with Rameau, since he most likely would have loudly proclaimed such a connection in his later defenses of what he viewed as Rameau's theories. While in Paris, he also probably lacked any personal contact with D'Alembert, whose *Elemens* he published in German in 1757. This is not surprising, considering that D'Alembert's interest in music theory did not begin until after Marpurg had left Paris. He probably met D'Alembert when the latter visited Berlin in 1763, but there seems to be no written record of their contact.

After he returned to Germany, Marpurg was in Leipzig for a short while, making the acquaintance of the Bach family. He then moved to Berlin, where in 1749 he began publishing music books and journals at an astounding pace. Within three years, his reputation was such that J. S. Bach's heirs turned to him to write a preface to the *Art of the Fugue* (published in 1752). Shortly thereafter, Marpurg published his two-volume *Abhandlung von der Fuge* (1753–1754), which remains a classic text.

Marpurg's three journals contain book reviews, biographies, translations of important foreign works, and articles on theory, aesthetics, and temperament. Their lively style was designed to attract professionals as well as musically literate amateurs:

1. *Critische Musicus an der Spree* (1749–1750), whose title honors earlier journals by Mattheson and Scheibe (the River Spree runs through Berlin).
2. *Historisch-kritische Beyträge zur Aufnahme der Musik* (1754–1762, 1778), with most entries signed with pseudonyms, hiding the fact that Marpurg wrote almost all the items.[1]

1. Daube, for instance, wrote to Marpurg in 1756 protesting an unfavorable review at the hands of a "Herr Gemmel," unaware that Marpurg himself was the author (Daube 1757). In 1772, Christoph Schröter still believed that the pseudonymous "Herr Gemmel" was Daube's reviewer (Schröter 1772, p. xviii).

3. *Kritische Briefe über die Tonkunst* (1759–1763) in the form of letters to famous musicians.

Other works from this period of activity include:

*Die Kunst das Clavier zu spielen,* in several editions (1750–1762) and two French translations.
*Anleitung zum Clavierspielen* (1755 and 1765).
*Anfangsgründe der Theoretischen Music* (1757) on temperament.
*Handbuch bey dem Generalbass und der Composition . . . für Anfänger und Geübter* (1757–1762), a comprehensive text.
*Anleitung zum Singcomposition* (1758), an exhaustive discussion of text-setting in German, Latin, and Italian (for example, pp. 122–134 categorize 2,130 ending-syllables in German).
*Anleitung zur Musik überhaupt* (1763), primarily on singing.

In addition, Marpurg translated D'Alembert's *Elemens* in 1757 and published a critique of Sorge's *Anleitung zum Generalbass* (1760). After this period of musical activity, during which he apparently was in continual financial hardship, Marpurg became director of the Prussian lottery, publishing only a few musical items:

*Versuch über die musikalische Temperatur, nebst einem Anhang über den Rameau- und Kirnbergerschen Grundbass* (1776).
A final volume of the *Historisch-kritische Beyträge zur Aufnahme der Musik* dealing with temperament (1778).
*Legende einer Musikheiligen* (1786), containing anecdotes and biographies of contemporaries (including Haydn and Vogler).

Overall, Marpurg's role in Berlin in the 1750s to 1770s is comparable to Mattheson's in Hamburg in the 1710s to 1730s. Like Mattheson, he broadcast a wide range of thinking. And his pugnacious nature, also like Mattheson's, brought many issues to the fore that might have otherwise remained unpublished. For instance, it is due to Marpurg's encouragement that Sorge wrote his *Compendium* (Sorge 1760, forward) to which Marpurg then responded.

SPECULATIVE AND PRACTICAL THEORY

Marpurg clearly recognized the difference between speculative and practical theory:

I can name no masters more distinguished than Rameau and [C. P. E.] Bach, the former in theory and the latter in practice.

Thoroughbass was invented for the facilitation of performance; fundamental bass, however, [was invented] to explain much more reasonably the relationship between the rules of composition and thoroughbass, and, so to say, to be able to survey them in one glance. (Marpurg 1755–1762, 1, fol. 3$^r$, p. 3)

His separation of these theoretical realms explains why he can adopt such rigid positions about the nature of fundamental bass (as quoted earlier in this chapter) and yet write influential practical works. It is why he can freely admit that "it was never a state secret" that suspensions arise from extending notes into the following chord, yet at the same time insist "that the question is, having discovered all the usable harmonies that arise from the process of suspension, how they should be presented systematically in a reasonable pedagogical method," which he believes can be done only via the theory of subposition. It is why he can assert that the fundamental bass, in which all chord inversions are functionally equivalent, is the proper way to understand harmonies, and yet criticize Sorge for having used 6/4 chords as if they were equivalent to root-position chords. It is why he can agree with Sorge that triads on scale-steps 1, 4, and 5 generate the major and minor scales, but disagree with Sorge's reasons for taking this position (Marpurg 1760, Chapter 3). And it is why he occasionally adopts a casual attitude toward systematic issues, such as during his dispute with Sorge when he allows that one could call a fourth a consonance or a dissonance, or call a suspended fourth a fourth or an eleventh—all that he cares about in a practical work is that its proper use be explained (Marpurg 1760, p. 145).

Marpurg's separation of speculative and practical theory also makes him much less dogmatic on certain issues than Rameau. On the contentious matter of the priority of harmony or melody, he sides with Rameau. But he also understands both positions:

> To have a harmony there must be at least two melodies, one higher and one lower, and consequently harmony is not really present before the melodies; therefore in this sense harmony always arises from melody. This is Herr von [!] Mattheson's opinion. But if one further considers that no simple melody can be conceived that does not have its basis in fundamental harmonies, then in this sense harmony precedes melody. This is Rameau's opinion. (Marpurg 1755–1762, 1, p. 26)

Many modern commentators on Marpurg's harmonic theories concentrate on his speculative ideas (Shirlaw 1917, pp. 308–316, Mekeel 1960). Even if this focus yields accurate statements about this side of his theorizing, it is insufficient to explain the popularity and influence of his practical works.

## MARPURG'S IDEAS AND RAMEAU'S THEORIES

Although Marpurg may have believed his views were consonant with those of Rameau, and attacked all who disagreed with him as departing from

*Example 9-1.* Marpurg 1755–1762, 1, p. 39 (scored from tablature)

Rameau's theories, in fact his own ideas often bear only a tangential relationship to those of the French theorist. Concerning chord generation, Marpurg insists on arranging all the possible notes in a diatonic and chromatic scale to form chords, where Rameau had done exactly the opposite, generating chords first and then creating scales out of the chords (Shirlaw 1917, pp. 309–310).

On many practical issues, Marpurg adopts a thoroughbass perspective, rather than a Rameauian outlook. For instance, in the *Handbuch* he discusses various uses of what he calls the second inversion of a diminished triad (see Example 9-1). To categorize the three highlighted chords as diminished triads is to concentrate solely on their pitch content, not their context, just as Heinichen or C. P. E. Bach might have done since in terms of their figuring, each chord is the same.

In another explanation reminiscent of Heinichen, Marpurg explains that the unprepared seventh over A shown in Example 9-2 arises from "the omission of an afterbeat chord [*nachschlagenden Harmonie*] in which the ninth and seventh should have resolved."

Similarly, pages 86 to 145 of the *Handbuch* discuss suspensions according to the interval involved. Although Marpurg explains many suspensions as members of seventh chords, the discussion as a whole is unlike any found in Rameau's works. In fact, when he discusses chord sevenths that form consonances against the bass (such as the fifth in a 6/5 chord), Marpurg speaks in the idiom of Gasparini's thoroughbass treatise. He denies the very basis of Rameau's inversional theory by calling such inter-

*Example 9-2.* Marpurg 1755–1762, 1, p. 55 (scored from tablature)

*Example 9-3.* Marpurg 1755–1762, 2, Table 2, Fig. 15a

vals "pseudo-dissonances" that must resolve even though they are consonant (Marpurg 1755–1762, 2, pp. 78–79; Gasparini 1708, p. 53).

Marpurg also speaks like a thoroughbass theorist in explaining other dissonances. For instance, he notes that sevenths generally resolve down. But some sevenths resolve up, like A-C-E-G♯ (Marpurg 1755–1762, 1, p. 54–55). For Rameau, G♯ in such a chord is not a seventh at all, but rather a leading tone in a chord by subposition.

Marpurg even invokes thoroughbass when he extends some of Rameau's tenets. When he adds thirteenths and even fifteenths to Rameau's category of subposed chords (Marpurg 1776, pp. 250, 260), he claims that he is acting not under Rameau's influence, but in imitation of two passages in C. P. E. Bach 1762 that deal with pedal points: Chapter 14, where Bach says that a 7/6/2 chord, "like others of its type, is best explained if the bass is removed" (Mitchell 1949, p. 284), and Chapter 24 on pedals, where Bach notes that "if one wishes to explain most clearly these alterations of the harmony and special juxtapositions of intervals, remove the bass" (ibid., p. 319).

In other matters, Marpurg simply rejects Rameauian tenets. Like Sorge, he finds dissonances within some types of triads. So he denies that the seventh is "the mother of all dissonant chords" (Marpurg 1755–1762, 1, p. 30), in the process rejecting a major motivation for Rameau's theory of subposition.

Likewise, Marpurg seems unaware of Rameau's notion of implied dissonances. Discussing Example 9-3, he challenges those theorists who insist that a dissonant fourth must be prepared (Marpurg 1755–1762, 2, p. 79). Rameau would have insisted that the upbeat chord contained an implied seventh preparing the C.

Marpurg also rejects added-sixth chords (Marpurg 1776, p. 279–280) and along with them double employment of dissonance and an interpretive role for fundamental bass progressions. In fact, when he discusses chord progressions (Marpurg 1755–1762, 1, pp. 84–100, 2, pp. 71–80), he never once mentions root motion. He also never notates a fundamental bass on a separate staff under any chord progression in any of his own works. Instead, he bases his discussion on Fux's four rules of voice leading

*Example 9-4.* Marpurg 1755–1762, 3, Plate 1, Fig. 20

(without crediting Fux). His instructions for harmonizing a melody are quite unlike the Rameau-style approach adopted by Mozart for Barbara Ployer. Instead, Marpurg begins with bass-melody structures in two voices, trying out eight bass lines to a given melody and evaluating each (see Example 9-4).

Comparing these basses, Marpurg comments on the contrapuntal interval structure as well as the harmonies. In contrast to Mozart's fundamental-bass approach to harmonization, where each version generally maintains the same harmonies, Marpurg freely changes chords from version to version. In this example, he complains that the first and second basses lack intervallic variety. The third merely interchanges G and D chords (Marpurg does not refer to them as tonic and dominant). The fourth bass has more variety, but the end lacks harmonic change. The fifth bass is the best yet, but Marpurg dislikes the D chord between two B-major triads. The sixth is the "true bass." The seventh and eighth are also good, although the first downbeat chord in the former is "rather hard right at the opening."

The order of instruction that Marpurg recommends for composition students agrees with neither a thoroughbass approach nor Rameau's theories. Musicians as diverse as Rameau, Niedt, J. S. Bach, C. P. E. Bach, and Kirnberger all recommend beginning instruction in composition with writing for four voices. But Marpurg begins with two-voice structures, as shown, and then works through combinations of from three to nine voices.

It should be clear that on a host of issues including chord types, chord inversions, dissonances, chord progressions, the use of fundamental bass, and compositional method—in brief, on most matters of harmonic theory—Marpurg differs substantially from Rameau's theories. Interestingly, Marpurg's brief summary of Rameau's harmonic theory in his *Kritische Briefe* (Marpurg 1759–1763, pp. 58–60) is accurate as far as it goes, even where Marpurg's own approach elsewhere differs from that of Rameau. But that brief summary does not touch on many of the areas in which he differs from Rameau's theories. As shown later in this chapter, on many points where Marpurg's approach differs from Rameau's, Kirnberger follows Rameau's theories. Thus, the readiness of German musicians to believe that Marpurg's works actually represented Rameau's theories, and the failure of a single German musician to challenge Marpurg on this issue during the 1750s, 1760s, or 1770s, is a sure indication of ignorance of Rameau's writings in their original form by German musicians.

## Kirnberger as Theorist

Johann Philipp Kirnberger is one of the major theorists of the late eighteenth century. Despite his admitted difficulties organizing his thoughts on paper (Bellermann 1872, col. 458), and despite his conservative attitude toward various aspects of newer music, his writings comprise the best-organized comprehensive approach to harmony and composition prior to Koch's treatise of the mid-1780s. He spent a few months in Leipzig in 1741, probably studying composition with J. S. Bach (Dadelsen 1980),[2] and eventually settled in Berlin, where he was active as a composer, violinist, and teacher. His major works are[3]

2. It was once thought he studied for a longer period with J. S. Bach.

3. The major studies of Kirnberger are Mekeel 1960, Beach 1974a, Grant 1976 and 1977, and Serwer 1970. Mekeel's and Beach's studies, despite disclaimers, take Marpurg at his word that he represents Rameau's ideas, thereby distorting the context of Kirnberger's theories and the Kirnberger-Marpurg disputes. Appendix B in Grant 1976 provides more details.

*Die Kunst des reinen Satzes (The Art of Strict Composition;* 1771–1779). Vol. 1 and Part 1 of Vol. 2 are on harmony and composition; the remainder (about one half the length of the whole) is on double (invertible) counterpoint.

Music articles in the encyclopedic *Allgemeine Theorie der schönen Kunste (General Theory of the Fine Arts)*,[4] 1771–1774, by Johann Georg Sulzer (1720–1779). Kirnberger's pupil Johann Abraham Peter Schulz (1747–1800) claimed in 1800 that Kirnberger wrote the music articles from A to I, and was assisted by Schulz in the articles from K to R. Schulz claims the articles from S to Z as his own (Schulz 1800, cols. 276–277; Spazier 1800, col. 593). But a 1783 letter by Kirnberger contradicts Schulz (Bellermann 1872).

*Die wahren Grundsätze zum Gebrauch der Harmonie* (1773), a short work summarizing *Die Kunst des reinen Satzes.*[5]

*Grundsätze des Generalbasses als erste Linien zur Composition* (c. 1781), a summary of Kirnberger's theories intended as a reader's introduction to the *Kunst des reinen Satzes.*

*Gedanken über die verschiedenen Lehrarten in der Komposition, als Vorbereitung zur Fugenkenntniss* (1782).

Two other works were written for amateurs: *Der allezeit fertige Polonoisen- und Menuettencomponist* (1757), a dice game for composing polonaises and minuets; *Methode, Sonaten aus'm Ermel zu schüddeln* (1783), explaining how to replace the melody and then the bass of an extant composition to create a new piece. Feil 1955 and Newman 1961 show how these lighthearted works underscore important aspects of musical thinking.

Probably without realizing how much he was borrowing, Kirnberger based much of his approach to harmony on Rameau's ideas, including

---

4. Or *The Theory of Polite Arts,* as Burney translated the title (Scholes 1959, p. 159).

5. Schulz claimed to have written this work but made his claim only after anyone who could contradict him was no longer alive (Schulz 1800, col. 278, fn.). Neither Marpurg, in attacking this work, nor C. P. E. Bach, in defending Kirnberger, questioned Kirnberger's authorship. There are discernible differences in writing style between *Die Kunst* and this work, but those can be attributed to the differences between a treatise and a summary. David Beach, who believes that Schulz was the author, argues that there are substantial differences in theoretical tenets between *Die Kunst* and this work and that therefore this work should be dissociated from Kirnberger's other writings (Beach 1974a, p. 9). Cecil Grant, however, argues convincingly that the supposedly new positions in this work are implicitly present in *Die Kunst* (Grant 1976, pp. 36–40). In addition, it strains credulity that Kirnberger would have published a work he disagreed with under his own name and then gone to great lengths to defend it. So for the purposes of the present discussion, it is assumed that Kirnberger agreed fully with the contents of *Die wahren Grundsätze,* whether or not he actually wrote it.

chord inversion, the seventh chord as a source of dissonance, fundamental bass to interpret chord progressions, and evaded cadences to promote harmonic continuity. He endorses Rameau's argument about the priority of harmony over melody: "Each piece always has as its basis a series of chords following one another according to certain rules; from these [chords] the melodies of single voices are in part determined" (Sulzer 1771–1774, *Accord;* compare *Bass*). He even echoes Rameau's 1732 suggestion to reform thoroughbass notation by using letters to represent chord roots (Sulzer 1771–1774, *Bezifferung*).

But in many areas of harmonic theory, Kirnberger avoids the most problematic aspects of Rameau's theorizing in favor of greater conceptual and pedagogical clarity. Most important, he omits or minimizes most of Rameau's speculative theories. He was aware of acoustic resonance (Sulzer 1771–1774, *Bass*). He invokes low interval ratios to explain consonance (Kirnberger 1771–1779, 1, pp. 23–24; Beach-Thym 1982, p. 38). And, like Sorge, he invokes the seventh partial (ibid., 2, pp. 68–69; Beach-Thym 1982, p. 337). But Kirnberger never makes such speculative points central to his theorizing, even when this leaves him without a systematic foundation. For instance, Kirnberger (like Marpurg) lists scales and then builds chords from the notes and intervals contained therein, bypassing the notion of intervallic roots which Rameau and Lippius before him found necessary to argue that the root-position form of chords is the origin of the inversions and not vice versa. Briefly put, the speculative issues that occupied so much of Rameau's energy simply did not interest him.

## CHORD CLASSIFICATIONS

Because he concentrates on applications, Kirnberger's writings offer a pedagogical clarity hitherto unknown in Rameauian harmonic theory. Right at the beginning of his discussion of chords (Kirnberger 1771–1779, Chapter 3, and Kirnberger 1773, opening), he presents a table with each chord type: there are triads, seventh chords, and these two chord types with added suspensions. Rameau, some of his pupils, and Sorge had implied such a classification, but never with such clarity, never as clearly separate categories, and never at the beginning of an exposition of harmony.

Like Marpurg, Kirnberger also does away with Rameau's added-sixth chords. Rameau had needed added-sixth chords to explain stepwise fundamental-bass progressions via *double emploi*. Kirnberger, like Rameau, believed that the fundamental bass should move primarily by the intervals in the triad (by fifths and thirds), insisting, for instance, that "the bass of a true seventh chord must progress up by four steps or down by five" (Kirnberger 1771–1779, 1, p. 66; Beach-Thym 1982, p. 85). But Kirnberger does not use *double emploi* to explain apparent root progressions by

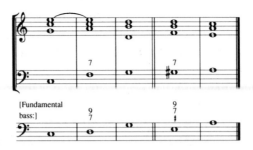

*Example 9-5.* Kirnberger 1771–1779, 1, p. 66; Beach-Thym 1982, p. 85

step, as Rameau did. Nor does he invoke compositional license—Rameau's convenient exit from various theoretical difficulties. Instead, Kirnberger argues that when seventh chords resolve by step, they are really ninth chords (see Example 9-5).[6] Kirnberger thereby develops his own form of implied bass progression akin to Rameau's subposed basses, but differing in substantial ways. Rameau uses subposition to explain suspended dissonances; Kirnberger uses his added fundamental bass to explain seventh chords resolving by step. Rameau's subposition adds a continuo bass below the fundamental bass; Kirnberger adds a new fundamental bass below the continuo bass. And Rameau's subposition is an attempt to explain the dissonances as parts of a seventh chord; Kirnberger changes the dissonances of a seventh chord into those of a ninth chord.

SUSPENSIONS: ESSENTIAL AND ACCIDENTAL DISSONANCES

Kirnberger does away with Rameau's subposed chords to explain suspensions. Instead, he employs the modern notion of nonharmonic-tone suspensions resolving into chord tones without a progression in the fundamental bass. He thus differentiates two types of suspended dissonances: those in which the suspended interval can resolve over the same chord root and those that require a new chord root to resolve. If a suspension can resolve into a chord with no other voice motion, it is an *incidental (zufällig) dissonance;* if other voices must move and a new harmony appears along with the resolution, the suspended tone is an *essential (wesentlich) dissonance,* a chordal seventh or ninth.

Rameau and his followers noted the relationship between suspensions and the theory of subposition, and Sorge anticipated Kirnberger's distinction and perhaps was the inspiration for it. But no theorist before Kirnberger so clearly distinguished between seventh chords and suspensions

6. A similar explanation of the stepwise resolution of a dominant seventh chord appears in Antoniotto 1760 (p. 98).

Compositional Theory in the Eighteenth Century

and recast subposed ninth and eleventh chords into 9–8 and 4–3 suspensions.

During the nineteenth century, this distinction between incidental and essential suspensions eventually joined the new perspective on nonsuspension dissonances, creating the modern distinction between chord tones and nonharmonic tones. Suspended dissonances were no longer considered a category entirely separate from all other dissonances, as they had been in counterpoint and thoroughbass methods. The modern distinction, which did not appear in a comprehensive fashion until the nineteenth century, replaced the traditional intervallic approach to dissonances with a chordal approach.

SUSPENSIONS: TWO TYPES OF 6/4 CHORDS

In addition to differentiating two types of suspended dissonances, Kirnberger establishes two separate categories of 6/4 chords: those that represent the second inversion of a chord (what we call passing, neighboring, and stationary 6/4 chords) and those that function as suspended tones over scale-step 5 resolving into the dominant (what we call the cadential 6/4). Rameau had already explained the cadential 6/4 as a pair of suspensions over the dominant in his *Code,* and it appears in his 1740s manuscript treatise on fundamental bass. And Charles Levens also included this interpretation of the cadential 6/4 in his 1743 treatise. But like other tenets that had appeared in earlier treatises, no one before Kirnberger expressed the distinction so categorically.

TWO FORMS OF THE DIMINISHED TRIAD

Kirnberger also clearly distinguishes two forms of the diminished triad: a "consonant" form that can appear in root progressions by fifth (especially as the supertonic chord in minor keys), and a dissonant form representing the upper three notes of a dominant seventh chord (a leading-tone triad). Once again, this distinction was not original with him. Thoroughbass methods recognized that sometimes it was appropriate to add a sixth to a diminished fifth (when the diminished triad functions as a leading-tone chord) and sometimes it was inappropriate to do so (when the diminished triad functions as a supertonic chord in minor). To facilitate making this distinction, Georg Philipp Telemann proposes placing an arc (a fermata without a dot) over a diminished fifth which did not permit a minor sixth to be played (a supertonic chord in minor), and C. P. E. Bach uses this notation consistently in his 1762 thoroughbass treatise. Rameau recognizes a comparable distinction between types of diminished triads in his 1722 *Traité* (Grant 1976, pp. 120–121). But once again, Kirnberger was the first to make the distinction so clearly.

OTHER INNOVATIONS

Like Rameau, Kirnberger believed that dissonances within harmonies help prevent premature closure within phrases (Kirnberger 1771–1779, 1, p. 31; Beach-Thym 1982, p. 45). But Kirnberger stresses more than Rameau how a complete harmonic progression and a cadence are necessary to establish a key (Kirnberger 1771–1779, 1, Chapter 6). With this larger conception of key, he is able to avoid the fear that bedeviled Rameau that a single triad without any dissonances might be a tonic. Kirnberger thus does not need Rameau's problematic notions of implied dissonance and implied chromaticism.

Kirnberger also replaces Rameau's cumbersome terminology of major and minor dissonances for the two sensitive notes in a dominant-seventh chord. He calls these notes leading tones, with scale-step 7 as an *apparent dissonance* (*scheinbaren Dissonanz;* Kirnberger c. 1781, pp. 42–43).

Kirnberger also explains more clearly than earlier theorists the distinction between what we call nowadays local tonicizations (secondary dominants) and larger changes of keys, as well as the difference between passing through keys and fully establishing a new key, which requires a cadence to confirm the new tonic (Kirnberger 1771–1779, 1, pp. 110, 120, Beach-Thym 1982, pp. 128, 136; Sulzer 1771–1774, *Ausweichung*). But unlike other areas listed above, Kirnberger does not introduce any clear term to refer to this distinction.

With a more secure basis for evaluating consonant and dissonant chords and chromaticism, Kirnberger has been credited with introducing the notion of passing progressions, in which several chords are viewed as connecting more fundamental harmonies. David Beach cites two passages in Example 9-6, a conjunct descending bass against a sustained chord, and a moving bass against a sustained upper-voice tone. Here Kirnberger was no innovator. His passing progressions are only apparent harmonies, merely the result of long nonharmonic tones. Similar passing dissonances against a sustained chord occur in virtually every extensive thoroughbass treatise of the century (as well as in Rameau 1737, Ex. 28). But in addition, some of Kirnberger's predecessors treat not only such extended dissonances but also consonant chords and functional progressions as passing chords. Heinichen discusses how several consonant and dissonant harmonies pass between two structural chords (Example 3-22). Rameau implies the notion of passing harmonies (Example 4-18). And Nichelmann uses a variety of interpolated progressions (passing chords, neighboring chords, repeated chords, tonicizing chords) to extend basic harmonies (Example 8-13). Recurring appearances of some form of the notion of passing harmonies, whether involving apparently functional harmonies or merely extended passing tones, most likely reflect the currency of this notion throughout the eighteenth-century. Explicit discussions probably

*Example 9-6.* Kirnberger 1771–1779, I, pp. 50–51, 86;
Beach-Thym 1982, pp. 72–73, 104

arose so rarely only because the notion essentially lies outside the formal theoretical traditions of the time, whether counterpoint, thoroughbass, or harmony.

Besides all the innovative aspects of harmonic theory and all the clarifications of terminology and concepts just outlined, Kirnberger's *Kunst des reinen Satzes* is also important for the successful linkage of that theory with the notion that the strict style is the basis of free composition. Kirnberger thereby unites the power of harmonic explanations with the teaching traditions associated with the very best treatises on thoroughbass and composition (Niedt, Heinichen, C. P. E. Bach) as well as strict counterpoint (Fux). As in the writings of Bernhard, Heinichen, and Niedt, Kirnberger repeatedly shows how complex compositional surfaces are based on simpler underlying structures (Kirnberger 1771–1779, I, Preface and p. 224; Beach-Thym, pp. 234–235).

His pedagogical clarity also emerges in the well-organized discussion of melodic harmonization in Chapter 1 of the second volume. He teaches how to harmonize a melody with tonic, dominant, and subdominant chords, then how to add other chords, and finally how to apply chromaticism to the simple structure, closing his discussion with a comparison of twenty-six different harmonizations of the same chorale melody. The manner of presentation is comparable to that of modern harmony texts.[7] Kirnberger also relates harmonic progressions to phrase structure more

7. Kirnberger's procedure and format may have been the model for a similar multiple harmonization exercise on an early Beethoven sketchbook leaf (Kramer 1975, pp. 76–82).

*Example 9-7.* Kirnberger's *Allegro*, mm. 1–6, with Marpurg's analysis

clearly than most of his predecessors (especially Kirnberger 1771–1779, 1, Chapter 10).

To be sure, Kirnberger was distinctly old-fashioned in some important respects, especially his wariness about common dissonance usages. His conservatism may have contributed to the absence of direct influence on many later theorists. Yet his *Kunst des reinen Satzes,* by presenting harmonic theory without many of the Rameauian trappings that seem irrelevant to modern theorists, stands alongside Mozart's pedagogical records and Koch's treatise in representing the manner in which the various traditions of eighteenth century theory could be combined in a comprehensive pedagogy.

## The Disputes between Marpurg and Kirnberger

The Berlin theorists engaged in two public disputes, one in 1759, the other in the mid-1770s. The first began with a characteristically harsh pseudonymous attack by Marpurg on an anonymous, unpublished two-voiced fugue (Marpurg 1759–1763, pp. 41–47). Kirnberger soon published the fugue, claimed it as his own, and defended it against Marpurg's charges (*Allegro für das Clavier allein,* 1759). Marpurg rejoined with an extensive rebuttal (Marpurg 1759–1763, pp. 175–220; the dispute is thoroughly surveyed in Serwer 1970).

Marpurg's critique mostly accuses Kirnberger of lacking compositional skill. But substantial theoretical issues also arise. Of particular significance is the recognition of chordal inversions and how chords and their inversions are relevant to two-part textures. Marpurg asserts that the chords implied in the fugue's exposition are those labeled below the score in Example 9-7. He finds the circled notes objectionable because each is the fifth of a triad and thus would produce an unacceptable 6/4 chord on the beat if the parts were inverted. Traditional rules for invertible counterpoint at the octave forbid a fifth in such circumstances because inversion produces an improper fourth. Marpurg, who six years earlier published his treatise on fugue, recasts this rule from intervallic into chordal terms, in

*Example 9-8.* J. S. Bach, *Fugue in F major, Well Tempered Clavier 2*

effect banning not the interval of a fifth but the fifth of a chord from such positions in invertible counterpoint.

In his response, Kirnberger fails to understand this criticism, merely citing instances of thirds and sixths in fugues by well-known composers, among them the J. S. Bach passage in Example 9-8. Marpurg countered that all these thirds and sixths involve roots and thirds of triads, but never fifths of triads (see Example 9-9). To be sure, there are examples of two-voice invertible counterpoint where J. S. Bach does place the fifth of a triad in an upper voice on a strong beat, such as in the *Fugue in D minor* from the first volume (in which the resulting 6/4 chord is treated appropriately when it occurs later in the fugue, as shown in Example 9-10). But Kirnberger does not tender any of these.

It is surprising that Kirnberger seems to have been unable to understand how full harmonies are to be found in a two-voiced texture, since a dozen

*Example 9-9.* Marpurg's analysis of the preceding example

*Example 9-10.* J. S. Bach, *Fugue in D minor, Well-Tempered Clavier 1*

*Example 9-11.* J. S. Bach, *Fugue in B minor, Well-Tempered Clavier* 1
as analyzed in Kirnberger 1773 (subject only)

years later, he argues in *Die Kunst des reinen Satzes* that two-voiced
counterpoint is based on a four-part texture. And *Die wahren Grundsätze*
(1773) concludes with fundamental-bass analyses of two compositions
from the *Well-Tempered* in which Kirnberger even provides a full-textured
harmonic analysis of the unaccompanied fugue subject. A portion of one
appears in Example 9-11.[8] Under the score is a full-voiced hypothetical
realization of the fugal texture, a fundamental bass with all suspended
dissonances, and a fundamental bass with only essential dissonances.

Kirnberger's seeming failure in 1759 to perceive chords in two-part
writing juxtaposed with this later analysis and his later insistence that
two-part writing is based on chords raises the question of when Kirnberger
developed his harmonic theories. Did Kirnberger did not learn harmonic
theory until after 1759? If so, did Kirnberger study Rameau's writings
more closely than has hitherto been thought by any scholar, or did Kirnberger work with some musician conversant with Rameau's theories? (We
can exclude Marpurg as his tutor because of their different interpretations
of Rameauian theory and because Marpurg surely would have claimed
Kirnberger as a pupil if this had been the case.) Or did Kirnberger under-

8. The opening of this analysis appears in Beach 1974, pp. 291–293. Beach accepts
Schulz's claim that *Die wahren Grundsätze* was not written by Kirnberger and argues that
"the analyses were done under [Kirnberger's] supervision by his student, J. A. P. Schulz."

*Example 9-12.* An alternative analysis of the preceding example

stand the issue in 1759 but fail to perceive that it was the point of Marpurg's criticism? The issue remains puzzling.

The analysis of Bach's *Fugue in B minor* also illustrates how Kirnberger's distinction between incidental and essential dissonances hampers his ability to perceive structures beyond the immediate foreground. When Kirnberger analyzes incidental dissonances, he can omit these tones to find a structural frame at a deeper level. In the first half of measure 2, for instance, he omits E and C and hears a single harmony: a B-triad becoming a B-dominant seventh chord on the lowest staff. But in the sequentially parallel second half of that measure, he felt bound to consider the implied B of his realization as an essential dissonance and to maintain two harmonies. Likewise, in the second half of the first measure, his perception that the B in the subject is a chord seventh requires him to retain eighth-note harmonic rhythm even in the lowest fundamental bass. Thus an analysis like the one shown in Example 9-12, which reduces all accented eighths that resolve by semitone (whether they are essential or incidental in Kirnberger's terms), was beyond him.

In the 1759 dispute, Kirnberger also fails to understand Marpurg's criticism of larger aspects of his fugue. Marpurg complains that there is insufficient tonal variety in the opening. There are three consecutive fugal expositions in the tonic (mm. 1, 12, and 24), all of which begin with the subject in the upper voice in the same register. Such repetitions violate recommendations common in fugue manuals favoring variety of keys (or modal placement) and voice placement of fugue-subject entries. Kirnberger counters that such repetitions are not problematic, noting that J. S. Bach's *Fugue in C-minor* from the *Well-Tempered Clavier* 1 presents the subject three times in the tonic. Marpurg points out that Bach's three statements are spread over the entire fugue and furthermore that the subject appears in different fugal voices. In contrast to Marpurg, Kirnberger seems unable to grasp either the larger tonal structure of the work or the variety that Bach's fugue offers.

*Example 9-13.* Kirnberger 1773, Supplement; Marpurg 1776, Fig. 70.
Marpurg omits the treble realization.

The second dispute became public when Marpurg appended a critique of Kirnberger's *Die wahren Grundsätze* and *Die Kunst des reinen Satzes* to his 1776 *Versuch über die musikalische Temperatur*. But it apparently had been simmering for a while. According to Marpurg, Kirnberger visited him often while preparing *Die wahren Grundsätze* for publication, boasting that this work would "drive the Rameauists into a corner" (Marpurg 1776, p. iii). And although Kirnberger angrily denies that he begged Marpurg to withhold a critique for a while so as "not to ruin sales of his *Grundsätze*" (ibid., p. iv), he acknowledges that the two engaged in theoretical discussions "from time to time" during this period (Kirnberger 1771–1779, 2, pp. 181–182).

The use of fundamental bass lies at the heart of the debate. As quoted above, Marpurg insists that a fundamental bass reflect the actual notes in a chord and not be altered to interpret a progression. For him, a fundamental bass that has notes not present in the music or that omits chords present in the music is like a table of contents that has more or fewer chapters than actually occur in a book (p. 277). He complains that Kirnberger often inserts a note not in the score into the fundamental bass in order to turn a step progression into a fifth progression, as on the second beat in Example 9-13.

Rameau would have agreed with Kirnberger's fundamental bass but would have explained it somewhat differently. For Rameau, the second chord, because it progresses by fifth, would have an implied seventh (as shown in Example 9-14). If the first chord had been a G triad, Rameau would again have insisted that the second chord contains an implied dissonance and would have used *double emploi* to explain the progression.

In all such examples, Marpurg rejects Rameau's belief that the fundamental bass should explain progressions. Kirnberger, like Rameau, uses the fundamental bass to interpret the progression.

Marpurg also rejects Kirnberger's addition of connecting chords not

*Example 9-14.* A Rameauian interpretation of the preceding example

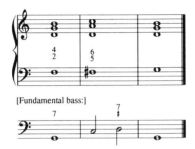

[Fundamental bass:]

*Example 9-15.* Kirnberger 1773, pp. 38–39 (Beach and Thym 1979, pp. 195–196); Marpurg 1776, Fig. 65. Marpurg omits the treble.

present in the music, as in Example 9-15. Kirnberger says the "fundamental harmony is to be understood" because it is necessary to explain the resolution of the seventh in the first chord.[9] Marpurg agrees that the progression arises from the omission of a chord but denies this has anything to do with fundamental bass. He also chides Kirnberger for saying that "via the omission of the resolution, the thread of the natural progression is not torn" (Kirnberger 1773, p. 43). If such gaps were natural, Marpurg asks, "why is it taught that dissonances must be resolved properly?" (Marpurg 1776, p. 278).

On other matters, Marpurg upholds Rameau's interpretations against Kirnberger's innovations. He challenges Kirnberger's distinction between incidental and essential dissonances, arguing that the term *incidental* should refer to those dissonances that occur in a melodic part, such as Fux's passing and changing notes. These are not essential notes because they do not affect the harmony. All types of suspensions, however, should be considered essential because they affect both melody and harmony. With this stance, Marpurg upholds a traditional thoroughbass perspective,

9. A nearly identical progression and explanation, though without a notated fundamental bass, appears in Kirnberger 1771–1779, I, p. 85; Beach and Thym 1982, p. 103.

*Example 9-16.* Marpurg 1776, Figs. 101, 102

asserting that suspensions create a new harmony, which is why they are notated in thoroughbass figures. That is why they are best explained by subposition. If incidental dissonances were merely notes resolving into chord tones, Marpurg asks why the suspensions shown in Example 9-16 would not be acceptable. Marpurg, like Rameau, insists that only knowing the origin of suspensions via subposition will prevent such "impure examples."

Marpurg and Kirnberger also disagree over what harmonies belong within a key. Marpurg refuses to recognize Kirnberger's notion of chromaticism within a key (what we call secondary or tonicizing dominants), rejecting his contention that the progression shown in Example 9-17 is within the key of C major. Marpurg contrasts this example with that in Example 9-18, where Kirnberger argues that the consecutive triads imply a sequence of keys. Marpurg ridicules the notion that a chromatic progression can be in one key, while a progression with only white-key notes offers tonal ambiguity. In both cases, Kirnberger upholds Rameau's interpretation. Kirnberger's notion of chromaticism within a key extends Rameau's suggestion discussed in connection with Example 4-21. And Kirnberger's interpretation of a simple sequence of first-inversion triads recalls Rameau's comparable trouble with similar progressions because he bans stepwise fundamental-bass progressions (Example 4-17 and Appendix 1).

The dispute also shows how even in the eighteenth century there were questions about the origin of commonly accepted tenets. Kirnberger argues that Rameau did not discover chordal inversion. This, of course, is true.

*Example 9-17.* Kirnberger 1771–1779, 1, p. 102 (Beach and Thym 1982, p. 120; Marpurg 1776, Fig. 131. Marpurg cites only the upper staff, and ends the example as shown.

*Example 9-18.* Kirnberger 1773, p. 45 (Beach and Thym 1979, p. 200);
Marpurg 1776, Figs. 132, 134. Marpurg cites only the bass.

But instead of citing any works prior to 1722 that explain inverted chords, Kirnberger lamely insists that inversional thinking was implicit in double counterpoint. Marpurg opposes this, arguing that Rameau did invent chordal inversion. He says he scoured treatises published before 1722 by Artusi, Berardi, Bononcini, Brossard, Fux, Glarean, Heinichen, Kircher, Mersenne, Zarlino, and others and found no mention of chord inversions (Marpurg 1776, pp. 271–272; he apparently overlooked Fux's explanation of triadic inversion).

## THE SIGNIFICANCE OF THE DISPUTE

It is clear from this survey that it distorts the dispute to characterize the issues debated by Marpurg and Kirnberger in terms of C. P. E. Bach's Rameau versus anti-Rameau remark. It is an even greater distortion to equate "Rameau vs. anti-Rameau" with a vertical, point-to-point perspective on harmony and voice leading versus a linear one, as some modern historians have done. Kirnberger supports Rameau's interpretive role for fundamental bass, while Marpurg argues that chordal structure, not chord progressions, should determine chordal roots. Marpurg supports Rameau's subposed bass, while Kirnberger turns triads into seventh chords and seventh chords into ninth chords in order to explain some progressions. If C. P. E. Bach's anti-Rameau remark supports Kirnberger's positions, should we interpret it to mean that Bach and his father agreed that fundamental bass should play an interpretive role and that seventh chords should be turned into ninth chords in stepwise root progressions, but did not believe that the root should be determined by the notes present in a chord and did not believe in subposed chords?

If the dispute does not represent a showdown between vertical and linear views of musical structure, one may properly ask what all the heat and sloganeering was about. An answer to this lies in ignorance of Rameau's actual writings as well as in nationalistic and philosophical issues not directly related to questions of musical structure.

Marpurg is probably correct when he claims that he was the first to make Rameau's name widely known in Germany (Marpurg 1776, p. 229). But he is wrong if he means to equate knowledge of Rameau's name with knowledge of Rameau's ideas. Marpurg claims that the appearance of fundamental bass in his 1757 D'Alembert translation and in his dispute with Sorge around 1760 was controversial because the concept was hitherto unknown in Germany. But Nichelmann's earlier use of fundamental bass in 1755 had aroused no questions. Hahn and Daube had incorporated many tenets of Rameau's harmonic theories into their thoroughbass treatises of 1751 and 1756 without any fanfare. Rameauian ideas appeared in Heinichen's 1728 and Kellner's 1732 thoroughbass treatises. And Schröter had studied Rameau's *Traité* in Jena as early as 1724.

Many of Rameau's ideas had become so pervasive that German musicians, who did not read Rameau's works directly, did not realize that they were the core of Rameau's theories. Quite possibly, Mattheson's recurring anti-Rameau remarks had given rise to a perception of Rameau's theories quite different from the Rameauian ideas in circulation. When Marpurg began espousing his own ideas as those of Rameau, and when he challenged other theorists from Sorge to Kirnberger, not a single German musician seems to have known Rameau's works well enough to argue that Marpurg had distorted the Frenchman's ideas.

There are several published indications of confusion over what Rameau represented. As noted in Chapter 8, Löhlein simply replaced Sorge's name with Rameau's between the 1765 and 1779 editions of his *Clavier-Schule,* leaving the theoretical contents unchanged. Apparently what he thought derived from Sorge in 1765 he later believed derived from Rameau. And Scheibe, after criticizing Rameau's theories in his *Ueber die Musikalische Composition* (1773), refers to the musical articles in Sulzer's recently published *Allgemeine Theorie,* complaining that "the author of the musical articles in this good work in most articles seems to have sworn an oath to D'Alembert's or Rameau's flag" (p. 383). There seems to be no reaction from Kirnberger or Schulz to Scheibe's assumption that their views echo Rameau.

Kirnberger claimed that his writings arose from the desire to reduce J. S. Bach's teaching to basic principles (Kirnberger 1782, pp. 4–5). What aspects of Bach's teachings are represented? David Beach argues that it was only the ordering of materials—beginning with four-part writing and gradually progressing to free composition (Beach-Thym 1982, pp. xvi–xvii). Certainly these are the aspects of Johann Sebastian's teaching described in C. P. E. Bach's letter of 1775 to assist Forkel in preparing his biography of Johann Sebastian (David and Mendel 1966, p. 279). There is no evidence that J. S. Bach knew of or taught any form of fundamental bass, the division of suspensions into essential and incidental, or any other specific tenets of Kirnberger's. But the similarities among treatment of fundamental bass in the writings of Nichelmann and Kirnberger (especially the use of fundamental bass to interpret progressions and their implicit assumption that fundamental-bass notation was common knowledge) and their common background in the Bach circle in Leipzig in the 1730s and 1740s suggest a common source for their fundamental-bass ideas. It will take further research, possibly into any extant manuscript teaching materials from the period, to determine the source of their common ideas.[10]

In evaluating the hostility to Rameau's name by Kirnberger and others who adopted various of Rameau's tenets, Cecil Grant calls attention to philosophical attitudes of the time (Grant 1976, pp. 16–34). Much of the practical side of Kirnberger's theory is based on Rameau, but the outlook of the two theorists was different and what they understood as a theory was different. Rameau was perceived in Germany as a representative of the French Enlightenment. There was considerable French influence at the court of Frederick the Great, including extended visits by Voltaire, D'Alembert, and other leading French figures. This inspired both nationalistic impulses (already adumbrated in music theory in Mattheson's anti-French and anti-Jesuit critiques of Rameau as well as in Sorge's reference to "Mr. Marpourg" who wished to bring Rameau's ideas to "our Germany"; Sorge 1767, dedication) and the pietism of the German Counter-Enlightenment. Sulzer, organizer of the *Allgemeine Theorie der Schönen Künste,* who encouraged Kirnberger to write *Die Kunst des reinen Satzes* (Schulz 1800, Beach-Thym 1982, p. xi), had studied with Johann Jakob Breitinger (1701–1776), a strenuous opponent of French influence in the arts and philosophy. It is quite possible that C. P. E. Bach's statement rejecting Rameau's influence on himself and his late father was more a critique of French influence and a rejection of the scientific side of Rameau's writings than of any specific tenets in the Kirnberger-Marpurg dispute. The contents of C. P. E.'s entire letter, if it still exists, would help reveal the context of the slogan Kirnberger cites.

Some previous interpretations of the Kirnberger-Marpurg disputes and

---

10. If it still exists, a lost treatise on harmony by W. F. Bach might provide clues; there was an announcement of the imminent publication of his *Abhandlung vom harmonischen Dreiklang* (c. 1754) in the spring of 1759, but the work never appeared.

of other aspects of eighteenth-century theory use theorists from the past as surrogates for twentieth-century theoretical battles. But because their perspective was quite different from ours, eighteenth-century musicians view various issues quite differently than we do. On numerous issues, theorists can be aligned with one another in ways that cut across modern differentiations. Some modern theorists align thoroughbass writers and contrapuntalists against supporters of harmonic theory. But C. P. E. Bach, apparently reflecting his father's views, sees thoroughbass and counterpoint as traditions opposed to one another, relating how J. S. Bach's teaching "omitted all the dry species of counterpoint that were given by Fux and others" (David and Mendel 1966, p. 279). Likewise, Fux builds his composition method from species counterpoint to oppose thoroughbass methods. J. S. Bach, Rameau, and Kirnberger argue that composition students should begin with four-voiced writing, while Fux and Marpurg insist on beginning with two voices. Marpurg sees no conflict in drawing upon the writings of both Rameau and C. P. E. Bach, just as W. A. Mozart incorporates both fundamental bass and Fuxian counterpoint (interpreted as expressing harmonies) into his teachings. Some fundamental-bass theorists imply the notion of passing harmonies (Rameau, Nichelmann), while contrapuntal and thoroughbass writers often insist that each verticality is a separate entity. Contrapuntalists like Fux insist on immediate resolution of linear dissonances, while some fundamental-bass theorists discuss polyphonic melodies with multiple voice-leading strands (Gianotti 1759, Part 2, Chapter 8). Padre Martini, who urges training in the polyphonic *stile antico,* interprets harmonies in that music according to Rameauian fundamental bass.

Clearly, the sharp separations some scholars draw between different theoretical traditions in the eighteenth century do not stand up to scrutiny. Perhaps the best indication of the unity perceived among various approaches during the latter part of the century—or at least of the consensus that each theoretical school had something important to contribute and that none had a monopoly on musical truth—is Leopold Mozart's reference to books by C. P. E. Bach, D'Alembert, Fux, Marpurg, Mattheson, Rameau, Riepel, Spiess, Scheibe, and Tosi-Agricola as sources of "sound stuff" (Anderson 1966, letter of June 11, 1778). Similarly, as Nottebohm pointed out over a century ago, the teaching materials Beethoven used as a student in the 1780s and early 1790s include species counterpoint, traditional thoroughbass methods, thoroughbass chords organized by chord types as found in Kirnberger's *Kunst des reinen Satzes,* and many of Marpurg's harmonic theories (including chords by subposition to explain suspensions), probably as presented in Türk 1791 (Nottebohm 1872, pp. 154–203).

# Harmonic Theory from the 1770s

This survey of Kirnberger and Marpurg completes this history of the contrapuntal, thoroughbass, and harmonic traditions as they evolved and interacted during the eighteenth century. By the 1770s, the contents of most contrapuntal and thoroughbass traditions had been absorbed by the harmonic approach. Whatever differences of opinion remained over important issues—and there were many—theorists agreed that chords were the building blocks of musical structure and that both the structure of chords and progressions from one to another were best understood in terms of their root movements. Marpurg and Kirnberger had provided the basis for understanding all the different types of nonharmonic tones in terms of a harmonic theory. As a result, writers with outlooks on musical style and pedagogy as different as those of Albrechtsberger, Kirnberger, Martini, and Marpurg, could agree on many essentials of musical structure.

The only exceptions to this consensus are some keyboard-instruction or thoroughbass manuals designed for amateurs or clearly based on earlier models. One such work is the *Unterricht im Generalbass Spielen* (1773) by Georg Michael Telemann (1748–1831), the grandson of the famous composer. Although the *Vorbericht* suggests that Telemann wished to modernize outdated thoroughbass rules, the contents suggest otherwise. Yet even in this work which presents materials much like pre-Rameau treatises, Telemann praises the "learned" Sorge's *Vorgemach,* Marpurg's "beloved" *Handbuch* to teach harmony, and C. P. E. Bach's "beautiful" *Versuch* for accompaniment, though he believes the last work is too learned for beginners (p. 10).[11]

What remains to be discussed is the growing awareness of musical phrasing and form during the eighteenth century, as well as the role of melodic construction in shaping the new music of the Classical era. This approach appears full-blown in Joseph Riepel's treatises of the 1750s and 1760s. Heinrich Christoph Koch then wedded this approach with harmonic theory in the 1780s, providing a new comprehensive vision of musical structure in his treatise of the mid-1780s. Riepel and Koch are the subjects of Chapters 10 and 11.

11. Page 11 of this book shares with p. xi of Vallotti 1779 the odd distinction of having a footnote to a footnote!

CHAPTER TEN

# Riepel on Melody and Phrases

*Even beyond these matters, composition is an inexhaustible sea.*

The concluding sentence of each
chapter of Riepel's Anfangsgründe

AS DESCRIBED in the preceding chapters, much of eighteenth-century theory, whether cast as species counterpoint, thoroughbass, or the study of harmony, addresses age-old questions: How do voices combine to form acceptable harmonies? What are the constraints on voice leading and the successions of harmonies? How must dissonances be treated? And how are these matters best explained? This agenda occupied much of the energy of theorists throughout the century.

While many theorists ardently debated these issues of chord definition and classification, dissonance classification, and the nature of harmonic continuity, essential elements of musical style were undergoing a profound transformation. By the middle of the century new musical issues demanded attention—issues that were not adequately addressed by any pre-existent approach. These issues primarily concerned melody and the structure of musical compositions.

These concerns had not been ignored by earlier theorists. In the early years of the century, Friedrich Erhard Niedt describes a close bond between thoroughbass practice and composition that is implicit in many thorough-bass treatises. He shows how rhythmicizing and expanding thoroughbass progressions could create a wide range of compositions. But except when he treats a few aspects of standardized dance movements, Niedt's approach does not directly address the nature of the resulting melodic structures, their motives, their articulation into phrases and phrase subdivisions, and the way phrases connect with one another to form larger musical structures. On these matters of melody and phrase structure, theorists were largely silent.

A major reason for this silence is that these topics were not as relevant to compositional styles at the turn of the eighteenth century as they soon became in the *galant* styles. Yet despite the growing prominence of articulated melodic phrases and periods in an increasing amount of contemporary music, only three theorists between the 1730s and the 1780s published anything substantial on melodic structure and phrase articulations. For whatever reasons, all were German: Johann Mattheson, Johann Riepel, and Heinrich Christoph Koch.[1]

Mattheson was hailed by his contemporaries for being the first to publish a book on melody: his *Kern melodischer Wissenschaft* of 1737, whose contents Mattheson incorporated into *Der vollkommene Capellmeister* of 1739. As described in Chapter 6, Mattheson discussed many important aspects of melodic construction. But much of his treatment deals only superficially if at all with those aspects that were important to later musicians. And, as several historians have commented, when Mattheson applies the jargon of rhetoric to musical structures, the reader often ends up learning more about Classical oratory than about music.

Little more than a decade after Mattheson's *Vollkommene Capellmeister,* the first of a series of works by Joseph Riepel appeared, reflecting a wholly new approach to melodic and compositional structure. Riepel placed melody and phrasing at the heart of musical structure in formulations that remained the sole detailed published discussion of these topics for three decades.

## Joseph Riepel

Riepel (1709–1782) apparently began his formal musical studies past the age of thirty. In the early 1740s, living in Dresden, he probably studied with the composer Jan Dismas Zelenka (1679–1745), a pupil of Fux and an assistant to Heinichen toward the end of the latter's life. By 1751, Riepel had settled in Regensburg, where he remained as violinist, composer, and author.[2] His major published work is a series of five chapters published one at a time between 1752 and 1768 under the general title

---

1. The discussions of melody and phrasing in the works of Kirnberger and Marpurg (also Germans) are substantially more limited and do not address the comprehensive agendas set by Riepel and Koch. The primary discussion of melody and phrasing in the works of Johann Friedrich Daube was not published until 1797, even though it was probably written in the 1770s.

2. Twittenhoff 1935 evaluates Riepel's career as composer and performer in Regensburg, including his angry reply to a negative assessment by Charles Burney (pp. 29–32).

*Anfangsgründe zur musicalischen Setzkunst (Rudiments of Musical Composition):*

Chapter 1: *De rhythmopoeïa, oder von der Tactordnung* (1752)
Chapter 2: *Grundregeln zur Tonordnung insgemein* (1755)
Chapter 3: *Gründliche Erklärung der Tonordnung insbesondere* (1757)
Chapter 4: *Erläuterung der betrüglichen Tonordnung* (1765)
Chapter 5: *Unentbehrliche Anmerkungen zum Contrapunct* (1768)

One additional chapter, entitled *Baßschlüssel,* was published posthumously in 1786, edited by Johann Kaspar Schubarth (1756–1810), Riepel's pupil and successor in Regensburg. Several other chapters remain in manuscript (summarized in Twittenhoff 1935). It is not clear whether Riepel substantially completed the *Anfangsgründe* by the early 1750s and then published the chapters one at a time, or whether he wrote the chapters separately as they were published. The five chapters published by Riepel are in dialogue format featuring a student *(Discantista)* and teacher *(Praeceptor)*, in obvious imitation of Fux's *Gradus.*[3]

Although he resided in Regensburg (not one of the main musical centers in Germany) while writing and publishing his *Anfangsgründe,* Riepel kept abreast of the latest writings in both German and French. For instance, in 1752 he refers to Rameau's recent *Démonstration* of 1750 (p. 75). And in 1755 he includes a critique of this treatise (p. 53) and also refers to the first part of C. P. E. Bach's *Versuch* of 1752 and Marpurg's *Abhandlung von der Fuge* of 1753–1754 (p. 129).

Despite his knowledge of a wide range of contemporary treatises—or perhaps precisely because of this knowledge—Riepel's *Anfangsgründe* is like no other work of its time. Riepel had little patience for the formalities of most of the published treatises of the day. He proudly proclaims his intention to write "ABCs for those who wish to comprehend the rules of composition, not for those who know how to dictate laws" (Riepel 1752,

3. There are several important studies of Riepel. Twittenhoff 1935 includes a valuable summary of the contents of each of his works. Schwarzmaier 1936, more comprehensive and more cognizant of Riepel's contemporaries than Twittenhoff, repeatedly compares Riepel's ideas to those of Koch, Marpurg, and Kirnberger and also uses passages by Haydn, Mozart, and Beethoven to illustrate various points. But Schwarzmaier insists on treating Riepel's teachings as a study of musical form in the nineteenth-century sense. And by applying Riepel's ideas directly to compositions from later in the Classical period, Schwarzmaier seems to ignore the major changes in style between the 1750s and the end of the century. Feil 1955 properly sees Riepel's works as a study of composition, not form. Reed 1983 is the only thorough summary of Riepel's ideas in English. Baker 1975 relates many of Koch's ideas to similar formulations of Riepel. Sisman 1982 demonstrates how Riepel's theories apply most particularly to music prior to and around 1750. In addition, Ratner 1980 contains numerous references to Riepel's works.

preface). He mocks what he regards as mathematical approaches to composition—nowhere in any of his published writings are there formal derivations of intervals, chords, and the like. (Riepel's mathematical predilections lie with permutations; he applies the *ars combinatoria* to such things as patterns of notes and rhythms, bowings, orderings of keys, and even harmonic combinations of notes, as discussed in Chapter 8). He disdains the pretensions of other theorists, even calling attention to the small size of his name on the title page of Chapter 1 and that he displays no self-portrait as a frontispiece (although the font in which his name is set on the title page does increase in size chapter by chapter!).

In line with his rejection of theoretical formalities, he opens the very first page of Chapter 1 with a discussion of how to compose a minuet. The student boldly offers a minuet, boasting that "it's no great honor to compose one," thereby launching an extensive discussion of its problems and possible emendations. Riepel uses this pedagogical method—introducing compositions and emending them—throughout all the chapters.

## Melody and Phrasing

Riepel's primary concern is melody, especially the articulation and joining of phrases. He rejects any and all studies of harmony or voice leading that have not first taught melody in the sense of melodic articulations and phrase structures: "Whoever wishes to build houses must first obtain the needed materials. For without knowledge of melody nothing can be accomplished with a bass" (Riepel 1768, p. 1). This criticism eschews the entire thoroughbass tradition of compositional instruction, all Rameauian harmony, and even the study of counterpoint. And it reflects a change in the role of the bass from its determining role in earlier music to its more supportive status in the newer styles around the middle of the century. Not until Chapter 5, published in 1768, does Riepel explain how to set a bass to a melody.

Unfortunately, Riepel's complaint that other methods put the cart before the horse can be applied to his own approach as well. Most of his copious examples are single-line articulated melodies. (Many other examples are in string quartet format; keyboard examples appears only occasionally.) These one-line melodic examples are always built on a clearly implied harmonic foundation, and he introduces many harmonic notions about cadences and keys long before he ever discusses harmony. Surely a student using the *Anfangsgründe* without prior grounding in thoroughbass, harmony, or counterpoint would encounter great difficulties writing in the style of Riepel's clearly articulated melodies.

Riepel deals with many aspects of melody: phrase length, cadential orientation, melodic contour, motives and motivic unity, common melodic shapes, rhythmic continuity, expansions and contractions of phrases, and the connection of phrases to one another. But he does not present comprehensive discussions of these and other issues (as Koch was to do some decades later). Rather, Riepel raises issues somewhat haphazardly as they arise in his extensive emendation and recomposition of examples. This discursiveness is to a large degree the result of the dialogue format. Much as in Fux's classic *Gradus,* it lends a welcome informality, heightened here by Riepel's colorful language. But whereas Fux almost always remained close to the topic at hand, Riepel often seems to ramble, explaining flute fingerings within a discussion of melodic ornamentation, and so forth.

Riepel classifies a *phrase (Absatz)* according to its length and cadential orientation. He indicates the length of a phrase by counting the number of measures it contains (*Zweyer, Dreyer, Vierer, Fünfer,* etc., through nine-measure units). Although he argues for the primacy of four-measure phrases, he also discusses extensively how phrases of other lengths may be used. He indicates the cadential orientation of a phrase by a prefix and an analytical symbol placed at the phrase ending in musical examples. A *fundamental phrase (Grundabsatz)* ends on the tonic, labeled with a black square. An *altered phrase (Aenderungsabsatz)* ends on the dominant, labeled with a white square (Riepel 1755, pp. 36ff.). Riepel extends his classification of phrases to include important changes of key; thus an altered phrase after a change of key to the dominant is a *fifth altered phrase (Quint-Aenderungs-Absatz),* sometimes labeled by a + (Riepel 1755, p. 64). A phrase may have more than one segment (*Einschnitt;* Riepel 1755, pp. 52ff.). Like phrases, segments also are differentiated according to the harmonic orientation of their ending.

Throughout the chapters, Riepel shows how phrases can be transformed by changing their endings, their contour, their motives, their meter, their ornamentation, their connection to preceding and following phrases, by partial or complete repetition *(Wiederhölung),* by iteration of the cadence *(Verdoppelung),* by an extension at the end of a phrase *(Verlängerung),* by expansion of material within a phrase *(Ausdähnung),* by abbreviation *(Verkürzung),* by the insertion of material within a phrase *(Einschiebel),* and so forth (Riepel 1755, p. 71, and passim). He begins with a minuet in Chapter 1 and returns often to discuss minuets. But he also explores other compositional genres.

Examples 10-1, 10-2, and 10-3, only some of the variants Riepel offers in an extended discussion of a symphonic allegro in Chapter 2 (1755; pp. 64–87), indicate the wealth of issues that Riepel discusses. Example 10-1 is a composite of four separate examples. Although Riepel discusses the entire allegro, only the first *part (Theil),* lasting up to the double bar, is illustrated here. Riepel never lines up any examples one under the other, as is done here. But his discussion demonstrates how these different versions are expansions, contractions, and transformations of one another, and how additional transformations could arise. The melody on staff number 3 is the first version he offers. A briefer version could simply omit measures 5 through 8. Or else, one could proceed directly from measures 1 through 6 to the four measures in brackets at the end of the example. Staffs 2 and 1 are progressively more condensed versions of the original version on staff 3.

Each version has its own integrity as a complete piece with balanced phrases and a combination of related and contrasting motives. Thus, the abbreviated version on staff 1 features an opening two-measure phrase divided into two segments and answered by a two-measure phrase. The reversal of the arpeggio to open the second phrase in measure 3 allows the two phrases to be contrasting while still remaining related. The version on staff 2 expands the concluding phrase to a pair of phrases, using the closing motive of measures 3 and 4 to open measures 5 and 6. In the original version on staff 3, the opening material forms a pair of two-measure phrases. The four-measure length of this opening material is reflected in the four measures for each of the two following phrases. The opening pair of phrases has its own motivic parallelisms; the phrase in measures 5 through 8 uses its opening motive as the basis of a sequence before returning to a motive from the very opening at its cadence in measure 8. The new theme beginning in measure 9 features a contour and rhythm reversal of this motive from the opening, thereby providing both thematic contrast and relationship.

The version on staff 4 is an expansion of the original version on staff 3, in which the opening two-measure phrases have become four-measure phrases covering the same ground. Riepel notes that the two measures after the + in this version could be repeated, expanding the version still further. Or this version could be expanded much further, appearing with a prefix and then a phrase in the parallel minor before proceeding to the next material, as in Example 10-2.

Riepel also offers other transformations of the versions in Example 10-1 that are not so much a matter of greater or lesser elaboration, but rather of different realizations of the material. For instance, he suggests that the version on staff 1 could appear with the first two cadences reversed, as shown in Example 10-3. This would lead to different realizations.

When depicted as in Example 10-1, Riepel's procedure seems to bear a striking resemblance to Schenkerian hierarchical analyses. As Riepel explains, the briefer versions of this allegro are condensations of the same content as the longer versions, "just as painters present a journey life size on a piece of paper only a hand's breadth wide in a so-called miniature" (p. 65). If one wished to reduce the entire movement to its barest essentials, "the miniature could be even smaller, namely only with letters, such as C-

*Example 10-1.* Riepel 1755, p. 65 (staffs 1 and 2), p. 64 (staff 3), p. 69 (staff 4)

G-C" (Riepel 1755, p. 65). At this level, which Riepel never depicts in musical notation, entire segments of the piece are subsumed under a single letter, all the characteristic shapes of the piece are absent, and issues of balanced phrasing, motivic contrast, and the like, are no longer relevant.

But at all levels above this representation of the main keys, Riepel does not view expansions and contractions as structural levels—as levels that stand for greater or lesser structural depth in the piece. In fact, none of these staffs on Example 10-1 are analyses at all in the sense of demonstrations or explanations of the structure of another realization. Rather,

each is a different possible foreground realization of the basic material. Riepel refers to a "miniature" as a complete painting, not as a sketch of a larger painting.

Riepel's different realizations are thus closer to thoroughbass realizations that are elaborated to a greater or lesser extent, such as those that Niedt demonstrates when he turns thoroughbass progressions into various dance types, or that Heinichen demonstrates when he notes that a bass line descending from tonic to dominant is an expanded half-cadence. And they are akin to the types of expansions noted by harmonic theorists such

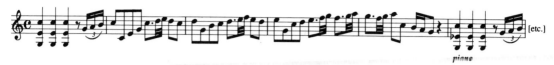

*Example 10-2.* Riepel 1755, p. 71. The chords appear as in a violin part; Riepel does not intend 6/4 harmonies.

as Nichelmann when he demonstrates how a chord progression can be realized by inserting additional harmonies between the originally adjacent chords.

Riepel's approach differs from these thoroughbass or harmonic alternatives in its concentration on melody. As long as expansions were perceived in terms of thoroughbass realizations or harmonic progressions, there was a limit to their structural dimensions. The realizations could be longer or shorter, elaborated to a greater or lesser extent. But there was little way to show how the results functioned as parts of pieces. Riepel, however, performs these structural transformations not on undifferentiated voice leadings or harmonic progressions, but rather on units that have specific functions within a composition: phrases that end on the tonic, on the dominant, on the dominant in the key of the dominant, and so forth; phrases that open an allegro, occur after the establishment of a new key in the allegro, and so forth. The transformations thus take place within a distinct position in a complete composition, and can be tailored to the compositional circumstances. For instance, the revised cadence scheme in measures 1 and 2 of Example 10-3 is a conceivable variant in part because of where the phrase occurs in the structure: different types of cadential rhymes are possible in an opening pair of phrases or segments. The same is true for the various ways of moving to the dominant key in the versions shown in Example 10-1. On staffs 2 and 3, there is a half cadence before the arrival on the tonic of the new key (m. 5 on staff 2; m. 8 on staff 3). But on staff 4, the corresponding cadence (m. 10) is on the tonic of the new key. To repeat, these separate versions are neither analyses of one another nor realizations of a single structure. They are explorations of the various paths that a piece may take and, implicitly, illustrations of the integrity that each realization must have.

Riepel applies his procedures not only to the construction of small

*Example 10-3.* Riepel 1755, p. 65

phrases and connections among them, but also to the construction of entire movements. For instance, his treatment of the entire symphonic allegro (of which the beginning is shown in Example 10-1) deals with the possible keys that might be present after the double bar, various thematic parallelisms between the first and second parts of the movement, and so forth. Just as his concern at the phrase level is with multiple possible realizations, on this larger scale too Riepel does not merely lay out one or two schemes for a movement. Rather, he considers a range of possible versions and their integrity. His is not a theory of form in the nineteenth-century sense, but an approach to composition.

Another primary difference between Riepel's transformations and those of thoroughbass methods concerns the manner in which the transformations are worked out. Niedt's thoroughbass method of composition clearly involves something that could be improvised and then set down on paper. Riepel's method, by contrast, is not one that he ever explains as performable. One can imagine Riepel working out a version by humming it or playing it on the violin, considering its good qualities and defects, and proceeding to improvise emended versions until a satisfactory entity arose. But he never describes it in such a manner. Likewise, Koch, Riepel's successor in these matters, and also a violinist, implies that his is a written method for composing, not one to be improvised, even though Koch argues that the creative act itself is a product of the imaginative genius. Much as the seventeenth century represents a transition from composition via vocal improvisation to composition via keyboard improvisation (thoroughbass), the treatises of Riepel and Koch appear to chronicle part of the transition from composition from a bass part that could well be the result of an act of improvisation to composition from an articulated melody that seems to be less related to performed improvisation.

## Riepel's Influence and Problematic Aspects

It is difficult to gauge the extent of Riepel's influence. His works were known and reviewed from the time they began to appear, yet they do not seem to have had much direct influence on any theorist other than Heinrich Christoph Koch, whose treatises of the 1780s and 1790s were profoundly influenced by Riepel. Marpurg gave glowing reviews to Chapters 1 through 3 in his *Historische-Kritische Beyträge* (1 [1755]: 340–343; 2 [1756]: 514–521; 3 [1757]: 396). Concerning Riepel's Chapter 1, Marpurg notes that "books like this merit being in the hands of each and every practicing composer, and ought to be read day and night." Likewise, in his *Handbuch* (p. 223), Marpurg recommends Riepel's Chapter 1 for the study of rhythm. But Marpurg also indicates that Riepel's works were apparently not easily available—in 1757 Marpurg reports that many readers of his earlier reviews had found it impossible to find copies of Riepel's works in any bookstore. Leopold Mozart apparently owned copies of one or more chapters and refers to Riepel in a 1778 letter to Wolfgang. In an earlier letter, Wolfgang mentions that he had borrowed a copy of an unspecified chapter.

With the sole exception of Koch's writings, Riepel's ideas do not seem to have been directly adopted by other theorists. But this does not mean his work may not have exerted a more indirect influence, or at least chronicled teaching methods in use at the time that were not reflected by other writings. Riepel's emphasis on writing minuets, for instance, is reflected in Wolfgang Mozart's own early education as well as his later compositional instruction. Without much more knowledge than we now possess on actual composition instruction (apart from published treatises on composition) from the 1750s onward, it is probably impossible to know whether such pedagogical similarities indicate a direct influence from Riepel to Leopold and Wolfgang Mozart, or merely show that Riepel himself was utilizing common methods that otherwise did not find their way into print.

The absence of a more direct influence on Riepel's contemporaries may be the result of several factors, including changing musical styles and inadequacies in Riepel's own works. In the rapidly evolving styles of the period, Riepel's musical examples may have quickly seemed dated. This is true both of the types of transformations that Riepel performs on his material to create different versions of a passage, and also of stylistic features in the examples themselves. When Riepel expands condensed musical materials into a symphonic movement as shown in Examples 10-1, he expands all the material more or less equally, regardless of the role that material plays in the structure of the movement. Thus, the 2+2 measure structure on staff 1 corresponds to an 8+9 measure structure on staff 4. This rough equivalence of length belies the rather different structural functions of the music in these phrases. Measures 1 and 2 of staff 1 expound the tonic key, while measures 3 and 4 change the key to the dominant, establish that key, and cadence in it. When Koch offers similarly related condensed and expanded structures in the 1780s, there is a striking difference between the extent to which he elaborates material of different structural functions. For instance, when Koch expands an eight-measure period into the thirty-two-measure first half of an allegro, he maintains some portions in their original dimensions while he considerably expands other portions (Example 11-14; Sisman 1982 explores this further).

In addition, Riepel often seems to regard the transformation of one set of cadential articulations to another as a relatively minor change. Switching closed and open cadences between staff 1 of Example 10-1 and Example 10-3 would give rise to profound effects in versions that elaborated

*Example 10-4.* Riepel 1757, p. 1

one or the other of these structures. Likewise, changing the cadential orientation before the new theme on staff 4 of Example 10-1 also carries major consequences. From the perspective of the musical styles around the middle of the century, Riepel may not have found these consequences to be so important. But by the 1770s and 1780s, such differences carried more weight.

Within his examples, Riepel cites various melodic-harmonic stereotypes that were apparently quite common before and around the 1750s but that were deemed obsolete by later generations. Example 10-4 shows one form each of the patterns he laconically entitles *Monte* (mountain), *Fonte* (fountain), and *Ponte* (bridge)—names that the *Discantista,* with Riepel's characteristic distaste for theoretical pretensions, accuses the *Praeceptor* of having introduced "only to poke fun at those foreign terms which most music writers throw in to cover their ignorance" (Riepel 1757, p. 1). Riepel refers to these stereotypes repeatedly, using them as the basis for melodic elaborations and discussing their roles within pieces. But he was aware that "in many areas—even in the main musical centers—they were discarded long ago, much like fake coinage" (Riepel 1765, p. 12). Koch, writing over two decades later, introduces a few phrases that are similar to these stereotypes. Without terming it a *Monte,* for instance, Koch comments on an example quite close to Riepel's, noting that "phrases that ascend sequentially by step were quite frequently used in older pieces, and to a certain extent have become obsolete" (*zum Ekel worden sind;* Koch 1782–1793, 2, par. 30). It is quite likely that by the 1770s and 1780s, musicians regarded other aspects of Riepel's examples and discussions as archaic as well.

If Riepel's ideas had been codified in a more systematic fashion, readers might have been able to apply the principles he enunciates to different styles more easily. (Such has been the case with Fuxian counterpoint, for instance.) But Riepel's discursive and frequently rambling dialogues can make it difficult for a reader to extract general principles. To be sure, it is probably unfair to charge Riepel with having failed to organize his material in a more lucid fashion, considering that he was the very first to try to put any of these ideas onto paper in any form at all. Viewed in this light, his achievements are indeed remarkable.

HARMONY

A more serious problem with Riepel's works, especially in the 1760s and 1770s, would have been his antiquated manner of dealing with harmony. Riepel is virtually alone among writers after the midcentury in failing to adopt the by-then universal vocabulary of harmonic theory. Riepel does know about chord inversions, explaining that a 5/3 chord changing to a 6/3 chord is a change from the *Grundnote* in the bass to the *Terzsprung* (Riepel 1757, p. 38). But he is quite inconsistent in applying these concepts. He lists the inversions of seventh chords in the order 6/5, 6/4/3, 4/2, and 7, not with the root-position form as the basis; this reflects earlier thinking that the 6/5 form was somehow more consonant since it does not feature a dissonance over the bass. Even though he recognizes the 6/4/3 position as an inversion of the others, Riepel seems unsure of the status of 6/4/3 chords; he questions them, noting that "Fux writes nothing of this derivation" (Riepel 1757, p. 40).[4] Indeed, he even returns to the seventeenth-century notion of the "irregular fourth" when he describes the fourth in a 6/4/3 chord as "freely inserted" and complains about those who have used this chord over scale-step 2 "during the past 50 years" (Riepel 1786, p. 2). Likewise, in an unpublished treatise on fugue, Riepel rejects Rameau's notion that the 7 chord is the parent sonority of the remaining inversions, explaining that "this is only based on numbers" (Twittenhoff 1935, p. 120). And finally, when Riepel changes the bass of a series of seventh chords so that the chords appear as 7 6/5 7 6/5, not 7 7 7 7, he recognizes that the new progression is related to the other progression by chordal inversion; but then explains that since half the chords are no longer figured with the number 7, "they can hardly be called seventh progressions any more" (Riepel 1765, p. 3).

At the same time that he seems to reject much of chordal theory, Riepel applies many aspects of Rameauian harmony. In his posthumous *Baßschlüssel* (1786), for instance, he explains that there are only three basic chords: those on scale-steps 1, 4, and 5. All other chords are built on *subsidiary* or *supplementary tones* or *intermediary bass notes* (*Neben-* or *Ausfüllungstöne* or *Mittelbassnoten;* p. 6). This leads him to harmonize melodies in a manner similar to that taught by Mozart in the 1784 studies.

4. Riepel frequently invokes Fux's "incomparable *Manuductio*" (Riepel 1752, p. 75), occasionally criticizing it. For instance, he faults Fux for rejecting the interval of an augmented sixth (Riepel 1757, p. 44). Riepel not only accepts augmented sixth chords but even presents them in all possible inversions (Riepel 1757, p. 64).

Compositional Theory in the Eighteenth Century

Example 10-5. Riepel 1768, p. 10

Riepel first applies root-position chords; then he changes the bass line to introduce inversions.

Other discussions demonstrate a full grasp of chord integrity and chord inversions. In Chapter 5 (1768), for instance, he warns that merely looking at the consonances and dissonances will not by itself explain which pitches are elaborations of the underlying chords. He illustrates with the two-part excerpt and various elaborations shown in Example 10-5, marking the elaborating notes. In the elaboration, note that Riepel properly understands the bass D in measure 1 as the added tone, even though that note makes a consonance with the melody's B♭ and the following E makes a dissonance. But he never explains how a reader might figure this out, either in terms of these examples, or via general principles.

Similarly, in discussing passing notes, he illustrates many examples where passing-tone patterns are allowed or prohibited because of the underlying harmony, although he never explains the issue in these terms (see Example 10-6).

Furthermore, in his own informal vocabulary, Riepel clearly recognizes various large-scale aspects of keys and harmonic structures. As previously noted, in Example 10-1, he labels the cadence in measure 8 of staff 3 as a *Quint-Aenderungs-Absatz*—a half cadence in the key of scale-step 5. But as with other tenets of harmonic theory, he never teaches the reader how to come to such a conclusion.

Whatever their problems, Riepel's works are a major source of infor-

Example 10-6. Riepel 1768, pp. 4–5

mation on a wide range of mid-eighteenth-century issues. He sheds light on numerous issues. And his copious examples compensate in large part for inadequacies in his presentation or vocabulary. His works, both published and unpublished, merit an adequate modern edition for a full assessment of his work.

Compositional Theory in the Eighteenth Century

# CHAPTER ELEVEN

# Koch: Toward a Comprehensive Approach to Musical Structure

*What is the highest degree of perfection of the creative spirit among composers? It is nothing other than the ability to conceive of melody harmonically; that is, to invent it so that one is capable of bringing forth simultaneously the main features of its harmonic accompaniment . . . "A painter who has conceived of the color and position of a head, if he is a Raphael or a Rubens, also sees at the very same moment the colors and folds of the garments with which he must dress the rest of the body." This description of a creative painter, applied to a creative composer, illuminates for us the creative method which the greatest masters of art have always used.*

*Koch 1782–1793, 2, pp. 81–82*

KOCH IS OFTEN thought of as a theorist who built on the ideas first enunciated by Riepel, treating melody, phrasing, and larger musical constructions more comprehensively and systematically than his predecessor and applying them to a later repertoire—including the earlier works of Haydn (some of whose compositions Koch discusses). This is certainly true. But Koch is equally important for placing this approach to composition into a comprehensive theoretical approach to the music of his time. Although his presentation of melody, phrasing, and what has come to be known as musical form is justly regarded as his major achievement, this aspect of his work cannot be fully appreciated outside the context of other topics he treats. He discusses the physical source of music, presents a comprehensive approach to harmony and counterpoint with several important innovations, and discusses aesthetics, all prior to an immensely detailed study of melody, of the larger structural aspects of compositions, and of compositional genres. Throughout, Koch's aim is instruction in composition. He thus draws together most of the theoretical domains of the eighteenth century and shows how they contribute to what he clearly regarded as the consummate musical activity—the creation of musical works.

All this material appears in his three-volume *Versuch einer Anleitung zur Composition* (1782–1793), the most informative treatise of the last quarter of the century. This work is important not only for its content, but also for its clarity and organization. Koch illustrates virtually every point with musical examples. And he systematically divides his material into volumes *(Theile)*, parts *(Abtheilungen)*, sections *(Abschnitte)*, chapters *(Kapitel)*, some with subdivisions *(Absätze)*, and clauses (numbered continuously in each volume)—an organization that parallels his hierarchical subdivisions of musical compositions and that betrays in its order his historical position at the end of the rationalist Enlightenment.

The organization of the *Versuch*—an exposition of the sources of music, of harmony and counterpoint, and of melody, form, and genre—became the model for several later generations of theorists.[1] Koch's ideas thus form a fitting conclusion to the present survey of eighteenth-century theory. The *Versuch* deals with many of the theoretical traditions of the eighteenth century, giving the opportunity to observe how several different theoretical approaches worked in concert and clashed with one another to create the musical universe of the Classic era: Rameauian harmony joined with thoroughbass concepts, counterpoint methodology applied to harmonization exercises, and so forth. Finally, both in its content and its organization the *Versuch* lays out the materials that occupied theorists for much of the nineteenth and early twentieth centuries.

Koch was associated from age fifteen until his death with the court chapel in Rudolstadt, where his father and grandfather had been instrumentalists and where he served as violinist, court musician *(Hofmusikus)*, chamber musician *(Kammermusikus)*, and, briefly, *Kapellmeister* (although he requested to be relieved of this latter post and return to the position of concertmaster). The *Versuch* was his first published work but by no means the last. He briefly edited a *Journal der Tonkunst* in 1795 and published the important *Musikalisches Lexikon* in 1802 (the first original large-scale dictionary of musical terms in German since Walther's 1732 *Lexicon*) as well as several other items. His ideas continued to evolve after the *Versuch*—for instance, in both the *Lexikon* and the *Journal der Tonkunst* he takes note of Mozart's works (mentioned only once in the *Versuch*). Because of the comprehensive nature of the *Versuch*, and because Koch's

---

1. This is true even of a work as late as Heinrich Schenker's *Neue musikalische Theorien und Phantasien* (1906–1935), which features a volume on the sources of sound and harmony, two volumes on counterpoint, and a volume on free composition, including a discussion of musical form and rhythm.

later works exceed the historical boundaries of this study, the present discussion is restricted to the *Versuch*.[2]

## Harmony and Counterpoint

HARMONY

The first volume of the *Versuch* is devoted entirely to harmony and counterpoint. Koch's focus here as elsewhere is primarily practical. Before the body of his text, he asks

> Who is so inexperienced in the pedagogical history of composition that he would deny that a beginner, when he has studied intervals, their combination into chords, their progression, and the usual rules that are commonly given for the preparation of a counterpoint, still remains in doubt and uncertainty with the majority of notes he sets as to whether or not he has selected the correct note? . . . Why this uncertainty? It can only arise from a much too obscure presentation of the diverse ways of connecting chords to make a whole, that is, from the diversity of composition itself . . . The leap from the simplest parts of composition, i.e., from chords, to all this diversity is too great [for the beginner], and he does not know how to bridge this gap. (1, pp. xv, xvii, xx)

Koch's solution lies in his approach to accompaniment, a novel formulation of what he calls five species of counterpoint that is in effect a series of harmonization exercises of increasingly complex harmonic vocabulary, quite similar in its practical effects to Kirnberger's method of harmonization in *Die Kunst des reinen Satzes* (1771–1779).

Before presenting this solution, Koch lays out his thoughts on the origins of tones, on intervals, on chords, and on chord progressions. As with many of his contemporaries, he draws on ideas from a variety of theoretical traditions but mostly from Marpurg's works. Like Marpurg in his *Handbuch* (1755–1762), Koch mixes Rameauian notions of the origins of chords and their invertibility with thoroughbass methodology and organization largely uninfluenced by root-progression thinking to explain the use of harmonies and the resolution of dissonances. Discussions of root progressions, as they occur in Rameau's or Kirnberger's writings, are absent.

Like Rameau, Koch explains that musical sounds arise from a sonorous body. Using a variety of experiments, he derives the major triad and links it with its transpositions up and down a perfect fifth to form the major

2. The major studies of Koch include Ratner 1949, 1956, and 1980; Baker 1975, 1976, 1977, 1983, 1988; Dahlhaus 1978; and Sisman 1982. These studies cover various aspects of Koch's works; there is as yet no comprehensive study of his entire theoretical output including his later works.

*Table 2.* Koch's matrix of triads in major keys

| The scale degrees | In the major key there are: | | | | | |
| --- | --- | --- | --- | --- | --- | --- |
| | Essential | | | Incidental | | |
| | Triads | 6-chords | 6/4-chords | Triads | 6-chords | 6/4-chords |
| On the tonic | ceg | | cfa | | cea | |
| On the second degree | | | dgb | dfa | | |
| On the third degree | | egc | | egb | | eac |
| On the fourth degree | fac | | | | fad | |
| On the fifth degree | gbd | | gce | | gbe | |
| On the sixth degree | | acf | | ace | | adf |
| On the seventh degree | | bdg | | | | beg |

*Source:* Koch 1782–1793, 1, p. 66.

scale. Koch then notes that the major scale includes three minor triads on steps 2, 3, and 6. Only in one area does Koch introduce a novel chord generation. Instead of generating seventh chords by adding a third above a triad so that a triad and seventh chord share the same function, Koch argues that all dissonant chords should be derived in a single manner (1, pp. xxii–xxiii). "Entirely contrary to the usual theory," he generates seventh chords by placing a new bass a third below a triad by subposition (*Untersetzen;* 1, p. 70). Thus, in C major he subposes G below a B triad to derive the dominant seventh chord, since "B, the bass of this triad, is a note that has the foundation of its existence in the note G" (1, p. 69). Koch does not draw any conclusions about the use of the dominant seventh chord from this idiosyncratic derivation, and it seems of no significance after this point in the *Versuch.*

Koch generates chords not only to show a systematic origin of the materials of music, but also to explore the role of the various triads in a key. The triads on scale-steps 1, 4, and 5, which give rise to the key, are the essential *(wesentlich)* chords, while the triads on scale-steps 2, 3, and 6 of a major key are incidental *(zufällig).*[3] Koch assigns each of the chords a fixed position within the key. Table 2 shows his matrix of the triads in a major key. He offers similar tables of the triads in a minor key and of seventh chords (1, pp. 67, 99). Rameau had assigned special roles to the tonic, dominant, and subdominant chords. But he had not specified any special status for the remaining chords in a key. Koch's classification of

3. Koch's use of *wesentlich* and *zufällig* is distinct from Kirnberger's use of the same terms to indicate different types of dissonances within a chord.

*Example 11-1.* Koch 1782–1793, 1, p. 180

chords into essential and incidental and the information in these tables provides the conceptual basis for much of his later discussions.

Koch is fully conversant with chord inversions. But although he recognizes and numbers chord inversions, surprisingly he has no term for the root of a chord. He uses the term *Grundton* to denote the bass of a sonority as well as the root of a chord (Baker 1983, p. 37). For instance, discussing the diminished triad built on the leading tone in C major, he first notes that "when scale-degree 4 of a given melody in the upper voice descends by step to scale-degree 3, the root [*Grundton*] of the diminished triad [the note B] can be set against it" (1, p. 270). In the very next sentence he explains that this F-E may be accompanied by "the bass note [*Grundton!*] D with its chord of the sixth, arising by means of the first inversion of the diminished triad to become a chord of the sixth" (1, p. 271). He also uses the term *Grundton* to refer to the tonic of a key (1, p. 180).

Like Marpurg, Koch never uses the root or fundamental bass of a chord to explain a progression. As a result, his extensive discussions of dissonance resolutions invoke chord inversions alongside explanations more typical of thoroughbass manuals. His discussion of "the progression of the major seventh accompanied by the major third and perfect fifth" (C-E-G-B) is representative. Koch first lists the chord and its inversions. Then he proceeds to harmonies that contain a major seventh but that are not at all functionally related to that seventh chord:

> After it has been prepared (in the strict as well as in the free style), the major seventh is resolved one step downwards. Its resolution to a third, as well as the chords arising from the inversion of this seventh chord, are those in [Example 11-1]. If this chord of the major seventh is formed on the tonic [*Grundton*] of a major key, its seventh can also be resolved a step upwards, either to an octave in [Example 11-2a] (if the bass [*Bass*[4]] is maintained on the same step), or to a third in [Example 11-2b] (if the bass moves a third

4. Here Koch uses the term *Bass* because he refers to the bass voice as an entity. This usage is distinct from *Grundton,* by which Koch refers quite literally to the "foundation tone" of a given harmony (either in the sense of the thoroughbass support for a chord or for the root on which the chord is built).

Koch: A Comprehensive Approach to Structure

*Example 11-2.* Koch 1782–1793, 1, p. 181

lower). If, however, as often happens, it appears on the tonic of the scale with the accompaniment of an eleventh,[5] then it must always be resolved upwards, as in [Example 11-2c]. (1, pp. 180–181)

The brief appendix to this chapter (1, pp. 213–218), dealing with the treatment of unusual dissonances, is in the tradition of Heinichen's explanation of dissonances in the theatrical style.

Koch uses both subposition and the combination of altered scale degrees to create various dissonant chords. Subposition yields ninth, eleventh, and thirteenth chords. Altered scale degrees yield chords including the diminished triad and half-diminished seventh chord built on the raised sixth step of the minor key and the augmented 6/4 on scale-step 7 in minor keys. Koch does not apply either of these methods of generating dissonant chords to explaining the resolution of the dissonance. As already noted, he treats dissonance resolutions in the manner of thoroughbass methods.

Koch omits any discussion of the functionally directed resolution of sensitive tones like the leading tone. The urge of the leading tone to resolve played an important role in Rameau's and Kirnberger's ideas of harmonic directionality. But Koch, following thoroughbass methods, offers only a brief discussion of the leading tone. And he places it not in Volume 1 within the study of harmony, but in Volume 2 amid a discussion of general aspects of melodic structure such as avoiding problematic interval successions, creating a sense of the key, and using rests properly (pp. 139–168). The absence of a discussion of the leading tone as a driving force in harmonic successions is not due to Koch's ignorance of the idea, since he prefaces his discussion of leading tones by citing Sulzer's *Allgemeine Theorie* (hence Kirnberger's ideas) and includes Kirnberger's extension of the term *leading tone* (*Leitton;* equivalent to Rameau's major and minor dissonance) to scale-step 4 in a dominant seventh chord, and to all chromatically raised and lowered tones in similar positions (2, pp. 157–158). Rather, Koch, like Marpurg, regards the linear context of harmonies to be best explained by the treatment of individual notes, not by harmonic

5. Note that since the fourth is a suspension here, Koch calls it an eleventh in the tradition of Rameau and Marpurg.

*Example 11-3.* Koch 1782–1793, 1, p. 162

progressions. In contrast to Rameau and Kirnberger, Koch does not view
the harmonic perspective as one that can deal with these matters.

Part of the reason that Koch does not treat leading tones as functionally
directed notes in a harmonic context has to do with his notion of cadences.
For Rameau and Kirnberger, cadences are models for harmonic progressions, generating voice motions such as leading-tone and chord-seventh
resolutions. And for Rameau, evasion of cadential progressions is the path
to understanding chordal connections. For Koch, a cadence *(Cadenz, Ton-
schluss)* is simply a conventional formal punctuation that ends a musical
period conclusively. A cadence must end on a tonic chord with scale-step
1 in both bass and melody, preceded by a root-position dominant chord
and any of a variety of antepenultimate chords (1, pp. 240–244). Anything
less formal than this is a caesura that ends an inconclusive phrase (*Cäsur
eines Absatzes;* 1, p. 239), most commonly a phrase ending on the chord
built on scale-step 1 *(Grundabsatz)* or on scale-step 5 *(Quintabsatz;* 2,
p. 415; Baker 1983, p. 36). His detailed explanation of the final, penultimate, and antepenultimate chords of a cadence illustrate numerous common cadential progressions. But he is quite informal when it comes to
deceptive cadences, reserving for a "remark" at the end of his discussion
the suggestion that "if the cadence is repeated, or if two cadences follow
one another, sometimes one uses an unauthentic bass note [a note other
than scale-step 1] for the first cadence, thereby making a so-called deceptive cadence [*Trugschluss*]" (1, p. 243).

By mixing inversional thinking with chord roots and thoroughbass
methods, Koch retains several problems that continued to plague harmonic
theory through the end of the century. For instance, in the progression in
Example 11-3, Koch notes that "the fourth is not resolved," in effect
resurrecting the "irregular fourth" of earlier thoroughbass methods. He
does not ban the progression; but he has no satisfactory explanation of
what we nowadays call passing second inversion chords. And Koch uses
Example 11-4 to explain "how a dissonance can be resolved by a regular
passing note." For Rameau (and for most composers of the time) a chord
seventh such as the F in measure 2 would have to resolve to a chord tone
in the next harmony.

Koch: A Comprehensive Approach to Structure

*Example 11-4.* Koch 1782–1793, I, p. 225

COUNTERPOINT

After expositing intervals and chords and explaining dissonance resolutions, Koch turns to "the centerpiece of my design, the position on which
[the first volume of] my *Versuch* must be judged" (1, p. xv). This is his
formulation of five species of counterpoint. His conception has little to do
with species counterpoint as presented by Fux (1725) or Albrechtsberger
(1790). Rather it is the manner by which

> we wish to put into use simple harmony (i.e., the origin and connection of
> tones, including the rules of their progression) . . . Nowadays one understands
> by making counterpoint [*contrapunctiren*] or by accompanying harmonically
> [*harmonisch begleiten*] that procedure whereby one sets to a given melody
> one or several additional series of tones, that is, one or several additional
> voices. The melody taken as the subject [*Gegenstand*] of the counterpoint is
> called the *fixed melody* [*feste Gesang*] or *cantus firmus*. (1, pp. 231, 232)

Koch's procedure is akin to the method of harmonization outlined by
Kirnberger in his *Kunst des reinen Satzes*. Like Kirnberger, Koch recommends that one begin with a simple harmonic vocabulary and gradually
add more and more chords. But Koch's gradations are more detailed and
systematic than Kirnberger's. First species uses only the essential triads in
root position, with inversions only when needed to avoid parallel fifths or
octaves, as when moving between chords on scale-steps 4 and 5. Second
species adds inversions and the leading-tone triad. Third species adds the
incidental chords of the key. Fourth species adds suspensions and unprepared sevenths on weak beats. And fifth species adds chromatic notes that
are not involved in large-scale key changes. Within each species, Koch
discusses separately setting a bass to a melody and setting a melody to a
bass. And within each species he treats *even counterpoint* (*gleiche,* or note
against note), *uneven counterpoint* (*ungleiche,* with rhythmically consistent melody or bass elaborations), and *mixed counterpoint* (*vermischte,*
with rhythmically free melody or bass elaborations). The discussion of
two-part counterpoint is rather long (1, pp. 257–331), since this is where
Koch explains how to create a soprano-bass framework. The discussions
of three- and four-part counterpoint are considerably shorter (1, pp. 332–
347, 348–365).

Both in his prefatory "general rules and maxims" (1, pp. 237–256) and
within the discussion of counterpoint itself, Koch offers a combination of

*Example 11-5*. Koch 1782–1793, I, p. 273

traditional rules of voice leading (such as recommending contrary motion), other voice-leading rules translated into harmonic terms, and various aspects of harmonic practice. Thus his first rule (1, p. 237) is that the counterpoint begin with the triad built on the tonic of the key with an octave or fifth between the outer voices (occasionally a third)—this is the centuries-old rule that a counterpoint should begin with a perfect interval, translated into tonal harmonic terms. His second rule recommends that whatever the harmonic vocabulary in use, the beginning of a harmonization should use mostly the essential chords of a key. Incidental chords and chromaticism should appear only later. In both rules, as elsewhere, Koch is thinking of the placement of the materials of music within phrases and pieces.

Throughout, Koch's viewpoint is fully harmonic. Two-part counterpoint for him (just as for Mozart and Albrechtsberger) represents chords, not merely intervals. And these chords always play specific roles within a key. The discussion of Example 11-5, an exercise in second species in two parts, is representative:

> The bass note F used below the note A in the second measure must not be regarded as the bass of the incidental triad FAC, but rather as the bass of the chord of the sixth that arises from the inversion of the essential triad DFA . . . The beginning of the second phrase in the first part can be accompanied harmonically in more than one manner with respect to its structure [*in Ansehung der Modulation*[6]]. The succession G/GFEA etc. can be regarded as entirely within the key of A minor (since the seventh degree of the minor scale can be minor when descending), in which case the bass voice must have the form shown [in Example 11-6] according to this species.

*Example 11-6*. Koch 1782–1793, I, p. 274
(realized from letter notation)

6. Koch uses the term *modulation* in its traditional sense of the structure or patterning of a melody ("the diversely changeable rise and fall of the tones within a fundamental key"; 2, p. 138).

Example 11-7. Koch 1782–1793, 1, p. 275
(realized from letter notation)

Example 11-8. Koch 1782–1793, 1, p. 292

Or else the opening note of this phrase (the G) can be regarded as a note with which a brief change of key [*einer kurzen Ausweichung*] to the key of C major should be made in the structure of the melody. This returns to the fundamental minor key at the note A on the last quarter note. And then the note G, with which the phrase begins, can be treated just like a note in the major key, as [shown in Example 11-7]. Or else this opening note G can even be considered as a note still contained within the key of A minor, after which the structure appears to go to the key of C major on the repetition of this note. With the note A, the structure returns once again to the principal key of the melody. The structure in [Example 11-5] is treated in this manner. (1, pp. 273–275)

With fifth species, Koch introduces what is probably the clearest explanation of any theorist in the eighteenth century of brief instances of chromaticism within a key (1, pp. 292–300). To emend the absence of terminology for this phenomenon, he labels it "an incidental, or still better, a brief optional change of key" (*zufällige* or *kurze willkührliche Ausweichung*; 1, p. 292):

Under the heading of optional change of key I do not understand those changes of key which the succession of notes of a given melody necessarily prolongs; thus, for example, the change of key [*Ausweichung*] from C major to the modified [*modificirte*] key[7] of G major in the phrase of the well-known chorale [shown in Example 11-8] is not optional, but necessary. Rather, I understand under the heading of such an optional change of key that procedure where one presents a succession of two or more notes of the given melody as a succession of notes in another key, and accompanies such a presentation accordingly. A few examples will make this more intelligible.

The phrase in [Example 11-9a] contains a succession of notes that truly

7. Koch means by this locution that G is a key that requires accidentals modifying the key signature. Elsewhere, he also uses the term *transposed* in this sense.

*Example 11-9.* Koch 1782–1793, 1, pp. 293–294

belongs entirely to the key of C major, and the accompaniment is arranged entirely according to this key. But the succession of notes EDCB in this phrase can be regarded (without considering the preceding or succeeding notes) as a succession of notes belonging to the key of A minor (as one can see in the phrase in [Example 11-9b]). One can also regard it as a succession of notes that belongs to the transposed key of G (as in [Example 11-9c]).

If we now consider the two notes DC in the accompanied phrase in [Example 11-9a] as a succession of notes belonging to A minor, but with the remainder belonging to the main key, then we can accompany the melody as in [Example 11-9d]. But if we regard the notes CB as a succession in the modified key of G, then the accompaniment can be arranged as in [Example 11-9e]. (1, pp. 292–293)

Other theorists had presented these ideas before—Rameau with his notion of the reigning key as opposed to temporary keys, and Kirnberger—but not with such clarity. And no other theorist had attempted to establish a terminology for this procedure (although Koch's terminology did not become standard).

Like Kirnberger, Koch extends the notion of optional changes of key to the phrase level: "What was said above concerning optional changes of key in the succession of individual notes can occasionally also be used for entire phrases" (1, p. 298). In Volume 2, Koch expatiates on optional changes of key within an extensive discussion of keys, their relationships, and the various ways of changing keys. He distinguishes three categories of key changes: incidental changes of key, which are quite brief, passing *(durchgehende)* changes of key, which either return shortly to the original key or proceed to a further key, and formal *(förmliche)* changes of key, which last a considerable amount of time and lead to a cadence in the new key.[8] Although incidental changes of key may be brief and may only momentarily disturb the continuity of the larger key, nevertheless such

8. Carl Dahlhaus argues that Koch lacks a distinction between sections that are tonally closed and those that are transitional (Dahlhaus 1978, pp. 158–159). But here and in his terminology for phrases that are tonally mobile *(Uebergang, Zurückgang, Zergliederungssatz)*, Koch does indeed make such differentiations.

*Example 11-10.* Koch 1782–1793, 2, p. 416

brief changes are indeed changes of key at the most local level. Thus the first phrase ending in Example 11-10 "cannot be considered as a phrase ending that is made on the triad on the fourth degree in C major; rather it must be considered as a tonic phrase-ending in F major" (2, p. 416).

## KOCH AND OTHER EIGHTEENTH-CENTURY THEORIES OF HARMONY

Koch does not explain chord-to-chord progressions as Rameau, Kirnberger, Martini, and others do via root movements and fundamental bass. In fact, it could be argued that Koch does not try to explain specific chord progressions at all. Rather, he describes innumerable harmonic usages via his notion of essential chords that enunciate a tonal area complemented by incidental chords that provide other avenues of harmonic motion, and via his notion of which chords can begin a phrase or section and how formal cadences provide a proper ending. He also differentiates harmonic progressions according to whether they are appropriate to strict style, fugal style, or free style.

By specifying where different types of chords may occur within phrases, Koch reverses Rameau's agenda. Rameau begins by questioning why it is that the arrival on a consonant chord does not cause a phrase to end. Building on Zarlino's notion of evaded cadences, Rameau studies root movements and chord types to understand how what might have been a point of repose is in fact an incomplete cadential progression demanding some sort of continuation until a true cadence occurs. Rameau thus implies that during a phrase, directed harmonic motions are continually evasive until a cadential progression appears.

Koch, by contrast, begins by assuming that a phrase is an entity, one that includes particular progressions at particular points because that is where they belong within a phrase. Cadential progressions belong at the end of a phrase; incidental chords are improper too early in a phrase or piece; and so forth. Although he may not be able to answer the questions that Rameau poses, he does impart advice about when to use various types of chords more successfully and systematically than most other late-eighteenth-century theorists.

Changing musical styles may have been a major factor in the different approaches to harmonic progressions taken by Rameau and Koch. Rameau in his early years was faced with a musical style that often features rapid harmonic changes and relatively long, unarticulated phrases. Koch, by contrast, was dealing with a style featuring relatively short, articulated phrases within which different types of chords appear at different points.

Another fundamental difference between Rameau and Koch concerns the relative status of bass and melody as the determining voice of a composition. Rameau, like thoroughbass theorists, always views the bass as a primary determinant of compositional structure. Koch, by contrast, lived in an era in which articulated melodies were the starting point for composition. Koch's goal in teaching harmony in the first volume of the *Versuch* is to prepare his readers to compose melodies. He agrees that deriving a melody from a sequence of chords is an important exercise (probably a reference to thoroughbass methods like Niedt's and funda-mental-bass treatises like Rameau's or Nichelmann's). But he insists that this approach is inadequate for modern music (2, p. 79–81).

Instead of relying on chords as the source of melody, Koch wants the composer to learn how to conceive of melodic ideas along with their supporting harmonies—"to think of the melody harmonically" (*die Mel-odie harmonisch zu denken;* 2, p. 76). This invocation to conceive of melody and harmony as complementary was Koch's answer to the burning issue of so much eighteenth-century polemic—the priority of melody versus harmony. A beginner might find it quite difficult to compose this way, but Koch believes that repeated practice with his five species of counterpoint will promote this ability (2, p. 92).

## Melody and Phrasing

Koch was proud of his contrapuntal species because they teach how melody and harmony are coordinated. For Koch, melody is the heart of a composition. As the principal voice *(Hauptstimme),* it contains "the out-line of the painting, the specific content of the composer's conception [*Ideal*]." The bass presents "the foundation of the harmonic fabric with which this picture is painted." And the middle, supporting, or secondary voices *(Mittel-, Füll-, oder Nebenstimmen)* provide "the drapery, decora-tion, and completion" (2, p. 4). Having demonstrated these relationships in volume 1, Koch was ready to proceed to the centerpiece of his treatise, the study of melody and larger constructions in Volumes 2 and 3.

Riepel too had made melody his centerpiece. But Koch, by first expos-iting his notion of harmonically conceived melody, constructs a far more compelling perspective. Koch may never have verbalized the idea in this fashion, but if melody is conceived harmonically, then a melodic phrase is also a harmonic motion writ large. Koch's extended presentation of melody and larger constructions that arise from melodic phrases deals with harmony—not only in the sense of the chords and voice leading that are the framework of the melodies, but also as the congruous union of all the elements of music on a large scale.

Koch recognizes two aspects of melody: its inner character, which is ultimately beyond explanation, and its outer aspect, which he believes can be explained according to "mechanical rules" (*mechanische Regeln; 2*, pp. 7–8). These rules form the core of Volumes 2 and 3 of the *Versuch* (2, pp. 135–464; 3, pp. 1–430; Baker 1983). Koch often restates the contents of Riepel's chapters: phrases are malleable units, transformable according to a number of specific techniques; and the connection of phrases one to another according to their cadential orientation creates the larger constructions of music.

But where Riepel presents his materials discursively in a dialogue, Koch offers a systematic exposition, proceeding from basic definitions to small phrases and small formal units, the techniques of phrase expansion and larger units, and then genres and their characteristics. Just as Koch organizes harmonization into five applicable species of counterpoint, he presents much of his discussion of melody via a series of compositional exercises. As in his earlier discussions of harmony and counterpoint, the text is illustrated with many hundreds of musical examples.

Responding to the lack of generally accepted terms for melodic constructions, Koch begins with definitions (2, pp. 342; Baker 1983, pp. 1). Although he realizes that analogies between the articulation of language and the structure of music can only be carried so far, he likens the subdivision of larger musical units to subdivisions in language. Superficially, Koch's analogies between music and language appear to put him in the same category as Mattheson and others who borrowed many concepts from rhetoric. But where Mattheson's application of rhetorical terms often fails to illuminate the musical structure on its own terms, Koch's emphasis is always on the music. Koch explains that he had extensively examined musical phrases as grammatical utterances with subject and predicate in earlier drafts, but that he found this approach unworkable (2, 350–356; Baker 1983, pp. 4–6).

A musical *period (Period)* is a complete thought ending with a strong punctuation. A *phrase (Satz)* is a part of a period and may be the *closing phrase* of a period *(Schlusssatz)* or an *inconclusive phrase (Absatz)*. A phrase is inconclusive either because it ends on the dominant or another nontonic chord, or because it ends without a formal cadence. For instance, all three phrases in Example 11-11 are inconclusive. The third phrase ends on "the fifth of an essential triad" (with the G supported by a tonic triad)—an inconclusive phrase may even end without any harmonic motion.

A phrase itself is divisible into *segments (Einschnitte; 2*, p. 346; Baker

*Example 11-11*. Koch 1782–1793, 2, pp. 359, 391; Baker 1983, Ex. 14, 15, and 67

1983, p. 2).[9] Koch frequently applies symbols akin to Riepel's black or white squares (which Riepel used for complete or incomplete phrases). Koch uses a white square to indicate the end of an inconclusive phrase and a white diamond to indicate the end of a segment. He has no symbol for closing phrases "because the cadential formula distinguishes them sufficiently" (2, p. 363; Baker 1983, p. 9).

Phrases and segments "are distinguished from one another as parts of the whole chiefly by two characteristics: first, the type of their endings . . . second, the length of these parts along with a certain symmetry or proportion, or a certain relationship of these parts which can be found in the number of measures they contain when they are reduced to their essential components" (2, p. 343; Baker 1983, pp. 2–3). An inconclusive phrase differs from a closing phrase by the type of ending (the first of these characteristics). And a segment is defined primarily by its length (it is too short to be a phrase).

A third aspect of phrases, the degree of completion, depends on length. An inconclusive phrase or a closing phrase may be a *basic phrase (enger Satz)* with only enough music to be complete, or it may be an *extended phrase (erweitere Satz;* 2, p. 346; Baker 1983, p. 3). Extended phrases may repeat part of a phrase (the beginning, middle, or end) or add an *appendix (Anhang)*. Koch treats each procedure in detail (2, pp. 424–453; Baker 1983, 41–54). A part of a phrase may be repeated on the same scale degree or on a different one. There may be only one repetition or there may be many. Repetitions may be literal, transposed to form a sequence within a key (*Progression;* 2, p. 431; Baker 1983, p. 43), transposed to form a sequence in another key (*Transposition;* 2, p. 432; Baker 1983, p. 44), or varied by figuration.

9. Baker and some others translate *Einschnitt* as *incise*. But *incise* is not a noun in English dictionaries. *Segment* includes the two relevant aspects of *Einschnitt:* that a segment is *a part* of a phrase and that it arises by *cutting* or *dividing (einschneiden)* a phrase.

Periodicity and balance are of central importance to Koch's notion of extended phrases. The proportion of preceding and following phrases should respond to the basic length of a phrase, not its apparent length. Thus a five-measure phrase arising from a four-measure phrase through the repetition of a measure "is considered as a four-measure phrase with regard to the rhythmic relation [*rythmischen Vergleichung*] of phrases" (2, 427–428; Baker 1983, p. 42). But Koch is ever the practical musician. If a repeated measure within a four-measure phrase is so varied that its status as a repetition is not entirely obvious, then the resulting unit should be treated as a five-measure phrase in its connection to other phrases. There are innumerable discussions like this, each illustrated by musical examples.

Phrases may be separate. Or several phrases may join to form a *compound phrase (zusammengeschobener Satz)* (2, pp. 453–464; Baker 1983, pp. 54–59). This can arise from suppression of a measure (*Tacterstickung, Tactunterdrückung;* 2, p. 453; Baker 1983, p. 55), making the last measure of one phrase the first measure of the next, compounding the two phrases. Or two segments may remain incomplete only to be answered by a longer phrase, as in a 2+2+4 construction. For modern musicians, these two procedures (suppressing a measure and building a 2+2+4 contruction) may seem separate; but Koch understands both under the rubric of compound phrases.

Koch does not discuss the thematic roles of phrases as systematically as he treats their structural properties. But various remarks show that he is aware of this aspect. The opening of a piece is often the *principal phrase (Hauptsatz)* or *theme (Thema)* containing the *principal idea (Hauptgedank)* of a piece, the idea "that defines the sentiment that the whole should arouse" (2, pp. 347–348; Baker 1983, p. 3). Later phrases, which "present various expressions of this sentiment," are *dissection phrases (Zergliederungssätze;* ibid.), probably so named because they dissect the piece into its parts. Earlier, Koch refers to "connecting and dissection phrases or *subsidiary ideas*" (*Verbindungs- und Zergliederungssätzen oder Nebengedanken;* 2, p. 99).[10] It is not entirely clear how the phrase "various expressions of this sentiment" is to be understood. If Koch means that a piece should express a single sentiment or affect, he is arguing that later phrases should retain the main sentiment of the movement. But if he is talking about *theme* in the sense of subject matter for development, then Koch may be arguing that all later musical materials should derive from the opening phrase.

Koch is interested not only in a phrase's content, structure, and role but also in its notation. He extensively discusses metric notation and its rela-

10. Baker interprets the term *Zergliederungssatz* differently (Baker 1983, p. 3).

*Example 11-12.* Koch 1782–1793, 2, pp. 397, 398; Baker 1983, Ex. 79, 81

*Example 11-13.* Koch 1782–1793, 2, p. 400; Baker 1983, Ex. 86

tion to phrase structure. Among the issues he raises is whether to notate in simple or compound meters (2/4 versus 4/4; 3/8 versus 6/8). The design of the phrase ending is an important factor. When melodic figuration continues past the downbeat into the middle of the compound measure in what he calls an *overhang (Ueberhang)* or *feminine ending (weiblichen Ausgang;* 2, p. 394; Baker 1983, p. 24), the cadential figuration should not extend into a new measure. In Example 11-12, where this happens, Koch insists that the phrase should be notated in cut C, not in 2/4.[11] Koch also differentiates the *basic (eigentlich)* form of a phrase ending, in which such figuration occurs only in the melody (as in the first phrase of Example 11-12) from the *figured* or *decorated (uneigentlich)* form of a phrase ending where even the harmonic motion extends past the downbeat, as in Example 11-13.[12]

11. In the first phrase, Koch places the squares indicating the endings of inconclusive phrases as shown here. In her translation, Baker frequently moves such squares in order to emend what seem to be inconsistencies in Koch's placement (Baker 1983, p. xxiv). Nola Reed Knouse argues that there may be consistencies underlying many of Koch's apparent misplacements (Knouse 1986, pp. 145–146). In the examples in the present study, the squares and triangles are placed where they appear in the *Versuch.*

12. Baker translates *eigentlich* and *uneigentlich* as *proper* and *improper,* making it seem as if Koch proscribes phrase endings where the harmonic motion continues past the downbeat (p. 28). But Koch more likely uses the dichotomy *eigentlich-uneigentlich* in the sense *literal-nonliteral* or *basic-figurative.* In any case, Koch introduces other such *uneigentlich* phrase endings without censuring them (as in 2, p. 408; Baker 1983, ex. 100).

## Larger Musical Constructions

Having explained the various types of melodic constructions and a vast range of their transformations, Koch turns in Volume 3 to "The Connection of Melodic Sections or the Construction of Periods." He proceeds from short compositions (dances, themes for variations) to larger constructions (such as the allegro of a symphony, sonata, or concerto). All these movement structures arise from evermore extended use of the techniques of phrase expansion applied both within phrases and to phrases themselves. Just as a portion of a phrase may be repeated, transposed, or otherwise transformed, phrases themselves are treated in that manner in larger compositions.

These discussions are extensive (pp. 39–152; Baker 1983, pp. 78–128 on short compositions alone). Koch repeatedly reworks several basic examples into a range of structures. In addition, he introduces compositions by others to illustrate various points. The composers Koch draws on include Haydn (cited the most frequently, including the entire slow movement of his *Symphony No. 42*), C. P. E. Bach, Carl Heinrich Graun (c. 1704–1759), Christian Gotthelf Scheinpflug (1722–1770; Koch's teacher and predecessor at Rudolstadt), and others.

At the very end of his discussion of such melodic extensions, Koch expands an eight-measure period into the first period of an allegro movement, thirty-two measures long. Triangles and squares label its various segments and inconclusive phrases, and annotations refer the reader to the appropriate discussion of each of the means of expansion. Example 11-14 arranges the original period and its expansion in the manner of a comparable set of examples by Riepel in Example 10-1. Each of Koch's cross-references is explained briefly.[13]

There are important differences between Koch's discussion and Riepel's similar examples. Whereas Riepel tends to expand all sections of his basic structure to form longer versions, Koch expands his basic version unevenly according to the structural role of the musical material. The opening pair of two-measure phrases in the original period appear as two five-measure phrases in the expansion. These two phrases, which establish the tonic key and move to prepare for the departure from that key, account for half of the entire period in the original version, but less than a third of the expansion. By contrast, the pair of two-measure phrases that follow, which move to and cadence in the dominant, are more extensively expanded (13 and 9 measures).

This difference between Riepel and Koch directly reflects changes in compositional styles from the music of the 1750s and earlier that formed

13. These two examples are discussed in Ratner 1956 and Sisman 1982.

*Example 11-14.* Koch 1782–1793, 3, pp. 226–230; Baker 1983, Ex. 361, 362

Koch: A Comprehensive Approach to Structure

the model for Riepel and the music of the 1770s that served as Koch's models.[14] In addition to the proportion of the expansion that presents the bulk of the music in the nontonic key, also significant is the extent to which the two opening phrases in the expansion (mm. 1–5, 6–10) are mostly expanded at their beginnings while the closing phrase is extended primarily via repetitions and the composition of a series of interlocking cadential phrases, directly mirroring allegro structures of the 1770s.

Whereas Riepel had suggested a range of alternate cadential patterns that would substantially change the nature of the form, Koch does not tamper with these articulative features. In fact, he probably designed the basic version in Example 11-14 with specific structural features of the expanded version in mind. The larger version has an air of authenticity to it. But the basic version, with its short subdivisions and their square endings, seems very much like a condensation of the longer version.

These features raise the same questions as with Riepel as to whether these examples of expansion and contraction should be understood as structural levels and not only as variable versions of a basic structure. As in Riepel, the examples are primarily separate realizations of a possible structure, not substructures of other levels. But at the same time, the analytic aspect is more convincing in Koch's *Versuch* than it is in Riepel's *Anfangsgründe* because of several factors. One is the much stronger sense of harmonic underpinning in Koch's work. Where Riepel presents only vaguely defined harmonic ideas, Koch builds his larger structures from "harmonically conceived melodies." Koch's more comprehensive harmonic perspective leads one to look at many of his expansions not only as extensions of a basic phrase, but also as prolongations of a basic harmony. In Example 11-14, for instance, there is a clear parallelism between the rise to scale-step 3 in the basic version and the motivic parallelism that Koch uses to ascend to scale-step 3 in measures 1 through 3 of the expanded version. Likewise, the phrase extension after measure 6 in the expanded version is based on an exchange with an inner voice in measure 7 and then the extension of the resulting structure—once again the result is an expansion of the phrase and a working out of its motives along with a prolongation of the underlying harmony. Similarly close relationships between the harmonic underpinnings of original versions and their expansions are pervasive throughout the *Versuch*. But Koch never treats these issues in his remarks.

Koch clearly has a sense of levels of essential structure and detail in a piece. Within a phrase or segment, he discusses harmony via his five species of counterpoint. From the level of the segment up to the extended and

14. Sisman 1982 and Wagner 1984 note the extent to which Koch's *Versuch* specifically pertains to music of the 1770s.

compounded phrases that constitute his extended periods, his focus is entirely different, using the language of phrase manipulation. But he could hardly have used any other language. His theories of harmony were a combination of vertical structures as in Marpurg's interpretations of Rameau, along with the isolated treatment of point-to-point relationships of thoroughbass approaches. The linkage that he makes with larger structures is through his notion of harmonically conceived melody. Melodic motions articulated into phrases are in effect also extended harmonic structures. Since phrases are in some sense harmony writ large, Koch's study of phrases and larger constructions (which are themselves the result of expansions of phrases) is in a very real sense a hierarchical view of music with changes in emphasis from the more immediate connections to the largest aspects of a piece.

Koch surely did not offer a fully developed theory of hierarchical structural levels. But at the same time, he did offer a comprehensive approach to music in which all the elements of a composition, from details of voice leading through the largest aspects of complete movements could be related to one another. No other theorist of the eighteenth century even came close to such an achievement.

## Complete Movements

Koch treats the structure of complete movements under the heading "The Connection of Melodic Sections into Periods of Greater Length, or the Arrangement of Larger Compositions" (3, pp. 231; Baker 1983, pp. 165). By viewing what later came to be known as musical form as a product of the connection of periods, Koch sees crucial aspects of movements in quite a different light than later theorists. What makes the matter more complex, however, is that Koch himself discusses various features of complete movements that are not compatible with his own notion of larger structures being formed by the connection of periods—features that are in fact those stressed by later theorists of musical form. The present discussion surveys Koch's ideas and compares them to some later notions.[15]

For Koch, periods, as composites of phrases, are defined by two primary characteristics, their length and the tonal orientation of their ending: "By a principal period I mean the connection of several phrases, of which the last closes with a formal cadence either in the principal key or in one closely related to it" (3, pp. 231–232; Baker 1983, p. 166). The length of a period depends on the length and structure of the relatively simple or

15. Dahlhaus 1978 raises some of the issues dealt with here along with others and draws some different conclusions. The modern scholar who first called attention to Koch's view of the period structure of a movement is Leonard Ratner in 1949.

complex phrases that constitute it. For example, each of the two versions in Example 11-14 presents a single period, even though the original version is eight measures long and the expansion thirty-two. According to Koch's notions of balance and proportion, the length of a period determines in part the balance required by later periods in the piece. Thus the eight-measure version in Example 11-14 would require later periods to be less extensive than those required by the thirty-two-measure expansion. The ending of a period is its formal cadence. This cadence is always, by Koch's definition, a full close on the tonic of some key, but not necessarily the principal key of the movement. The period in both versions in Example 11-14 ends in the key on scale-step 5.

The structure of a movement depends on the number of periods and the tonal orientation of their endings. The allegro of a symphony, for instance, has three periods, corresponding to the three principal sections of sonata form that we know as the exposition, the development, and the recapitulation. Since the terms *sonata form, exposition, development,* and *recapitulation* were unknown to the eighteenth century, the present discussion follows Koch and refers to such movements as allegros and to their parts as the first, second, and third periods.

Koch's description of an allegro as the connection of periods is problematic in several ways. First, it ignores the larger repetition scheme of the movement. Koch recognizes that allegros have two repeatable parts *(Theile),* with period 1 comprising the first part, and periods 2 and 3 forming the second part (3, pp. 304, 307; Baker 1983, pp. 199). If the parts are repeated as commonly indicated in scores of the time, then the sequence of periods in the movement would be 1 1 2 3 2 3. This differs from periods 1 2 3, as Koch lists them. Apparently he did not consider large-scale repetition of parts as an essential feature of movement construction.

A second problem concerns the adequacy of defining the status of a period solely by the tonal orientation of its ending. As Koch himself discusses, the beginnings of each of the three periods in an allegro also present important features. Although his most extended discussion of allegros occurs in Volume 3 (pp. 304–311; Baker 1983, pp. 199–201), Koch deals with the tonal orientation of these periods in Volume 2 even before he discusses melody. As part of his explanation of keys, key changes, and the role of various keys in a movement, Koch surveys the tonal structure commonly used in unspecified movements of symphonies, quartets, trios, and sonatas. In a major key, the first period establishes the tonic and then shifts to the fifth, cadencing there. The second period begins in this key and moves to the minor key on scale-step 6. After a cadence in this key, there is either an immediate return to the opening phrase *(Anfangssatz)* in the tonic, or else there is a transition back *(Zurückgang)* to the tonic, usually via passing changes of key *(durchgehenden Ausweich-ungen)*. Alternatively, the second period can leave the key of scale-step 6 without a cadence and proceed to the key of scale-step 4 and cadence there. Or else it may go to scale-step 3 or even 2. The third period is a concluding period *(Schlussperiod)*, primarily in the principal key, although the key of scale-step 4 sometimes appears temporarily without a formal cadence (2, pp. 223–225). In minor keys, the first period generally goes to the major key on scale-step 3 and the second period moves to the minor key on scale-step 5. Or else this is reversed, and the first period moves to the minor key on 5 and the second period moves to the major key on 3 (2, pp. 237–238).

Thus, in each of the periods of an allegro, critical features occur prior to the ending orientation, despite Koch's basic definition of a period's structure being determined by its length and ending. Period 1 terminates in a nontonic key, but its beginning announces the principal key of the movement. Period 2 may well begin in an important key other than where it cadences. And the beginning of period 3 is defined primarily by the arrival on the tonic key; without this criterion, the transition after a cadence in the key of 6 in the second period could be the beginning of the third period.

A third problem with Koch's definition concerns whether period 2 qualifies to be a period at all. If periods must end with a formal cadence, then period 2 often does not meet the definition of a period, since its main cadence may occur before the end of the period. If there is a transition following a cadence in the key of 6, is the transition part of the second period, in which case the second period defies the definition of a period by not ending with a cadence? Or does the transition begin the third period, which contradicts Koch's musical sense that period 3 begins with the firm arrival back on the tonic? Or does the transition belong to neither period, in which case the movement does not in fact consist only of the connection of periods? Koch neither raises nor answers these questions. His silence on such definitional distinctions implies that he recognizes movements arising not only from the cadential orientation of the constit-uent periods, but also from the tonal orientation of the sections represented by these periods.

A fourth inadequacy of Koch's basic definition of a movement as a composite of periods concerns the absence of thematic functions in this perspective. He recognizes that a successful movement needs to have "an adequate variety of parts, or a sufficient interchange and alternation be-tween the principal ideas combined with the connecting phrases and dis-section phrases or subsidiary ideas, and a precise and completely suitable connection of all these ideas" (2, p. 99). The opening phrase of a movement is generally the principal phrase or theme *(Hauptsatz, Thema; 2, pp. 347–*

348; Baker 1983, p. 3). Likewise, the third period "begins most frequently with the theme, but sometimes also with another principal melodic idea" (*mit einem andern melodischen Haupttheile;* 3, p. 311; Baker 1983, p. 201). "Another principal melodic idea" probably refers to the beginning of music in the contrasting key in period 1, because earlier, Koch had explained that a movement features "a principal idea [*Hauptgedank*] connected to a subsidiary idea [*Nebengedank*] which leads to another principal idea" (2, p. 98). In fact, Koch specifies precisely where "another principal melodic idea" might occur within the first period. He recognizes that the arrival on the second key area is commonly the point at which a lyrical theme appears: "quite often one hears no absolutely clear phrase ending [*keinen förmlichen Absatz;* no clear ending of an inconclusive phrase] until rushing and sonorous phrases are replaced by a more singing phrase [*ein mehr singbarer Satz*], usually performed at a lower dynamic level. Thus one finds quite a few such [first] periods in which an absolutely clear phrase ending is not heard until the piece has been led into the most closely related key" (3, p. 306; Baker 1983, p. 199). Koch also refers in two other passages to "the singing phrase [*cantabler Satz*] after the phrase ending on scale-step 5 in the key on 5" (3, pp. 334, 385; Baker 1983, p. 210, 230).

A further thematic aspect recognized by Koch is the transposition of the themes stated in the nontonic key in period 1 to the tonic key in period 3. "The second half of the first period, or those melodic ideas which followed the cadence on scale-degree 5 in the key on 5, is repeated in the principal key" (3, p. 311; Baker 1983, p. 201).

As a result, Koch's full view of the structure of allegros recognizes several separate structural aspects: the tonal orientation of periods throughout their length, the cadential orientation of periods, connections between periods, and thematic content and function. These issues—tonal structure, cadences, and themes—are in fact the primary features dealt with by later theory. But Koch relates these features in a manner quite different from later theory. First, nineteenth-century theorists viewed thematic contrast as a primary determinant of sonata form. There is thematic contrast within the exposition, heightened by tonal contrast. In the recapitulation, the return of the contrasting theme in the tonic key assuages these contrasts. Although Koch does deal with the placement of themes and is aware of the presence of contrasting themes (rushing versus singing phrases) within the first period, he never mentions thematic contrast as an issue needing resolution in a movement. In addition, nowhere in Koch's discussion of allegros does he make a strong statement about contrast of any type— theme or tonality—within the first period. For Koch, the first period of the movement is a single unit, not a dichotomous entity.

Additionally, a thematic view of sonata form often regards the development section as a place where the themes are taken apart, prior to their restatement in a form close to their original presentation in the recapitulation. This promotes the view that the exposition and recapitulation are the relatively stable parts of the form supporting the variable development in the middle. But Koch does not view the overall dynamic of the form in this way. He does recognize that period 3 (corresponding to the recapitulation) is a stable section. But its stability derives from its tonal structure, from the fact that the closing period "is primarily in the principal key of the piece because thus far this key has been heard only a little in the execution of the movement" (2, pp. 224–225). Because it is grounded in the tonic, period 3 thus stands in contrast to both the first and second periods—both of which end away from the tonic—not merely the second part of period 1.

Indeed, Koch's view of the stability of period 3 in contrast to the first two periods offers a perspective that differs not only from a thematic perspective on sonata form but also from the harmonic perspective that is in vogue nowadays. To repeat, Koch contrasts the tonal stability of period 3 with the mobile character of both periods 1 and 2; he regards period 1 as a single unit, not as two units, one in the principal key and one elsewhere, that need to be reconciled.

## Compositional Method

Koch's thoughts on complete movements are related to his ideas on compositional method, set forth in the extended essay "on the nature of composition" *(von der Entstehungsart der Tonstücke)* that opens Volume 2.[16] Koch builds on ideas in the articles on general aesthetic issues written by Johann Georg Sulzer (1720–1779) for his encyclopedia, *Allgemeine Theorie der schönen Künste* (1771–1774). Sulzer's ideas as they pertain to music are in turn partly based on Mattheson's *Der vollkommene Capellmeister* (1739) and the influential *Les beaux-arts réduits à un même principe* (1746) by the French aesthetician Charles Batteux (1713–1780), which was translated into German in 1758 by the Berlin poet Karl Ramler (1725–1798).

As elsewhere, Koch generally steers clear of abstractions. He suggests that composing a musical work occurs in three stages: a *plan (Anlage)*, its *execution (Ausführung)*, and its *elaboration (Ausarbeitung)*. This notion, adopted from Sulzer, is similar to Mattheson's *dispositio, elaboratio,* and *decoratio,* itself drawn from classical rhetoric, where it pertains to the composition of a speech. The plan contains a work's main ideas and

16. Baker 1977 is the most extensive discussion in English on this aspect of Koch's writings.

harmonic accompaniment in the first stage of creation. The execution and elaboration are later stages of the compositional process.

Koch never fully specifies exactly what any of these stages would contain, although he does present his own plan for an aria by Graun (2, pp 60–62 and following discussion). This plan is not an outline of the entire aria. Rather, like the original version of the period in Example 11-14, it contains only a single period that begins in the principal key and ends in the dominant. Unlike the original period in Example 11-14, however, Koch's plan for this aria is much more detailed in that it contains recognizable themes from the completed aria, not merely a condensation of the essential motions of a section, as in Example 11-14. The act of composing the sections missing from the plan presumably belongs to the execution of the plan.

The plan lacks many features of the finished work, such as expansions within the given period and also all those sections that are derived from the first period but not present in it. In many movement constructions, the sections missing from the plan are the later periods. Thus in an allegro (corresponding to what we know as sonata form), the music in period 1 is the source for much of period 3 and also many of the ideas in period 2. But in some constructions, such as concerto allegros and arias, the plan corresponds not to the music that opens the movement, but rather to the music in a later section. In a concerto allegro, the plan is the basic content of the first solo section. Thus, the opening music of the movement—the opening ritornello—is derived from the plan but is not actually present in it. When the teenaged Wolfgang Mozart transformed keyboard sonatas of J. C. Bach into concertos, he proceeded in just this fashion (Rosen 1980, pp. 73–76). He used the first period of the sonata allegros as the direct basis of the first solo in the concerto and derived the ritornello from materials in that solo.[17]

Koch does not specify how or whether the plan relates to appreciation of the finished piece. If, as Carl Dahlhaus argues, Koch regards the plan as the essence of a piece, then in a concerto movement, for instance, the results of viewing the music from the perspective of the plan stand in stark opposition to the results of a thematic view. From a thematic view we might regard a concerto movement built from its opening themes; but the opening ritornello and its themes do not even appear in Koch's plan. However, Koch suggests the plan as a path toward composition, not as a perspective through which the finished piece is to be viewed. Furthermore, Koch nowhere argues that the plan is heard by the audience of a piece. For how could listeners know, and what difference would it make, that

17. Stevens 1971 discussions Koch's views on concertos.

the opening themes they were hearing in a concerto ritornello were conceptually added to the piece after some later music had been worked out?

## Concluding Remarks

This survey of Koch's theories concludes this historical chronicle. Koch's works draw together many of the theoretical traditions of the eighteenth century. He assembled notions of counterpoint, thoroughbass, harmony, melody, phrasing, what we call musical form, and compositional process into a more coherent universal view of musical structure than that achieved by any other theorist of the age. If his work bypasses some of the aspects of contrapuntal theory that were more thoroughly explored by Fux and others, that probably reflects the diminished presence of contrapuntal surface textures in the music of his generation. If his work does not deal explicitly with the root-progression aspect of harmony, this reflects the continuing influence of thoroughbass thinking on harmony in the works of Marpurg, which were the primary influence on harmony in Koch and many other German musicians of the time. His perspective is at once individual in the sense that it represents the thinking of one musician, and universal in the sense that it draws upon all the major theoretical themes of the time. Despite the lack of a direct influence from Koch to many later theorists, his agenda became that of many of the principal nineteenth-century theorists.

# Epilogue

IF THERE IS A THEME to this study, it is the remarkable diversity of theoretical traditions within the eighteenth century and their extraordinarily complex interactions. Previous studies parsed the traditions of the time much more simply. Shirlaw drew a line between harmonic theory and thoroughbass tradition. Likewise, many Schenkerian theorists draw a line between harmonic theory on one side and the traditions of thoroughbass and species counterpoint on the other. These dichotomies do not stand up to critical scrutiny. There are a great number of features linking Rameauian ideas and those of the thoroughbass methods. And musicians of the time found no close affinity between species counterpoint and thoroughbass. Furthermore, considering eighteenth-century writings according to the three traditions of species counterpoint, thoroughbass, and harmony omits many important works of the age: the melodic studies of Mattheson, Riepel, and Koch, the different interpretations of counterpoint from Niedt through Kirnberger and Koch, and what might be called general composition texts such as Mattheson's *Der vollkommene Capellmeister*. All these traditions are interrelated, with writers continually borrowing tenets that we most closely associate with one tradition in works that primarily deal with another.

Simplistic divisions of the theoretical traditions of the time have often led to interpretations of eighteenth-century ideas along the lines of twentieth-century theoretical disputes. The notion of a split between those theorists who thought of music vertically and those who thought linearly, for example, may be germane to the differences between Schenkerian and Riemannian perspectives in the twentieth century. But it hardly applies to the differences among theorists in the eighteenth century. Eighteenth-century applications of species counterpoint, for instance, frequently incorporated harmonic thinking, whether in the form of Fux's discussions of triads and inversions and of rules for unfigured basses, or of the more thoroughgoing harmonic approaches of Mozart and Albrechtsberger. And theorists adopting a Rameauian approach—Nichelmann, for instance—

imply a more comprehensive notion of complex diminutions than any contrapuntal theorist of the age.

In short, the interactions within and among theoretical traditions of the eighteenth century are both much more complex and much richer than has hitherto been imagined. It is my hope that from this more comprehensive perspective, the eighteenth century will be viewed less as an arena in which good theorists riding white horses who stand for a favored modern perspective did battle with bad theorists riding black horses who stand for perspectives that are now out of favor. Instead it will be recognized that modern ideas have been nourished by a wide range of theoretical traditions.

Einstein once suggested that our knowledge might be likened to a circle of light amid the surrounding darkness of our ignorance. As we increase our knowledge and thereby increase the diameter of the circle of light, the circumference representing our awareness of the surrounding darkness grows geometrically. The present study, which I hope increases that circle of light, makes it all the more imperative that we learn much more about areas of eighteenth-century theory that have hardly been explored at all to date. One of these is the relationship between improvisation and composition as composition methods and models changed. From earlier eras until the seventeenth century, vocal improvisation (both polyphonic improvisation against a given part and ornamentation of a completed composition) was an important part of a composer's training. During the seventeenth century, thoroughbass improvisation—realizing bass parts as well as preluding, fantasizing, and even improvising complete pieces—largely replaced vocal improvisation in providing compositional models. To what extent did this affect compositional theory and practice during and after the seventeenth century? And what happened to compositional process when the *galant* style put a new focus on melodic articulations and phrase expansions that seem to be less directly related to real-time improvisation? Was improvisation inspired by *galant* melody as much a part of compositional method in the new styles as thoroughbass improvisation had been earlier in the century?

Likewise, a virtually unknown body of compositional pedagogy awaits exploration. The relatively few items that have surfaced (manuscripts of J. S. Bach compositions from the Leipzig circle with analytic annotations; the studies of Mozart's students in composition) have revealed that methods as they appeared in published works were applied rather freely in pedagogical situations. Even the existence of other similar pedagogical source materials is barely known. Are there extant student exercises from those who studied with Rameau, with Kirnberger, or with Koch? What do they show?

Finally, a host of less wide-ranging issues await attention. For instance, the transmission of ideas and approaches needs to be much better documented. The spread of Rameau's theories to Germany is one such topic. An informative review of his 1722 *Traité* appeared in Leipzig in 1723; at least two German theorists (Christoph Schröter and his teacher Johann Nicolaus Bach) worked through the treatise in 1724; and Heinichen probably adopted some of its ideas for his 1728 thoroughbass manual. Yet many scholars assert that Rameau's ideas remained virtually unknown for more than nearly three decades. Once again, hitherto unexplored manuscript sources may help to round out the picture.

As the eighteenth century recedes ever farther into the past, its repertoire (the works of Bach and Handel, Couperin and Rameau, Vivaldi and the Scarlattis, Haydn and Mozart, early Beethoven, and a host of others) will be kept alive as it remains meaningful to our own times. It will remain important to interpret that legacy and its structural bases in ways that inform us how and why the music remains alive to us in the present. At the same time, it is important to maintain a focus on how the structural bases of this music were conceived by its own time. A step toward that goal is the study of compositional theory in the eighteenth century.

Appendixes

Bibliography

Index

# Rameau, *Nouveau systême de musique theorique* (1726): Chapter 23, "Examples of Errors Found in the Figures of Corelli's op. 5"

All emphases and capitalizations are Rameau's. Cross-references to other sections of the *Nouveau systême* are omitted. Also omitted is Rameau's explanation of various abbreviations he uses to refer to the movements. The annotations in brackets following many paragraphs highlight important issues. These annotations often use modern terminology instead of Rameau's. Numbers in brackets are page numbers in the original. According to Lee Brentlinger, who is studying the transmission of Corelli's op. 5, Rameau's source for these pieces was undoubtedly a French manuscript, not a published edition. The thoroughbass figures he cites agree with no published edition, but are close to those in a Parisian edition of the 1730s by LeClerc.

[95] We shall see by placing the Fundamental Bass beneath Corelli's Basso Continuo the true chords which must be found there as a consequence of the *Connection* [*Liaison*] that the fundamental progression of a *Fifth* must support most naturally within each harmonic *Motion* [*Modulation*]. This progression [of a fifth] can only be broken off after a *principal Tone* [a tonic chord], except in the case of *broken* or *interrupted Cadences*.

[Rameau insists that all progressions in the fundamental bass (all root progressions) follow the pattern of cadences: root progression down by a fifth in a perfect cadence, up by a fifth in an irregular cadence, up by step in a broken cadence (*cadence rompuë*), or down by third in an interrupted cadence (*cadence interrompuë*). In each of these cadences, the first chord is dissonant: a seventh chord in the perfect, broken, and interrupted cadence; an added-sixth chord in the irregular cadence. (Note that a 6 above a note in the fundamental bass refers to an added-sixth chord, not to a first-inversion triad.) Among these cadences, the perfect and irregular,

*Example A1-1.* Sonata No. 1, first Allegro, m. 5; mm. 9–10

in which the root progression is by fifth, are the models for other progressions. Only after a tonic chord may the fundamental bass move freely.]

We will see that Corelli, when he figured the Chords that this Bass must carry, was guided much less by knowledge than by the Intervals that his ear made him use between the *Violin* [*Dessus*] and the *Bass*.

[Rameau stresses that he is not criticizing the compositions, which he regards as the result of Corelli's genius, but the thoroughbass figures that Corelli added to the completed composition. Rameau states this position repeatedly during the chapter. He thereby implies that he views working out the voices of a composition as an act distinct from and prior to the application of thoroughbass figures.]

Since the source of the Harmony is the same in these two different progressions A-B and C-D [in Example A1-1], consequently the Notes A and C must be figured the same. But Corelli seems to have judged them only according to the *Violin*, which makes a *Sixth* and *Fifth* from Note A, while it only makes a *Sixth* from Note C. The same problem appears in numerous other passages in the same Allegro and elsewhere.

[Two issues are involved here: Explicitly, Rameau criticizes Corelli's inconsistency. Implicitly, Rameau favors the first figuring because he believes that a proper approach to a dominant-seventh chord (a *dominant-tonic* in his terminology) is a root progression down by fifth from a seventh chord, not a root progression up by step from a triad. There are two reasons for his position. First, he believes that a triad (on scale-step 4) would imply the stability of a temporary tonic arrival on that scale step. Second, a seventh chord built on scale-step 2 allows a root progression by fifth imitating a perfect cadence, which is for him a stronger motion than a root-progression up by step which might imitate a broken cadence.]

[97] Although one could give a 6/4 Chord to Note A [in Example A1-2], conforming to the Fundamental Bass indicated by a custos below Note A, the 4/2 Chord that Corelli figured elsewhere is even more apt, conforming to the Fundamental-Bass Note placed below Note A. This is because we are in the *Key* of D, and not at all in the *Key* of G, which 6/4 represents.

*Example A1-2.* Other examples on the same topic [that when Corelli added figures, he was guided primarily by the intervals between the *violin* and the *bass*]:
Sonata No. 1, first Adagio; Sonata No. 1, first Allegro, mm. 29–30;
Sonata No. 1, first Allegro, mm. 38–39; Sonata No. 1, second Adagio, mm. 23–24;
Sonata No. 2, first Adagio, mm. 8–9; Sonata No. 3, first Allegro, m. 28;
Sonata No. 10, first Adagio, m. 17

[Two issues influence Rameau's argument. Explicitly, the 6/4 represents a triad, hence a tonic. This 6/4 therefore implies for Rameau the key of G, which contradicts the prevailing key of D major. In addition, as already noted, Rameau prefers a descending fifth in the fundamental bass to approach the dominant.]

6/4 must be figured above Note C to indicate the *perfect Chord* of the *principal Tone,* which must naturally follow the *Dominant* heard at Note B. This 6/4 is even more necessary because Note D is in the Chord of that *principal Tone* and not at all in the Chord of the *Dominant.*

[For Rameau, the F♯ and D on the second beat imply a B-minor tonic triad that resolves the dominant, thereby creating a quarter-note harmonic rhythm. Corelli's figuring implies a half-note harmonic rhythm with a neighboring chord between two dominants, and with the bass D as a rather complex dissonance functioning as a dominant of the G. See Example A1-3.]

If Note L is figured correctly, then Notes G and J are figured incorrectly, since each of these notes has a different fundamental bass.

*Example A1-3.*

Note L represents the *principal Tone;* Note G makes the *Fifth* of a *Dominant* [i.e., of a seventh chord], and Note J makes the *third* [of a *Dominant*]. Thus, each of these Notes must be figured in relation to the Chord of the fundamental Tone that they represent [i.e., in relation to the root of that chord], conforming to the style of figuring adopted by Corelli. Consequently, 6/4 must be figured for a Note a *Fifth* above a *principal Tone* [i.e., a fifth above the root of a chord], as at L; 4/3 for a Note which is a *Fifth* above a *Dominant* or a *Third* above a *Subdominant* [i.e., a fifth above the root of a seventh chord or a third above the root of an added-sixth chord], as at N; and 6/5 for a note a *Third* above a *Dominant,* as at A in [Example A1-1].

[As in preceding examples, Rameau implies that a triad is improper for note G because the chord is not a tonic. Rameau addresses note J again on his p. 98.]

If Note P is figured correctly, then Note E and also Note C in [Example A1-1] are figured incorrectly, because each of these Notes represents a different fundamental Tone, or at least is a different distance [from the fundamental Tone]. Consequently, 6 must be figured for a Note which is the *Third* of a *principal Tone,* as at P; 4/3 for a Note which is the *Fifth* of a *Dominant,* such as Note E; and 6/5 for a Note which is the *Third* of a *Dominant,* such as Note C in [Example A1-1].

[As in preceding examples, Rameau implies that a triad is improper for note E in Example A1-2 and note C in A1-1 because the chord is not a tonic.]

If 4/3 is figured correctly at N, then it is incorrect at M. Even worse, the Chord at M designated 4/3♯ is worthless. It is from this very type of error that one can judge the difference that existed between knowledge and feeling in such an excellent musician as Corelli.

If that Composer had known that of two Stepwise Notes that fill one single *Beat* of the *Measure* [such as the D♯ and E above Note M] one is the master in deciding which Note one wishes to have carry the Harmony, he would have seen that of the two Notes of the *Violin* that go along with Note M, that which makes the *Fourth* [over the *Bass*] should have been chosen for the Harmony. He would have felt it himself if he had been able

*Example A1-4.* Sonata No. 9, second Allegro, mm. 12–13

to think about it. And he would have had no doubt if he had known of the Fundamental Bass, from which he would have been convinced that he had to figure that Note M with a 6/4, and not with a 4/3♯, which has not even a shadow of the Harmony.

[Rameau reads the progression from X-M as an irregular cadence. Hence he only wants a 6/4 chord over note M. Once again, Rameau acknowledges Corelli's genius in composing the sonatas at the same time that he faults Corelli for not understanding his own composition well enough to figure it properly.]

[98] The same error is found in [Example A1-4].

The *Violin* alone should have informed Corelli that Note Q carries no Harmony, and that on the contrary it is Note R that carries the Harmony. Consequently, the 7/5 figured on Note Q is worthless.

[Rameau implies here that notes not part of the harmony—nonharmonic tones in our modern terminology—should not be given figures. Thus, instead of Corelli's thoroughbass figures, which here simply tell the performer what to play, Rameau wants a notation that will indicate the functional harmony. Perhaps he was already thinking ahead to his proposal published in 1732 that thoroughbass figuring should be replaced with a notation that listed the chord roots and chord types. In such a notation, many problematic figurings that arise from the presence of nonharmonic tones in the bass would never arise; see the reference to *figured Melody* two paragraphs below.]

It must also be noted in [Example A1-2] that the 6/4 figured on Note J is even more incorrect [than was discussed above], since the *Dissonance* represented by Note H is not *resolved* until Note K. Therefore Note J must carry the same Chord as Note H; instead of 6/4, 6/5 must be figured there according to the Fundamental Bass.

When Corelli employed the harmony of an *irregular Cadence* from N to P in [Example A1-2] (as can be recognized by the *Sixth* added to the *perfect Chord* of the *Subdominant,* which then descends immediately by a *Fourth* in the Fundamental Bass), he could well have anticipated that the same *Cadence* takes place from X to M in [Example A1-2] and from Q to S in [Example A1-4]. But when one does not know the source of the Harmony, the *figured Melody [Chant figuré]* sometimes disguises it so much that the Ear can be fooled, as one sees here.

And if one wished to go by the most perfect progression in the Fundamental Bass at Note F in [Example A1-2], one would see that Note F must instead be figured with a 9 rather than with a 7, since the Note stipulating the 9 would have been expressly written in the Fundamental Bass, while only a custos would have marked the note which stipulates the 7.

The 7 which the Fundamental Bass stipulates at Note F introduces an imitation of the *interrupted Cadence* into [the piece],[1] whereas the 9 that [the Fundamental Bass] stipulates there introduces an imitation of the *perfect Cadence*. Now this is not a *Harmonic Connection* where the *Key* changes, which must happen in *interrupted Cadences*. Moreover, when *interrupted Cadences* are thus used [where there is no key change], this is done more by accident and involuntarily than by knowledge.

[For Rameau, an interrupted cadence (motion from a seventh chord down by third to another seventh chord, such as $G^7$ to $E^7$) always indicates a change of key, however temporary. Since there is no key change here, Rameau rejects this cadence as a possible explanation for the progression.]

People who accompany on the Clavecin will be able to see that the 9 is much easier to use here than the 7, and if it did not require such a detailed digression, we would also give a reason for it much more satisfactory than that of the *Connection* within the same *Key*. Corelli's Works are full of this little fault, [99] which has rightfully been deemed less important than the beauties which abound there.

[Perhaps Rameau's "much more satisfactory reason" is that "chords by subposition serve only to suspend sounds which should be heard naturally" (Rameau 1722, Book 3, Chapter 31). Hence, explaining note F as a subposed ninth chord defines the role of the notes in this chord more fully.]

## Example on Another Topic. [Example A1-5][2]

The *Dot* of Note A, which *syncopates* that Note, carries a Harmony. Because of that, Corelli figured it with a 5/2. But that Note A, which therefore represents the *Dissonance* and which has already sounded with the *Leading Tone* B, cannot exist together with Note C which is the

---

1. Rameau writes *broken Cadence (Cadence rompuë)* throughout this paragraph, clearly an error for *interrupted Cadence (Cadence interrompuë)*.
2. The third note in the fundamental bass is an A in the original.

*Example A1-5.* Sonata No. 2, first Adagio, m. 7

*principal Tone* announced by the *Leading Tone;* for no *Dissonance* may exist in the chord where it is to be *resolved.* Thus that *Syncopation* Note A is out of place in such a case. The Fundamental Bass allows us to see that the Note which follows A ought to be at the place of the *Dot A.*

[For Rameau, the term *Dissonance* here refers to suspensions. Hence his explanation that "all *Dissonances* cannot exist in the chord where they must be *resolved.*"]

Therefore note well that sometimes the Intervals used by Corelli between the *Violin* and *Bass,* sometimes habit, as with that ill-conceived *Syncopation* in [Example A1-5] (for this Composer was particularly fond of *Syncopation*), and sometimes his Ear all guided him in his figures much more than his understanding; for the same Chord that he might have seen between the *Violin* and the *Bass,* or that he was in the habit of figuring in a certain manner, or that his Ear made him perceive in certain passages issued forth from him more often than he hit upon [the right chord for the right reasons], leaving aside the familiar Chords with which even the weakest Musicians do not make errors. But we will not stop there, instead going on to other remarks no less important than the preceding.

[Here Rameau reverses his earlier stance and criticizes the written parts for being guided by the figuring. It is not clear why Rameau finds the suspended *Bb* so troublesome and does not merely regard it as a 4–3 suspension and/or as part of a subposed chord.]

For example, what can one think of the manner of figuring many Notes that rise by Step [*Diatoniquement;* Example A1-6], where nearly all the 5s and 6s must indicate a different Chord, according to [Example A1-7].

[100] Corelli knew of all these last figures to designate the very Chords

*Example A1-6.*

*Example A1-7.*

that are set down in the Fundamental Bass. Undoubtedly, if he had recognized these Chords, he would have figured them there as he did elsewhere.

Corelli's manner of figuring [in Ex. A1-6] is an evasion which almost all Musicians make use of quite willingly, and on account of their using it, one can accuse them of not knowing what they have practiced in such cases.

[However useful Rameau's insistence on seeing all chordal connections as cadences or imitated cadences may be in explaining many progressions, it is hopelessly inadequate in sequential motions as in Example A1-6. In his contorted attempt to deal with this progression, Rameau even violates his usual practice of avoiding syncopated harmonic rhythm by tying the G-seventh chord over the first barline.]

There is another thing to take note of in this Composer: when he uses some quarter-note rests in his Basso Continuo, he does not indicate the Chord that must be played during that rest [Example A1-8].

If the rest followed a *principal Tone,* there would be nothing to say in such a case. But since this rest is between two *Dissonances,* of which the first must be *resolved* and of which the second must be *prepared,* one cannot then dispense with sounding the Harmony that exists during that rest.

Since it is up to the Accompaniment to furnish the source of the Harmony, it is absolutely obligatory always to make the necessary *Connection* felt there. Without this *Connection* a defective gap is found there, at least in a passage where the rest not only interrupts the necessary *Connection,*

*Example A1-8.* Sonata No. 6, first Allegro, m. 42

*Example A1-9.* Sonata No. 7, first Allegro, mm. 26–31

but destroys it. This is so because the [proper] manner of laying out a Basso Continuo can never suspend that *Connection.*

[Here Rameau criticizes a common feature of thoroughbass figuring that does not provide a full accounting of the harmonic structure of a passage. Once again, he seems to be looking ahead to his 1732 proposal for a new system of chord labeling to replace thoroughbass figures.]

See [Example A1-9] on the same topic.

[102] The first Fundamental Bass ends here in the *Key* of *F major* at A, and resumes immediately afterward in *D minor* at D, which is related to it.

The second Fundamental Bass maintains the *Key of D minor* by means of an *irregular Cadence* between G and H.

The third Fundamental Bass once again maintains the *Key of D minor* by means of an *interrupted Cadence* between J and L.

Note here that one can cause a listener to confuse the *irregular Cadence* G-H and the imitation of the *perfect* [*Cadence*] L-M. The first Note of each of these *Cadences* (G and L) gives the same harmonic source. But by virtue of the *Cadences* that they announce, one can take either one or the other as fundamental.

[Rameau here explains the essentials of *double emploi* without using that term.]

Not one of the three types of Harmony indicated by these three Fundamental Basses is announced to us by Corelli's figuring; but let us return to the beginning of the Example.

The first rest can be realized as is, because the [preceding] Connection ends there on the *principal Tone.*

The other rests cannot do without the source of the Harmony which must support the Connection there.

In any case, if one could provide a *Connection* during this example solely by means of the Chords that Corelli figured, we would be wrong to condemn him. But note well that according to the *Connection* of the Basso Continuo Melody and that of the *Violin*, only the Key [*Modulation*] of D can be understood, and that that *Key* is absolutely destroyed by the Chord figured at N, which according to the *Violin* must impart to us the *Key* of F.

We do not insist on this source of the *Key*, if it could be brought about and followed by a *Connection* relative to that of the Melody. But on the contrary, one cannot follow Corelli's figuring thereby considering the *Violin* line, without sounding some *unprepared minor Dissonances* [chord sevenths], or without imitating a *broken Cadence*, while the Melody gives no occasion for such a cadence.

[Rameau insists, as he did in connection with Example A1-6, that what Corelli marks as a sequential progression must be interpreted in terms of cadential progressions. When he speaks of unprepared chord sevenths that would arise by following Corelli's figures, he may be referring to the progression from measure 29 to measure 30: even if the end of measure 29 is read as an F-major triad, Rameau would insist that the E-diminished triad in measure 30 represents a C dominant-seventh chord with an un-prepared B♭. When Rameau speaks of imitating a *broken Cadence*, he is referring to the progression from measure 30 to measure 31, in which Corelli's figures imply a C-seventh chord (because a diminished triad is for Rameau the upper portion of a dominant-seventh chord) moving to a D-minor triad.]

Should Musicians sensitive to the Harmony try to accompany Corelli's Basso Continuo by considering the *Violin*, they will soon sense its flaw and will acknowledge the necessity of filling in the rests there according to the Harmony announced by the Fundamental Bass.

See [Example A1-10] on the same topic.

[103] It must be noted here (and this must be applied to the preceding Example as well) that in every Melody that touches two Strings of the same Harmony (which one calls an arpeggio [*Batterie*]), [each Note of the Melody] is expected to remain on the same String that it leaves [when it] passes to the other note. Otherwise the *Dissonance* which can appear next would be intolerable, having only been *prepared*, in this case, by the String where the Sound has not remained until that *Dissonance*.

Thus the String (i.e., Note A of the *Violin*) is expected to remain until the *Dissonance* D which it *prepares*. It remains to note that D makes a

*Example A1-10.* Sonata No. 5, first Allegro, mm. 59–62

*Dissonance* with M which here represents the Basso Continuo and even the Fundamental Bass.

Thus, the *Dissonance* D will be *resolved* on the *Consonance* G; at the same time that *Consonance* G *prepares* the *Dissonance* H, which will be *resolved* on the *Consonance* I, and that in turn *prepares* the *Dissonance* L, etc.

[Along with many thoroughbass writers, Rameau here notes that in an arpeggiation one must follow each line within the arpeggiation and not necessarily the note-to-note sequence in order to understand properly the preparation and resolution of dissonances.]

One can judge from these remarks that Corelli's figuring is worthless [here] and that he absolutely did not understand what his Ear made him apply successfully in this passage, for because the *Dissonance* D is expected to remain until the *Consonance* G which *resolves* it, Note N had to be figured with a 7 and not with a 6; and the following Note P should have been figured with the Chord that *resolves,* in this case, with the *Seventh.* The same goes for Notes Q, R, etc.

The rests can take place in the Harmony of the last Example, [104] by inserting the Basso Continuo figured in our manner there. For the rests only serve to delay [*suspendre*] the *Connection* without destroying it.

One cannot say that this is a misprint here, for it is repeated in the text in two consecutive *Measures,* and it is in the piece in the form of a series of three or four *Measures* figured in the same manner; and it does not seem that the intention was to figure a Chord on each quarter-note there, as should have happened, and as in fact happens in the two *Measures* preceding those in this example.

## Example on Another Topic [Example A1-11]

In these last two examples there is a *Connection* that terminates only on the 6 that follows the 7 at Note G, as one can also learn from the melody

*Example A1-11.* Sonata No. 5, second Adagio, mm. 10–11 and 25–26

of the *Violin* in the Composer's score. The *leading Tone* which announces the end of this *Connection* is marked there precisely by a *sharp* or a *natural;* thus there must not be any Chords between that of the *Dominant* A and that of the *principal Tone* D. Nevertheless, Corelli figures one new [Chord] between that of the *Dominant* A and that of the *principal Tone* D in the first passage, and two new Chords in the other. What does one conclude from such an error?

If Corelli really meant to claim that the Chord figured with a 7 on the Notes labelled G was the same as the Chord on the *Dominants* at Notes A, he could have easily seen that this 7 in no way indicated such a Chord. Moreover, seeing as he was careful to mark the *leading Tone* everywhere with a *sharp* or with a *natural* (which must indicate the *leading Tone*), how would he have forgotten this here if he had been aware that the *leading Tone* must remain in the Harmony until the *principal Tone,* D at Note D?

Musicians who care about *consecutive Octaves* would perhaps not wish to allow the *Ninth* to be used here on a Note that descends immediately by Step. But isn't the source of the Harmony the most advisable? And if one can attribute to error the Harmony that we indicate here, then the fault is in the Basso Continuo [105] and not at all in the source which cannot be excluded from it. In any case, let us reject all scruples when considering a Composition that pleases us; and let us wait until we know perfectly the principle of our rules before basing any judgement on these rules.

[In that Rameau's fundamental bass remains on scale-step 5 under each 7–6 suspension, he understands each of these suspensions to arise from a subposed ninth chord. For example, the first chord is for him a D-seventh chord with a subposed B♭. Within the progression from that suspended D-seventh chord to the following G-minor triad, an upper voice will proceed from C-B♭, thereby implying parallel octaves with the immediately preceding C-B♭ in the bass. On a separate topic, note that Rameau figures the 4–3 suspension in the second passage as a suspension, not as a subposed chord.]

*Example A1-12.* Sonata No. 8, first Allegro, mm. 12–14

What does this 6 figured above Note A [in Example A1-12] mean? Is this how one resolves *Dissonances?*

[The following discussion concerns the resolution of the A within what Rameau regards as the implied B-seventh chord over note G.]

Note well the order of the Melody in the *Violin,* and you will find there a kind of repose on Note D. However, this repose, which is less noticeable than that which comes immediately afterwards, is adroitly broken by Corelli's Basso Continuo at Note A. But at the same time, this Composer destroys the effect with his Figuring.

The *Seventh* figured at Note G must *resolve* by descending Stepwise to the first place where the repose announced by the *leading Tone* that carries the *Dominant* G appears. Accordingly, this *Seventh* must *resolve* to the *Fifth* above Note A; and the *Sixth* there is worthless.

[Although the details differ, the progression here is similar to the one that Rameau objects to in the second progression in Example A1-2. In both cases, a dominant seventh moves to a 6 chord on the next higher degree before returning and resolving in a more emphatic manner shortly thereafter. Even though Rameau recognizes that the resolution of the dominant from notes G-A is "less noticeable" than the coming cadence (a remark that could have applied to the progression in Example A1-2 as well), he still insists that the seventh of the dominant chord resolve properly in the ensuing harmony.]

The *Cadence* is *broken* from G to A, or from G to H [in the Fundamental Bass], and the *Cadence* is *irregular* from J to L [both times].

We do not know if the faulty passage indicated here has been taken as a model, but many Musicians have many fewer scruples about using it than they have about making *two consecutive Octaves.*

Such a fault [moving to a 6 chord a step above a dominant seventh] may be excusable in one situation but not in another. For instance, whenever one can assume that the Notes carry no Harmony, or whenever one separates the *Dissonance* from the Harmony, provided that the natural progression of a *minor Third* does not suffer; in such cases the *Sixth* figured on Note A is good.

[When Rameau speaks of the "natural progression of a *minor Third*," he means the usual downward resolution of a chord seventh (because a chord seventh is the *minor* dissonance that arises from the addition of a minor third above a triad). Thus, when he says one can "retake the *Dissonance*" instead of resolving the chord seventh, he means sustaining the seventh of the dominant into the next harmony, as in the progression from notes G-A. Presumably, such a chord that retakes the chord seventh without resolving it will then return to the dominant seventh and then resolve properly. This is, of course, the basis of the progression in the second passage in Example A1-2, which Rameau censures as well as the progression here. But in both cases, the simplicity of the progression is clouded by several other dissonances. It seems that Rameau is objecting to those complicating factors here, not to the progression itself.]

If we would examine the Works of this Composer for all the omitted Figures, we would never be done; no less than if we would list all the passages where the errors that we have just condemned here appear. But we believe we have said enough to prove that Musicians recognized as the most skillful are not always free from faults—not in the source of their compositions (for one can suppose that they are all as sensitive to Harmony as Corelli seems to have been [judging] by his excellent Works), [106] but where they are obliged to give proof of their knowledge, such as in the Figures.

When we compose Music, that is not the time to recall the rules that could enslave our genius. In composing, we must only have recourse to the rules when genius and the ear seem to deny us what we seek. But when we wish to make known to others the source of Harmony that exists there, and to do that through the Basso Continuo Figures, that is the time when we must recall these Rules. If these Rules were worthless, our Ear could hardly protect us from errors to which they subjected us. In this case, all reason prohibits judging by Ear; and for most Musicians, to prohibit judging by Ear is to deprive them of all their knowledge.

One must conclude from this Chapter's argument that whoever only knows how to Accompany according to the figures does not know Accompaniment. For to know Accompaniment, one must be able to correct these Figures, and consequently one must know Composition in a manner different from they way it has ever been known.

In condemning some Figures by Corelli, we do not claim to thereby condemn his Works. On the contrary, we have chosen them from all Works that are among the best in the matter of Harmony in order to make known that reason and Ear do not always agree among Musicians—not that they could not be in a state of proving the contrary nowadays.

Accordingly, our critical remarks apply more to the past than to the present.

[In these last two sentences, Rameau seems to be taking note of changes in compositional style between Corelli's generation and the music of the 1720s. One of these stylistic changes is the gradual reduction in a fast harmonic rhythm featuring many sequential progressions in favor of a slower harmonic rhythm featuring more root progressions by fifths. As a result, from Rameau's perspective, the progressions that he found most problematic in the works of Corelli were less common in more recent music.]

In debating the value of Science with Musicians, we have at the same time opened up the paths [to Science] for them. Thus, we soon hope to see Musicians more animated than ever in the noble rivalry which must make them distinguish themselves in their Art. In fact, will showing that they are as capable of illuminating the spirit as amusing the ear not greatly add to their merit? Hence, let us no longer be lulled by the frivolous pleasure of the senses; let us carry our ideas even further. For who better than one who is already experienced in an Art can carry it to its last degree of perfection? Let us begin now by laying down all prejudice. Instead of maintaining that our errors are correct, let us take pride in confessing them. That will yield a first proof of one's knowledge, that of acceding to the truth, whereas in opposing it, one remains forever in an ignorance that is uncovered sooner or later.

# Concerning the Authenticity
# of Thoroughbass Methods Attributed
# to Albrechtsberger

After living and teaching in Vienna since the 1760s, Johann Georg Albrechtsberger turned in 1790 to the publisher Breitkopf in Leipzig to produce a handsome edition of his 400-page *Gründliche Anweisung zur Composition*. In nearly every conceivable way, there are stark contrasts between this work and the *Kurzgefasste Methode den General Bass zu erlernen* that was published without a date (probably 1791) by Artaria in Vienna and Mainz. The *Anweisung* is set in type; the *Methode* is inexpensively hand-engraved. The *Anweisung* spells out Albrechtsberger's full name on the title page; the *Methode* uses initials for his first and middle names. The *Anweisung* uses standard German spellings; the *Methode* is replete with Viennese dialect (such as *Regln* in a heading on page 1). The *Anweisung*, like almost all formal works after the middle of the century, is wholly in German; the *Methode* is in an antiquated macaronic German replete with inconsistencies (*Sext minor oder Major* on p. 5 versus *Kleine Sext* on p. 7). The *Anweisung* uses standard music notation; the *Methode* features some unorthodox notations (the key signature for C♯ major simply lists all the sharps in a scale in both clefs, p. 4). The *Anweisung* is comprehensive and clearly organized; the *Methode* is quite sketchy and poorly organized on every level. Sometimes topics run into one another within paragraphs. Other times a single topic is broken into two paragraphs, each of which contains other topics. This poor organization is cited by an anonymous reviewer of a later Leipzig edition who urges readers seeking a methodical presentation of thoroughbass to look elsewhere (*Berlinische Musikalische Zeitung*, 2 [1806]:52). Briefly put, it is hard to imagine that Albrechtsberger, who had just produced a work as well organized and well produced as the *Anweisung* could have had anything directly to do with the *Methode* a year later.

The *Methode* reappeared in several different editions over the next decades, some entitled *Generalbassschule*. Some of these are printed (no longer engraved) and use more standard German spellings (such as an edition by C. F. Peters in Leipzig, again without a date, in the library of New York University). But there are still problems with the contents, and the macaronic German remains (*Terz-minor-Sprung*, p. 4.)

Additional types of evidence also separate the *Methode* from the *Anweisung*. *Thayer's Life of Beethoven* notes that Beethoven's studies with Albrechtsberger in the mid-1790s were based on the *Anweisung* (Forbes 1967, pp. 146–147). But no mention is made of any thoroughbass method by Albrechtsberger.

Finally, there is the statement of Ignaz Xaver Ritter von Seyfried (1776–1841), a pupil of Albrechtsberger's who published a complete edition of his teacher's writings (Seyfried [c. 1825]). Although the sections that correspond to Albrechtsberger's *Anweisung* faithfully copy that work, the *General-bass-schule* that Seyfried included differs substantially in content from the *Methode* under discussion here, including quite a bit more harmonic theory. Seyfried has gained a deserved notoriety for the numerous inaccuracies in his publication of Beethoven's student work (Seyfried 1832). But it is hard to question statements he made in the preface to the 1837 edition of his publication of Albrechtsberger's theoretical works. To answer the criticism that there were inconsistencies within Albrechtsberger's teachings, he explained his sources: "The first volume, the *General-bass-schule,* had to be compiled almost from scratch [*schlechterdings bey-nahe neu erschaffen werden*] since only a very small portion of the necessary materials existed. On the other hand, Albrechtsberger completed in his own hand with the greatest precision the material of the last two parts, the *Anweisung zur Composition*" (Seyfried [1837], preface). Surely Seyfried knew of the *Methode* and *Generalbassschule;* he must have had some reasons to doubt that it represented Albrechtsberger's teaching of thoroughbass.

Thus, there are substantial reasons to doubt that Albrechtsberger had much to do with any of the editions of the *Methode*. Possibly, the Viennese publisher Artaria, seeing the success of the *Anweisung,* located a Viennese pupil of Albrechtsberger (quite possibly someone who had studied with him years earlier) and published a compendium assembled from that student's notes. Once the work had been published in the late-eighteenth-century world without copyright restrictions, it assumed a life of its own, probably in a manner quite similar to the thoroughbass manual falsely ascribed to Mozart, which has repeatedly been published under Mozart's name, most recently in the 1950s in New York.

# Bibliography

This is not a comprehensive bibliography for eighteenth-century theory. Only primary and secondary literature on music cited in the course of this study appears here. Thus, standard encyclopedia entries, such as those in *MGG* or *The New Grove*, may be important sources of information, but they are listed only if explicitly cited in the text. Many eighteenth-century titles have been shortened. Original spellings are retained for all names and titles, except that capitalization has been changed to conform to standard practice, and umlauts over capital letters have been changed to an *e* after the vowel with the umlaut. A date in brackets indicates that in the publication the date is absent from the title page (or copyright page for modern works) or that the date on the title page is not accurate. *Facsimiles* (Facs.) are photocopies of the original; *reprints* are reset in type from the original. Translations appear under the translator's name, with both original and translation cross-referenced. Publishers are not listed for works before 1900.

Adlung, Jacob. 1758. *Anleitung zu der musikalischen Gelahrtheit*. Erfurt. Facs. Kassel: Bärenreiter, 1953.

Agricola, Johann Friedrich. 1786. "Beleuchtung der Frage von dem Vorzuge der Melodie vor der Harmonie." *Magazin der Musik* 2:809–829. Facs. Hildesheim: Olms, 1971.

Albert, Heinrich. 1643. *Ander Theil der Arien*. Königsberg.

Albrechtsberger, Johann Georg. 1790. *Gründliche Anweisung zur Composition . . . zum Selbstunterrichte*. Leipzig. Editions and translations into French and English, 1814–1834. Partial English transl. in Mann 1965b.

———? [c. 1791]. *Kurzgefasste Methode den Generalbass zu erlernen*. Vienna, Mainz. Editions, some entitled *Generalbaß-schule*, through 1822. See Appendix 2 concerning authorship.

D'Alembert, Jean le Rond. 1752. *Elemens de musique, théorique et pratique, suivant les principes de M. Rameau*. Paris. Facs. New York: Broude, 1966. Reprint in 1759. 2nd ed. 1762. Reprints in 1766, 1772, and 1779. Facs. of 1779 print. Les introuvables, France: Editions d'aujourd'hui, 1984. German translation of 1752 ed. in Marpurg 1757. Partial English transl. in *Encyclopaedia Britannica,* 2nd ed., 1784; 3rd ed., 1797.

D'Alembert, Jean le Rond, and Denis Diderot. 1751–1765. *Encyclopédie, ou dictionnaire raisonné des sciences, des arts et des métiers.* Paris.

Allerup, Albert. 1931. *Die 'Musica Practica' des Johann Andreas Herbst und ihre entwicklungsgeschichtliche Bedeutung: Ein Beitrag zur Geschichte der deutschen Schulmusik.* Kassel: Bärenreiter.

Amat, Joan Carlos. 1627. *Guitarra española.* Lérida. Numerous editions into the eighteenth century.

Anderson, Emily, editor and translator. 1966. *The Letters of Mozart and His Family.* 2nd ed. New York: St. Martin's Press.

Antoniotto, Giorgio. 1760. *L'Arte Armonica; or, A Treatise on the Composition of Musick.* London.

Arnold, Franck Thomas. 1931. *The Art of Accompaniment from a Thoroughbass.* London: Oxford University Press. Facs. New York: Dover, 1965.

Artusi, Giovanni Maria. 1586. *L'Arte del contraponto ridotta in tavole.* Venice.

———. 1589. *Seconda parte dell'arte del contraponto.* Venice.

———. 1598. *L'Arte del contraponto.* Venice, 1598.

———. 1600. *L'Artusi, ovvero Delle imperfettioni della moderna musica.* Venice. Partial English translation in Strunk 1950. References are to this translation.

———. 1603. *Seconda parte dell'Artusi, overo Delle imperfettioni della moderna musica.* Venice.

Avianius, Johannes. 1581. *Isagoge in libros musicae poeticae.* Erfurt. Partial reprint and English translation in Rivera 1978.

Azopardi, Francesco. 1786. *Le musicien pratique ou leçons . . . dans l'art du contrepoint . . . composé dans les principes des conservatoires d'Italie.* French transl. by Nicolas Framery. Paris.

Bach, Carl Philipp Emanuel. 1753. *Versuch über die wahre Art das Clavier zu spielen.* [First part.] Berlin. Facs. Leipzig: Breitkopf & Härtel, 1957 and 1969. Numerous later editions. English translation in Mitchell 1949.

———. 1757. "Einfall, einen doppelten Contrapunct in der Octave von sechs Tacten zu machen, ohne die Regeln davon zu wissen." In Marpurg 1754–1778 3 (1757):167–174.

———. 1762. *Versuch über die wahre Art das Clavier zu spielen.* [Second Part.] Berlin. Numerous later editions. Facsimiles and translation listed under Bach 1753. May have circulated in some form before 1760; Sorge [1760] (Chapter 23, par. 29) refers to C. P. E. Bach writing on accompaniment.

Baker, Nancy. 1975. "From Teil to Tonstück: The Significance of the Versuch . . . by Heinrich Christoph Koch." Ph.D. diss., Yale University.

———. 1976. "Heinrich Koch and the Theory of Melody." *Journal of Music Theory* 20:1–48.

———. 1977. "The Aesthetic Theories of Heinrich Christoph Koch." *International Review of the Aesthetics and Sociology of Music* 8:183–209.

———. 1983. *Introductory Essay on Composition.* New Haven: Yale University Press. Partial translation of Koch 1782–1793.

———. 1988. "'Der Urstoff der Musik': Implications for Harmony and Melody in the Theory of Heinrich Koch." *Music Analysis* 7:3–30.

Baron, Ernst Gottlieb. 1727. *Historisch-Theoretisch und Practische Untersuchung des Instruments der Lauten.* Nürnberg.

———. 1756. *Abriss einer Abhandlung von der Melodie.* Berlin. Partial reprint in Benary [1961].

Bartolomi, Angelo Michele. 1669. *Table pour apprendre facilement à toucher le theorbe sur la basse continue.* Paris.

Batteux, Charles. 1746. *Les beaux-arts réduits à un même principe.* Paris. German translation in Ramler 1758.

Beach, David. 1974a. "The Harmonic Theories of Johann Philipp Kirnberger." Ph.D. diss., Yale University.

———. 1974b. "The Origins of Harmonic Analysis." *Journal of Music Theory* 18:274–306.

Beach, David, and Jürgen Thym. 1979. "'The True Principles for the Practice of Harmony' by Johann Philipp Kirnberger." *Journal of Music Theory* 23:163–225. Translation of Kirnberger 1773.

———. 1982. *The Art of Strict Musical Composition by Johann Philipp Kirnberger.* New Haven: Yale University Press. Partial translation of Kirnberger 1771–1779.

Beck, Lewis White. 1969. *Early German Philosophy.* Cambridge, Mass.: Harvard University Press.

Bellermann, Heinrich. 1872. "Nachtrag zu Kirnberger's Briefen." *Allgemeine musikalische Zeitung* 7:457–459.

Bemetzrieder, Anton. 1771. *Leçons de clavecin, et principes d'harmonie.* Paris. Facs. New York: Broude, 1966. Reprints in Denis Diderot's *Oeuvres complètes.*

Benary, Peter. [1961]. *Die deutsche Kompositionslehre des 18. Jahrhunderts.* Leipzig: Breitkopf & Härtel.

Berardi, Angel. 1687. *Documenti armonici.* Bologna. Facs. Bologna: Forni, 1970.

———. 1689. *Miscellanea musicale.* Bologna. Facs. Bologna: Forni, 1970.

Berger, Karol. 1987. *Musica ficta.* Cambridge: Cambridge University Press.

Bernard, Jonathan. 1989. "The Marpurg-Sorge Controversy." *Music Theory Spectrum* 11:164–186.

Bernhard, Christoph. [c. 1655]. *Tractatus compositionis augmentatus.* Ms. published in Müller-Blattau 1926. English translation in Hilse 1973. All references are to this translation.

Béthizy, Jean Laurent de. 1754. *Exposition de la théorie et de la pratique de la musique.* Paris. 2nd ed. 1764. Facs. Geneva: Minkoff, 1972.

Bewerunge, Henry. [1895]. *Harmony Simplified.* London. Translation of Riemann 1893.

Bianciardi, Francesco. 1607. *Breve regola per imparar' a sonare sopra il basso.* Siena. Facs. Milan, 1965. German translation in Haas 1929. Partial English translation in Arnold 1931.

Blainville, Charles. 1746. *Harmonie theorico-pratique.* Paris.

Blankenburg, Quirinus van. 1739. *Elementa musica, of Niew licht tot het welverstaan van de musiec en de bas-continuo*. The Hague. Facs. Amsterdam: Frits Knuf, 1972.

Blow, John. [c. 1670?]. *Rules for Playing of a Through Bass*. Ms. published in Arnold 1931, pp. 163–172.

Bononcini, Giovanni Maria. 1673. *Musico prattico*. Bologna. Facs. Hildesheim: Olms, 1969 and New York: Broude, 1969. Later editions Venice, 1678 and Bologna, 1688. German translation. Stuttgart, 1701.

Bontempi, Andrea. 1660. *Nova quatuor vocibus componendi methodus*. Dresden.

———. 1695. *Historia musica*. Perugia. Facs. Bologna: Forni, 1971 and Geneva: Minkoff, 1975.

Bradshaw, Murray, and Edward Soehnlen. 1984. English translation of Diruta 1609. Henryville: Institute of Mediaeval Music.

Brenet, Michel. 1888. "La règle de l'octave et ses inventeurs." *Le Guide Musicale* 34:235–237, 243–244.

———. 1906–1907. "La librarie musicale en France de 1653 à 1790 d'après les Registres de privilèges." *Sammelbände der Internationalen Musik-Gesellschaft* 8:401–466.

Briscoe, Roger. 1975. "Rameau's 'Démonstration du principe de l'harmonie and Nouvelles réflexions': An Annotated Translation." Ph.D. diss., Indiana University.

Brofsky, Howard. 1980. "Giovanni Battista Martini." In *The New Grove*.

Brossard, Sébastien de. 1703. *Dictionaire de musique*. Paris. Facs. Amsterdam: Antiqua, 1964.

Buelow, George. 1962. "Heinichen's Treatment of Dissonance." *Journal of Music Theory* 6:216–274. Reprinted in 1986 edition of Buelow 1966a.

———. 1966a. *Thorough-bass Accompaniment According to Johann David Heinichen*. Los Angeles: University of California Press. 2nd ed. Ann Arbor: UMI Research Press, 1986.

———. 1966b. "The *Loci topici* and Affect in Late Baroque Music: Heinichen's Practical Demonstration." *Music Review* 27:161–176.

———. 1980a. "Affections, Doctrine of the." "Figures, Doctrine of the." "Rhetoric and Music." In *The New Grove*.

———. 1980b. "Schröter, Christoph Gottlob." In *The New Grove*.

Burmeister, Joachim. 1599. *Hypomnematum musicae poeticae*. Rostock.

———. 1606. *Musica poetica*. Rostock. Facs. Kassel: Bärenreiter, 1955.

Burrigel, Johann Georg. 1737. *Compendiose musicalische Machine*. Augsburg.

Busch, Hermann. 1970. *Leonhard Eulers Beitrag zur Musiktheorie*. Regensburg: Bosse.

Buttstett, Johann Heinrich. [c. 1715]. *Ut mi sol, re fa la, Tota Musica et Harmonia Aeterna*. Erfurt. See Lester 1989, p. 119, concerning the date.

Calvisius, Sethus. 1592. *Melopoeia*. Erfurt. 2nd ed. Edited by Heinrich Grimm. Magdeburg, 1630.

Campion, François. 1716. *Traité d'accompagnement et de composition, selon la regle des octaves*. Paris. Facs. Geneva: Minkoff, 1976.

Campion, Thomas. [c. 1613]. *A New Way of Making Fowre Parts in Counterpoint*. London. See Lester 1989, p. 33, concerning the date. Reprinted in Vivian 1909. All references are to that reprint.

Caplin, William. 1981. "Theories of Harmonic-Metric Relationships from Rameau to Riemann." Ph.D. diss., University of Chicago.

Capri, Antonio. 1945. *Giuseppe Tartini*. Milan: Garzanti.

Castel, Louis Bertrand. 1722. Review of Rameau 1722. *Journal de Trévoux*, pp. 1713–1743, 1876–1910. Partial German translation in *Neuer Zeitungen von Gelehrten Sachen*, 1723:818–821, 878–880. Facs. of review and translation in Rameau CTW 1.

———. 1728. Review of Rameau 1726. *Journal de Trévoux*, pp. 472–481. Facsimile in Rameau CTW 2.

———. 1737. Review of Rameau 1737. *Journal de Trévoux*, pp. 2142–2167. Printed in Rameau CTW 6.

Catel, Charles-Simon. 1802. *Traité d'harmonie . . . adopté par le Conservatoire*. Paris.

Chailley, Jacques. 1965. "Rameau et la théorie musicale." *La Revue musicale*. Number 260:65–95.

Chandler, Glenn. 1975. "Rameau's 'Nouveau système de musique théorique': An Annotated Translation with Commentary." Ph.D. diss., Indiana University.

Choron, Alexandre-Etienne, and François Joseph Fayolle. 1810–1811. *Dictionnaire historique des musiciens*. Paris. Facs. Hildesheim: Olms, 1970.

Christensen, Thomas. 1985. "Science and Music Theory in the Enlightenment; D'Alembert's Critique of Rameau." Ph.D. diss., Yale University.

———. 1987a. "Rameau's 'L'Art de la Basse Fondamentale.'" *Music Theory Spectrum* 9:18–41. Addendum in Christensen 1990a.

———. 1987b. "Eighteenth-Century Science and the *Corps sonore*: The Scientific Background to Rameau's Principle of Harmony." *Journal of Music Theory* 31:23–50.

———. 1989. "Music Theory as Scientific Propaganda: The Case of D'Alembert's *Élémens de musique*." *Journal of the History of Ideas* 50:409–427.

———. 1990a. "Communication." *Music Theory Spectrum* 12:276–277.

———. 1990b. "Nichelmann contra C. Ph. E. Bach: Harmonic Theory and Musical Politics at the Court of Frederick the Great." In *Carl Philipp Emanuel Bach und die europäische Musikkultur des mittleren 18. Jahrhunderts*, pp. 189–220. Edited by Hans Joachim Marx. Göttingen.

———. 1992a. "The Spanish Baroque Guitar and Seventeenth-Century Triadic Theory." *Journal of Music Theory*.

———. 1992b. "The Rule of the Octave in Thorough-Bass Theory and Practice." *Acta Musicologica*.

———. 1993. *Jean-Philippe Rameau: The Science of Music Theory in the Enlightenment*. Cambridge: Cambridge University Press.

Clement. 1758. *Essai sur l'accompagnement*. Paris.

Cohen, Albert. 1971. "*La Supposition* and the Changing Concept of Dissonance in Baroque Theory." *Journal of the American Musicological Society* 24:63–84.

———. 1980. "Rameau." In *The New Grove*.

———. 1981. *Music in the French Royal Academy of Sciences: A Study in the Evolution of Musical Thought*. Princeton: Princeton University Press.

Cohen, Vered. 1983. *On the Modes*. New Haven: Yale University Press. Translation of Book 4 of Zarlino 1558.

Corrette, Michel. 1753. *Le maitre de clavecin pour l'accompagnement . . . le tout selon la règle de l'octave et de la basse fondamentale*. Paris. Partial facs. Geneva: Minkoff, 1976.

Couperin, François. [undated]. *Regle pour l'accompagnement*. Ms. published in *Oeuvres complètes de François Couperin, Oeuvres didactiques*. Paris, 1933, pp. 13–17. A published version (before 1722) is lost but was listed in Ballard's catalog of his publications at the back of Rameau 1722 and 1726 (see also pp. 7–8 of the *Oeuvres*).

———. 1716. *L'Art de toucher le clavecin*. Paris.

Cyr, Mary. 1980b. "Rameau." In *The New Grove*, work list.

Dadelsen, Georg von. 1980. "Johann Philipp Kirnberger." In *The New Grove*.

Dahlhaus, Carl. 1957. "War Zarlino Dualist?" *Musikforschung* 10:286–290.

———. 1978. "Der rhetorische Formbegriff H. Chr. Kochs und die Theorie der Sonatenform." *Archiv für Musikwissenschaft* 35:155–177.

———. 1984. *Die Musiktheorie im 18. und 19. Jahrhundert: 1, Grundzüge einer Systematik*. Darmstadt: Wissenschaftliche Buchgesellschaft.

———. 1985. *Realism in Nineteenth-Century Music*. Translated by Mary Whittall. Cambridge: Cambridge University Press.

———. 1986a. "The Eighteenth Century as a Music-Historical Epoch." Translated by Ernest Harriss. *College Music Symposium* 26:1–6.

———. 1986b. "Ist Rameaus *Traité de l'harmonie* eine Harmonielehre?" *Musiktheorie* 1:123–127.

———. 1989. *Die Musiktheorie im 18. und 19. Jahrhundert: 2, Deutschland*. Darmstadt: Wissenschaftliche Buchgesellschaft.

Damschroder, David, and David Russell Williams. 1990. *Music Theory from Zarlino to Schenker: A Bibliography and Guide*. Stuyvesant, N.Y.: Pendragon.

Dandrieu, Jean-François. [c. 1719]. *Principes de l'acompagnement du clavecin*. Paris. Later editions through the 1760s.

Daube, Johann Friedrich. 1756. *General-Bass in drey Accorden*. Leipzig. The preface is dated 1754. English translation in Wallace 1983.

———. 1757. Letter to Marpurg, dated November 30, 1756, printed in Marpurg 1754–1778, 3 (1757):69–70.

———. 1770–1771. *Der musikalische Dilettant; eine Abhandlung des Generalbasses*. Vienna. English translation in Snook 1978.

———. 1773. *Der musikalische Dilettant; eine Abhandlung der Komposition*. Vienna. English translation in Snook 1978.

———. 1797–1798. *Anleitung zur Erfindung der Melodie und ihrer Fortsetzung*. Vienna and Linz. Some printings under the title *Anleitung zur Selbstunterricht in der musikalischen Komposition, sowohl für die Instrumental- als Vocal-*

*musik.* May have been completed by 1773 (Snook 1978, pp. 458, 469).

David, Hans T., and Arthur Mendel. 1966. *The Bach Reader.* Revised ed. New York: W. W. Norton.

Delair, Denis. 1690. *Traité d'acompagnement pour le theorbe et le clavessin . . . aussi à acompagner les basses qui ne sont pas chifréez.* Paris. Facs. Geneva: Minkoff, 1972. 2nd ed. Paris, 1723 (according to title page) or 1724 (according to final page). Rameau 1732 and Rousseau 1768 cite a 1700 edition, but no copy survives.

de Laisement, Ballière. 1764. *Théorie de la musique.* Paris.

Denis, Pietro. 1773. *Traité de composition musicale.* Paris. Reprinted 1780, 1788. Translation of Fux 1725.

De Podio, Guillermus. 1495. *Ars musicorum.* Valencia. Facs. Bologna: Forni, 1975. Partial English translation in Seay 1978.

Deppert, Heinrich. 1987. *"Anmerkungen zu Alfred Dürr."* Musiktheorie 2:107–108.

Descartes, René. 1618. *Compendium musicae.* Ms. published Utrecht, 1650. Facs. Strasbourg: Heitz, [1965] and New York: Broude, 1968. English translation in Robert 1961. All references are to this English translation.

Deshayes, Thérèse. 1737. Review of Rameau 1737. *Le pour et contre* 13, no. 179:34–48. Facs. in Rameau CTW 6.

Deutsch, Otto Erich. 1952. "Ink-Pot and Squirt-Gun." *Musical Times* 93:401–403.

Diderot, Denis. [c. 1761]. *Rameau's Nephew.* English translation by Leonard Tancock. London: Penguin, 1966.

Diruta, Girolamo. 1609. *Il transilvano, seconda parte.* Venice. Later edition in 1622. Facs. of the 1622 ed. Bologna: Forni, 1969. English translation in Bradshaw and Soehnlen 1984.

Duchez, Marie-Elisabeth. 1986. *"Valeur épistémologique de la théorie de la basse fondamentale de Jean-Philippe Rameau: connaissance scientifique et représentation de la musique."* Studies on Voltaire and the 18th Century 245:91–130.

Duckles, Vincent. 1970. "Johann Adam Hiller's 'Critical Prospectus for a Music Library.'" In *Studies in Eighteenth-Century Music,* pp. 177–185. Ed. R. E. Chapman and H. C. Robbins Landon. New York: Oxford University Press.

———. 1980. "Johann Nicolaus Forkel." In *The New Grove.*

Dünkelfeind, Caspar (pseud.). 1755. *Gedanken eines Liebhabers der Tonkunst über Herrn Nichelmanns Tractat von der Melodie.* Berlin.

Dürr, Alfred. 1986. *"Ein Dokument aus dem Unterricht Bachs?"* Musiktheorie 1:163–170.

Earhart, A. Louise Hall. 1985. "The Music Theories of Jean-Laurent de Béthizy and Their Relationship to Those of Rameau and D'Alembert." Ph.D. diss., Ohio State University.

Ebner, Wolfgang. 1653. *Eine Instruction und Unterweisung zum Generalbass.* In Herbst 1653.

Estève Pierre. 1751. *Nouvelle découverte du principe de l'harmonie avec un exa-*

*men de ce que Ms. Rameau a publie sous le titre de demonstration de ce principe.* Paris. Reprinted in 1752.

Euler, Leonhard. 1739. *Tentamen novae theoriae musicae.* St. Petersburg. Facs. New York: Broude, 1968. English translation in Smith 1960.

Faber, Heinrich. 1548. *Compendiolum musicae pro incipientibus.* Braunschweig.

Federhofer, Hellmut. 1957. "Der Gradus ad Parnassum von Johann Joseph Fux und seine Vorläufer in Oesterreich." *Musikerziehung* 11:31–35.

———. 1958. "Zur handschriftlichen Ueberlieferung der Musiktheorie in Oesterreich in der zweiten Hälfte des 17. Jahrhunderts." *Musikforschung* 11:264–269.

———. 1962. "Johann Joseph Fux als Musiktheoretiker." In *Hans Albrecht in Memoriam,* pp. 109–115. Kassel: Bärenreiter.

———. 1964. "Marco Scacchis 'Cribrum musicum' 1643 und die Kompositionslehre von Christoph Bernhard." In *Festschrift Hans Engel,* pp. 76–90. Edited by Horst Heussner. Kassel: Bärenreiter.

———. 1970. "Johann Joseph Fux und Johann Mattheson im Urteil Lorenz Christoph Mizlers." In *Speculum musicae artis, Festgabe für Heinrich Husman,* pp. 111–124. Edited by Heinz Becker and Reinhard Gerlach. Munich: Fink.

———. 1971–1972. "Mozart als Schüler und Lehrer in der Musiktheorie." *Mozart Jahrbuch,* pp. 89–106.

———. 1978–1979. "Mozart und die Musiktheorie seiner Zeit." *Mozart Jahrbuch,* pp. 172–175.

———. 1982. "Fux's *Gradus ad Parnassum* as Viewed by Heinrich Schenker." *Music Theory Spectrum* 4:66–75.

Feil, Arnold. 1955. *Satztechnische Fragen in den Kompositionslehren von F. E. Niedt, J. Riepel und H. Chr. Koch.* Heidelberg: Gehrer & Grosch.

———. 1957. "Zum *Gradus ad parnassum* von J. J. Fux." *Archiv für Musikwissenschaft* 14:184–192.

Fellerer, Karl Gustav. 1962. "Zur Melodielehre in 18. Jahrhundert." *Studia musicologica* 3: 109–115.

Ferris, Joan. 1959. "The Evolution of Rameau's Harmonic Theories." *Journal of Music Theory* 3:231–256.

Fétis, François-Joseph. 1833–1844. *Biographie universelle des musiciens.* Brussels. Later editions. Paris, 1860–1865 and 1870–1875.

Fleury, Nicolas. 1660. *Methode pour apprendre facilement à toucher le theorbe sur la basse continue.* Paris. Facs. Geneva: Minkoff, 1972.

Fontenelle, Bernard. 1707. "Sur un nouveau système de musique." In *Histoire de l'Académie royale des sciences 1701,* pp. 155–175. Amsterdam.

Forbes, Elliott. 1967. *Thayer's Life of Beethoven.* Princeton: Princeton University Press.

Forkel, Johann Nicolaus. 1777. *Ueber die Theorie der Musik, insofern sie Liebhabern und Kennern nothwendig und nützlich ist.* Göttingen.

Förster, Emanuel Aloys. 1805. *Anleitung zum General Bass.* Vienna.

Frère, Alexandre. 1706. *Transpositions de musique.* Paris.

Fuller, David. 1980. "Jean-François Dandrieu." In *The New Grove.*

Fux, Johann Joseph. 1725. *Gradus ad parnassum*. Vienna. Facs. *Fux Sämtliche Werke*, vii/1 with preface and critical notes by Alfred Mann. Kassel: Bärenreiter, 1967. Facs. New York: Broude, 1974. German translation in Mizler 1742. Italian translation in Manfredi 1761. English translation in [Heck? 1767?]. French edition in Denis 1773. German translation of portion on species counterpoint in Mann 1938. English translation of portion on species counterpoint in Mann 1943 and 1965a. English translation of portion on fugue and invertible counterpoint in Mann 1965b. English translation of miscellaneous later portions in Lester 1989. All page references are to Mann's or Lester's English translations, except for untranslated passages.

Gafori, Franchino. 1496. *Practica musicae*. Milan. Facs. Farnborough: 1967. English translations in Miller 1968 and Young 1969. All references are to Miller 1968.

Galilei, Vincenzo. 1581. *Dialogo della musica antica et della moderna*. Florence. Facs. New York: Broude, 1967.

———. 1588. *Discorso intorno all'uso delle dissonanze*. Ms. Published in Rempp 1980.

Gasparini, Francesco. 1708. *L'armonico pratico al cimbalo*. Venice. Facs. New York: Broude, [1967]. Several editions through 1802. English translation in Stillings 1963.

Geminiani, Francesco. [c. 1754]. *Guida armonica, o dizionario armonico*. London.

———. [after 1754]. *A Supplement to the Guida Armonica, with Examples*. London.

Gerber, Ernst Ludwig. 1790. *Historisch-Biographisches Lexikon der Tonkünstler*. Leipzig. Facs. Graz: Akademische Druck- und Verlagsanstalt, 1977.

Gerigk, Herbert. 1934. "Würfelmusik." *Zeitschrift für Musikwissenschaft* 16:359–363.

Gessele, Cynthia. 1989. "The Institutionalization of Music Theory in France: 1764–1802." Ph.D. diss., Princeton University.

Gianotti [Pietro]. 1759. *Le Guide du Compositeur*. Paris. Closely based on Rameau [c. 1740] (Christensen 1990a). *RISM* and Eitner do not list a 1755 edition cited in *MGG* and *The New Grove*.

Girdlestone, Cuthbert. 1969. *Jean-Philippe Rameau: His Life and Work*. 2nd ed. New York: Dover.

Goldschmidt, Hugo. 1915. *Die Musikästhetik des 18. Jahrhunderts und ihre Beziehungen zu seinem Kunstschaffen*. Zürich and Leipzig. Facs. Hildesheim: Olms, 1968.

Gossett, Philip. 1971. *Treatise on Harmony*. Translation of Rameau 1722.

Gotwals, Vernon. 1963. *Joseph Haydn, Eighteenth-Century Gentleman and Genius*. Madison: University of Wisconsin Press. Translation of Griesinger 1810.

Grant, Cecil Powell. 1976. "Kirnberger versus Rameau: Toward a New Approach to Comparative Theory." Ph.D. diss., University of Cincinnati.

———. 1977. "The Real Relationship between Kirnberger's and Rameau's Concept of Fundamental Bass." *Journal of Music Theory* 21:324–338.

Grave, Floyd, and Margaret Grave. 1987. *In Praise of Harmony; The Teachings of Abbé Georg Joseph Vogler*. Lincoln: University of Nebraska Press.

Grenerin, Henri. [c. 1670]. *Livre de theorbe . . . avec une nouvelle methode tres facile pour apprendre à joüer les basses continues.* Paris.

Gribenski, Jean. 1980. "A propos des 'Leçons de clavecin' (1771): Diderot et Bemetzrieder." *Revue de musicologie* 66:125–178.

Griesinger, Georg August. 1810. *Biographische Notizen über Joseph Haydn.* Leipzig. English translation in Gotwals 1963.

Grout, Donald. 1965. *A Short History of Opera.* 2nd ed. New York: Columbia University Press.

Gunn, Barnabas. 1752. *Twelve English Songs . . . Set to Musick by the New-Invented method of Composing with the Spruzzarino.* London.

Haas, Robert. 1929. "Das Generalbassflugblatt Francesco Bianciardis." In *Musikwissenschaftliche Beiträge: Festschrift für Johannes Wolf,* pp. 48–56. Edited by Walter Lott, Helmuth Osthoff, and Werner Wolffheim. Berlin: Breslauer.

Haggh, Raymond. 1962. *Hugo Riemann's 'Geschichte der Musiktheorie' . . . Books I and II.* Lincoln: University of Nebraska Press. Partial translation of Riemann 1898.

———. 1982. *School of Clavier Playing.* Lincoln: University of Nebraska Press. English translation of Türk 1789.

Hahn, Georg Joachim Joseph. 1751. *Der wohl unterweisene General-Bass-Schüler.* Augspurg. 2nd ed. 1768.

Hahn, Kurt. 1957. "Johann Kuhnaus 'Fundamenta compositionis'." In *Bericht Hamburg* 1956:103–105.

Handel, George Frideric. [undated]. Ms. treatise for Princess Anne. Published in Mann 1987, pp. 21–32.

Harnish, Otto. 1608. *Artis musicae.* Frankfurt.

Harris-Warrick, Rebecca. 1984. *'Principles of the Harpsichord' by Monsieur de Saint Lambert.* Cambridge: Cambridge University Press. Translation of Saint Lambert 1702.

Harriss, Ernest. *Johann Mattheson's 'Der vollkommene Capellmeister': A Translation and Commentary.* Ann Arbor: UMI Research Press, 1981. Translation of Mattheson 1739.

Hayes, Deborah. 1974a. *Dissertation on the Different Methods of Accompaniment.* Ann Arbor: University Microfilms. Translation of Rameau 1732.

———. 1974b. *Harmonic Generation.* Ann Arbor: University Microfilms. Translation of Rameau 1737.

———. 1974c. "Rameau's 'Nouvelle méthode.'" *Journal of the American Musicological Society* 27:61–74.

Hayes, Elizabeth. 1977. "F. W. Marpurg's 'Anleitung zum Clavierspielen' . . . Translation and Commentary." Ph.D. diss., Stanford University.

Hayes, William. 1751. *The Art of Composing Music by a Method entirely New, suited to the meanest capacity.* London.

Heck, John Jasper. [c. 1760?]. *Short and Fundamental Instructions for Learning Thorough Bass.* London.

———? [1767?]. *Practical Rules for Learning Counterpoint.* Translation of Fux 1725. Later prints through c. 1787.

———? [c. 1776]. *A Complete Treatise of Thorough Bass.* London. Partial translation of Mattheson 1735.

Heinichen, Johann David. 1711. *Neu erfundene und gründliche Anweisung . . . des General-Basses.* Hamburg. Author's name is spelled Heinchen on title page.

———. 1728. *Der General-Bass in der Composition.* Dresden. Facs. Hildesheim: Olms, 1969.

Helm, Ernest Eugene. 1960. *Music at the Court of Frederick the Great.* Norman: University of Oklahoma Press.

———. 1966. "Six Random Measures of C. P. E. Bach." *Journal of Music Theory* 10:139–151.

Herbst, Johann Andreas. 1642. *Musica practica sive instructio pro symphoniacis . . . auff jetzige Italienische Manier.* Nuremberg.

———. 1653. *Arte pratica et poëtica.* Frankfurt.

Hesse, Johann Heinrich. [1776]. *Kurze, doch hinlängliche Anweisung zum General-Bass.* Hamburg. Date is at end of *Vorrede.*

Hiller, Johann Adam. 1766–1770. *Wöchentliche Nachrichten und Anmerkungen.* Leipzig.

Hilse, Walter. 1973. "The Treatises of Christoph Bernhard." *Music Forum* 3: 1–196. Translation of Bernhard [c. 1655].

Holden, John. 1770. *Essay Towards a Rational System of Music.* Glasgow and London.

Holder, William. 1731. *A Treatise of the Natural Grounds, and Principles of Harmony.* London. Includes Keller 1707.

Horsley, Imogene. 1966. *Fugue: History and Practice.* New York: Free Press.

Jacobi, Erwin. 1958. "Jean-Adam Serre, ein vergessener Schweizer Musiktheoretiker." *Schweizerische Musikzeitung* 98:145–148.

———. 1964. "Rameau and Padre Martini." *Musical Quarterly* 50:452–475.

Jamard, Canon. 1769. *Recherches sur la théorie de la musique.* Paris.

Janowka, Thomas Balthasar. 1701. *Clavis ad thesaurum magnae artis musicae.* Prague. Partial English translation in Lester 1989.

Jeppesen, Knud. 1939. *Counterpoint: The Polyphonic Vocal Style of the Sixteenth Century.* Translated by Glen Haydon. New York: Prentice-Hall, 1939. Danish edition, 1931.

———. 1970. *The Style of Palestrina and the Dissonance.* Translated by Margaret Hamerik. 3rd ed. New York: Dover, 1970. Danish edition, 1923.

Johnson, Fredric. 1985. "Tartini's *Trattato* . . . An Annotated Translation with Commentary." Ph.D. diss., Indiana University. Translation of Tartini 1754.

Kalib, Sylvan. 1973. "Thirteen Essays from the Three Yearbooks *Das Meisterwerk in der Musik* by Heinrich Schenker." Ph.D. diss., Northwestern University.

Kassler, Jamie Croy, and Michael Kassler. 1980. "John Jasper Heck." In *The New Grove.*

Keane, Sister Mary. 1961. *The Theoretical Writings of Jean-Philippe Rameau.* Washington: Catholic University of America Press.

Keiler, Allan. 1981. "Music as Metalanguage: Rameau's Fundamental Bass." In

*Music Theory: Special Topics,* pp. 83–100. Edited by Richmond Browne. New York: Academic Press.

Keller, Gottfried. 1707. *Rules for Playing a Thorough Bass.* London. Earlier edition in 1705. Later editions as *A Compleat Method . . .,* 1717–c. 1731. Reprinted in Holder 1731. All editions contain numerous errors.

Kellner, David. 1732. *Treulicher Unterricht im General-Bass.* Hamburg. Editions through 1796. Facs. of 1737 edition. Hildesheim: Georg Olms, 1979. Facs. of 1743 edition. Laaber: Laaber-Verlag, 1980. Swedish, Dutch, and Russian translations, 1739–1791.

Kirnberger, Johann Philipp. 1757. *Der allezeit fertige Polonoisen- und Menuetten-componist.* Berlin. French translation. Berlin, 1757.

———. 1759. *Allegro für das Clavier allein.* Berlin.

———. 1771–1779. *Die Kunst des reinen Satzes.* Vol. 1. Berlin, 1771; Berlin and Königsberg, 1774. Revised edition, Berlin, c. 1776. Vol. 2. Berlin and Königsberg, 1776–1779. Facs., supposedly of the Berlin and Königsberg 1776 and 1776–1779 editions, Hildesheim: Olms, 1968 (see Beach-Thym 1982, p. xviii, concerning the probable source of volume 1 of this facsimile). English translation in Beach and Thym 1982.

———. 1773. *Die wahren Grundsätze zum Gebrauch der Harmonie.* Berlin and Königsberg. Possibly written by Johann Abraham Peter Schulz (see p. 240). Facs. Hildesheim: Olms, 1970. English translation in Beach and Thym 1979. 2nd ed. Vienna, 1793.

———. [c. 1781]. *Grundsätze des Generalbasses als erste Linien zur Composition.* Berlin.

———. 1782. *Gedanken über die verschiedenen Lehrarten in der Komposition, als Vorbereitung zur Fugenkenntniss.* Berlin. Facs. Hildesheim: Olms, 1974. 2nd ed. Vienna, 1793. English translation in Nelson and Boomgaarden 1986.

———. 1783. *Methode, Sonaten aus'm Ermel zu schüddeln.* Berlin. English translation in Newman 1961.

Knouse, Nola Reed. 1986. Review of Baker 1983. *Music Theory Spectrum* 8:143–148.

Koch, Heinrich Christoph. 1782–1793. *Versuch einer Anleitung zur Composition.* Rudolstadt and Leipzig. 3 vols. Facs. Hildesheim: Georg Olms, 1969. Partial English translation in Baker 1983. Complete table of contents in Baker 1983, pp. 249–252.

———. 1795. *Journal der Tonkunst.* Erfurt.

———. 1802. *Musikalisches Lexikon.* Frankfurt. Editions through 1865. Facs. Hildesheim: Olms, 1964.

Kohlschütter, Bernd. 1978. "Die musikalische Ausbildung auf Salzburger Boden im 18. Jahrhundert." *Mozart Jahrbuch,* pp. 200–202.

Kramer, Richard. 1975. "Notes to Beethoven's Education." *Journal of the American Musicological Society* 28:72–101.

Krehbiel, James. 1964. "Harmonic Principles of Jean-Philippe Rameau and His Contemporaries." Ph.D. diss., Indiana University.

Lach, Robert. 1918. *W. A. Mozart als Theoretiker.* Vienna. Includes facsimile and transcription of Mozart 1784.

Ladewig, James. 1980. "Geminiani." In *The New Grove*, work list.

Laisement, Ballière de. 1764. *Théorie de la musique*. Paris.

Lampe, John Frederick. 1737. *A Plain and Compendious Method of Teaching Thorough Bass, After the most Rational Manner*. London. Facs. New York: Broude, 1969.

——. 1740. *The Art of Musick*. London.

Lanfranco, Giovanni Maria. 1533. *Scintille di Musica*. Brescia. Facs. Bologna: Forni, 1970. English translation in Lee 1961.

Langner, Thomas. 1980. Article "Christoph Nichelmann." In *The New Grove*.

Larsen, Arved. 1980. "Berardi." In *The New Grove*.

Lee, Barbara. 1961. "Giovanni Maria Lanfranco's *Scintille di musica* and Its Relation to 16th-Century Music Theory." Ph.D. diss., Cornell University. Translation of Lanfranco 1533.

Lester, Joel. 1973. Review of Busch 1970. *Notes* 29:450–451.

——. 1974. "Root-Position and Inverted Triads in Theory around 1600." *Journal of the American Musicological Society* 27:110–119.

——. 1977. "The Fux-Mattheson Correspondence: An Annotated Translation." *Current Musicology* 24:37–62.

——. 1978. "Simultaneity Structures and Harmonic Functions in Tonal Music." *In Theory Only* 5:65–103.

——. 1989. *Between Modes and Keys: German Theory 1592–1802*. Stuyvesant, N.Y.: Pendragon.

——. 1990. "A 17th-Century Publication Including Christoph Bernhard's *Figurenlehre*." *Israel Studies in Musicology* 5:97–111.

——. 1993. "Mozart as Composition Teacher and Late Eighteenth Century Theory." In *Report of the Hofstra Mozart Bicentennial Conference, 1991*.

Levens, Charles. 1743. *Abregé des regles de l'harmonie, pour apprendre la composition*. Bourdeaux.

Lewin, David. 1978. "Two Interesting Passages in Rameau's *Traité de l'harmonie*." *In Theory Only* 4:3–11.

——. 1979. "Comment." *In Theory Only* 5:12–14.

Lippius, Johannes. 1610. *Disputatio musica tertia*. Wittenberg.

——. 1612. *Synopsis musicae novae*. Strassburg. English translation in Rivera 1977.

Locke, Matthew. 1673. *Melothesia*. London. Facs. New York: Broude, 1975.

Löfgrön, Antonius. 1728. *De basso fundamentali*. Uppsala.

Löhlein, Georg Simon. 1765. *Clavier-Schule oder kurze und gründliche Anweisung zur Melodie und Harmonie*. Leipzig and Züllichau. Editions through 1848. Russian translation. Moscow, 1773–1774. English translation in Wilson 1979.

——. 1781. *Clavier-Schule, zweyter Band, worinnen eine vollständige Anweisung zur Begleitung der unbezifferten Bässe*. Leipzig and Züllichau. Editions through 1848. English translation in Wilson 1979.

Lusitano, Vicente. 1553. *Introduttione facilissima, et novissima, di canto fermo, figurato, contraponto semplice, et in concerto*. Rome. Later editions, Venice, 1558, 1561. All references are to the 1561 edition.

Madin, Henri. 1742. *Traité, du contrepoint simple, ou du chant sur le livre.* Paris.

Malcolm, Alexander. 1721. *A Treatise of Musick.* Edinburgh. Facs. New York: Da Capo, 1970.

Manfredi, Alessandro. 1761. *Salita al Parnasso.* Carpi. Italian translation of Fux 1725.

Manfredini, Vincenzo. 1775. *Regole armoniche.* Venice. Facs. New York: Broude, 1966.

Mann, Alfred. 1938. *Die Lehre vom Kontrapunkt.* Celle: Hermann Moeck. Reprinted 1951. Translation of species counterpoint portion of Fux 1725.

————. 1943. *Steps to Parnassus.* New York: W. W. Norton. Translation of species counterpoint portion of Fux 1725.

————. 1965a. *The Study of Counterpoint.* New York: W. W. Norton. 2nd ed. of Mann 1943 with new preface and same pagination.

————. 1965b. *The Study of Fugue.* New York: W. W. Norton. Includes partial translations of Albrechtsberger 1790, Fux 1725, Marpurg 1753–1754, Martini [1774–1775].

————. 1967. Preface to *Fux Sämtliche Werke,* vii/1. Kassel: Bärenreiter.

————. 1973. "Haydn's *Elementarbuch.*" *The Music Forum* 3:197–237.

————. 1978–1979. "Zur Kontrapunktlehre Haydns und Mozarts." *Mozart Jahrbuch,* pp. 195–199.

————. 1987. *Theory and Practice.* New York: W. W. Norton, 1987.

Marco, Guy, and Claude Palisca. 1968. *The Art of Counterpoint.* New Haven: Yale University Press. Translation of Book 3 of Zarlino 1558.

Marpurg, Friedrich Wilhelm. 1749–1750. *Critische Musicus an der Spree.* Berlin. Facs. Hildesheim: Olms, 1970.

————. 1750–1762. *Die Kunst das Clavier zu spielen.* Berlin. Two vols.: Vol. 1 reprinted Berlin, 1751, 1760, 1761 and Augsburg, 1761; Vol. 2 in 1762. French translations. Facs. of the 1762 edition and the 1761 second part on accompaniment. Hildesheim: Olms, 1969.

————. 1753–1754. *Abhandlung von der Fuge.* Berlin. Facs. Hildesheim: Olms, 1970. Editions and translations through 1858. Partial English translation in Mann 1965b. (Mann's fine translation is considerably abridged in text and a number of musical examples).

————. 1754–1778. *Historisch-kritische Beyträge zur Aufnahme der Musik.* Berlin. Published continuously through 1762, and then again in 1778. Facs. Hildesheim: Olms, 1970.

————. 1755. *Anleitung zum Clavierspielen.* Berlin. English translation in Hayes 1977. Reprinted 1765. Facs. New York: Broude, 1969; Hildesheim: Olms, 1970. French translation. Berlin, 1756. Facs. Bologna: Forni, 1971; Geneva: Minkoff, 1973. Dutch translation. Amsterdam, 1760. All references are to the 1765 print.

————. 1755–1762. *Handbuch bey dem Generalbasse und der Composition.* 3 vols and appendix. Berlin, 1755, 1757, 1758, 1760. Facs. Hildesheim: Olms, 1974. 2nd ed. of Vol. 1. Berlin, 1762. All references to Vol. 1 are to the second edition. Swedish translation. Stockholm, 1782. Annotated English edition in Sheldon 1989.

————. 1757a. *Systematische Einleitung in die musicalische Setzkunst, nach den Lehrsätzen des Herrn Rameau*. Leipzig. Translation of D'Alembert 1752. Facs. Leipzig: Zentralantiquariat der DDR, 1980.

————. 1757b. *Anfangsgründe der Theoretischen Music*. Berlin. Facs. New York: Broude, 1966.

————. 1758. *Anleitung zum Singcomposition*. Berlin.

————. 1759–1763. *Kritische Briefe über die Tonkunst*. Berlin. Issued weekly, then collected in three volumes in Berlin, 1760–1764. Facs. Hildesheim: Olms, 1974.

————. 1760. *Herrn Georg Andreas Sorgens Anleitung zum Generalbass und zur Composition*. Berlin. Extensive quotations from Sorge [1760] with commentary.

————. 1763. *Anleitung zur Musik überhaupt*. Berlin. Facs. Leipzig: Zentralantiquariat der DDR, 1975.

————. 1776. *Versuch über die musikalische Temperatur, nebst einem Anhang über den Rameau- und Kirnbergerischen Grundbass*. Breslau.

————. 1786. *Legende einer Musikheiligen*. Berlin.

Martin, James. 1981. "The *Compendium harmonicum* (1760) of Georg Andreas Sorge (1703–1778): A Translation and Critical Commentary." Ph.D. diss., Catholic University. Translation of Sorge [1760].

Martini, Giovanni Battista (Padre). [1756]. *Regola ogli organisti per accompagnare il Canto fermo*. Bologna. Reprinted Bologna: Forni, 1969.

————. 1757–1781. *Storia della musica*. Bologna. Facs. Graz: Akademische Druck- und Verlagsanstalt, 1967.

————. [1774–1775]. *Esemplare o sia saggio fondamentale pratico di contrappunto sopra il canto fermo*. 2 vols. Bologna, [1774 and 1775] (dates on p. viii in Vol. 1 and at end of dedication in Vol. 2). Facs. Ridgewood: Gregg Press, 1965. Partial English translation in Mann 1965b.

Mason, Kevin. 1981. "François Campion's Secret Art of Accompaniment for the Theorbo, Guitar, and Lute." *Journal of the Lute Society of America* 14:69–94.

Masson, Charles. 1699. *Nouveau traité des regles pour la composition de la musique*. 2nd ed. Paris. The first edition is lost. Facs. with introduction by Imogene Horsley. New York: Da Capo, 1967. (See Schneider 1973, p. 246, concerning this introduction.) Editions in Paris and Amsterdam through 1755. Facs. of the 1705 edition. Geneva: Minkoff, 1971.

Mattheson, Johann. 1713. *Das neu-eröffnete Orchestre*. Hamburg.

————. 1717. *Das beschützte Orchestre*. Hamburg.

————. 1719. *Exemplarische Organisten-Probe im Artikel vom General-Bass*. Hamburg. An earlier version of Mattheson 1731.

————. 1721. *Das forschende Orchestre*. Hamburg. Facs. Hildesheim: Olms, 1976.

————. 1722. *Critica Musica*. Hamburg. Facs. Amsterdam: Frits Knuf, 1964.

————. 1725. *Criticae Musicae*. Hamburg. Facs. Amsterdam: Frits Knuf, 1964.

————. 1731. *Grosse General-Bass-Schule*. Hamburg. Facs. Hildesheim: Olms, 1968.

————. 1735. *Kleine General-Bass Schule*. Hamburg. Facs. Laaber: Laaber Verlag, 1980. Partial English translation in Heck [c. 1776].

————. 1737. *Kern melodischer Wissenschaft*. Hamburg. Facs. Hildesheim: Olms, 1976.

————. 1739. *Der vollkommene Capellmeister*. Hamburg. Facs. Kassel: Bärenreiter, 1954. English translation in Harriss 1981.

McArtor, Marion. 1951. "Francesco Geminiani, Composer and Theorist." Ph.D. diss., University of Michigan.

Mekeel, Joyce. 1960. "The Harmonic Theories of Kirnberger and Marpurg." *Journal of Music Theory* 4:169–193

Mickelsen, William. 1977. *Hugo Riemann's Theory of Harmony, with a Translation of Riemann's "History of Theory," Book 3*. Lincoln: University of Nebraska Press. Partial translation of Riemann 1898.

Miller, Clement. A. 1968. English translation of Gafori 1496. [Rome]: American Institute of Musicology, 1968.

Mitchell, William. 1949. *Essay on the True Art of Playing Keyboard Instruments*. New York: W. W. Norton, 1949. Translation of C. P. E. Bach 1753 and 1762. Mitchell combines the 41 chapters of Vol. 2 into 7 chapters and adds some of the added passages in the 1797 edition.

Mizler, Lorenz. 1736–1754. *Musikalischen Bibliothek*. Leipzig. Facs. Hilversum: Frits Knuf, 1966.

————. 1739. *Anfangsgründe des Generalbasses*. Leipzig, 1739.

————. 1742. *Gradus ad parnassum*. Leipzig. Facs. Hildesheim, 1984. German translation of Fux 1725.

Montéclair, Michel Pignolet de. 1709. *Nouvelle methode pour apprendre la musique, dèdiée a Monsieur Couperin*. Paris.

————. 1736. *Principes de musique*. Paris.

Monteverdi, Claudio. 1605. "Studiosi lettori." Preface to *Il quinto libro de' madrigali*. Venice. Facs. *Claudio Monteverdi: Tutte le opera*, 5. Edited by G. Francesco Malipiero. English translation in Strunk 1950.

Monteverdi, Giulio Cesare. 1607. "Dichiaratione." In Claudio Monteverdi, *Scherzi musicali*. Venice. English translation in Strunk 1950.

Mozart, Wolfgang. 1784. *Barbara Ployers Theorie- und Kompositionsstudien bei Mozart*. Facs. and transcriptions in Lach 1918 and *W. A. Mozart Neue Ausgabe* X,30,2 (1989).

————. 1785–1786. *Thomas Attwoods Theorie- und Kompositionsstudien bei Mozart*. In *W. A. Mozart Neue Ausgabe* X,30,1 (1965).

Muffat, Georg. 1699. *Regulae concentuum partiturae*. Ms. published in *An Essay on Thoroughbass*. Edited by Helmut Federhofer. N.p.: American Institute of Musicology, 1961.

Müller-Blattau, Joseph Maria. 1926. *Die Kompositionslehre Heinrich Schützens in der Fassung seines Schülers Christoph Bernhard*. Leipzig: Breitkopf & Härtel, 1926.

Murschhauser, Franz Xaver Anton. 1721. *Academia musico-poetica*. Nuremberg.

Nelson, Richard, and Donald Boomgaarden. 1986. "Kirnberger's 'Thoughts on the Different Methods of Teaching Composition as Preparation for Understanding Fugue.'" *Journal of Music Theory* 30:71–94. Translation of Kirnberger 1782.

Newman, William. 1961. "Kirnberger's Method for Tossing Off Sonatas." *Musical Quarterly* 47:517–525. Contains English translation of Kirnberger 1783.

Nichelmann, Christoph. 1755. *Die Melodie nach ihrem Wesen sowohl, als nach ihren Eigenschaften*. Danzig.

Niedt, Friderich Erhard. 1700. *Musicalische Handleitung*, Part 1 *Handelt vom General-Bass*. Hamburg. 2nd ed. 1710. Facs. Buren: Frits Knuf, 1976. English translation in Poulin-Taylor 1988. All references here are to the 1710 edition.

———. 1706. *Musicalische Handleitung*, Part 2 *Handleitung zur Variation, wie man den General-Bass und darüber gesetzte Zahlen variiren, artige Inventiones machen, und aus einen schlechten General-Bass Praeludia, Ciaconnen . . . leichtlich verfertigen können*. Hamburg. 2nd ed. edited by Johann Mattheson. Hamburg, 1721. Facs. Buren: Frits Knuf, 1976. English translation in Poulin-Taylor 1988. All references here are to the 1721 edition.

———. 1717. *Musicalische Handleitung*, Part 3 *Handlend vom Contra-Punct*. Edited by Johann Mattheson. Hamburg. Facs. Buren: Frits Knuf, 1976. English translation in Poulin-Taylor 1988.

Nottebohm, Gustav. 1872. *Beethoveniana*. Leipzig and Winterthur.

———. 1873. *Beethoven's Studien I*. Leipzig and Winterthur. Facs. Wiesbaden: Söndig, 1971.

Osborne, Richard. 1966. "The Theoretical Writings of Abbé Pierre-Joseph Roussier." Ph.D. diss., Ohio State University.

Ozanam. 1691. *Dictionaire mathematique*. Amsterdam.

Palisca, Claude. 1956. "Vincenzo Galilei's Counterpoint Treatise: A Code for the *Seconda Pratica*." *Journal of the American Musicological Society* 9:81–96.

———. 1958. Article "Kontrapunkt" in *MGG*.

———. 1972a. "Marco Scacchi's Defense of Modern Music 1649." In *Words and Music*, pp. 189–235. Edited by Laurence Berman. Cambridge, Mass.: Harvard University Press.

———. 1972b. "*Ut oratoria musica:* The Rhetorical Basis of Musical Mannerism." In *The Meaning of Mannerism*, pp. 37–61. Edited by Franklin Robinson and Stephen Nichols, Jr. Hanover: University Press of New England.

———. 1983. "The Artusi-Monteverdi Controversy." In *The Monteverdi Companion*. Edited by Denis Arnold and Nigel Fortune. 2nd. ed. London: Faber & Faber.

Paolucci, Giuseppe. 1765–1772. *Arte pratica di contrappunto dimostrata con esempi di vari autori e con osservazioni*. 3 vols. Venice.

Pascal, Blaise. [c. 1658]. *Pensées*. In *Pascal Oeuvres Complètes*. N.p.: Macmillan, 1963.

Pasquali, Nicolo. 1757. *Thorough-Bass Made Easy*. Edinburgh. Editions and French translation through c. 1810. Facs. of London, [c. 1765]. London: Oxford University Press, c. 1974.

Paul, Charles. 1971. "Music and Ideology: Rameau, Rousseau, and 1789." *Journal of the History of Ideas* 32:395–410.

Penna, Lorenzo. 1684. *Li primi albori musicali.* Bologna. Facs. Bologna: Forni, 1969. Other editions in 1672, 1679, 1696, and Antwerp, 1690. All references are to 1684.

Pischner, Hans. 1963. *Die Harmonielehre Jean-Philippe Rameaus: Ihre historischen Voraussetzungen und ihre Auswirkungen im französischen, italienischen und deutschen musiktheoretischen Schrifttum des 18. Jahrhunderts.* Leipzig: Breitkopf & Härtel.

Planchart, Alejandro. 1960. "A Study of the Theories of Giuseppe Tartini." *Journal of Music Theory* 4: 32–61.

Pohl, Carl Ferdinand. 1875. *Joseph Haydn.* Berlin.

Poulin, Pamela, and Irmgard Taylor, 1988. *The Musical Guide.* Oxford: Clarendon Press. Translation of Niedt 1700/1710, 1717, 1721.

Praetorius Michael. 1619. *Syntagma musicum,* 3. Wolfenbüttel. Facs. Kassel: Bärenreiter, 1959. Reprinted, edited by Eduard Bernoulli. Leipzig, 1916.

Preussner, Eberhard. 1924. *Die Methodik im Schulgesang der evangelischen Lateinschulen des 17. Jahrhunderts.* Dissertation, University of Berlin.

Printz, Wolfgang Caspar. 1676–1696. *Phrynis Mytilenaeus oder Satyrischer Componist.* Vol. 1: Quedlinburg, 1676; Vol. 2: Sagan, 1677; Vols. 1–3: Dresden and Leipzig, 1696. Reprint. Dresden, 1744.

Purcell, Henry. 1694. "A Brief Introduction to the Art of Descant; or, Composing Music in Parts." In John Playford, *A Breefe Introduction to the Skill of Musick,* 1694 ed. Facs. New York: Da Capo, 1972.

Quantz, Johann Joachim. 1752. *Versuch einer Anweisung, die Flöte traversiere zu spielen.* Berlin. Reprinted Wroclaw, 1780, 1789. Translations into French, Dutch, English, 1752-c. 1780.

Quirsfeld, Johann. 1675. *Breviarium musicum.* Dresden. Later editions through 1717.

Rameau, Jean-Philippe. 1722. *Traité de l'harmonie.* Paris. Facs. in Rameau CTW 1. English translation of Book 3. London, 1752, 1779. English translation of Book 4. London, c. 1795, c. 1805. English translation in Gossett 1971.

———. 1726. *Nouveau Système de musique théorique . . . pour servir d'introduction au traité de l'harmonie.* Paris. Facs. in Rameau CTW 2. English translation in Chandler 1975.

———. 1729–1731. Article exchange (possibly with Michel Pignolet de Montéclair) in *Mercure de France.* Facs. in Rameau CTW 6. Partial English translation in Keane 1961, pp. 81–112.

———. 1732. *Dissertation sur les différentes métodes d'accompagnement . . . avec le plan d'une nouvelle métode.* Facs. in Rameau CTW 5. 2nd ed. c. 1772. English translation in Hayes 1974a.

———. 1736. "Lettre de M. Rameau au R. P. Castel." *Journal de Trévoux,* pp. 1691–1709. Facs. in Rameau CTW 6.

———. 1737. *Generation harmonique, ou Traité de musique théorique et pratique.* Facs. in Rameau CTW 3. English translation in Hayes 1974b.

———. c. 1740. *L'Art de la basse fondamentale.* Ms. (see Christensen 1987a). Gianotti 1759 is closely based on this treatise (Christensen 1990a).

———. 1750. *Démonstration du principe de l'harmonie, servant de base à tout l'art musical théorique & pratique.* Facs. in Rameau CTW 3. English translation in Briscoe 1975.

———. 1752. "*Extrait d'une réponse de M. Rameau à M. Euler, sur l'identité des octaves.*" *Mercure de France,* December, 1752, pp. 6–31. Facs. in Rameau CTW 5. Published Paris, 1753.

———. 1754. *Observations sur notre instinct pour la musique, et sur son principe.* Facs. in Rameau CTW 3.

———. [1761]. *Code de musique pratique . . . avec de nouvelles réflexions sur le principe sonore.* Facs. in Rameau CTW 4. Dated 1760 on title page (see Rameau CTW 4, pp. xxxix–xl).

———. 1762. *Origine des sciences.* Facs. in Rameau CTW 4.

———. 1763–1764. *Vérités également ignorées et intéressantes tirées du sein de la nature.* Ms. published in Schneider 1986.

———. CTW. *The Complete Theoretical Writings of Jean-Philippe Rameau.* 6 vols. Edited by Erwin Jacobi. N.p.: American Institute of Musicology, 1967–1972.

Ramler, Karl. 1758. *Einleitung in die schönen Wissenschaften.* Berlin. Translation of Batteux 1746. Later editions.

Ratner, Leonard. 1949. "Harmonic Aspects of Classic Form." *Journal of the American Musicological Society* 2: 159–168.

———. 1956. "Eighteenth-Century Theories of Musical Period Structure." *Musical Quarterly* 42:439–454.

———. 1970. "*Ars combinatoria,* Chance and Choice in Eighteenth-Century Music." In *Studies in Eighteenth-Century Music,* pp. 343–63. Edited by R. E. Chapman and H. C. Robbins Landon. New York: Oxford University Press.

———. 1980. *Classic Music: Expression, Form, and Style.* New York: Schirmer Books.

Reed, Nola. 1983. "The Theories of Joseph Riepel as Expressed in His *Anfangsgründe zur Musicalischen Setzkunst.*" Ph.D. diss., University of Rochester.

Reilly, Allyn. 1980. "Georg Andreas Sorge's *Vorgemach der musicalischen Composition*: A Translation and Commentary." Ph.D. diss., Northwestern University. Translation of Sorge [1745].

Rempp, Frieder. 1980. *Die Kontrapunkttraktate Vincenzo Galileis.* Cologne: Arno Volk Verlag.

Riedt, Friedrich Wilhelm. 1756. "Tabellen über alle drey- und vierstimmige . . . Grundaccorde." In Marpurg 1754–1778, 2:387–413.

Riemann, Hugo. 1893. *Vereinfachte Harmonielehre.* London. English translation in Bewerunge [1895].

———. 1898. *Geschichte der Musiktheorie im IX.-XIX. Jahrhundert.* Leipzig. 2nd ed. 1921. Facs. Hildesheim: Olms, 1961. English translation in Haggh 1962 and Mickelsen 1977.

Riepel, Joseph. 1752. *Anfangsgründe zur musicalischen Setzkunst: De rhythmopoeïa, oder von der Tactordnung.* Frankfurt and Leipzig.

———. 1755. *Grundregeln zur Tonordnung insgemein.* Frankfurt and Leipzig.

———. 1757. *Gründliche Erklärung der Tonordnung insbesondere.* Frankfurt and Leipzig.

———. 1765. *Erläuterung der betrüglichen Tonordnung.* Augsburg.

———. 1768. *Unentbehrliche Anmerkungen zum Contrapunct.* Augsburg.

———. 1786. *Baßschlüssel.* Regensburg. Edited by Johann Kaspar Schubarth.

Rivera, Benito. 1977. *Synopsis of New Music.* Colorado Springs: Colorado College Music Press. Translation of Lipplus 1612.

———. 1978. "The *Isagoge* (1581) of Johannes Avianius: An Early Formulation of Triadic Theory." *Journal of Music Theory* 22:43–64.

———. 1979. "Harmonic Theory in Musical Treatises of the Late Fifteenth and Early Sixteenth Centuries." *Music Theory Spectrum* 1:80–95.

———. 1980. *German Music Theory in the Early Seventeenth Century: The Treatises of Johannes Lippius.* Ann Arbor: UMI Research Press.

Robert, Walter. 1961. *Compendium of Music.* N.p.: American Institute of Musicology. Translation of Descartes 1618.

Rosen, Charles. 1980. *Sonata Forms.* New York: W. W. Norton.

Rousseau, Jean Jacques. 1753. *Lettre sur la musique française.* Paris. Partial English translation in Strunk 1950.

———. 1768. *Dictionnaire de musique.* Paris. Facs. Hildesheim: Olms, 1969. Many later transformations. English translation, London, [c. 1775].

Roussier, Pierre-Joseph. 1764. *Traité des accords, et leur succession, selon le systéme de la basse-fondamentale.* Paris and Lyon.

———. [1765]. *Observations sur différens points d'harmonie.* Geneva and Paris. Erroneously dated 1755 on the title page; p. 29 refers to reviews of Roussier 1764 that appeared early in 1765.

St. Lambert. 1702. *Les principes du clavecin.* Paris. Facs. Geneva: Minkoff, 1974. English translation in Harris-Warrick 1984. See Harris-Warrick 1984, p. ix, concerning the erroneous use of Michel as his given name.

———. 1707. *Nouveau traité de l'accompagnement.* Paris. Reprint Amsterdam, c. 1710. Facs. Geneva: Minkoff, 1974. See Harris-Warrick 1984, pp. viii–ix and Arnold 1931, pp. 900–901 concerning the lingering error that there was a 1680 edition.

Scheibe, Johann Adolph. c. 1730. *Compendium musices.* Ms. published in Benary [1961].

———. 1737–1740. *Der critische Musicus.* Hamburg. Facs. Amsterdam: Antiqua, 1966.

———. 1773. *Ueber die Musikalische Composition; Die Theorie der Melodie und Harmonie.* Leipzig, 1773.

Schenker, Heinrich. 1930. "Rameau oder Beethoven? Erstarrung oder geistiges Leben in der Musik?" *Das Meisterwerk in der Musik* 3:9–24. Facs. Hildesheim: Olms, 1974. English translation in Kalib 1973.

———. 1954. *Harmony.* Chicago: University of Chicago Press. Translation by Elisabeth Mann Borgese of *Neue Musikalische Theorien und Phantasien, I: Harmonielehre.* Stuttgart, Berlin, and Vienna, 1906.

———. 1987. *Counterpoint.* New York: G. Schirmer. Translation by John Rothgeb of *Neue Musikalische Theorien und Phantasien, II: Kontrapunkt.* Stuttgart, Berlin, and Vienna, 1910–1922.

Schering, Arnold. 1931. *Geschichte der Musik in Beispielen.* Leipzig.

Schneider, Herbert. 1973. "Charles Masson und sein *Nouveau traité.*" *Archiv für Musikwissenschaft* 30:245–274.

———. 1986. *Jean-Philippe Rameaus letzter Musiktraktat.* Stuttgart: Franz Steiner Verlag. Publication of Rameau 1763–1764.

Schnoebelen, Anne. 1979. *Padre Martini's Collection of Letters in the Civico Museo Bibliografico Musicale in Bologna.* New York: Pendragon.

Schoenberg, Arnold. 1946. "Criteria for the Evaluation of Music." In *Style and Idea,* pp. 124–136. Edited by Leonard Stein. Berkeley and Los Angeles: University of California Press, 1975.

———. 1950. "Composition with Twelve Tones." In *Style and Idea,* pp. 214–245. Edited by Leonard Stein. Berkeley and Los Angeles: University of California Press, 1975.

Scholes, Percy. 1959. *Charles Burney: An 18th-Century Musical Tour.* London: Oxford University Press.

Schröter, Christoph Gottlob. 1772. *Deutliche Anweisung zum General-Bass.* Halberstadt. Possibly completed by 1754 (date in preface; see Buelow 1980b).

Schulz, Johann Abraham Peter. 1800. "*Ueber die in Sulzers Theorie der schönen Künste . . .*" *Allgemeine musikalische Zeitung,* 2:257–265, 273–280.

Schulze, Hans-Joachim. 1972. *Dokumente zum Nachwirken J. S. Bachs 1750–1800.* Kassel: Bärenreiter.

———. 1984. *Studien zur Bach-Ueberlieferung im 18. Jahrhundert.* Leipzig: Edition Peters.

Schwarzmaier, Ernst. 1936. *Die Takt- und Tonordnung Joseph Riepels: Ein Beitrag zur Geschichte der Formenlehre im 18. Jahrhundert.* Wolfenbüttel: Verlag für musikalische Kultur und Wissenschaft.

Seay, Albert. 1961. *The Art of Counterpoint.* Translation of Tinctoris 1477. N.p.: American Institute of Musicology.

Serre, Jean-Adam. 1753. *Essais sur les principes de l'harmonie.* Paris. Probably appeared in late 1752 (Rameau CTW 3, p. lxv). Facs. New York: Broude, 1967.

———. 1763. *Observations sur les principes de l'harmonie.* Geneva. Facs. New York: Broude, 1967.

Serwer, Howard. 1970. "Marpurg vs. Kirnberger: Theories of Fugal Composition." *Journal of Music Theory* 14:209–236.

———. 1980. "Johann Friedrich Marpurg." In *The New Grove.*

Seyfried, Ignaz Xaver Ritter von. [c. 1825]. *J. G. Albrechtsberger's sämmtliche Schriften.* Vienna. Facs. Kassel: Bärenreiter, 1975. 2nd ed., 1837. Translations into French (1830) and English (c. 1834, 1842, and 1855).

———. 1832. *Ludwig van Beethoven's Studien im Generalbasse, Contrapuncte und in der Compositions-Lehre.* Vienna. Several later editions and translations.

Sheldon, David. 1989. *Marpurg's 'Thoroughbass and Composition Handbook': A Narrative Translation and Critical Study.* Stuyvesant, N.Y.: Pendragon Press.

Shirlaw, Matthew. 1917. *The Theory of Harmony.* London: Novello. Facs.

DeKalb, Ill.: Coar, 1955; New York: Da Capo Press, 1969; Sarasota, Fla.: Coar, 1970 (as *The Theory and Nature of Harmony,* with an appended essay).

Signoretti. 1777. *Traité du Contrepoint par P. Signoretti dédié a Mrs. les amateurs.* Rennes.

Sisman, Elaine. 1982. "Small and Expanded Forms: Koch's Model and Haydn's Music." *Musical Quarterly* 68: 444–475.

Smith, Charles S. 1960. "Leonhard Euler's *Tentamen novae theoriae musicae:* A Translation and Commentary." Translation of Euler 1739. Ph.D. diss., University of Indiana.

Snook, Susan. 1978. "J. F. Daube's *Der musikalischen Dilettant: Eine Abhandlung der Komposition* (1773): A Translation and Commentary." Ph.D. diss., Stanford University.

Soler, Antonio. 1762. *Llave de la modulación . . . theorica y práctica . . . desde el tiempo de Juan de Muris, hasta hoy.* Madrid. Facs. New York: Broude, 1967.

Sorge, Georg Andreas. [1745–1747]. *Vorgemach der musicalischen Composition; oder . . . Anweisung zum General-Bass.* Lobenstein. 3 vols. Dates at end of dedication. English translation in Reilly 1980.

———. [1753]. *Ausweichungs-Tabellen, in welchen auf vierfache Art gezeiget wird, wie eine jede Tonart in ihre Neben-Tonarten ausweichen könne.* Nuremberg.

———. [1760]. *Compendium harmonicum; oder, kurzer Begrif der Lehre von der Harmonie, vor diejenigen, welche den Generalbass und die Composition studiren.* Lobenstein. Date at end of dedication. Partial reprint in Marpurg 1760. English translation in Martin 1981.

———. [1767]. *Anleitung zur Fantasie . . . nach theoretischen und practischen Grundsätzen, wie solche die Natur des Klangs lehret.* Lobenstein. Date at end of dedication.

Spazier, Karl. 1800. "Einige Worte zur Rechtfertigung Marpurgs, und zur Erinnerung an seine Verdienste." *Allgemeine musikalische Zeitung,* 2:593–600.

Speer, Daniel. 1697. *Grund-richtiger/ kurtz-leicht-und Nöthiger/ jetzt Wol-vermehrter Unterricht der Musicalischen Kunst.* Ulm. Expanded 2nd ed. of 1687 work. Facs. Leipzig: VEB Edition Peters, 1974.

Spiess, Meinrad. 1745. *Tractatus musicus compositorio-practicus.* Augsburg. 2nd ed. 1746.

Spitta, Philipp. 1889. *Johann Sebastian Bach.* English translation by Clara Bell and J. A. Fuller-Maitland. London, 1889. Facs. New York: Dover, 1951. Original edition, Leipzig, 1873–1880.

Stevens, Jane. 1971. "An Eighteenth-Century Description of Concerto First-Movement Form." *Journal of the American Musicological Society* 24:85–95.

Stierlein, Johann Christoph. 1691. *Trifolium musicale.* Stuttgart.

Stillingfleet, Benjamin. 1771. *Principles and Power of Harmony.* London.

Stillings, Frank. 1963. *The Practical Harmonist at the Harpsichord.* New Haven: Yale School of Music, and Yale University Press, 1968. Translation of Gasparini 1708.

Strunk, Oliver. 1950. *Source Readings in Music History.* New York: W. W. Norton.

Suaudeau, René. 1958. *Le Premier système harmonique (dit Clermontois) de Jean-Philippe Rameau.* Typescript. Clermont-Ferrand. Summary in Chailley 1965, pp. 77–79.

———. 1960. *Introduction à l'harmonie de Rameau.* Clermont-Ferrand: Ecole Nationale de Musique de Clermont-Ferrand.

Sulzer, Johann Georg. 1771–1774. *Allgemeine Theorie der schönen Künste.* Leipzig. Numerous reprints through 1798. Facs. of the 1792–1794 edition. Hildesheim: Olms, 1967–1970. The music articles were written by Kirnberger and, probably, his pupil Johann Abraham Peter Schulz (see p. 240).

Tartini, Giuseppe. 1754. *Trattato di musica secondo la vera scienza dell' armonia.* Padua. Facs. New York: Broude, 1966; *Le Opere di Giuseppe Tartini* II/1 (Padua, 1973). English translation in Johnson 1985.

———. 1767. *Riposta . . . alla critica del di lui Trattato di musica di Mons. Le Serre.* Venice.

Telemann, Georg Michael. 1773. *Unterricht im Generalbass Spielen.* Hamburg.

Telemann, Georg Philipp. 1730. *Fast allgemeines Evangelisch-Musicalisches Lieder-Buch . . . [mit] Unterrichte, der unter andern zur vierstimmigen Composition und zum damit verknüpften General-Basse anleitet.* Hamburg.

———. 1733–1734. *Singe-, Spiel- und General-Bass-Uebungen.* Hamburg.

Tigrini, Orazio. 1588. *Il compendio della musica.* Venice. Facs. New York: Broude, 1966.

Tinctoris, Johannes. 1477. *Liber de arte contrapuncti.* Ms. English translation in Seay 1961. All references are to this translation.

Treiber, Johann Philipp. 1704. *Der accurate Organist im General-Bass.* Jena.

Trydell, John. 1766. *Two Essays on the Theory and Practice of Music.* Dublin. Reprinted as "Music" in the *Encyclopaedia Britannica,* 1st ed., Edinburgh, 1771.

Türk, Daniel Gottlob. 1789. *Klavierschule.* Leipzig and Halle. Later editions 1800 and Vienna, 1798. Facs. of the 1789 edition. Kassel: Bärenreiter, 1962, 1967. English translations by C. G. Naumberger (London, 1804) and in Haggh 1982.

———. 1791. *Kurze Anweisung zum Generalbaßspielen.* Halle and Leipzig. Reprint in 1800. Facs. Amsterdam: Frits Knuf, 1971.

Twittenhoff, Wilhelm. 1935. *Die musiktheoretischen Schriften Joseph Riepels.* Halle/Salle: Buchhandlung des Waisenhauses.

Vallotti, Francesco Antonio. 1779. *Della scienza teorica e pratica.* Padua. Remainder of the treatise in Vallotti 1950.

———. 1950. *Trattato della moderna musica.* Padua: Il Messaggero di S. Antonio. Includes Vallotti 1779 and three additional parts.

Vandermonde, Alexandre-Théophile. 1778. *Second Mémoire sur un nouveau système d'harmonie applicable à l'état de la musique.* N.p.

Verba, Cynthia. 1973. "The Development of Rameau's Thoughts on Modulation and Chromatics." *Journal of the American Musicological Society* 26:69–91.

————. 1978. "Rameau's Views on Modulation and Their Background in French Theory." *Journal of the American Musicological Society* 31:467–479.

Viadana, Lodovico Grossi da. 1602. *Cento concerti ecclesiastici . . . con il basso continuo*. Venice. Many later editions. English translation in Arnold 1931.

Vial, François-Guillaume. [c. 1767]. *Arbre Généalogique de l'harmonie*. Paris. Date according to publication privilege dated January 9, 1767 (Brenet 1906–1907:456).

Vicentino, Nicola. 1555. *L'antica musica ridotta alla moderna prattica*. Rome. Facs. Kassel: Bärenreiter, 1956.

Vion, Charles Antoine. 1742. *La musique pratique et theorique, réduite a ses principes naturels*. Paris.

Vivian, Percival. 1909. *Campion's Works*. London: Oxford, 1909.

Vogler, Georg Joseph. 1776. *Tonwissenschaft und Tonsezkunst*. Mannheim. Facs. Hildesheim: Olms, 1970.

————. [1778]. *Kuhrpfälzische Tonschule*. 2 vols. Mannheim.

————. 1778–1781. *Betrachtungen der Mannheimer Tonschule*. 3 vols. Mannheim. Facs. Hildesheim: Olms, 1974.

Wagner, Günther. 1984. "Anmerkungen zur Formtheorie H. C. Kochs." *Archiv für Musikwissenschaft* 41:86–112.

Wallace, Barbara. 1983. "J. F. Daube's *General-Bass in drey Accorden* (1756): A Translation and Commentary." Ph.D. diss., North Texas University.

Walther, Johann Gottfried. 1708. *Praecepta der musicalischen Composition*. Ms. published by Peter Benary. Leipzig: Breitkopf & Härtel, 1955. All references are to this edition.

————. 1732. *Musicalisches Lexicon*. Leipzig. Facs. Kassel: Bärenreiter, 1953.

Wason, Robert. 1985. *Viennese Harmonic Theory from Albrechtsberger to Schenker and Schoenberg*. Ann Arbor: UMI Research Press.

Werckmeister, Andreas. 1697. *Hypomnemata musica . . . insonderheit von der Composition und Temperatur*. Quedlinburg. Facs. Hildesheim: Olms, 1970.

————. [1698]. *Die nothwendigsten Anmerkungen und Regeln wie der Bassus continuus oder General-Bass wol könne tractiret werden*. Aschersleben. Date appears in the introduction to Werckmeister 1702. Reprinted 1715.

————. 1700. *Cribrum musicum*. Quedlinburg. Facs. Hildesheim: Olms, 1970.

————. 1702. *Harmonologia musica, oder kurtze Anleitung zur musicalischen Composition, wie man vermittels der Regeln und Anmerckungen bey den General-Bass einen Contrapunctum simplicem . . . componiren und ex tempore spielen*. Frankfurt and Leipzig. Facs. Hildesheim: Olms, 1970.

Westbladh, Tobias. 1727. *De triade harmonica*. Uppsala.

Wideburg, Johann Friedrich Michael. 1765–1775. *Der sich selbst informirende Clavierspieler*. 3 vols. Leipzig and Halle, 1765; Halle, 1767 and 1775. Author's name spelled Wiedeburg in volume 1.

Wilson, Dora Jean. 1979. "Georg Simon Löhlein's Klavierschule: Translation and Commentary." Ph.D. diss., University of Southern California. Translation of Löhlein 1765 and 1781.

Wolff, Christoph. 1968. *Der stile antico in der Musik Johann Sebastian Bachs*. Wiesbaden: F. Steiner, 1968.

Wollenberg, Susan. 1970. "The Unknown 'Gradus.'" *Music and Letters* 51:423–434.

Young, Irwin. 1969. English translation of Gafori 1496. Madison: 1969.

Zacconi, Lodovico. 1622. *Prattica di musica seconda parte*. Venice. Facs. Bologna: Forni, 1967; Hildesheim: Olms, 1982.

Zarlino, Gioseffo. 1558. *Istitutioni harmoniche*. Venice. Facs. New York: Broude, 1965. Reprinted 1561, 1562, 1572. English translation of Book 3 in Marco-Palisca 1968. English translation of Book 4 in Vered Cohen 1983. All references are to these translations.

———. 1562. *Nove madrigali a cinque voci*. Reprinted, edited by Siro Cisilino. Venice: Istituto per la collaborazioni culturale, [1963].

———. 1571. *Dimostrationi harmoniche*. Venice. Facs. Ridgewood, New Jersey: Gregg, 1966.

———. 1573. *Istitutioni harmoniche*. 2nd ed. Venice. Facs. Ridgewood, New Jersey: Gregg, 1966.

———. 1588. *Sopplimenti musicali*. Venice. Facs. New York: Broude, 1979.

# Index

Key signatures, 59, 73
Kircher, Athanasius, 253
Kirnberger, Johann Philipp, 93, 135, 170,
    176, 177, 196, 197, 207, 208, 209,
    211–212, 217, 223–224, 239–257,
    259n, 260n, 275, 276n, 278–279, 280,
    283; on fundamental bass, 186n,
    241–243, 250–251; on counterpoint,
    190; on permutations, 228; dispute with
    Marpurg, 231–243; on suspensions,
    242–243; on 6/4 chords, 243
Knouse, Nola Reed, 289n. See also Reed,
    Nola
Koch, Heinrich Christoph, 27, 66n, 93,
    121, 124, 135, 177, 204, 210, 217,
    260n, 267, 269, 273–302; on harmony,
    275–285; on melody and phrasing,
    285–289; on form, 290–297; on
    compositional method, 297–299
Kohlschütter, Bernd, 51
Kramer, Richard, 168, 245n
Krehbiel, James, 153, 197n
Kuhnau, Johann, 166, 215

Ladewig, James, 173
Laisement, Ballière de, 194
Lampe, John Frederick, 151–152, 207
Lanfranco, Giovanni Maria, 26, 30
Langner, Thomas, 218n
Lassus, Roland de, 10
Levens, Charles, 140, 152–155, 243
Lewin, David, 115, 228n
Lippius, Johannes, 27, 37, 42, 55, 97–98,
    190, 229, 241
Locke, John, 91
Locke, Matthew, 49n
Löfgrön, Antonius, 125
Löhlein, Georg Simon, 74, 176, 196, 205,
    206, 210, 224, 254
Lully, Jean-Baptiste, 131, 137–138, 147,
    150, 219
Lusitano, Vicente, 30
Lute, 51

Madin, Henri, 30
Major and minor dissonance, 107, 116,
    244
Malcolm, Alexander, 76–77
Manfredini, Vincenzo, 226
Mann, Alfred, 31, 34n, 36, 60, 185n, 187,
    191
Marcello, Benedetto, 165
Marpurg, Friedrich Wilhelm, 56, 135, 175,
    177, 205, 218, 228, 229, 231–239,
    246–257, 259n, 260, 275, 293;
    translator of D'Alembert, 144, 146, 194,

219, 223, 254; and Rameau's theories,
    150; as journalist, 168, 233–234; on
    fundamental bass, 186n, 234–235,
    250–251; on fugue, 191, 246–249; and
    Sorge, 194–197, 205–206, 211–212,
    254; and Daube, 201; on subposition,
    210–212, 251–252; on passing
    dissonances, 212–214; dispute with
    Kirnberger, 231–233, 246–257; on
    Riepel, 267–268
Martini, Giovanni Battista, 30, 32, 44, 47,
    69n, 74, 135, 147, 148, 177, 183, 190,
    209, 213, 214, 256, 257; composition
    method, 178–182
Mason, Kevin, 72, 99n
Masson, Charles, 23, 116–117, 158
Mattheson, Johann, 31n, 35, 50, 53, 60,
    66, 86, 98, 150, 151, 158–174, 190,
    196, 197, 201, 215–216, 218, 223, 224,
    233, 234, 254, 255, 256, 286, 297; on
    harmony and melody, 123, 235; on
    melodic structure, 161–168, 259
McArtor, Marion, 173n
Mekeel, Joyce, 235, 239n
Mersenne, Marin, 253
Mitchell, William, 56, 93
Mizler, Lorenz, 54, 89, 92, 151, 168; and
    Fux, 31n, 47; and chord inversion, 98
Modes, 31n, 33, 35, 46, 169–171
Modulation, as a term, 2, 87, 153, 281,
    305, 314
Monody, 162, 219–220
Montéclair, Michel Pignolet de, 144
Monteverdi, Claudio and Giulio, 20–21
Morales, Cristóbal, 35
Mozart, Leopold, 197, 256, 268
Mozart, Wolfgang Amadeus, 135,
    182–187, 190, 228, 256, 260n, 268,
    274, 298, 321; and species counterpoint,
    31, 36, 45, 47, 93, 177, 281; and
    secondary dominants, 86; and
    fundamental bass, 142–143, 203, 226;
    and passing dissonances, 212; and key
    change, 217
Muffat, Georg, 53, 54
Murschhauser, Franz Anton Xaver, 171

Newman, William, 240
Newton, Isaac, 127, 128, 143
Nichelmann, Christoph, 93, 135, 142,
    218–224, 229, 254, 255, 256, 265, 285
Niedt, Friderich Erhard, 27, 37, 50, 52,
    53, 190, 229, 239, 258–259;
    composition method, 66–68, 142–143,
    162, 164, 265–267, 285
Ninth chords. See Subposition

Sammartini, Giovanni Battista, 180
Sauveur, Joseph, 127, 128, 130, 172
Scacchi, Marco, 24
Scarlatti, Alessandro, 79
Scheibe, Johann Adolph, 98, 133, 158, 168, 193, 195, 197, 233, 254, 256
Scheinpflug, Christoph Gotthelf, 290
Schenker, Heinrich, 36, 96, 106, 150, 157, 214, 274n
Schenkerian theory, 35–37, 219, 263
Schering, Arnold, 79
Schneider, Herbert, 95n
Schoenberg, Arnold, 139, 156
Schröter, Christoph, 13, 124–125, 194, 233n, 254
Schubarth, Johann Kaspar, 260
Schulz, Johann Abraham Peter, 240, 248n, 254
Schulze, Hans-Joachim, 221n
Schütz, Heinrich, 21
Schwarzmaier, Ernst, 260n
*Seconda pratica*, 19–25, 28, 39, 49
Secondary dominant, 82–87, 217; in Heinichen, 81; in Rameau, 122–123; in Kirnberger, 244, 252; in Koch, 282–284
Serre, Jean-Adam, 173n, 200
Serwer, Howard, 233, 239n, 246
Seventh chords, 45–46, 55; in thoroughbass, 62; in Rameau, 100, 106–108; vs. suspensions, 114; in D'Alembert, 145–146; in Sorge, 195; in Kirnberger, 241–243, 250–251; in Koch, 276. *See also* Subposition
Seyfried, Ignaz Xaver Ritter von, 321
Shirlaw, Matthew, 4, 49n, 94n, 96, 103, 104, 109, 133, 235, 236
Siefert, Paul, 21
Signoretti, 192
Sisman, Elaine, 260n, 268, 275n, 290n
Six-four chord, 10, 65, 116–117, 140, 184, 205–206, 243
Snook, Susan, 200n, 204
Solmization, six-syllable, 31n, 46, 171–172, 188
Sorge, Georg Andreas, 150, 193–197, 198, 205–206, 207, 216, 217, 231, 234, 235, 237, 241, 255, 257
Soriano, Francesco, 35
Species counterpoint, 26–48; early formulations, 27–30; improvised, 30–31; in *Gradus ad parnassum*, 31–48; in Haydn, 31, 32, 34, 35, 177, 187, 191, 234, 273, 290; in Mozart, 182, 186–187; in Albrechtsberger, 187–189

Speer, Daniel, 54, 70
Spiess, Meinrad, 256
Spitta, Philipp, 82n
Stevens, Jane, 298n
Stierlein, Johann Christoph, 21, 30, 163
Stillingfleet, Benjamin, 198
String divisions, 9, 101–105, 194
Suaudeau, René, 95n
Subposition: in Rameau, 100, 108–114, 140; in Levens, 153; in Marpurg, 210–212, 213, 237, 251–252; in Beethoven, Löhlein, Türk, 210; in Koch, 210, 276, 278. *See also* Supposition
Sulzer, Johann Georg, 240, 255, 297
Supposition, 101, 108–109. *See also* Subposition
Suspensions, in Zarlino, 13–14. *See also* Subposition

Tartini, Giuseppe, 197–200, 209
Telemann, Georg Michael, 257
Telemann, Georg Philipp, 31n, 50, 65, 202, 218, 219, 222, 224, 243
Temperament, 103
Theorbo, 51, 76, 99
Thoroughbass, 49–89, 182–183; and diminution, 37, 63–68, 80–81; and chords, 53–61; and dissonance, 61–65, 209–210; and composition, 65–68; and unfigured basses, 69–82; compared to Rameau, 142–143; in Daube, 200–204; compared to Riepel, 265–267
Tinctoris, Joannes, 15, 27, 30, 118, 178n
Treiber, Johann Philipp, 50
*Trias harmonica*, 11, 97
Triple proportion, 132
Trydell, John, 207–208
Türk, Daniel Gottlob, 50, 59, 93, 135, 210, 256
Twelve-tone row, 173
Twittenhoff, Wilhelm, 259, 260

Underlying voice leading: in Artusi, 20–21; in Heinichen, 64, 79–81; in Kirnberger, 245; in Riepel, 263–266; in Koch, 285–286, 292–293
Unfigured basses, rules for, 43, 51, 69–82; interpreted by Rameau, 119–122

Vallotti, Francesco Antonio, 182, 190, 209, 211, 257n
Verba, Cynthia, 131, 138n
Viadana, Lodovico Grossi da, 49, 50, 69n
Vial, François-Guillaume, 229, 230
Vicentino, Nicola, 19